# Welsh Americans

A HISTORY OF ASSIMILATION
IN THE COALFIELDS

# Welsh Americans

The
University of
North Carolina
Press
Chapel Hill

Ronald L. Lewis

Designed by Kimberly Bryant
Set in Scala and Scala Sans
by Keystone Typesetting, Inc.
Manufactured in the United States of America

The paper in this book meets the guidelines for permanence
and durability of the Committee on Production Guidelines for
Book Longevity of the Council on Library Resources.

The University of North Carolina Press has been a member
of the Green Press Initiative since 1993.

Library of Congress Cataloging-in-Publication Data
Lewis, Ronald L., 1940–
Welsh Americans : a history of assimilation in the coalfields /
Ronald L. Lewis.
p. cm.
Includes bibliographical references and index.
ISBN 978-0-8078-3220-2 (cloth : alk. paper)
1. Welsh Americans—Cultural assimilation. 2. Welsh Americans—
Ethnic identity. 3. Welsh Americans—Social conditions. 4. Welsh
Americans—History. 5. Immigrants—United States—History.
6. Coal miners—United States—History. 7. Coal mines and
mining—Social aspects—United States—History. 8. Middle West—
Ethnic relations. 9. Pennsylvania—Ethnic relations. 10. West
Virginia—Ethnic relations. I. Title.
E184.W4L49 2008
973.0491′66—dc22                                    2008009930

12 11 10 09 08   5 4 3 2 1

# CONTENTS

## ILLUSTRATIONS, MAPS, & TABLES

### Illustrations

## Maps

## Tables

## PREFACE

This book has its earliest origin in family history, dating back more than twenty years to a long conversation I had in Justus, Ohio, with the lone family elder who possessed any knowledge of our common Lewis ancestors. While I scribbled copious notes, Laverne Lewis passed on this oral history. He told of Howell Lewis, my great-grandfather, and four of his brothers who emigrated from near Rhymney in the 1860s, how they scattered across the American coalfields and eventually lost contact with one another, and how my great-grandfather became embroiled in the Tuscarawas, Ohio, coalfield strike in 1880. Laverne described how my great-grandfather and several of his colleagues, disguised in women's dresses and blackened faces reminiscent of the "Scotch Cattle" of the South Wales coalfield, tied up the mine guards and set fire to the tipple. Hunted by Pinkerton detectives, "the union" transported Howell Lewis, his wife, Frances, and their children by train to Braceville, Illinois (which is next door to the more famous coal town of Braidwood). There my great-grandfather was given a job in the mine and his true identity was kept a secret. When he and his butty were killed by a rock fall in 1890, my great-grandmother and her four children returned to the small Welsh community in North Lawrence, Ohio, which they had departed in haste ten years before.

My later research into local archives over the years documented the essential accuracy of this oral tradition. Along the way, I came to realize that the Welsh, and other British immigrants, were instrumental in establishing the American coal industry and in shaping it into the engine of the American industrial revolution. I also became keenly aware of the extent to which the Welsh were/are invisible in American historiography. As a specialist in the social history of race, ethnicity, and labor, I found the challenge of that vacuum too powerful to resist.

The pages that follow present a unified treatment of Welsh immigration to the American coalfields, scattered though it was, and of a group of immigrants whose importance to industrializing America was far greater than their comparatively modest numbers would suggest. My primary focus is not only the role of the Welsh in transferring their mining skills to establish the American coal industry, but also the process by which this relatively small, welcome group of craftsmen reconstructed their identity and became Americanized. I also explore why this experience for the Welsh was at variance with that of the mass labor migrations from Europe.

As a group, the Welsh may have been nearly "invisible" to most Americans, but the Welsh identity of the first generation of immigrants was constructed from a strong cultural memory that they transferred along with their mining skills to the American coalfields. In America, however, Welsh culture receded into the shadows of memory and then was nearly forgotten altogether. The loss of cultural memory extends to Wales itself, for, even though historical writing on the South Wales coalfield has blossomed in recent years, it has not incorporated the experiences of Welsh miners abroad. For readers interested in the ebb and flow, as well as the theoretical and analytic framework, of immigration scholarship, the introduction provides a brief overview; other readers my wish to skip ahead to chapter 1 and begin their journey of discovery there. The scholars and archivists to whom I am indebted are recognized in the acknowledgments, for no one makes such a journey alone.

My great-grandparents Howell and Frances Lewis were full partners in this transatlantic Welsh migration project, and it is to them and their scattered descendants that this book is dedicated.

# Welsh Americans

# INTRODUCTION

The collapse of the coal-mining industry in post–World War II Wales left this small nation with an "identity crisis." R. Merfyn Jones has observed that a previously homogeneous Wales has dissolved into an "unfamiliar pluralism" of fragmented images. These images range from "short dark men singing hymns in the shadow of slag heaps," on the one hand, to a restructured society "dripping with microchips" on the other.[1] It is probably safe to say that Americans still identify Wales with coal rather than microchips.

This traditional identity with coal mining rests on solid ground. Though in the nineteenth century coal was a significant presence in Wales, it was the massive late Victorian and Edwardian expansion of the industry that established coal mining's dominance as the popular image of Wales. During this expansionary period the number of miners employed in the British coal industry rose exponentially from 57,000 in 1871, nearly tripled to 150,000 in 1901, and reached more than 230,000 in 1913. By 1921 one of every three Welsh males, more than one quarter of a million men and boys, were employed in mining.[2]

Forging the indelible identity of coal-mining Wales was essentially a twentieth-century phenomenon in Britain. In the nineteenth century the British public imagined Wales, as R. M. Jones observed, in "a benign if patronizing fashion as an honest, industrious, pious people wedded to their mountains and to the Welsh language and culture."[3] They lived in a state of freedom close to nature and were characterized by travelers as the "wild Welsh." By the end of the nineteenth century, however, the image of the wild Welsh in their brooding mountains gave way to the coal miner personified as the "proletarian hero" or the "lumpen threat" of the South Wales Valleys. This Wales was not so much a place as a political position expressed in the values and achievements of the South Wales coalfield: international socialism, the Labour Party, strikes and lockouts, choirs, and rugby. Novels, poetry, and film documentaries reinforced this twentieth-century image. Again, according to R. M. Jones, "the Welsh male came even to be associated, in some imaginations, with a particular physical type, evolved for mining: 'strongly built, broad-shouldered and short' as if a racial Darwinism had prepared the Welsh especially for labor underground."[4]

In America, construction of the Welshman as coal miner probably predated the British version. American capitalists began to recruit Welsh miners in the mid-nineteenth century to establish the coal industry; as a result, the Welsh dominated the emerging American coal industry. The overwhelmingly agrarian Americans recognized early on that the Welsh possessed a superior knowledge of mining and the idea readily mutated into the myth of the Welsh as masters of the mines. But just at the moment when the number of miners peaked in Wales, and coal miners acquired the status of distinctive subterranean proletarians, their Welsh colleagues in America found themselves in a losing struggle to maintain their privileged position in the industry.

Partly because of this mythologizing, a clear understanding of the Welsh experience as working-class immigrants in America is difficult to reconstruct. From the American perspective on immigration history, the challenge is to find an interpretive framework that accounts for the fragmented identities attached to incoming migrant groups and that of the people themselves. The very term "immigrants" distinguishes a group as an other, "them" as opposed to "us." Therefore, "immigrant" is packed with meanings constructed by natives, but there is no convenient term to replace it. Scholarship on immigration during the early twentieth century reflected the major concern of Americans over the potential for assimilating the great diversity of people who entered the country at the turn of the century. Early historians, such as Carl Wittke, were optimistic that the European nationals arriving on America's shores would all be assimilated eventually. America was exceptional, and the source of its genius lay in its ability to absorb different peoples and meld them into one. Americans were, after all, a singular people composed of the assimilated populations of the world. People from Africa and Asia posed a problem that was generally ignored, but traditional interpretations accepted the idea that immigration and assimilation played a critical role in forging the American character. America was a "melting pot" even though Britain was the dominant contributor.[5]

Beginning in the 1960s revisionists abandoned this homogenizing paradigm by shifting away from assimilation and focusing on race, ethnicity, and cultural pluralism. They found precedent in the work of Marcus Lee Hansen, who wrote in the 1930s. He argued that, even though British culture was dominant in America, it was only one of the cultures from which America was fashioned, an opinion that prompted some to declare Hansen the first "transethnic" American historian. Realizing that immigration and assimilation was a two-way street, new conceptual approaches emerged to explain the intercontinental mass movement of people. Richard A. Easterlin's "push-pull" model explained immigration within the processes of economic modernization, as rapid industrialization in the United States created a great demand for labor while undermining the ability of other national economies to sustain their own people. American scholarship on immigration still retained the internal perspective, however, concentrating on particular ethnic cultures in specific communities. Within this framework historians generally portrayed immigrants as "proud retainers" of their culture within ethnic enclaves, or as "aspiring modernizers" who abandoned the old culture for the new for rational economic reasons.[6] In either case, scholars were preoccupied with ethnic conflicts with the dominant group, and ethnic cultures in their own right. Far from passively conforming to American values, immigrants actively protected their own cultural identities.

John Bodnar's *The Transplanted* (1985) attempted to synthesize immigration and assimilation within the framework of capitalism and to explore how old-world values were adapted, rather than abandoned, in the New World. He located this dynamic within the family, community, and workplace, a personal world further influenced by class, kinship, and ethnicity. Bodnar belongs to that group John Higham called "soft pluralists," who "perceive cultural differences as intrinsic assets, to be cherished for their own sake," as opposed to "hard pluralists," who concerned themselves principally with class rather than culture, and the issues of "struggle and exploitation."[7] Bodnar's thesis is that immigrants brought their cultures with them, retaining what was useful of the old culture and adopting what they found useful in the new.[8]

Since the 1990s the drumbeat in immigration history has been for scholars to expand their approach beyond the American focus and beyond the nation-state in order to internationalize the field in its global context. The Organization of American Historians and the American Historical Association have taken the lead in fostering this approach. A four-year collaborative effort, led by Thomas Bender, produced the *La Pietra Report*, calling on a more international approach to American history, and a major collection of essays entitled *Rethinking American History in a Global Age*.[9]

Kevin Kenny has pointed out in an important recent article that this literature has been torn between the two approaches to comparative history by the effort to transcend the dead ends inherent in focusing on the nation-state and cultural enclaves. The diasporic, or "transnational," approach looks for "reciprocal interactions and the sensibilities they nurture among globally scattered communities." The comparative, or "cross-national," approach, on the other hand, "examines specific similarities and differences in the experiences of similar migrants who have settled in different nations." Kenny argues that neither perspective by itself will yield satisfactory results. Comparisons based on nationality do not "capture the fluid and interactive processes at the heart of migration history," such as the international mass movement of people, the persistence of identification with the homeland and participation in national events there, or the articulation of artistic, political, or emotional sensibilities that tie people together even when separated by vast distances. The transnational approach alone, however, does not account for the persistent power of nation-states to attract loyalty, or the sharp regional, cultural, and political differences that may fragment a single nationality, such as the Scots, Welsh, and English, not to mention the Irish, within Great Britain.[10] Kenny recognizes both approaches to immigration history, but his primary concern is with the similarities and differences between migrant groups abroad, in his case the Irish in America and other destinations in the diaspora. This study, on the other hand, takes the other transnational approach by examining continuity and change among Welsh immigrants within the framework of the homeland and the hostland. The transatlantic transfer of Welsh culture and skills, and how the migrants adapted them to American circumstances in order to succeed, is a major theme in this study.

This study of Welsh coal miners is built upon the conceptual foundation of both the transnational and the cross-national perspectives, both being vital in telling the story of British immigration and assimilation into American society. Unlike the southern and eastern European mass migrations, Americans either welcomed the British or their presence was no cause for comment. In his popular book *The American Commonwealth* (1888), James Bryce claimed that the English, Welsh, and Scottish migrants were "absorbed into the general mass of native citizens," and tended to "lose their identity almost immediately" in the United States. Although they numbered in the millions, their political footprint was invisible because they had "either been indifferent to political struggles or have voted from the same motives as an average American."[11] Andrew Carnegie went even further in *Triumphant Democracy* (1886), claiming that the British held a privileged position in America because they played a leading role in building the country. British immigrants not only created the industries, like the Welsh-man David Thomas, credited as "the father of the anthracite iron industry in America," but as industrial workers performed much of the labor as well. Carnegie claimed that British immigrants had a monopoly on industrial invention and the skills to run those industries. In the nineteenth century almost half of the manufacturing workforce was British, while Americans were primarily engaged in agriculture. Moreover, this near monopoly in manufacturing and the skilled trades was passed on to their children.[12]

Unlike the southern and eastern Europeans, not to mention the Asians and Africans, whom many Americans regarded as too alien to be assimilable, British immigrants thought of themselves and were seen as "valuable reinforcements" to the British stock that had built America. They occupied an ambiguous status between native and immigrant, comfortable living among "cousins" but not necessarily at home. The British identity was a fragmented one contingent upon the circumstances. Constructed to meet the needs of empire, "British" incorporated the distinct nationalities of the English, Welsh, and Scots, and represented expansion, global power, imperialism, and civilizing the heathens of remote places. Emigrants did not always share this identity in equal portions. The Scots and Welsh each maintained their distinctive cultural and national identities in the United States in a way the English did not, even though Americans drew little distinction between them. The paucity of scholarship on the subject indicates that, at least in the literature, British immigrants were, in Charlotte Erickson's memorable phrase, nearly "invisible."[13]

While the original American immigrants between the seventeenth and early nineteenth century were predominantly British and Irish, it was the transportation revolution of the mid-nineteenth century that transformed emigration in British history. Steamships greatly reduced the perils of sea travel and made migration a much less irreversible decision, and railroads opened the American interior to settlement and development. The cost of transportation also fell, and the emigration process itself was opened up to ordinary workers who sought to improve their lives abroad. Industrialization attracted skilled British workers who were quick to take advantage of the new opportunities. Their privileged status was reflected in the immigrant experience of Welsh coal miners, whose identity was anchored in their unique work culture and nineteenth-century Welsh nationalism. The culture they transplanted to America was particularly visible in religion, politics, cultural practices, and labor-industrial relations. Their reception and social position stood in stark contrast to that of the millions of Europeans who entered the U.S. labor market at the lowest rung, resulting in a stratified and segmented labor market rather than actual job competition.[14]

Welsh immigration to the United States was chronologically, geographically, and occupationally concentrated. Eighteenth- and early-nineteenth-century Welsh immigrants to the United States were primarily farmers seeking better land. By far the greatest influx, however, came in oscillating waves between the 1840s and 1900 with the migration of industrial workers. In 1850 there were only 30,000 foreign-born Welsh in the United States, but that number more than trebled by 1890 to reach a historic peak of 100,079. Due to undercounting, the actual figures were undoubtedly higher, perhaps double the official figure. The motivations for emigrating from Wales also shifted from the acquisition of farmland to better industrial jobs primarily in the coal and iron industries.[15]

On both sides of the Atlantic, coal not only heated homes and fired the ironworks, but also powered the steam-driven factories, railroad locomotives, and steamships. The burgeoning demand for coal prompted American capitalists to import British miners as early as 1827 to inaugurate a more "methodical system" for the extraction of coal, according to a report in the *Pottsville Miners' Journal*. Coal miners were as skilled as any of the immigrants who crossed the Atlantic to industrializing America. The rise of the United States as an industrial power is measured by the dramatic expansion of the basic industries and their respective workforces. The U.S. census counted only 6,800 mine workers in 1840, but their numbers grew to 36,500 by 1860, doubled during the Civil War decade, surpassed 127,000 in 1900, and peaked at over 650,000 in 1920.[16]

Along with their English, and to a lesser extent Scottish, colleagues, Welsh miners first came to the anthracite fields of eastern Pennsylvania as those fields began to open in the 1820s. English miners became more prevalent in the southern anthracite fields, and the Welsh in the northern fields of the upper Schuylkill and Susquehanna valleys from Pottsville to Carbondale. Scranton became the largest single Welsh population center in America. In the words of one authority, this was "the epicenter of Welsh-America."[17]

Until after the Civil War most of the coal raised in America was anthracite, and because the Welsh were accustomed to mining anthracite and hard steam coal, their skills were highly prized. Their skills were also transferable to the softer bituminous coal found further west, and, with the development of those fields, Welshmen set out for the coal and steel districts of western Pennsylvania, Maryland, and Ohio. Johnstown, in Cambria

County, Pennsylvania, grew under the stimulus of a major steel mill, and satellite coal-mining communities provided the great quantities of coal consumed by the furnaces. The large Welsh colony that hunkered down around the mills and mines prompted one Welshman to call the Cambria works the "Dowlais of America."[18]

By midcentury the iron and coal industries had also established an embryonic presence in Ohio, which expanded rapidly during the Civil War and postwar years. In the northeastern Ohio triangle between the industrial cities of Youngstown, Cleveland, and Canton, thousands of Welsh coal and iron workers converged between the 1850s and the 1890s. In many of these towns the Welsh presence was prominent; a native of Llanelli reported that Youngstown was "the Welsh metropolis of America."[19] During the late nineteenth century the growth of the tinplate industry at the tristate headwaters of the Ohio between Youngstown, Pittsburgh, and Wheeling also stimulated production and sparked another influx of Welsh miners and mill workers.[20]

The population and markets expanded westward and Welsh miners advanced with the mineral frontier to the bituminous coalfields of Indiana, Illinois, Iowa, Missouri, Kansas, Colorado, Utah, Idaho, Wyoming, and Washington. Adamantly anti-slavery, Republican in politics, and equally supportive of labor unions, Welsh immigrants found little attraction in settling in the southern states, where they would have to compete with oppressed African American labor. Of course, this form of exploitation reduced the need for immigrant labor of any kind. There were important exceptions. The vast coal reserves of Central Appalachia were developed just as Welsh immigration began to decline, but Welsh mining families did settle for a time in Soddy, Tennessee, and in the Birmingham mineral district where they were conspicuous for their hold on the managerial positions. However, the overwhelming majority of Welsh miners settled north of the Ohio River, thinning on the ground the further west they migrated.[21]

Welsh miners and iron mill men, along with their English and Scottish counterparts, pioneered these industries in the United States. Iron and steel mills were erected in close proximity to coking coal supplies and numerous small coal towns. By the 1850s well-established Welsh industrial communities emerged in the coal and iron districts of Pennsylvania and Ohio, and they became magnets for the earliest and the largest concentrations of Welsh Americans.[22]

The 1900 census recorded the Welsh in every state of the union, but they were concentrated in several particular states. Out of a total 267,000 Welsh immigrants and their children in the United States (93,744 immigrants and 173,416 children of immigrants), 100,143 of them lived in Pennsylvania alone. Ohio was a distant second with 35,971. These two states also contained the two largest concentrations of Welsh in the coal and iron districts. More than 40,000 lived in adjacent Luzerne and Lackawanna Counties with the centers of Scranton and Wilkes-Barre. Of the 35,971 total Welsh stock in Ohio, 24,312 lived in the coal and iron districts of northeastern Ohio and along the Ohio River. By the end of the nineteenth century conditions in the American coal industry became less favorable as technology began to undermine traditional manual skills, and unskilled eastern and southern European immigrants were preferred to British miners who insisted on protecting their status and higher pay. As the incentive to migrate faded, British immigration to America generally declined in the first decade of the twentieth century, and then dropped off dramatically to a mere trickle of hundreds per decade.[23]

This study explores the formative influence of the Welsh on the American coal industry by examining their role in establishing technical and work practices, in safety legislation and enforcement, and in the labor organizations that represented the miners' interests. It also explores the transnational cultural spaces they created in coalfield communities. The Welsh carried with them similar cultural markers that worked against other immigrants. They spoke their own language and used it in the religious services of their own national church denominations and organizational structures. Welsh communities tended to cluster around these churches, and their tendency to intermarry and to employ workers from their own group exposed them to charges of clannishness. They also had their own fraternal orders and literary societies, and brought with them the eisteddfod (pronounced "ice-stéth-vod"; literally, "session"), a cultural festival usually conducted in Welsh. While all this was noted by Americans, these cultural differences prompted no serious negative reaction as they did against the Irish, Slavs, and Italians. This book explores why, even though the Welsh were so "foreign," they encountered so little discrimination.

As Welsh immigrants became Americanized, their transplanted institutions and customs went into decline and then all but disappeared. Over time the Wales they remembered existed only in memory. Their children had no memory of Wales to perpetuate, and no history of discrimination or struggle for survival to generate the kind of distinctive experience that would unite them. Hardly a ray of light could pass between what it meant to be "Welsh

American" and "American," and within a generation the Welsh had been "transformed" into Americans.

Welsh coal miners constituted one of the largest and most distinctive elements within the industrial labor migrations from Britain. Therefore, they provide an excellent focus group for demonstrating the breadth of skills, cultures, and experiences within the mass labor migrations to America between the Civil War and World War I. The fulcrum of this study is the intersection where "transnational" immigration history, ethnic history, and labor history converge. In the end this study demonstrates the continuity and change within both an internal and comparative framework, and analyzes how Americanization worked within a small, privileged, working-class ethnic group. The United States built its industrial empire on coal and steel, and, despite their comparatively small numbers, no immigrant group played a more strategic role per capita in advancing basic industry in America than the Welsh.

# EMIGRATION, IMMIGRATION

Americans and Welshmen think of the industrial migration of the mid-to-late nineteenth century as the historical tissue connecting the two nations, but the links actually stretch back to the origins of the United States. Although an indeterminate number of Welsh went to the American colonies, they were few in number and they went as individuals. This changed with the Restoration of the monarchy in 1660 when a significant number of Quakers, Baptists, and Presbyterians departed for the New World. The victory of Oliver Cromwell and the Protestants over the royalists in 1645 during the first civil war stimulated the growth of Protestantism in Wales. The inability to preach in the Welsh language also rooted out many Anglican clergy, further weakening the power of the established church in Wales. Restoration of the British monarchy, however, threatened the Nonconformists with persecution, and emigration became an avenue of escape.[1]

The first individuals to migrate to the American colonies were led by the Swansea Baptist, John Miles, who led his congregation to New England in 1663. Finding the Plymouth Puritans too repressive, he established the permanent and prosperous colony of Swanzey in Rhode Island. Other Nonconformist groups motivated by similar pressures created by the Restoration soon followed. The first major Welsh migration to Pennsylvania came with the Quakers and Baptists from northern and western Wales, who settled on William Penn's lands. Penn himself thought about naming the colony "New Wales," but Charles II, who granted the charter, christened it "Pennsylvania." Hoping to attract Welsh Quakers, Penn agreed that a large forty- or-fifty-thousand-acre tract known as the "Welsh Tract" (present-day Bala Cynwyd) would be set aside for the Welsh to control. Led by Richard Davies, the first group of Welsh sailed for Pennsylvania in 1682, and many more followed. The migrants were disappointed, however, when Penn surveyed the Welsh Tract and divided it into townships. Whatever hope remained for establishing a Welsh domain were put to rest in 1691 when the Welsh Tract was opened to non-Welsh settlers. Welsh Anglicans and Welsh

Baptists were also attracted to Pennsylvania. The Baptists' tendency to splinter soon overtook them, and in 1703 those who wanted services in Welsh split from those who did not and moved to the Welsh Tract near present-day Newark, Delaware. Another group established a colony along the Black River in North Carolina in the 1730s, and a third established Welsh Neck on the Pee Dee River in South Carolina in 1737. By the 1790s, the inability of the Welsh to maintain compact ethnic settlements, the drying up of new immigrants from Wales to replenish the culture, and the economic advantages of assimilation led to the decline in Welsh language and customs in the American colonies.[2]

It would be natural to attribute the motives of these early emigrants to rural poverty and agricultural distress, for both were plentiful, but most of them were people with some means. Moreover, they had a broader political and religious consciousness than is generally ascribed to peasants. Several prominent Nonconformist clergymen with a wide following in Wales and a deep understanding of American affairs embraced the American War for Independence and took the lead in defending it from opponents in Britain. In his *Observations on the Nature of Civil Liberty* (1776), the dissenter Richard Price anticipated Thomas Paine's application of the "rights of man" to the Revolution, and David Williams, another Welsh dissenter who knew Benjamin Franklin, advanced an intellectual defense of the Americans in *Letters on Political Liberty* (1782). Both argued for the God-given right to national self-determination, and Williams went a step further by advocating universal manhood suffrage, the ballot, payment of MPs, annual parliaments, and smaller constituencies—reforms that presaged the Chartist Manifesto. The identification of America with radical democratic ideals had a strong appeal in Wales, particularly coming from these highly respected religious leaders, and while they did not stimulate emigration, they did keep America in the collective thought as a legitimate alternative for Welsh settlement.[3]

Welsh emigration in the nineteenth century was divided into two phases characterized by occupation, first an agricultural migration from 1815 to the 1840s, and then an industrial migration from the 1840s to the 1920s. The Welsh agricultural migration was generated by major social and economic changes on the land similar to those stimulating the mass migrations in Europe following the Napoleonic wars. For most of the nineteenth century, Wales was two nations, according to historian Alan Conway. The rural areas were occupied by a "Welsh-speaking, non-conformist, politically Liberal Welsh peasantry and an English-speaking, Anglican, politically Tory landowner class." In the industrial districts "the same linguistic, ethnic, religious, and political differences divided the foundry men from the iron-masters." This was more or less true for the colliers as well, who were employed in the captive mines belonging to the iron companies, but less so in the sale-coal segment of the industry where more Welshmen could be found among the owners. Nevertheless, in the heavily capitalized segments of the iron and coal district of South Wales, the Royal Commission on the State of Education in Wales emphasized this division in 1847: "In the works the Welsh workman never finds his way into the office. He never becomes either clerk or agent. . . . Equally in his new, as in his old, home, his language keeps him under the hatches, being one in which he can neither acquire nor communicate the necessary information. It is a language of old-fashioned agriculture, of theology and of simple rustic life, while the entire world about him is English."[4]

In the early nineteenth century, life in rural Wales remained much as it had been for centuries. People clothed themselves in homemade woolens, their diet was poor, and so was their health. Housing was primitive, with families of a dozen children sharing small cottages with the pigs and poultry. The English village was rare in the rural areas of North and mid-Wales, where the prevailing pattern was scattered farmsteads and squatters occupying the high wasteland. The economy depended upon cattle, sheep, and goats, and, since roads were almost nonexistent, Welsh drovers herded their stock to markets over trails followed by their ancestors since medieval times.[5]

The agricultural revolution that transformed England in the eighteenth century was slow in coming to Wales. The rugged terrain to the west of the South Wales coalfield was remote from major cities, and landowners with the capital to promote improvements generally were nonresidents more concerned with their English lands, while the resident gentry lacked the capital and landholdings were much smaller. This meant that Wales was unprepared for the great population explosion that began in the early nineteenth century and doubled the population of Wales by midcentury. The enclosure movement disrupted traditional patterns of landholding and land use by changing the rules of the "moral economy," which gave the poor access to commons they could use to sustain themselves. In Wales the enclosure movement was precipitated by the dramatic increase in the price for corn during the wars with France between 1793 and 1815, which made it attractive to enclose uplands formerly regarded as wastelands suitable only for the poor. The impact was felt throughout the British countryside. In Ireland plots traditionally used by the poor to grow potatoes were fenced off.

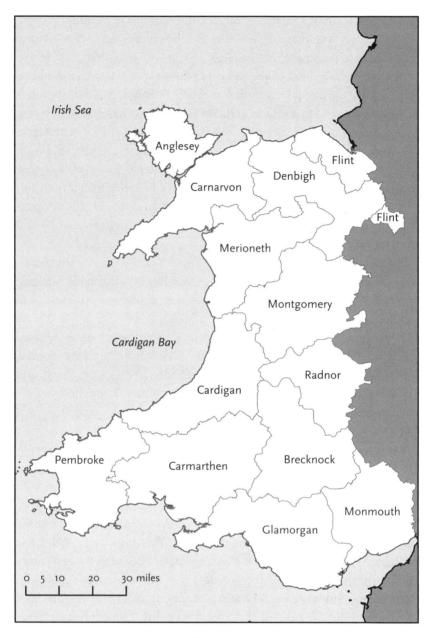

Irish Sea

Anglesey

Flint

Denbigh

Carnarvon

Flint

Merioneth

Montgomery

Cardigan Bay

Radnor

Cardigan

Pembroke

Brecknock

Carmarthen

Monmouth

Glamorgan

o  5  10      20      30 miles

MAP 1. Counties of nineteenth-century Wales. Map by Sue Bergeron,
adapted in part from Alexander K. Johnston, *England and Wales*.

Welsh farmers removed from the moorland grew into an "army of landless farm laborers" forced to migrate to the burgeoning South Wales coal and iron district, or to immigrate to America where cheap land was available.[6]

Corn prices collapsed with the end of war, and depression ensued. By 1817 Wales was in the throes of a famine. Although not quite so desperate as in Ireland, the experience in Wales was not entirely dissimilar. The agricultural crisis in Wales was compounded by the government in 1836 when commutation of tithes to money payments became compulsory, an act that was deeply resented in a segment of the population whose religious Nonconformity was becoming nearly universal. To the class and language antagonisms dividing the gentry and tenants was added religion. Like their Irish counterparts, the normally conservative Welsh peasants became radicalized, and their grievances exploded in the Rebecca Riots following passage of the Highways Act of 1835. The act initiated a turnpike system in Wales, maintained by tolls collected at gates erected every few miles. The first riot erupted in 1839 in West Wales and spread to South Wales during the early forties. Like the better-known rural violence of the Whiteboys, Ribbonmen, and Molly Maguires in Ireland, Welshmen with their faces blackened and disguised in women's clothes destroyed tollgates and drove off the keepers and constables attempting to protect them. Initial success prompted an expansion of the attacks against the barns of grasping landowners and the hated workhouses. By the mid-forties the authorities had stamped out these protests, and the main Rebecca leaders had been transported to the penal colony in Australia.[7]

The agrarian unrest had major implications, however, as the Welsh became much more politically conscious. The Nonconformist ministers emerged from the smoke of cultural war as the uncontested leaders of the people in the struggle against the Anglican, English-speaking, Tory landowners who still controlled society. The rising tide of Welsh nationalism broke in full force over the "Treachery of the Blue Books" (*Brad y Llyfrau Gleision*), an inquiry conducted for Parliament by the Royal Commission on the State of Education in Wales and released in 1847. The three commissioners were English Anglicans ignorant of the Welsh language and culture who conducted themselves with an arrogance that exceeded what even the Welsh had come to expect from the English. The reports contained a wealth of social information, but the commissioners managed to insult patriotic Welshmen with their conclusions that the indigenous language, culture, and institutions of Wales were inferior. The most hostile response was prompted by the commissioners' characterization of rural Welsh women as "almost universally unchaste." The report was received in Wales with bitter indignation, and galvanized the Welsh behind the Noncomformist ministers who launched a counterattack against English imperialism.[8]

The "Treachery of the Blue Books" shifted the balance of power in the political struggle for the hearts and minds of the Welsh-speaking Nonconformist ministers who rose up in unison to denounce the Blue Books. Their position was heightened by the great religious revival of 1859, and by the actions of landowners who evicted tenants who refused to become Anglican or to vote for politicians the landowners found acceptable. The politics of dissent attracted some notable candidates into the field during the general elections of 1868. Perhaps most prominent was the election to Parliament of the Reverend Henry Richard of Merthyr, a leading Nonconformist spokesman in Wales and outraged critic of the Blue Books. He and several other dissenters were elected that year, and they brought the issue of disestablishment of the Anglican church as the official state church to the forefront of Welsh politics.[9]

In this context, one can readily understand why the idea of establishing a new Welsh nation abroad, one that would preserve the language and culture of Wales, gained urgency during the nineteenth century. Nonconformist ministers, such as Morgan John Rhys, Rev. Benjamin Chidlaw, Rev. Samuel Roberts, and Rev. Michael D. Jones, played a prominent role in this movement, leading thousands of Welsh to new colonies abroad. Rhys, a Baptist preacher, began his search for a location for the new *Gwalya*, or homeland, in the American backcountry in 1794. The new colony, "Beulah Land," was established in Ebensburgh, Cambria County, Pennsylvania, and hundreds of settlers sailed from Wales over the ensuing decade. Some of them continued down the Ohio River to found sister colonies in southwestern Ohio. One of them, Benjamin Chidlaw, had immigrated to Ohio with his parents as a youth but returned to Wales to complete his education. Shortly after he finished his studies, Chidlaw became the Congregationalist minister at the Welsh settlement of Paddy's Run (now Shandon), near Cincinnati. He returned to Wales again in 1836 and 1839 to revitalize his command of Welsh and to preach the advantages of colonization. In 1840 he published his widely distributed *Immigrant's Guide to America* to help newcomers.[10]

The Reverend Samuel Roberts of Llanbrynmair, Montgomeryshire, a close friend of Chidlaw, proclaimed that only by immigrating to the United States could Welsh farmers become landowners and preserve the Welsh language and culture. In establishing the Welsh colony of Brynffynon in Tennessee, Roberts received assistance from his cousin William Bebb of

Ohio. William was born in 1802 to Edward and Margarett Bebb, who emigrated from Llanbrynmair with the first settlers of Paddy's Run. Their son William became the first native-born governor of Ohio, serving from 1846 to 1848. Although Roberts's experiment failed, he was instrumental in creating awareness in Wales of the benefits of emigration through his journal *Y Cronicl*, and a widely circulated pamphlet in Wales, *Farmer Careful of Cil-Haul Uchaf.* The third prominent minister seeking to establish a haven for the preservation of the Welsh language and culture was the Congregationalist preacher Michael D. Jones of Bala, Merionethshire. Former governor William Bebb seems to have had some influence on Jones as well. Jones's sister, Mary Ann, had immigrated to Ohio in the 1830s and grew up in the Bebb household. Bebb encouraged Jones to migrate to Ohio in 1847, but Jones believed that Americanization was too powerful for Welsh culture to survive in the United States, so in 1865 he established a new Welsh colony in the Chubut Valley in Patagonia, Argentina.[11] If a separate nation for the preservation of the Welsh language and culture are the only measurement, these colonies failed.

Undoubtedly, the promotional activities of these preachers stimulated interest and general awareness of emigration among the rural Welsh population. The vast majority of those who left for America went for pragmatic rather than idealistic reasons. Even though the vast majority did not seek an exclusive Welsh existence, the pre-1840s agrarian migrants tended to join family and friends in the Welsh agricultural communities of Pennsylvania, New York, and eastern Ohio, where they continued their familiar ways with little interference. Welsh settlers followed the American western agricultural migration into the fertile flatlands of the Midwest. Important Welsh settlements were established early in Ohio's Western Reserve at Palmyra, and then in central Ohio at Gomer, and in the southern part of the state in Gallia and Jackson Counties, which became known as "Little Cardiganshire." Continuing the westward migration, large concentrations of Welsh settled in Wisconsin, and others moved to Iowa, Missouri, and Kansas. The Welsh certainly were not averse to being pioneers, but, compared with other immigrant groups, their numbers were small, and the further west they migrated the thinner and more dispersed on the land they became. It is also clear that they emigrated individually or in family groups, relying on family to assist them in settling the new land. One section of the United States Welsh farmers avoided was the South. In 1860 the census reported that fewer than 500 of the 45,500 foreign-born Welsh lived below the Mason-Dixon Line. If the Welsh ethnic press and prominent chapel leaders are an indication, Welsh immigrants avoided the South because ideologically they found slavery repugnant. Solid material reasons also motivated their avoidance, however, for there was little cheap land available in the South, and there was little demand for their labor in a region dependent on oppressed African American workers.[12]

Occupying a unique place in the history of Welsh emigration in the mid-nineteenth century was the large number of Mormon converts who settled in Utah. In 1840 Dan Jones, a native of Flintshire, immigrated to Illinois, and by 1843 was owner of a schooner that transported settlers westward over the Ohio and Mississippi Rivers. In 1843 he met Joseph Smith and became a convert and close confidant of the prophet. Mormon scholar Douglas Davies argues that Jones was the embodiment of the movement. He was a convert, an eyewitness, and a participant, but he was a Welshman fluent in the Welsh language who delighted in missionary work. Captain Dan Jones was sent to Wales as a missionary in 1845, and two years later reported converting more than nine hundred. By the end of 1848 the number of converts in Wales had grown to 4,654. Against the fierce opposition of the Nonconformist ministers, the focus of his work was in the coal and iron producing center of Merthyr Tydfil, Glamorganshire. Severe unemployment coincided with Mormon teachings that a bright future lay ahead in "Zion," which they called America at the time. Captain Dan Jones led the first Welsh migrants from Wales to America in 1849.[13] Thousands followed him to Utah where they created small Welsh communities within the new Mormon society; many found their way to the coal-mining areas of Utah. Douglas Davies claims that approximately one-third of the 60,033 Welsh immigrants to the United States between 1847 and 1890 were Mormons. According to his calculations, in 1887 the Welsh population reached about 17,000, or about 15 percent of the population in Utah. Another authority claims this figure is too low, and estimates that the Welsh population was closer to 25,000.[14]

### Industrial Migration within Wales

By the end of the 1840s the emigration from rural Wales to the United States faded with the return of more prosperous times in the 1850s and 1860s. They did not last long, for in the late 1870s the Welsh countryside was plunged into a severe depression that lasted for the next two decades. Once again poverty forced people to migrate, but this time they moved to the rapidly expanding South Wales coal and iron district.[15]

In the nineteenth century Welsh industry was defined regionally. Slate mines and quarries dominated the northwestern county of Gwynedd; Cardiganshire was noted for its woolens manufactured in small shops and homes throughout the western counties; in the lower Swansea Valley copper ore was imported and smelted along the Tawe River, where water, limestone, timber, and coal were plentiful. Before 1850 the noxious gases from eleven major copper works spanning a radius of three miles of "Copperopolis" darkened the sky and killed plant life. A few miles west, in Llanelli and adjacent towns, the Welsh tinplate industry dominated British production to the point of monopoly, provided the United States with over 70 percent of its needs, and challenged competitors in the world market. But it was the ironworks, born out of the demands of the almost continuous wars with France from 1757 to 1815, that stood testimony to the religion of progress and the Welsh future in the first half of the nineteenth century. Eight great ironworks, and many smaller ones amongst them, sprang up to cast guns and munitions, each "the love child of war and empire," as the Welsh historian Dai Smith has aptly characterized them. At the center of the iron industry was Merthyr, the Iron Capital of the world, encircled by the giant Cyfarthfa, Dowlais, Penydarren, and Plymouth works.[16]

The use of anthracite for smelting iron was pioneered in the 1830s by ironworks owner George Crane and his inventive superintendent David Thomas at the Ynyscedwyn Ironworks, thirteen miles up the River Tawe from Swansea in the village of Ystrdgynlais. In 1839 Thomas was persuaded to immigrate to Pennsylvania and erect an ironworks on the Lehigh River near Allentown that would use the extensive measures of anthracite coal found there. Thomas became the "Father of American Anthracite Iron" and succeeded in igniting the American industrial revolution. Thousands of skilled Welsh miners and ironworkers would soon follow Thomas's path to the American anthracite fields.[17]

By the mid-nineteenth century, the advantages of location at the upper rim of the South Wales coalfield dimmed as the ores played out and technological changes forced the iron and steel industry to move out of the valleys to the coast. The South Wales coal industry became the engine of the Welsh economy for the next three-quarters of a century. The coal resources found in South Wales were among the richest deposits in the world. Within this one-thousand-square-mile coal region were anthracite measures rivaled only by those found in Pennsylvania; the smokeless quality of the bituminous steam coal was unmatched anywhere in the world until the southern West Virginia coalfields were developed at the turn of the twentieth century. In addition there was an abundance of excellent coking coal

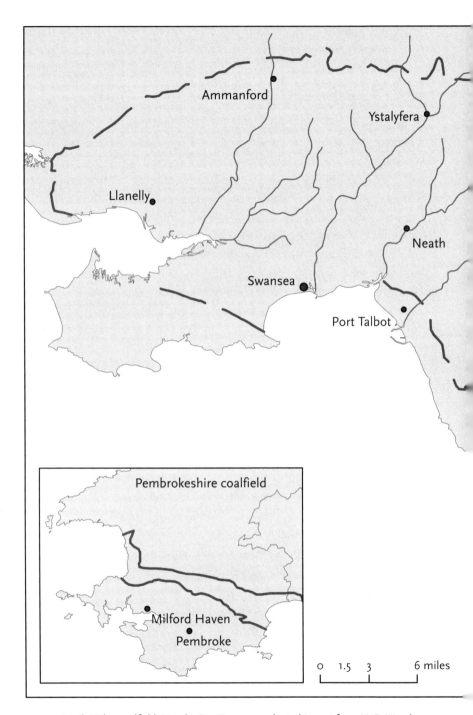

MAP 2. South Wales coalfield. Map by Sue Bergeron, adapted in part from H. B. Woodward, ed., *Stanford's Geological Atlas of Great Britain and Ireland*, 3rd ed. (London: Edward Stanford Ltd., 1914).

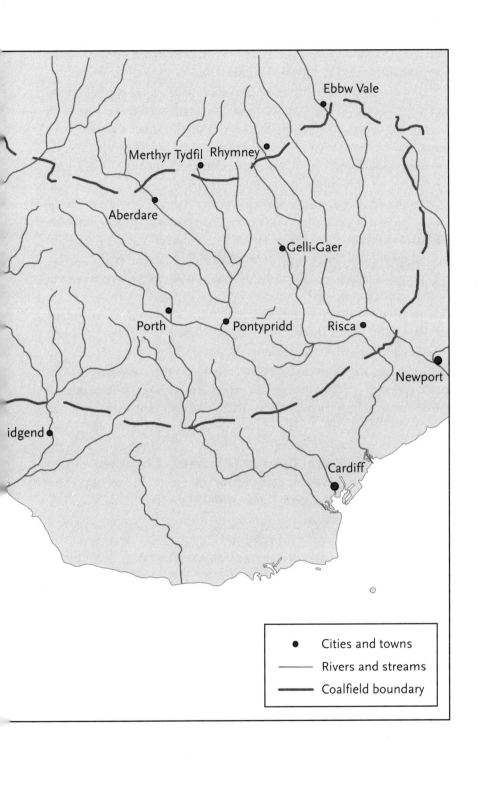

Ebbw Vale

Merthyr Tydfil  Rhymney

Aberdare

Gelli-Gaer

Porth      Pontypridd      Risca

Newport

idgend

Cardiff

Cities and towns

Rivers and streams

Coalfield boundary

for steel production. The export trade was assured by the opening of the Bute docks in Cardiff in 1839, and railroads penetrated the valleys reaching from the coastal docks to the top of the valleys at the lower edge of central Wales. Finally, in the 1850s, all the pieces were in place for an explosion in the export coal trade when the British Admiralty declared South Wales steam coal the best available for naval requirements. Meanwhile the deepest coal seams, found in the central section of the basin-shaped coalfield, were tapped in 1837, and methods for sinking shafts of up to 2,000 feet deep were worked out by several pioneering entrepreneurs. The widespread belief that the steam coal lay too deep to recover profitably was put to rest when the Bute Merthyr pit was sunk, and the first trainload of steam coal chugged down the Rhondda Valley to the docks at Cardiff in December 1855. Welsh entrepreneurs established the industry that would rule the economy until the collapse of the 1920s.[18]

Until the mid-nineteenth century, coal was mined in levels or drifts at the perimeter of the basin-shaped South Wales coalfield where the coal seams were closer to the surface. Shafts were few and shallow until the 1860s when the deep seams (some 2,000 feet) of the Rhondda Valleys were finally penetrated. Although the iron industry was controlled by English investors, the coal industry was developed by the Welsh. In both industries, however, workmen were primarily Welsh. Initially, the coal industry serviced the iron and steel industry, but a sale-coal segment of the industry soon developed that was primarily for export. Growth came as a result of the conversion from sail to steam power, producing some 60 million tons of smokeless coal for the naval shipping industry by the onset of World War I. Canals and railroads were constructed by the great companies to transport their products down the valleys to the busy docks of Cardiff and Swansea to be loaded on ocean-going vessels. Thousands of workers were required for this great industrial expansion, and, fortunately for the capitalists, a great pool of labor was available amongst the displaced rural population. In the 1880s, 100,000 people abandoned rural Wales mostly for the industrializing coal valleys.[19]

The rise of the steam coal industry had national implications for Wales. With some of the richest coal seams in the world, the South Wales coalfield developed into one of the world's greatest coal-producing regions. By the turn of the twentieth century more than five hundred mines were in operation, shipping coal by rail to the docks at Swansea, Newport, and Cardiff, which for two decades exported more coal than any other port in the world.[20]

The industrial transformation of Wales in the nineteenth century is documented statistically by the growth in population from about half a million in 1800, 80 percent of whom depended on agriculture, to more than 2.5 million in 1914, 80 percent of whom lived in urban areas and were employed in non-agricultural pursuits. By 1850 industrial workers already outnumbered farmers, but, by 1910, 388,000 people had abandoned the Welsh countryside primarily for the South Wales coalfield. The two major coal-producing counties, Glamorganshire and Monmouthshire, contained one-quarter of the Welsh population in 1801, but, by 1911, three-quarters of them resided there. Most of the workforce was Welsh at midcentury, but Wales became an importer of labor. By the first decade of the twentieth century the population of Glamorgan topped one million, and fully one-third were born outside the country. More than one-half of the entire workforce of South Wales was employed in the coal industry. By 1921, King Coal commanded 270,000 miners, and one in every four Welshmen depended on the pits for a livelihood. Famous for their natural beauty before coal, the valleys of the Rhondda Fach and Fawr (little and big) had a population of less than 1,000, but by 1921 it was 163,000; the forests were gone and the streams were dead from pollution. Production indicates the expansion as well, from 4.5 million tons in 1840 to 8.5 million tons in 1854. By 1913 Wales produced 56.8 million of the total 287 million tons of coal brought to the surface in Britain. By 1900 South Wales was the leading coal exporting region in the United Kingdom, and, for the two decades from 1890 to 1910, South Wales shipped nearly one-third of the world's total coal exports.[21]

### Grievances and Conditions

The rapid industrialization of the South Wales coalfield, particularly the most explosive growth area between Merthyr Tydfil and Pontypool, was the center of social turmoil during the first half of the nineteenth century. Social services failed to keep pace with the burgeoning population. Conditions were poor enough in the 1840s that H. Seymour Tremenheere, a government inspector, described the coalfield as a neglected society and laid blame for this negligence on the employers. In 1847 a commissioner of education concurred: "I regard their degraded condition as entirely the fault of their employers, who give them far less tendance [sic] and care than they bestow upon their cattle, and who, with a few exceptions, use and regard them as so much brute force instrumental to wealth, but as nowise involving claims on human sympathy."[22]

One of the social problems to attract the attention of reformers was the practice of employing women and children in the mines. This was a widespread practice and not confined to Wales, but in 1847 the Children's Employment Commission found boys as young as four employed in the South Wales collieries. The youngest tended ventilation doors or helped their fathers. Boys were found dragging small sledges of coal on hands and knees out of the thin seams to the main entries for pick up. Older children became hauliers or loaders before graduating to hewing at the face. The incentive was strong for fathers to take their children into the mines at a young age. Until a lad was seventeen (adulthood for a collier) his earnings were paid to the father, providing supplemental income for the family, and the hewer-father could also claim another tram for a helper further increasing the family income. Employment of girls in Welsh mines was not common, and the employment of women was confined primarily to the older Pembroke-shire field where they screened and sorted the coal at the surface or worked on the windless, hoisting coal from underground.[23]

An act passed by Parliament in 1842 excluded women and children under ten from underground work in collieries, a sharp change in policy for most British mining regions. During the forties the act was evaded, and in 1850 Commissioner Tremenheere reported that women and boys under ten continued to work in the pits. The managers claimed that the mines were accessible through the levels on the sides of the hills, and that the boys and women entered before it was light and exited after dark. They easily hid themselves when a search was made for them. Even on the surface, women were seldom found employed at the mines. The practice of employing women and young children had died out in the old coalfields by the 1860s, and the new deep mines being opened in the valleys ended the practice of entering and leaving at will. For the most part, companies complied with the act from its initiation. By the 1860s, women were absent from the pits entirely, and the miners themselves were demanding that the age for boys be raised to twelve.[24]

Life was bleak in coal regions wherever they were located, and many of the same conditions awaited those Welsh miners who emigrated to the United States. In Wales coal mines were developed in the moorland and steep, narrow valleys. Since little in the way of infrastructure was present, the companies shouldered the responsibility for recruiting and accommodating an ever-expanding labor force and their families. The narrow valleys presented no alternative to building terrace or row housing for the miners. Often they were dark and dank, lacked proper sewage and sanitation, and built in the shadow of the black mountains of slag waste behind the housing. Generally two rooms down and two up, the miners' houses were a step up from the older rural dwellings, but they were usually crowded by large families and the practice of taking in single male boarders. Not surprisingly, they were vulnerable to diseases. Ribbon villages developed in the narrow valleys, providing little opportunity for the growth of community life until early in the twentieth century. The coal industry generally does not stimulate other industries, so few employment alternatives existed.[25]

In the 1840s schools for children in the South Wales coalfield were rare, but with each decade the employers became more aware of the importance of educational facilities in maintaining their employees' families. Generally, a deduction was made from the miner's pay determined by the number of children in the family. Medical facilities also were lacking in the beginning but improved throughout the century. To pay for medical services, which were often called for in an occupation with a high death and casualty rate, the company took another deduction from the miner's paycheck. Supplementing the company-supplied services, Welsh miners joined benefit societies and clubs that provided insurance against the costs arising from sickness, accidents, and funerals. As the century wore on, the amenities of life were improved in coalfield towns as basic social services improved substantially, and places of worship, libraries, and other forms of recreation and leisure outside the pub greatly enhanced the quality of life for miners and their families.[26]

Many of the miners' worst aggravations were not about conditions, which gradually improved, but rather a cluster of grievances rooted in not only the amount of wages, but also the employers' method of paying wages generally known as the "truck" system. From the 1840s through the 1870s, truck was a prominent feature of life in the South Wales coalfield. There were many miners in Glamorganshire and Monmouthshire who received their wages at the company or local shop rather than in cash. Advances in goods were taken by miners against their earnings. The books were reconciled at the end of the pay period, and the miner received the balance due if any. Miners disliked the system and complained that the prices were higher than elsewhere, by about 15 percent according to general consensus. The shop established by a company developing a mine in an isolated area would provide an important service to the employees, and higher prices might reflect higher costs. A company shop at Cwmavon was established to guard against price gouging from independent shopkeepers, and such shops often provided miners with the necessities during a business downturn.[27]

By the 1870s these justifications for the truck shop were no longer important. And yet the truck continued to survive; the main reason was the long period between paydays, known as the "long pays." Colliers were normally paid once a month, with a "draw" every two weeks, generally in cash for the miner to spend as he saw fit. If colliers took an "advance" between the payday and the draw, the company expected most of the advance to be spent at the company shop, which generally was in the same building as the pay office. Those who did not abide by this practice might be discharged or discriminated against in work assignments by the company. Most of the better paid or more provident men did not deal at the company store, but there were many who could not survive without advances. Once the stores were established, they provided another source of profit for the company, and also increased the degree of control it could exert over colliers. While the long pay survived, therefore, so too did the truck shop. Understandably, the miner, joined just as forcefully by his wife, regarded the truck shop as a wage-reducing mechanism, which mired them in debt to the company.[28]

The Welsh coal miner's life during the great expansion period was plagued by unpredictability and the lack of control over his own destiny. When miners went on strike, the mine owners in Wales, as in the United States, evicted them from company houses, "blacklisted" them so they could not get employment elsewhere, and replaced them with strikebreakers, or "blacklegs." Miners who went on strike were liable to run afoul of the law if they had not given notice a month in advance as required, and the operators would mark their discharge note as a warning to the next employer that the miner was a troublemaker. Some employers also brought charges against strikers for breach of the contract they signed upon employment. If these measures failed, they called on the government to send in the troops. Black-listing in the late 1860s left few alternatives to active unionists but to migrate to the United States; sometimes their passage was paid by the union.[29] In addition to the market booms and busts that characterize the coal industry generally, mining life was further destabilized by the frequent failure of coal companies. One study traced the longevity of fifty-three out of sixty-four companies formed during the years 1856 to 1867, and found that three were aborted, ten had failed by 1864, and thirty-one had failed by the end of 1870, as did two more by 1874. In 1875 only seven were still in existence.[30]

### Rebellion and Organization

The exact timing of Wales's industrialization is subject to interpretation, but the process was rooted at least in the seventeenth century. Nevertheless, prior to the major phase of industrial expansion in the nineteenth century Wales was overwhelmingly pastoral, and the workforce that gathered in the new coal and iron towns lacked a tradition of class cohesion. Little wonder then that, before the formation of the union, protest bore the hallmarks of a primitive folk movement to defend former standards of the "moral economy." Of the fifty or so strikes and riots in South Wales between 1800 and 1830, all but a handful were defensive actions against wage reductions. The Scotch Cattle was the quintessential expression of primitive action in the South Wales coalfield, an organization intended to enforce community morality against blacklegs, merchants who overcharged, and the overly ambitious. The Scotch Cattle were the coalfield's version of the Daughters of Rebecca; their ritualistic behavior echoes the charivari, the *ceffyl pren*, of earlier times: a warning note over the red bull's head, "To all Colliers, Traitors, Turncoats and Others"; then the night visit by a "herd" from the next valley, faces blackened and clad in animal hides or women's clothes, led by a horned bull; then the ritualistic breaking of the window sash and furniture, and sometimes beating up the offender. Similarly, the primitive food riot was imported into the towns, as were the armed "marching gangs" that appeared when the folk now living in the industrial towns were upset with another wage reduction and fought pitched battles with the constabulary. The old communal discipline of the village adapted to life in the coalfield, with the colliers in the lead of the emerging proletarian consciousness.[31]

During the crisis years of depression and the First Reform Bill, 1829–31, the working class in Wales first took shape as a national force. The climax was reached with the Merthyr Rising of May 1831, when the miners filled the streets of Merthyr Tydfil in political demonstrations, and a great rally was held on an overlooking hill under a red banner. The crowd stormed the town shouting "Reform for Ever," sacked the debtors' court, and returned confiscated goods to their owners. A dozen men died when the crowd attacked the soldiers and drove them from town. The towns at the upper rim of the coalfield joined in with strikes and demonstrations. Recapturing Merthyr after four days of control by the crowd came only after three pitched battles between rebels and soldiers. Several of the leaders were convicted and transported to Australia; Richard Lewis, known as "Dic Penderyn," a young miner of twenty-three, and most likely innocent, was sent to the gallows in August, and began his mythical career as martyr of the Welsh working class.[32]

Eight years after the Merthyr Rising, Chartism, the first attempt to build an independent political party representing the interests of the working classes, took form in the Welsh valleys. The Chartists took their name from their charter, first published in 1838, demanding universal manhood suffrage; annual parliaments; the secret ballot; abolition of property qualifications for Members of Parliament; payment to MPs; and equal electoral districts. They intended to make the charter a part of the constitution, "peaceably if we can, forcibly if we must." Scholars do not know how Chartism came to the South Wales coalfield, but it gathered old and new radicals, Scotch Cattle, and union men into one great movement for political democracy. A petition signed by more than one million Britons and presented to the House of Commons was rejected in June 1839. Thereafter, the movement split into two factions, one favoring moral appeal, and the other physical force. Chartism in the valleys remains a mystery at its vital points, particularly the ill-fated March on Newport in November 1839, when soldiers fortified at the Westgate Hotel fired on the crowd of 2,000 miners. When the smoke cleared twenty-two Chartists were either dead or dying; three of the leaders were transported to Australia for life. Whether the celebrated March on Newport was an insurrection, as some believe, or a mass demonstration gone wrong, as others regard it, the miners had another important milepost on the road to class consciousness.[33]

Despite the labor unrest of the nineteenth century, the militant trade unionism with which Welsh miners became synonymous in the twentieth century was slow to find organization. For most of the nineteenth century, Welsh miners were not ideological radicals; in fact, they were preoccupied with wages even to the exclusion of hours of labor, safety, and working conditions. It must be understood that there were legitimate reasons for this: wage rates were substantially lower in South Wales than in other British coalfields for most of the century after 1850; they also worked longer hours than their English counterparts; and retail prices in South Wales mining districts were probably higher than the national average because of the rapid expansion. In other words, they worked longer and received lower wages, while the cost of living was higher.[34]

It was this preoccupation with wages that shaped their attitudes toward unionism: when the union promised to raise wages, miners joined; when it failed to keep that promise, they lost interest. Consequently, no permanent coalfield-wide labor organization was established in Wales until 1898. Many reasons have been offered for this lack of unionism: the virulent opposition of employers; the difficulty of uniting a heterogeneous labor force in small isolated communities; and reluctance to pay union wages out of meager earnings. Moreover, the idea that miners and mine owners shared a common interest probably weakened the growth of unionism based on class conflict, as in those organizations that emerged at the end of the century. In the 1870s the automatic wage regulator, the sliding scale, and the regulatory committee, established to deal with grievances, undoubtedly weakened the perceived need for strong labor unions. Also, the Nonconformist denominations, which were particularly strong among the miners, threw their weight against unions. The strike weapon was the only instrument left to the miners, therefore, and for most of the century it was used in generally unsuccessful attempts to prevent a cut in wages rather than to seek wage advances. Limiting the supply of labor offered an alternative to the strike, but this policy was never implemented other than in the 1880s when miners encouraged emigration in order to reduce the supply of labor to raise the wages of those who remained. A second approach, to curtail coal production, was not implemented either. Miners were loath to accept tactics that called for slowing down production, or curtailing actual time at work, because as tonnage workers they would suffer a loss of earnings.[35]

Strong unionism was slow to take hold in the South Wales coalfield, but there had been brief attempts at organization during crises. The Rhondda miners were organized briefly in 1847, and in Aberdare they formed the Glamorgan Union of Colliers in 1850. Delegates from England occasionally tried to organize the Welsh miners. In 1831, they introduced the Friendly Society of Coal Mining; in the late forties the Miners' Association of Great Britain made a brief appearance. Both attempts were ephemeral. Welsh delegates attended a Leeds conference in 1863 when the Miners' National Union was established, and some Welshmen were active with the National Association of Practical Miners formed shortly thereafter. Both organizations, however, soon failed, and there is little evidence that these organizations gained much traction among the South Wales miners. In the place of the MNU emerged the more militant Amalgamated Association of Miners, which did generate some interest among the colliers of Glamorgan and Monmouthshire. During three bitter strikes between 1873 and 1875, a powerful organization of owners destroyed the fledgling union movement. In 1875 the owners locked out the miners, but offered a settlement of a smaller wage reduction and a sliding scale determined by the market price of coal and supervised by a joint committee of owners and miners. The men accepted the settlement and thereby accepted the principle that the owners and miners had a common set of interests. The miners embraced the sliding scale because it brought an end to the turmoil in the South Wales coalfield and removed the wage rate from the arbitrary actions of the employers. It also undermined the need for a strong labor union.[36] The commitment of Welsh miners who emigrated to America to the sliding scale and arbitration of grievances was, therefore, deeply rooted in their experience back in Wales.

## Nonconformity and the Miners

The great influx of people seeking employment in the burgeoning South Wales coal and iron district came primarily from rural Wales, displaced agricultural laborers who brought with them their own traditions and religious practices. In the years prior to the 1850s, Nonconformist Protestantism, as represented by the Unitarians, Congregationalists, Presbyterians, Baptists, Calvinistic Methodists, and Independents, was the religion of the Welsh. Many Welsh rejected the Established Church, the Anglican, as an imposition and symbol of their subordinate position to England. Also, they found comfort in the simplicity of the denominational structure of Nonconformism in which control rested with the local congregations. They also shared the evangelical belief in the personal relationship between God and human beings, that faith alone could save one's soul, and, to some degree, the Calvinistic theology of predestination. Nonconformity enabled the Welsh to claim some control over their lives, and therefore 87 percent of them attended Nonconformist chapels while only 9 percent of Welsh churchgoers attended the official Church of England.[37]

Noted for its powerful preaching, thorough grounding in doctrine, solemnity, and directness of approach, Nonconformism attracted many talented Welsh ministers. Its anti-establishment stance carried within it the roots of Welsh nationalism, but what made Nonconformism the religion of Wales were the nonreligious institutions it created. Dissenting chapels became educational centers for working-class children and adults, whom British institutions ignored, by operating tuition-free day schools and Sunday schools. Moreover, unlike the Anglican churches, which were strictly devotional places, the chapels also served as community centers providing educational activities, such as lectures, eisteddfodau, concerts, readings, and meeting places.[38]

The Nonconformist chapel also provided an alternative to the pub, "the masculine republic," as it has been called. Drunkenness was a serious problem in the new industrial centers. The Nonconformists struggled against drink as the source of poverty and other social and moral deviations, and incorporated moderation and teetotalism into Dissenter culture as an antidote. The temperance movement originated in America during the 1820s, had spread to Wales by 1833, and the emphasis on self-respect and setting a good example through teetotalism became a dominant theme within Welsh Nonconformism. Even though the vast majority of Welshmen either ignored or were openly hostile to the moral and religious crusade against John Barleycorn, Dissenter ministers embraced the idea that abstinence was a sign of respectability. The churches' response to industrialization in South Wales emphasized the "centrality of individual responsibility and worth, and claimed that individual evils were responsible for the social iniquities of the period," not the capitalists, not the economic system, not the complicity of government. The emphasis was on personal respectability rather than social change. Therefore, with the exception of the free-thinking Unitarians, the denominations were either lukewarm or hostile to the social revolts of the day, such as the Scotch Cattle, the Rebecca Riots, the Merthyr Rising of 1831, and the Chartist Movement.[39]

Even though the denominations generally did not support labor activism, there were radical Dissenter ministers who did play an active role in the Chartist movement. The leaders of Chartism were in the main craftsmen, tailors, shopkeepers, master colliers, printers, and others of the respectable middle class. Their only commonality was religious affiliation, and the radical ministers provided their chapels as sanctuaries. The small radical strain in Welsh Nonconformism was indebted to Oliver Cromwell and the American revolutionaries, a tradition inherited through men like Richard Price and his writings on the nature of liberty. There was another point of convergence for labor and Dissenter radicalism, and that was the growing importance of Disestablishment, the movement for religious freedom and independence of the Nonconformist denominations from the official state church. Through political reform a greater representation could be achieved in Parliament, providing the power to repeal laws that prevented freedom of religious expression. By the 1840s a united Nonconformist front had emerged on this issue.[40]

The chapel, then, played an important role in the secular as well as the religious life of the Welsh. Particularly in industrializing South Wales, the chapel was an institution in which old traditions converged and new ones were created. Within this chapel-centered society there emerged a culture of the ordinary folk, who yearned to acquire, at least in humble measure, the enjoyment, prestige, and status of a more cultured society. The society they sought would represent the strivings of working people, share the basic desire for the elevation of a submerged people, and promote self-improvement through personal initiative. These ideas were rooted in the optimistic nineteenth-century belief that through individual initiative one could be reborn, and in what Max Weber famously called the "Protestant Ethic," the conception that one's self-worth, or respectability, was revealed in personal achievement. Attributing worldly success to divine approval was a significant bastardization of Calvinism, and was antithetical to the doctrine that salvation was achieved through faith and divine grace, not good works. The growth of Welsh Nonconformism, which was strongly Calvinistic, was accelerated by the libelous 1847 parliamentary commission *Report into the State of Education in Wales*. The report presented in very unflattering terms everything Welsh: the language, education, religion, family life, and morality.[41]

The Welsh were outraged by the degree of disrespect exhibited by the English commissioners, and the Nonconformists led a counteroffensive that portrayed the Welsh, according to one scholar, "as the most virtuous people in Europe, the most hard-working, the most God-fearing, the best at observing the Sabbath, the most temperate, and the most deeply devoted to educational improvement." In all of their institutions, religious and secular, the Welsh were encouraged "to work hard, to elevate themselves, to liberate themselves from obscurity, and to wear the badges of progress, industriousness and self-improvement." In other words, they should become respectable middle-class Victorians.[42]

Early Welsh Nonconformity was antagonistic toward labor associations, partly because of the secrecy oaths, and partly because they met in public houses. By the turn of the twentieth century, with the notable exception of more than a few Radical ministers, the denominations and organized labor maintained an uneasy truce as new labor leaders, such as William Brace, Vernon Hartshorn, and James Keir Hardie, emerged to challenge the chapels for the miners' loyalty.[43] On both sides of the Atlantic the clergy kept their distance from trade unionists but embraced the mine managers. Welshmen who migrated from the Rhondda Valley in Wales to the Wyoming Valley in Pennsylvania found the chapels headed by like-minded ministers, and leadership positions were controlled by the under managers, the foremen, fire bosses, subcontractors, as well as tradesmen and shopkeepers. As the class divisions within the congregations became widened, the democracy of the chapels weakened. By the 1880s, the chapels ceased to provide meaningful leadership for the miners in either country except in spiritual matters.[44]

Notwithstanding the stirrings of conscience among some individual clerics, official Nonconformism in Wales took no stand on social or political issues unless they directly affected the denominations. They seemed indifferent to the social problems that affected the tens of thousands of their adherents. Their aloofness, and occasional hostility, toward labor unions was duly noted by the Welsh miners. Like most churches in Victorian Britain and America, the Christian message from pulpits in the coalfields was purely individualistic to the exclusion of larger community needs or material conditions. However, some ministers and many laymen became disenchanted with an approach that inevitably led to a rejection of the world and excessive moralizing about personal vices. The struggle between labor and capital intensified as the nineteenth century waned, but organized religion seemed obsessed with prohibitions and blind to social injustice. One miner complained that, "instead of giving men justice, they want to make them better, more sober, more humble and contrite in heart." The chapels were good for "Psalm singing, tea meetings, and pious sentiments," he continued, but "their influence is always on the side of the oppressors, the capitalists."[45]

The chapels, miners believed, tilted the playing field toward the powerful, and away from the working class. George Davey, a miners' leader in the Ogmore Valley, observed that "when occasionally the preacher touched upon better working conditions there was a responsive throb in many hearts, but those moments were few and far between. . . . Hence we looked more closely to the emerging Labour Party and we recognized that therein lay salvation." According to one scholar, there was a growing rebellion among many intelligent miners against the insularity of the chapels. Miners needed humane working conditions, but "with the exception of a few ministers, the chapels were presenting a message in which personal virtues were given an exclusive place and the world of affairs regarded as an alien province."[46]

Welsh coal miners brought their criticism of Nonconformist ministers to America. For example, during the Colorado Mine War of 1913–14, a Reverend Pingree, of Denver, announced that "iron and steel and the bayonet are the means by which to rule the striking coal miners." In reply, George Jenkins questioned that a man of Pingree's stripe should be in the pulpit, and worse, whether or not he was even a Christian. "Would not a true preacher go down among the poor, ignorant miners and encourage and cheer them . . . just to show them that the spirit of Christ, that friend of the poor, was in him?"[47]

Edward C. Evans, a former miner from Broughton, near Wrexham, North Wales, emigrated in 1869, at age twenty-five, and settled in Shenandoah, Pennsylvania. Because of a shortage of preachers he agreed to serve in that capacity. He prepared himself through long hours of study and was admitted to Princeton Theological Seminary, and then was given a scholarship to study at Oxford University for two years. While serving at the Welsh settlement of Remsen, New York, Evans launched the *Cambrian* in 1880, a Welsh American periodical. The magazine published a series of articles by ministers defending the church against charges from workers that the institution served the interests of capital rather than labor. The split in Wales between the Radical Dissenters and traditional Nonconformist ministers was also apparent in the United States. The Reverend D. T. Jenkins, who declared that Christianity "teaches the true Socialism, and condemns in no uncertain tones the present state of society," was clearly one of those of the Radical tradition. He claimed that "because the Christian Church has allowed in silence tyranny and oppression on the part of the rich to exist; because its sympathies have been in the main, with the rich and opulent, the hearts of the common people have been lost to the church." There was, he charged, a "monstrous contradiction between the ethics of Christ and the state of society which Christians tolerate."[48]

The Reverend Morgan P. Jones declared that the vast majority of the church's members were from the working class, so it was imperative that "the impression existing in some quarters that the church is unfriendly to the interests of the laboring classes" must be seriously examined. While he did not think this impression was correct, he believed that, in its devotion to philosophical and theological questions, the church's "ecclesiastical conservatism" was one reason ministers often neglected the physical and spiritual welfare of men and was so "enamored of dogmas that it forgot the practical side of religion almost entirely." The workingman is entitled to justice, but with industrial problems "the church should be impartial. . . . If employers have a right to combine for self-protection, the church should not denounce workingmen for banding together in defense of the rights of labor."[49] This kind of fair-minded fence-straddling in an age when the conditions for miners were deteriorating only offered comfort to the capitalists who would deny miners an equal opportunity to succeed by using their power to trap them in a permanent lower-class status.

### Bound for America

It is against this backdrop of poor living and working conditions, violence, the unpredictability of employment and wages, and growing power of Nonconformity that the emigration from the Welsh coalfields must be understood. Those who emigrated did so before conditions and militant unionism emerged in 1898 with the formation of the South Wales Miners' Federation, popularly known as "the Fed."[50] Ethnically, these mining families were very cohesively Welsh, and, while they were not far distant from the culture rooted in rural Wales, they had, nonetheless, already severed ties once by moving from the farm to the alien environment of the industrial valleys. Many who had become industrial workers were still capable of returning to the land if that became possible. Increasingly, most were the children of the migrants who moved from the land to the mines and mills, and this was the only life they had known. Therefore, when difficulties mounted in the Welsh coalfields, the lure of a rapidly industrializing America, where skilled labor was in demand and an abundance of cheap land was still available, was irresistible for many. And the Welsh were fully apprised of developments in the United States. The movement of thousands of Mormon converts to Utah, the gold rush of 1849, and the thousands of farmers who took up land from Ohio to Wisconsin kept America in the Welsh consciousness because of letter writing and newspaper exchanges. Lectures on the United States by Nonconformist ministers were common and attracted considerable attention in Wales. But the United States as an emigrant destination also generated points of controversy. Harriet Beecher Stowe's *Uncle Tom's Cabin* was translated into Welsh and serialized in the Welsh press, reinforcing Welsh hostility to slavery. One writer in *Baner Cymru* suggested in 1859 that migration to the United States was not an intelligent choice because "3,000,000 people are slaves" there, and the country would soon be torn asunder.[51] In a rejoinder, another writer responded that "slavery in America does not appear to be any less praiseworthy than the eviction of tenants from their farms by landlords in an attempt to coerce the farmers into following the religious beliefs [Anglican] and political ideas [Tory] of the squirearchy."[52]

The Civil War stirred a great interest in Wales, and also dampened the emigration spirit until it became clear that the Union would prevail. The Welsh clergy and the press spoke in a unified voice against slavery, and public opinion in Wales was strongly supportive of the Union during the Civil War, which they viewed as a struggle to end the evil of slavery. Nearly all of the Welsh in America had settled in the northern states, particularly New York, Pennsylvania, Ohio, Illinois, and Wisconsin, at least in part because of an abhorrence of slavery. Almost without exception, therefore, those who fought were enlisted into the Union ranks. Prior to 1863, President Lincoln occasionally was chastised in the Welsh press for not emancipating the slaves.[53] Even with the disruptions in transportation, however, a number of Welsh workers embarked for America during the war years, most of them skilled ironworkers and colliers. Skilled American workmen were being enlisted in the military, so newly arrived British replacements readily found work at high wages. The *Merthyr Telegraph* editorialized on the reasons for the emigration of industrial workers, noting first low wages, followed by a glut of labor in the mines and mills, and the almost constant strife between workers and operators over low wages and poor living and working condi-

Emigration agent lecturing in the Temperance Hall at Merthyr Tydfil, 1875.
*Illustrated London News* 66 (March 6, 1875): 224.

tions. Consequently, even with the attendant risks, the potential for prosperity in America was preferable to the certain misery of remaining at
home.[54] The outflow strengthened as the war proceeded, and its conclusion
in 1865 triggered a surge in Welshmen heading for the United States.

What motivated individual Welsh emigrants to leave for the United
States is central to understanding the process, but very difficult to weigh
with certainty. Some left a record in the biographical sketches found in
ethnic newspapers, such as *Y Drych* and the *Druid*, or the county histories.
Newspapers of the period commented extensively on the larger forces that
compelled Welsh industrial workers to seek their fortunes abroad. Welsh
historian Bill Jones has shown it was "a very difficult and complex decision
for the majority of individuals involved."[55] There can be little doubt that
economic advancement was one of the principal motivations for emigration. The magnetic "pull" of better-paying jobs, land, or religious and political freedom in the United States on the one hand and the "push" of poverty,

Exodus of miners from Merthyr Tydfil, 1873.
*Illustrated London News* 62 (January 18, 1873): 52.

declining availability of land, or religious and linguistic tensions between elites and non-elites in Wales on the other provided what historical geographer Anne Kelly Knowles has called the "context of choice" for potential emigrants.[56]

The decision to emigrate was a multidimensional choice conditioned by a range of personal reasons within the context of broader social and economic forces. Consequently, individual decisions varied widely according to occupation, age, sex, family circumstances, stage in the life cycle, and psychological makeup. Perception of America as a land of opportunity also was important. One man remembered that his parents had migrated to America in the 1880s because his father was possessed of an "adventurous spirit." Moreover, some "enterprising villagers," including his brother, had already gone there, and he was assured of work at higher wages and a place to live.[57]

A small minority emigrated for less than honorable reasons, such as to escape debts, and others left their place of employment without proper notice, or to elude the consequences of some other misdeed. Accumulating debts and intentionally leaving town without paying them stirred considerable comment in the local press. Aberdare merchants reportedly were reluctant to extend credit because "America was so close." One Aberdare grocer published a list of seventy-five debtors who owed him a total of 652 British pound sterling.[58] The practice was common enough that people walking to the next railroad station to catch the train were recognized as departing emigrants attempting to avoid their creditors. Some correspondents in the local press claimed that this charge was exaggerated because news spread quickly when a person's departure became known. A few workmen might have fled their debts, one correspondent observed, but merchants and tradesmen were more likely to be thieves than workmen.[59] Another letter writer decried those who emigrated to avoid paying their debts or being jailed for breaking the law, but the "most disgraceful of all the classes that emigrate illegally is that class of men who led young women astray and then abandoned them."[60]

Financial loss to absconding debtors undoubtedly was a short-term worry in nineteenth-century Wales, as it was in the United States and elsewhere, but the long-term concern about emigration among local elites was that "emigration fever" would spread like a "contagion" throughout the South Wales coalfield and "drain" the region of its most skilled workmen. The waves of departures occurred almost annually between the 1850s and the 1890s among colliers and the iron-steel-tin craftsmen. There was, therefore, a constant and nagging fear among civic leaders that the best and most respectable families were migrating to America and leaving behind the less desirable elements who were not capable of leaving. In his study of emigration from Merthyr Tydfil, Bill Jones found that, until the end of the 1860s, most commentators in the local press viewed emigration as a rational response among working families confronting industrial recessions and wage cuts, "a laudable attempt by workers to seek their own independence and improvement as well as being an instrument for reducing the labour supply and raising the wages of those who remained."[61]

By the end of the 1860s, however, there was a growing concern among newspapers of the South Wales coalfield over a perceived mass migration. It was not in Merthyr's interest to export their best workmen, city papers pointed out, for local industry would be deprived of their services, while, at the same time, they would be in the United States helping to advance the industrial interests of Merthyr's competitors. The *Telegraph* editorialized in 1869 that, with the "excessive course of depletion" from the coal and iron district, "we lose our best workmen and our competitors gain their services; and while we suffer they are advantaged."[62] The *Merthyr Express* complained in 1868, under the heading "Emigration: its advantages and disadvantages," that people were still keen to go abroad, and "our best men have been scattered to the four corners of the earth."[63] At the beginning of the decade, the *Merthyr Telegraph* declared that it was proud to acknowledge "the advancement of Merthyrians be it at home or at the antipodes."[64] By the end of the decade, "contagion" of emigration was resurrected as a source of criticism of the owners for neglecting their civic responsibilities by not paying these skilled men a proper wage, or giving them the respect they deserved.[65] Bill Jones suggests that Merthyr, and by implication other cities on the coalfield that experienced long-term out-migration, is best understood if we acknowledge that Merthyr was a "transnational" city to some degree. The press played an influential role in constructing an international Merthyr and nurturing an awareness of a wider world with the town at its nerve center. The city's newspapers carried news of former Merthyrians, printed letters from them, and reprinted extracts from overseas papers sent to them by emigrants.[66]

Like most of the major trade unions during the mid-nineteenth century, the miners' unions embraced emigration as a way of alleviating the distress caused by irregular employment, low wages, strikes and lock-outs, black lists, and other grievances common to all British colliers, including those of South Wales. The Miners' National Association of Great Britain and Ireland collapsed in 1848. Sporadic attempts to resurrect a national union all failed, but in 1863 county unions in Scotland, England, and Wales organized the National Association of Coal Miners of Great Britain and chose the head of the Scottish miners, Alexander McDonald, to serve as president of the federation. No stronger proponent of union-sponsored emigration could have been chosen, and, although not a new idea, emigration was more openly advocated by the miners and their organizations than ever before. Espousing the wage-fund theory, union leaders believed that diminishing the labor supply would give workers more bargaining power, force the mine owners to improve conditions for those who remained at home, and, at the same time, benefit those who went abroad. According to the theory, the need to restrict the supply of labor was greatest in hard times; in actual practice, however, most plans were less than successful because funds for emigration were available when work was plentiful rather than when it was not.[67]

Miners in Aberdare in 1863 advised the editor of the *Miner and Workman's Advocate* that they intended to "liberate" themselves from their "present slavery," and invited other miners in the valley to join them in establishing a General Emigration Fund. In the same issue appeared a letter from a union official at Blaina suggesting that a national emigration fund be established to aid miners who wished to relocate abroad.[68] Although unlikely to have been related to the proposed General Emigration Fund, the same paper noted in July that "every week a large number of able-bodied men leave this neighbourhood for America."[69]

By 1868 the South Wales coalfield had many emigration societies, particularly in the towns at the heads of the Taff, Cynon, and Rhondda Valleys where there was serious economic distress, and a significant number of people were leaving, mostly for the United States. The *Merthyr Star* reported a meeting in the Temperance Hall in March 1868 featuring Edward's Panorama, with American music, anecdotes, and sights of the United States, a very good program for a venue like Merthyr "where so many people look forward to the States as their future home."[70] Two societies were launched in Merthyr in 1868, the Merthyr Tydfil Emigration Society and the Cambrian Emigration Society, both organized by workmen themselves, and both hoping to relieve the labor surplus. Beyond what the local newspapers published, little is known about these organizations or why there were two of them in the same town trying to attract the same colliers and iron mill workers. The MTES intended to purchase land in America, Missouri in particular. Welsh communities, like New Cambria, were being established, and families of colliers were preferred.[71]

The Cambrian Emigration Society, established shortly after the MTES, had similar motives and goals. The CES seems to have been directed by John Morgan. Little is known about Morgan before his arrival in Merthyr, but he was the Secretary of the Trades Council and the editor of the *Workman's Advocate* and *Amddiffynydd y Gweithwr*. Morgan also was the local agent for the Royal London Friendly Society, so his motives for promoting emigrations might have been more complex than simply improving the condition of labor through emigration. Although both organizations had the same goals and hoped to settle miners in Missouri, the CES emphasized temperance and the MTES did not. In the end, neither provided the funding for the "indiscriminate stampede" that the local press feared most. The historical significance of both organizations, and others like them, is in the evidence that emigration was considered by many workmen of South Wales, as in Britain generally, to be a legitimate alternative during times of economic stress. But the greatest majority of those who emigrated did so with their own financing, and relied on their own networks of family and friends to make the passage.[72] In 1869, the *London Times* observed that it was disheartening "to witness the large number of colliers and miners who are constantly leaving the iron and coal districts of South Wales from Merthyr, Aberdare, Pontypool, and other centres of population." Each week 100 to 120 were departing, "the passage money of a large number of them has been paid by relatives and friends who left their native home years ago, and who have since so far prospered as to be able to render this assistance to their connexions. As usual a large majority of the emigrants are leaving for the United States."[73]

A unique business emerged to promote emigration and provide services to those who made the transit. The emigration business in Wales has not been thoroughly studied yet, but its outward visages must have been conspicuous to the public. Agents, generally out of Liverpool, advertised in newspapers and posted broadsides throughout Wales claiming that they would make travel arrangements for migrants bound for America. An emigrant company based in Aberdare posted an advertisement in 1879 claiming that its agent, Gomer Roberts (Cymro Dof, or Tame Welshman), would accompany emigrants by train to Liverpool, provide lodging en route, and see that they boarded the proper ship for embarkation. All of this, and Roberts would be sober as well. Moreover, his partner, John Williams, would meet passengers at dockside in New York.[74] Nearly all of the South Wales coalfield towns had one or more emigration sub-agents, often local leaders, such as the Merthyr newspaper editor and union leader John T. Morgan. A number of Welsh agents in Liverpool offered accommodations to Welsh emigrants waiting for passage to America. One of the most famous was the former miner and writer, Noah M. Jones, whose bardic name "Cymro Gwyllt" (Wild Welshman) suggests a much different personality from that of Gomer Roberts. Although Liverpool, which was home to the largest concentration of Welsh outside of Wales, was the principal port of debarkation for Welsh emigrants to America, shipmasters in most of the small ports along the coast of Wales also carried passengers across the Atlantic.[75]

The emergence of the emigrant steamship lines as a mature business transformed traveling conditions and significantly lowered the barriers to crossing the Atlantic. Steamships first plied the Atlantic in the 1840s, but they carried only a few cabin passengers who could afford the trip. In 1856, 96 percent of all British passengers entering the United States through New York arrived by sailing vessels, mostly American packets; as late as 1862 more than 80 percent still traveled by sail. The threat of attack by Confederate ships, however, pushed the cost of insurance so high that American vessels remained in port. In their place, British steamships owned by newly founded passenger lines, such as the Allan, Cunard, Guion, Inman, National, and the

White Star lines, established regular timetables and departure schedules. The rapid shift to steam had important repercussions on the emigration business: by 1865 nearly three-quarters, and in 1867 more than 90 percent, of British passengers bound for North America arrived by steamship. Most South Walian emigrants traveled over the newly built railroad lines to Liverpool where the major lines operated, but by the 1870s local companies began to offer services, such as the South Wales Atlantic Steam Ship Company located in Cardiff, or the Great Western Steam Ship Company from Bristol. By the end of the decade travel by sail was a thing of the past.[76]

Large-scale migration to America would not have been possible without the shift to steam, for crossing the Atlantic Ocean in a sailing ship was a monumental psychological barrier for most people. Passage from Liverpool to New York took about five weeks by sail, and foul weather could easily lengthen the voyage to fourteen weeks. The steamship reduced the length of the voyage to two weeks or less, and was far less traumatic even if still fraught with danger. Steamships made the world smaller so that crossing the Atlantic seemed less irreversible, and if one was disappointed with America, or wanted to visit family, returning was not unreasonable or impractical. It also made seasonal migration possible for workers who could sojourn to America when work was dull in Britain, and return when the economy picked up back home.[77]

Although passage aboard a nineteenth-century steamship was no pleasure cruise, particularly in steerage, it was infinitely easier than aboard a sailing vessel. In addition to the length of the voyage, conditions aboard the wooden sailing ships were cramped, poorly ventilated, and crude by any standard. In the early days passengers had to bring their own food, which often was inadequate or ruined at sea. A ship sinking during a storm or striking an iceberg was not a remote possibility. Epidemics of cholera or typhus occasionally rampaged through the passengers, killing them in sufficient numbers that they were called "coffin ships." Seasickness was not fatal, but it turned the voyage into a living hell for the afflicted and for the others who were forced to endure in the filthy conditions it created below decks. For most, therefore, crossing the Atlantic in a sailing ship was undertaken but once, and those who migrated to America generally did not return. The steamship passenger business changed the one-way journey into an experience that could be reversed. Almost from the inception of the steamship, fear of the transatlantic journey to America began to diminish. Reporting on the departure of a group of emigrants from Beaufort, at the head of the Ebbw Fawr valley in Monmouthshire, a Merthyr newspaper account observed that "the difficulty of getting to America is of little moment or consideration" for the journey to America "is now looked upon as a mere excursion."[78]

Typically, men would precede their wives to America and, once they had earned sufficient money, send them "passes," or tickets to join them. In October 1869, the *Baner ac Amserau Cymru* correspondent in Aberdare reported that scores of wives were leaving the train station to join their husbands in America.[79] An unknown number of Welsh women went to America on their own volition, but the vast majority of them were part of a family migration. Women generally played an important, although understudied, role in emigration. Immigration historian William Van Vugt states that women certainly were not "just wives, mothers, and daughters who were dragged across the Atlantic by men; they often made that migration possible and participated fully in the decision to leave for America."[80] A woman who stayed behind lived in a state of uncertainty for months, and sometimes years, until her husband finally sent the money for her to join him. In the meantime she had to support herself and the children between very irregular remittances. At a meeting of the Bridgend Board of Guardians in 1879, it was reported that men of the mining district were ready to emigrate and "leave their wives to the tender mercies of the ratepayers at home." The vice-chairman warned that men who left their wives behind to fend for themselves would condemn them to "the cold cheer of the workhouse, as out-door relief will be refused."[81] The incident of a Mountain Ash wife who appealed to the Board of Guardians for assistance after her husband emigrated without providing for her and their three children probably was not that unusual.[82] Family abandonment consigned women to pauperism if they had no other recourse. In 1880, John Jones ran off with another woman in Pennsylvania even though he had a wife and eight children back in the Rhondda who were waiting to join him in America.[83] Similarly, in 1912 Thomas Thomas abandoned his wife Mary and two children in Nantymoel, Ogmore Valley, for a better job in America. Mary refused to accept abandonment, however, and, having learned he was in Colorado, the following year she and the children booked passage for America to confront her husband with his responsibilities (see chapter 9).[84]

Even under the best of circumstances departures were dramatic, disruptive events for families and communities. Considering the magnitude of the event, many thought emigration was undertaken with too little forethought.

The *Merthyr Telegraph* opined in 1865 that emigrants took "but little time to make up their minds, and just as little to get ready." Another report claimed that on the morning of departure "a broker or an auctioneer is called in, a bargain struck, the cash received, and the train taken, all in one hour."[85] Farewell and departure rituals, sometimes with concerts, poetry reading, and speeches, provided the emigrants a proper send-off, but they also testify to the impact of emigration on the family and community. Large crowds often escorted emigrants to the train station amidst exhibitions of great joy and sorrow. In Aberdare hundreds paraded the streets, some apparently inebriated, cheering and waving handkerchiefs as a farewell to a party of emigrants. Men and women standing along the track for two miles did the same as the train passed by.[86]

Emigration triggered social repercussions in Wales and America on a very personal level. Families were the principal links in the networks that supported the chain migration and forged transnational identities among families both in Wales and America. It created distinctive ethnic occupational communities in the United States, which, as long as memory and communication lasted, made America an extension of "home."

### Patterns of Migration

In the second half of the nineteenth century and the early decades of the twentieth century, Wales came closest to experiencing a mass migration to the United States, and Welsh immigrants exerted their greatest influence. The British statistics of those emigrating for America between 1871 and 1920 suggest a much larger number than the official count of the United States: 3 million English and Welsh together; 650,000 Scots; 2,200,000 Irish. Between 1881 and 1931, Wales lost to the United States an average of less than 7 per 10,000 of population, whereas England lost 14, Scotland 25, and Ireland 89 per 10,000. Accurate data are hard to come by because of the differences in the American and British definitions of an emigrant and an immigrant. Until 1909 the United States counted only steerage passengers as immigrants when a significant number of British booked second- or even first-class passage to America. Until 1914, on the other hand, the British government classified as emigrants all passengers whether or not they intended to remain in America. Therefore, the American figures are too low while the British statistics are too high. Also, the British did not differentiate between the Welsh and English, while in 1860 the U.S. Immigration Service became the first to recognize the Welsh as a distinct nationality. Further confounding the calculations, the British did not distinguish those who

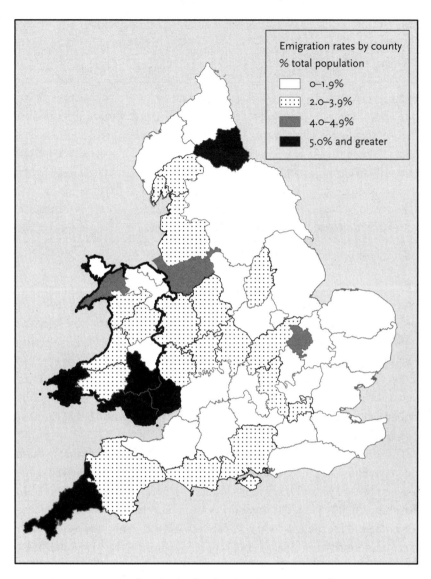

MAP 3. Native emigration from England and Wales, 1861–1900. Map by Sue Bergeron, adapted in part from Baines, *Migration in a Mature Economy*, 188.

TABLE I. British-Born Population of the United States, 1850–1920

| Year | Total Population | Total Foreign-Born | English | Welsh | Scottish | Irish |
|---|---|---|---|---|---|---|
| 1850 | 23,191,876 | 2,244,602 | 278,675 | 29,868 | 70,550 | 961,719 |
| 1860 | 31,443,321 | 4,136,175 | 431,692 | 45,763 | 108,518 | 1,611,304 |
| 1870 | 38,558,371 | 5,567,229 | 555,046 | 74,533 | 140,835 | 1,855,827 |
| 1880 | 50,155,783 | 6,679,943 | 664,160 | 83,302 | 170,136 | 1,854,571 |
| 1890 | 62,947,714 | 9,249,560 | 909,092 | 100,079 | 242,231 | 1,871,509 |
| 1900 | 75,994,575 | 10,341,276 | 840,513 | 93,586 | 233,524 | 1,615,459 |
| 1910 | 91,972,266 | 13,515,886 | 877,719 | 82,488 | 261,076 | 1,352,251 |
| 1920 | 105,710,620 | 13,920,692 | 813,853 | 67,066 | 254,570 | 1,037,234 |

Source: *Sixteenth Census of the United States, 1940: Population*, 2:43.

returned until 1895, and the United States did not record those who re-turned until 1908. Even though precise numbers are not possible, the trends are clear: far more English, Scots, and Irish came to the America than did Welsh, both numerically and as a percentage of their respective national populations. As may be seen in Table 1, the vast majority migrated between the Civil War and World War I. The number of immigrants in the United States born in Wales was 29,868 in 1850, but by 1890 that number rose to 100,079 and declined in subsequent decades.[87]

The historically significant issue is why the Welsh migration was so much smaller than the tens of millions of European immigrants who came between the 1880s and the 1920s, and but a trickle of the emigration from elsewhere in the United Kingdom, both in absolute numbers and as a percentage. Why, then, were the Welsh less likely to emigrate even though the conditions that stimulated emigration elsewhere in the British Isles also were present in Wales? The answer is found in the growth of the Welsh industrial economy, and its articulation with the British and American econ-omies. During the second half of the nineteenth century and beginning of the twentieth century, emigration from Britain and investment in the United States was positively correlated. When British capitalists invested in the U.S. industrial expansion, economic activity at home stagnated, and excess labor migrated to the United States. When British capitalists invested at home, the reverse occurred, emigration declined, and internal migration to British urban-industrial centers accelerated. During the entire period between 1851 and 1911, Britain lost population through emigration, mostly to the United States, but emigration fluctuated with these economic cycles with peak periods during the years 1851–61, the 1880s, and 1901–11.[88]

Wales, more specifically the South Wales coalfield, was a mirror image that moved in opposite directions from the British pattern. Emigration spiked in the 1860s and increased slightly in the 1880s; then, in the first decade of the twentieth century, Wales had a significant net gain in population from in-migration and absorbed population at a rate second only to the United States. Nearly the opposite occurred in England and Scotland. Wales's distinctive migration pattern is directly related to the growth of the South Wales coalfield during the second half of the nineteenth century. Because of this rapid industrialization, the surplus rural population was absorbed into the workforce within Wales. In effect, the South Wales coal and iron industry held back what might have been a flood of emigration to the growing economies of England and the United States. Employment in the industry provided an intermediate step in the migration off the land to England or America by providing migrants with an opportunity to earn some cash to pay for their passage, and provided a "springboard" as well as a "dam." Displaced rural people simply moved to the nearest urban-industrial center, which accounts for the comparatively small out-migration from Wales.[89] This was not an option elsewhere on Britain's "Celtic Fringe," particularly Ireland, where no similar expansion of industry provided the rural poor with other employment options.

The option of migrating to the coalfield explains why "only" tens of thousands of Welsh emigrated, a significant movement even if it was not a diaspora. The influence of the Welsh migration in the United States, however, far surpasses the measure of their removal. This was overwhelmingly an industrial migration of skilled workers following ethnic and occupational networks in the coal, iron, steel, and tinplate industries in which the Welsh were experts. According to the U.S. Immigration Commission of 1907–10, only 15 percent of all immigrants working in industry had done so in the old country. The numbers were much higher for the British: 58 percent of the Welsh, 50 percent of the English, and 36 percent of the Scots. Only 5 percent of the British industrial workers previously had worked on the land. The Immigration Commission reported that a much larger proportion of the British than other nationalities in the United States resumed their old trades in America. Among all British-born coal miners in the United States, 88 percent of the Welsh and Scots and 83 percent of the English had been miners prior to their emigration. Among the British iron, steel, and tin workers, fully 72 percent of the Welsh resumed their previous line of work in the United States, while 48 percent of the English and 43 percent of Scots did so—a high percentage compared with 21 percent of the Swedes and 17 percent of the Germans, two other nationalities with a significant presence in the U.S. steel industry. Similarly, the highest wages in coal, iron, and steel went to the English, Welsh, and Scots.[90]

Rowland Berthoff's observation that the nineteenth-century British migration to the United States "ran not in a broad, undifferentiated stream but rather in many parallel channels" has particular poignancy for the Welsh. As Berthoff noted, they did not come merely to find work, but rather migrated from jobs in specific industries to find comparable jobs in America's mines and mills. None of the British workingmen were likely to cross the ocean unless they expected to find work in their proper trade. The historical significance of the migration, therefore, lies not so much in its numbers as in the fact that they "directly transfused the skills and experience of the premier industrial nation of the early nineteenth century into the veins of the rising giant of the twentieth."[91]

On arrival in the United States, the Welsh flocked to colonies where they would be welcomed by relatives and friends. It was said that the Lonaconing, Maryland, miners were "all uncles and cousins." Welsh settlements in America were generally small and widely scattered. The Reverend R. D. Thomas counted two hundred Welsh settlements in 1870. Other than the Welsh communities in urban-industrial centers, such as Scranton, Wilkes-Barre, Pittsburgh, and Youngstown, Thomas reported that Welsh settlements were "small everywhere except some agricultural districts and in the coal fields." Moreover, he declared, while there were some rich and famous among the Welsh in the large cities, "farmers, laborers, craftsmen, and miners, make up the majority of the Welsh in America." The 100,079 Welsh in America in 1890 were not widely dispersed, as shown in Map 4. Instead, the industrial migrants concentrated in the coal and iron centers of Pennsylvania and Ohio, where nearly one-half the Welsh lived, while the Welsh agricultural migrants were concentrated in Ohio and Wisconsin. They nearly always settled north of the Mason-Dixon Line, where the demand for industrial labor was strongest. Four of every five Welsh immigrants lived in Pennsylvania, New York, Ohio, or Wisconsin in 1880. As late as 1900, after decades of American westward migration, two of every three Welsh still lived in these states and Minnesota.[92]

The notion that the Welsh were much less likely to emigrate than the English or Scots does not fit comfortably into Welsh thought, or the popular perception of the Welsh. The "exiles" (*Cymry a Wasga*) occupy a special place

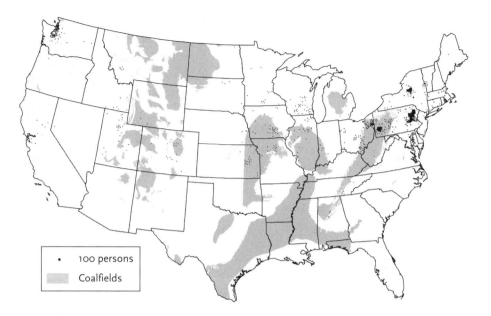

MAP 4. Welsh-born immigrants in the United States, 1880. Map by Sue Bergeron, adapted in part from Berthoff, *British Immigrants in Industrial America, 1790–1950*, 26, and *Tenth Census of the United States, 1880*.

in Welsh life, symbolized by the special day set aside for them at the annual national eisteddfod in Wales until that tradition ended in 2005. The reason the émigrés have not been forgotten is that Welsh Americans, perhaps even more so than emigrants who settled in the Commonwealth nations, were literally and figuratively family. The farmers, colliers, and steel workers who missed their family and friends subscribed to local and trade newspapers, wrote letters, and in many cases returned to visit. Industrial modernization had fractured their families, but locations where they settled—Scranton, Pittsburgh, Youngstown, and the countless small coal towns—became virtually household names to kith and kin in Wales. The idea that relatively few Welshmen went to America contradicts received wisdom in Wales because there are few families, and hardly any extended families, which do not have an American branch. Welsh historian Gwyn A. Williams has suggested that "this truth registers so powerfully on the Welsh imagination precisely because the Welsh . . . remained in objective terms a small people. It does not take many of them to create an American dimension." If Wales had not industrialized in the nineteenth century, he wrote, its people almost certainly would have suffered the same disintegrative migration as the Irish.[93] Even though Ireland had the heaviest migration rate to America and Wales the least, the two countries shared many similarities in the nineteenth century, including poor conditions of rural life, rapid population growth, the enclosure movement and the violence it sparked in the countryside, as well as the rise of cultural nationalism and the growing awareness that relief might be found in America. But the heavy out-migration from Ireland was not duplicated in Wales, where the economy was exploding while the Irish economy was imploding. Perhaps the Welsh realized that they had dodged the Irish fate, and the loss of those who did leave was all the more forcefully imprinted on the Welsh psyche.

## SUPERINTENDENTS, NETWORKS, & WELSH SETTLEMENT PATTERNS

In his notable work *One Hundred Years of Welsh Calvinistic Methodism in America*, the Reverend Daniel Jenkins Williams provided a survey of the development of his denomination by state and community. He lamented the extraordinary difficulties encountered by Welsh churches in keeping up with shifts and changes in the mining conditions of the districts. The closure of mines due to the suspension of operations, strikes, or lockouts "played havoc" with churches and other social institutions; coal communities "grew up in a night and might vanish in a night." Such unsettled conditions made it difficult to maintain Welsh institutions, but economics trumped religion in matters of family security, for "it was the habit of Welsh miners to follow their leader from one location to another," he observed. "When a Welsh superintendent was transferred from one place to another, or found a more lucrative and inviting position elsewhere, many of those in his employ followed him to the new location to work."[1]

Construction of the mining facilities and the workforce to operate them was determined to a large degree by the geographical location of the coal itself, but Welsh miners nearly everywhere in America saw more opportunity when one of their own was in charge. This pattern was more observable earlier in the industrial migration than later, but remained a prominent feature of Welsh mining settlement patterns during the nineteenth century. Eastern Pennsylvania, the earliest of the coalfield settlements, reveals the pattern very clearly.

### Pennsylvania

Large numbers of Welsh were attracted to the developing coal and iron industries of Scranton beginning in the mid-1840s. George W. Scranton founded a rolling mill company in 1846, and John R. Williams, a Welsh immigrant working in Wilkes-Barre, was recruited to organize and supervise the mill that rolled the first rails in the town of Scranton. As the number of Welsh grew they began to concentrate in their own neighborhoods. One

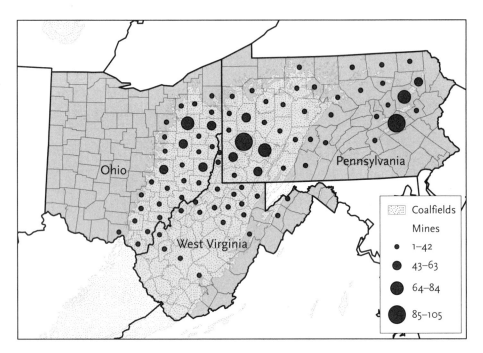

MAP 5. Coal mines in Pennsylvania, Ohio, and West Virginia, 1880. Map by Sue Bergeron. Source: *Tenth Census of the United States, 1880.*

of these was Bellevue, where in the mid-1850s Walter Phillips superintended the coal mine and successfully recruited Welsh miners and their families. In 1858 the Scranton Welsh began to move to another section known as Hyde Park, a neighborhood that eventually became the largest single concentration of Welsh in America. Mine and mill managers often were the leaders in the social, cultural, and economic affairs of their respective communities. John Williams and Walter Phillips were key figures in the establishment and maintenance of their respective churches; in fact, Williams himself was a minister, and Phillips was instrumental in establishing the Calvinistic Methodist church in Bellevue as well as in Hyde Park.[2]

The Wilkes-Barre Welsh grew with the city and the presence of Welsh owners and bosses. John T. Griffiths was appointed general superintendent of the Wilkes-Barre Consolidated Coal Company in 1863 with instructions to increase the number of Welsh miners. Griffiths and his Welsh friend Lewis S. Jones, the superintendent of Empire Mine, succeeded in luring many Welsh laborers to the mines. Griffiths and Jones both had been influential in the Calvinistic Methodist church, and were instrumental in establishing the church in Wilkes-Barre. Jones himself was an elder who preached the first service held in the new church when it opened in 1864. The Wilkes-Barre Calvinist Methodist church became the "mother" of numerous branches in the surrounding Welsh coal communities, such as Baltimore Mines, Mill Creek, and Miners Mills.[3]

Welsh operators and managers opened mines throughout the northern anthracite district and recruited Welsh colliers to operate them. As the industry mushroomed in the mid-nineteenth century, Welsh anthracite settlements like Plymouth, Edwardsville, Jermyn, Kingston, Providence, and Ashley proliferated on the landscape and became familiar American place names in Wales. The shifting nature of these early Welsh settlements is illustrated in the case of Ashley, where D. R. Roberts was appointed superintendent of the Lehigh and Wilkes-Barre Coal Company in 1879, and Welsh miners and their families joined him. True to form, when Roberts left that mine in 1888 for Avoca, the Welsh community in Ashley went into decline because so many Welsh went with him. But Avoca eventually suffered the same fate as Ashley on the departure of Roberts. Similarly, when William T. Smith left the Lehigh and Wilkes-Barre Coal Company in 1889 and bought a coal mine near Avoca, his Welsh miners relocated with him. The migratory Welsh reestablished their churches and stayed for awhile, but soon took flight again when Smith sold his company. When the Welsh miners came they brought their institutions, particularly the church, with them, and when they departed the church did too, a victim of shifting conditions that Rev. Williams described as "common to other churches in coal mining regions."[4]

Even though the northern anthracite field was their principal domain in Pennsylvania, thousands of Welsh also settled in the middle and southern anthracite fields, particularly in Schuylkill County. As early as the 1830s and 1840s Pottsville and St. Clair drew numerous Welsh immigrants to the newly opening coal mines after the railroad linked the field with Philadelphia in 1842. Welsh operators and bosses lured 800 to Pottstown, and about 600 to St. Clair during the early 1870s. The Welsh began moving into Minersville in the 1850s, and, over the next few decades, a strong community took form, replete with several Welsh churches, literary societies, and an annual eisteddfod. During the 1870s, the Minersville Welsh community began to weaken. Nevertheless, about 1,500 Welsh still called it home and counted their own among the most successful businessmen of the community. Ashland numbered approximately 1,200 Welsh residents in the early 1870s by the "many rich and respected [Welsh] mine owners such as David Evans, Esq., Thomas Davies, Esq., and others," according to Rev. R. D.

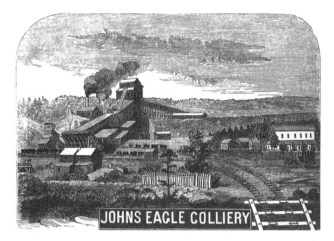

Johns Eagle Colliery. From Samuel Harris Daddow and Benjamin Bannan, *Coal, Iron, and Oil; or the Practical American Miner* (Philadelphia: J. B. Lippincott, 1866; Pottsville: Benjamin Bannan, 1866), 768.

Thomas. About 600 Welsh lived in Shenandoah where several Welshmen held responsible positions, such as "Mr. Davies," a coal operator.[5]

Similarly, Mahanoy City's 6,000 residents were of diverse nationalities, but the 1,000 Welsh represented a significant element in the population and were among the conspicuously successful. Rev. Thomas observed in 1872 that among the Shenandoah Welsh were "many respected miners who have built their own homes. Some of them are skillful and accountable bosses in the coal fields: John W. Williams, Rees P. Jones, John Powell, Thomas R. Williams, Thomas Lewis, Lewis Evans, William J. Watkins, and perhaps others. The present contractors of the old Meyers coal mine are also Welsh, and the Welsh also own the successful Union Co-operative Store in the town." Along with the numerous Welsh churches, the Ivorite Society and two literary meetings had been established, and two successful eisteddfodau had been held.[6]

Just outside St. Clair, Schuylkill County, William and Thomas Johns leased coal lands in 1846 and built Johns Eagle Colliery, one of the most substantial of the early coal mines in the anthracite region. Originally from the South Wales coalfield, the Johns brothers were experienced operators who lived in a house that stood within 100 yards of the breaker and was exposed to all the noise, soot, and mud that afflicted their Welsh employees. Nevertheless, they did not move away even after they were worth millions. Their mine bosses were also experienced Welsh miners too, Protestants and Republicans like the Johns. Johns Eagle Colliery was a "Welsh mine" from 1846 to 1888.[7]

Pennsylvania anthracite mining became synonymous with the Welsh between the 1850s and the 1880s, but not all Welsh observers regarded this as desirable. The Rev. R. D. Thomas, a Welsh minister and resident of Mahanoy City, Pennsylvania, in 1871, writing in his native language, observed in his oft-cited *Hanes Cymry America* (A History of the Welsh in America) that "there are *already entirely too many* MINERS and *laborers* in the COAL mines. It would be better for thousands of them if they would immigrate to some of the western and southern states and attempt to gain their livelihood more comfortably through working on the land." Welsh ministers generally associated rural life with a higher standard of morality, and urban or industrial life with sinfulness, but Rev. Thomas also advanced an economic motive for settling American farmland. "The *miners* will never be able through *strikes* and *suspensions* to get the wages which they *ought to get* for their hard and dangerous work while there are so MANY *workers* in the *coalfields*. In addition, there is now very little hope that the Welsh THEMSELVES will be able *to gain control of the coal mines* in Pennsylvania because those of other nationalities already own them."[8]

The explosive growth of the anthracite coal industry was a direct result of the discovery of how to use it as a fuel in the making of iron. The market for anthracite in the 1830s was household heating, but leaders in the coal and iron industries were busy exploring smelting techniques that used raw anthracite as fuel. The traditional "cold blast" method, which forced outside air into the furnace, chilled the inside to below the ignition point of anthracite. The "hot blast" forced hot air into the furnace and made possible the use of anthracite in the smelting of iron, a process that was much more efficient than the traditional method.[9] George Crane, an English furnace owner, had been trying unsuccessfully since 1826 to smelt iron with anthracite at his cold blast furnace in his Yniscedwyn works, situated in the village of Ystradgynlais, thirteen miles up the valley from Swansea, South Wales. In the early 1830s, he sent his ironmaster, David Thomas, to Scotland to observe James Neilson's recently patented method for heating the blast. On returning to Wales, Thomas built a hot-blast furnace and successfully smelted iron with anthracite at the Yniscedwyn works in 1837.[10]

Two competing companies in Pennsylvania followed these developments closely and eagerly anticipated their adaptation in the United States. One of the iron men, Josiah White of the Lehigh Coal and Navigation Company at Mauch Chunk, had been trying to make anthracite iron since 1826. In 1838 the Lehigh Company enticed Crane's ironmaster, David Thomas, to Pennsylvania to build a furnace based on the new technology. Thomas began work on the new furnace in July 1839 at Catasauqua, near

David Thomas, "Father of the American Anthracite Iron Industry." Courtesy of Hagley Museum and Library, Wilmington, Delaware.

Bethlehem, and successfully put it into blast in July 1840.[11] Meanwhile, the competing Pottsville group also learned of the successful trial at Crane's South Wales works, and during the winter of 1837–38 began to plan the construction of its own furnace. Where they obtained the technical knowledge to construct the works is unclear, but Welsh coal miner Richard Jones was reported to have returned to Pottsville from a visit to Yniscedwyn in April 1838 bearing samples of coal, iron ore, and pig iron. The following year David Thomas provided the Pottstown group with the technical knowledge to build Pioneer Furnace on the same plan as Catasauqua. Benjamin Perry, a Welsh furnace manager familiar with the Yniscedwyn works back in Wales, was employed as overseer. The Pioneer Furnace at Pottstown was blown in during October 1839, and the Lehigh Crane furnace at Catasauqua went into blast in July 1840. The new technology not only transformed the iron industry, but also led to an explosion in anthracite coal production, spawned America's rise as an industrial power, and anointed David Thomas as "father of the anthracite iron industry."[12]

One of the technological innovations in the iron industry that also helped to transform the bituminous coal industry was the substitution of coke for charcoal, and anthracite after the 1870s, in the manufacture of iron. As early as 1759 colonists were aware of the bituminous coal deposits in western Pennsylvania; they could not have known then that the rich seams underlying the recently platted town of Pittsburgh fanned out in a sixty-mile radius. By the early nineteenth century, Pittsburgh coal was being exported to the new towns springing up along the Ohio River for blacksmithing and domestic heating purposes; therefore, mining was small-scale and seasonal. Charcoal still fueled the pig iron furnaces, but it required an extensive workforce and denuded the countryside to produce a relatively small amount of iron. Although English ironmasters had discovered how to use bituminous coal to fire their furnaces by the early eighteenth century, their American counterparts were slow to adopt the process. Both charcoal and coke were made by covering a pile of timber or coal with earth, leaving holes to vent the gases while it smoldered. This process was later greatly improved by development of the coke, or beehive, oven. By 1817 Colonel Isaac Meason was using coke at his forge where, according to tradition, the Welshman Samuel Lewis supervised the construction of the puddling furnaces, and perhaps shared his knowledge of coke production.[13]

Coal, coke, and iron were too heavy to ship by wagon, and before midcentury water was the only efficient mode of transportation. The domestic demand for coal was limited, but the opportunity to expand coal production increased significantly if the iron industry adopted coke as the fuel of choice. In the early 1830s Norton's Iron Works in Connellsville used coke that was made in a stone coke oven, possibly the first in the region. During the 1840s, the Great Western Iron Company at Brady's Bend, about sixty miles up the Allegheny River from Pittsburgh, began to produce coke iron, and other companies in the region soon followed. The Civil War saw a major spike in demand for iron, and the higher prices encouraged iron makers to invest in another technology that increased production. The hot blast furnace overcame the disadvantages of using regular air to fan the flames by substituting heated air, which helped to maintain the high temperatures necessary to smelt iron. Development of the Bessemer process for converting pig iron into steel made it possible beginning in the 1870s to mass-produce steel, further stimulating the demand for more pig iron and, therefore, western Pennsylvania coal. Transportation improvements were the final component in the construction of the Pittsburgh coal and iron region as a leading industrial center. The railroads required to haul the heavy raw materials to the mills and the iron and steel to metal manufacturers all over America became a reality during the decades after the Civil

War. Two measures of the resulting expansion were the number of coke ovens, which by 1882 reached 8,400, and coal production in the coke region, which grew 300 percent between 1870 and 1884.[14]

Most of the coal mines producing coke were owned by the tycoon Henry Clay Frick, a protégé of the iron magnate Andrew Carnegie. Almost from the beginning Frick hired eastern and southern European immigrants to work his mines and ovens. Some Welsh were employed in the mining industry of western Pennsylvania from early times, but it is impossible to determine the number, and their influence paled in comparison with the anthracite region or the Ohio coalfields. The 1870 census found only 1,036 natives of Wales residing in the city of Pittsburgh. Although the 1880 census enumerated the population by nativity and county, they were not delineated by occupation. Moreover, the Welsh were incorporated in the nativity of "English and Welsh." In the eight largest coal-producing counties of western Pennsylvania there were 26,589 "English and Welsh," and if the Welsh are generously estimated at one-quarter of this group, the Welsh population would have been 6,647, including women and children. Assuming male breadwinners were one-third of the total, again a generous estimate, there would have been 2,216 Welshmen. It is most likely that most of these men worked in the iron industry because they were overwhelmingly located in Allegheny County in which Pittsburgh is located. This general profile would seem to hold true for 1900 as well, when the census takers found a total of 8,971 natives of Wales in these leading coal counties, and even more overwhelmingly located in Allegheny County.[15] The Pennsylvania mine inspectors' *Reports* did not provide an ethnic breakdown by location until 1915, and by then the Welsh were abandoning the industry (see chapter 7).

The Reverend R. D. Thomas's generally reliable 1872 survey of Welsh communities in the United States cites only a few of those communities in western Pennsylvania. By far the largest, Pittsburgh was home to about 3,000 Welsh who "began to populate it over 30 years ago and miners, craftsmen, and 'fire workers' [ironworkers] have continued to immigrate there over the years." Clearly Pittsburgh attracted a diversified workforce, not just coal miners. Ebensburgh, which was originally settled by Welsh followers of Morgan John Rees (see chapter 1), was still a settlement of farmers, and Johnstown was the home of the Cambrian Iron Company and about 1,500 Welsh. Some of them were skilled miners or bosses, but most were ironworkers or in business for themselves. Rev. Thomas also mentioned Brady's Bend in Armstrong County, but this too was a small ironworks community where some Welsh worked in the local mines. The only

Means of entry to the coal seam. From Samuel Harris Daddow and Benjamin Bannan, *Coal, Iron, and Oil; or the Practical American Miner* (Philadelphia: J. B. Lippincott, 1866; Pottsville: Benjamin Bannan, 1866), 414.

other Welsh settlements he thought worthy of note in western Pennsylvania were Blossburgh and Morris Run in Tioga County. These were coal towns, and the three Congregationalist chapels served by a Welsh minister testify to the presence of a small Welsh community living there, due, perhaps, to the Welsh superintendent Alfred Jones.[16]

The British miners transferred their scientific knowledge of underground mining to America as well as their practical skills as craftsmen. The Welsh were part of this same talent pool and trained in the same mining systems adapted throughout the British Isles. The United States coalfields presented a greater range of challenges, however, and mining methods were adapted to a diversity of geological conditions. Nevertheless, the British mining system was the common starting point for mining in America, so a brief description of the basic method of mining will be useful to readers.

Generally, underground coal mining has been characterized by the means of entry to the coal seam. Local physical conditions determined which approach was used. The *drift* mine was used when the seam was exposed as an outcrop in the side of a hill, the entry being driven directly into the coal and its removal accomplished with a minimum of cost and effort. If the seam was on a downward incline for more than one hundred feet, the most cost-effective method was a *slope* mine that was sunk to the intersection with the coal seam. A *shaft* mine was called for when the coal was so deep that a slope would have been too long to pump water or pull the coal out efficiently. The shaft was sunk vertically from the surface to the

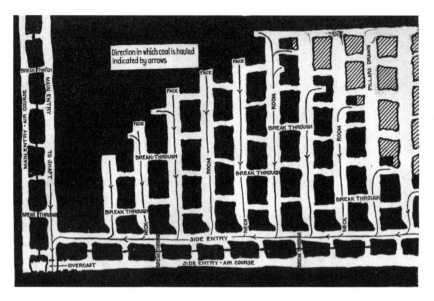

Traditional pillar and breast system. From Isador Lubin, *Miners' Wages and the Cost of Coal: An Inquiry into the Wages System in the Bituminous Coal Industry and Its Effects on Coal Costs and Coal Conservation* (New York: McGraw-Hill, 1924), 19.

seam. Hoisting machinery lowered and raised men, equipment, and coal to the preparation plant or tipple (or anthracite breaker) where the coal was sized and deposited in waiting railroad cars or barges. If the coal lay close enough to the surface, the overburden was removed and a strip, trench, or open quarry mine was installed to extract the coal.[17]

The room (or breast) and pillar method was the most widespread system for extracting coal in America, as it was in Britain. Tunnels, called entries when cut through coal, were driven horizontally into the coal seam from the bottom of the shaft or slope. Every several hundred feet along the main entry, *side* or *cross* entries about ten feet wide were driven at right angles, blocking out rectangular panels of coal. From these cross entries fourteen or more *rooms* were opened up on each panel. Depending on the quality of the top, or *roof*, these rooms were on average about twenty feet wide. Here miners brought down the coal from the *coal face*, or leading edge of the extraction process. Rooms were connected by periodic *breakthroughs* driven between the walls separating the rooms. The entries, cross entries, and breakthroughs also served as the ventilation system through which fresh air coursed through the mine. When all of the rooms in a panel had been mined out, the pillars of coal holding up the roof were "pulled" by starting at the end of the panel and "retreating" to the main entry.[18]

One very notable exception to the basic room and pillar mining system was carried out in the Schuylkill anthracite region of Pennsylvania, where the coal seams were very steeply inclined and erratically undulating. Here, pitch mining had to be employed whereby a gangway was driven beneath the coal seam, and a timber chute was constructed into the upward angling coal seam. A narrow manway also was built to give the miner access to the "breast," where he freed the coal which fell into the chute and was directed into a coal car.[19]

Mining involved four basic steps in this system. The miner first *undercut* the coal face by lying on his side and using a long pick. Then he manually *drilled* a hole several feet into the coal with an auger and *blasted* the coal down. He then *shoveled* the coal into a car that was gathered for hoisting topside. This labor process prevailed in underground mining throughout the hand-loading era, which was coming to a close during the early twentieth century. Timbers and track were provided by the company, but as a craftsman the miner was responsible for his own tools. Paid by the ton, miners worked largely without company supervision and independently in their own rooms, where they passed on the craft to laborers serving an informal apprenticeship. The miners exercised considerable control over their jobs, and acquired a proprietary interest in their rooms. Their independence under the room and pillar system was described by scientific management expert Carter Goodrich as the "miner's freedom," a freedom they guarded jealously.[20]

### Ohio

The American industrial revolution can be read as a story of Welsh technical skills being transferred to Pennsylvania and from there dispersed to other regions as the market economy expanded, with the Welsh mine and mill managers in the vanguard. After Pennsylvania, Ohio claimed the second-largest population of immigrant Welsh miners in the nineteenth century. Most of them were concentrated in the Mahoning Valley near Youngstown, the Tuscarawas Valley near Canton and Massillon, or in the Hocking and Ohio River mining towns of southeastern Ohio. These fields developed rapidly between the 1860s and 1880s; these were peak years in the Welsh industrial migration, and Welshmen flocked to these coalfields until they began to decline toward the end of the century.

The importance of the Welsh miners and ironworkers in the founding of the industrial center around Youngstown can hardly be overestimated. Both industries were, in effect, founded by skilled Welsh managers. John Davis was hired by David Tod, the Civil War governor of Ohio, to develop the coal found on Tod's farm, "Brier Hill," which now lies within the city of Youngstown. During the 1830s and 1840s, Davis recruited Welsh miners, returning to Wales himself to lead a "substantial number" to the Mahoning Valley. Thomas Davis and Morgan Reese were the first to cut what became known as "Brier Hill Block." Another Welshman, William Philpot, erected the Eagle Furnace at Brier Hill (the first in this famous iron and steel center), which was managed by another Welshman, William Richards.[21]

The pioneering commercial mine in adjoining Trumbull County was the Cambria, opened in 1850 by Welshman John Morris, and subsequently operated by W. T. Williams. It was not until 1854, when John Lewis, a miner from Monmouthshire, recognized that the bottom of this little mine was not worthless blackstone but rather black-band ore, that the industry attracted significant investment.[22]

Trumbull and Mahoning Counties became a major Welsh destination during the last half of the nineteenth century. In 1880, the area was home to thousands of Welsh immigrants. Because the 1890 census was destroyed by fire, and the 1880 census combined the English and Welsh into one category, it is difficult to say precisely how many Welsh there were. A manual count of the Welsh-born in the Trumbull County census index for 1880 totaled 1,237 heads of household. Assuming a very conservative average family of three, the number of people living in Welsh households was at least 3,700. The census listed English and Welsh at 4,569, but the Welsh far exceeded the English in Trumbull. This is consistent with local history. A similar census index does not exist for Mahoning County, where 3,280 English and Welsh were listed in the 1880 census, but it shared a coal, iron, and metal manufacturing economy with neighboring Trumbull County, and was recognized as one of the most influential Welsh concentrations in the United States. It is impossible to determine how many were coal miners from the census, but from manual counts in strategic locations, two-thirds of the Welsh heads of household in Trumbull worked in the coal industry in 1880.[23]

Even though it would be impossible to directly link the thousands who depended on mining with the number of Welsh mine owners and managers, the positive correlation is unmistakable. In the mine-by-mine survey

## THE CAMBRIAN.

Now, go write it before them in a table, and note it in a book, that it maybe for the time to come for ever and ever.

| Vol. XII. | FEBRUARY, 1892. | No. 2. |

Ohio coal operator, businessman, and politician Anthony Howells. *Cambrian* 12 (February 1892): 33.

conducted by the Ohio Inspector of Mines in 1875, a total of twenty-four mine managers were listed for Trumbull County. The nativity of twenty of them have been identified: thirteen were Welsh-born, two others probably were Welsh, so over half of them were definitely Welsh. For Mahoning County, eighteen mine managers have been identified, ten of whom were Welsh-born, and another was married to a woman of Welsh birth.[24]

The Mahoning Valley was often the first American home for Welsh miners and managers. The large Welsh mining community provided a receptive location for immigrants to acquire an economic foothold and get their bearings before moving on to other Ohio mining districts or further west. Anthony Howells, for example, was born in Dowlais and worked underground until 1850, when he immigrated to the United States. He headed straight for the Brier Hill mine in Youngstown, and, after five years underground in Governor Tod's mine, Howells went into the mine provisioning business. In 1870 he moved to Massillon, Ohio, where he launched Howells Coal Company. Howells hired another Welshman, Evan Evans, as his superintendent, and he in turn recruited a Welsh workforce. The town of Justus grew up around the mine and descendants of those early families still reside there. Incidentally, after serving as Ohio state treasurer and state senator,

Howells was the U.S. Consul to Cardiff from 1893 to 1897. In 1901 he sold his mining interests and constructed the luxurious Courtland Hotel in Canton, Ohio. At home, President William McKinley was his next-door neighbor.[25]

Adjacent to Justus was North Lawrence, the principal mining community in Lawrence Township, laid out after the Pennsylvania Railroad came through in 1852. During the late 1860s and 1870s, many Welsh settled in this section of the Tuscarawas field. By 1880 the English and Welsh, just about evenly divided, represented half of all miners in the township. The first coal seams in Summit County were found accidentally in 1808, and were worked as wagon mines from local farms. The Tallmadge Coal Company was chartered in 1838.[26] It built a tramway from the mines to the Pennsylvania and Ohio Canal to carry coal for Lake Erie steamers. After the Civil War numerous mines were opened in Springfield and Coventry Townships. Straddling the township line was Thomastown. According to one source, "the industry was particularly active during the 1880s and during that period many Welshmen came to work as miners and formed a little settlement on Triplet Boulevard near Arlington Street called Thomastown."[27] A county history published in 1892 described Thomastown as "a considerable village . . . two miles south of Akron—composed largely of coal miners, mostly Welsh, who have for several years worked the coal mines of that vicinity—with church, school house, store, post office, etc."[28]

Thomastown was a decidedly Welsh town. Its name was probably derived from Llewelyn Thomas, one of the original coal mine owners. According to the manuscript census for 1880, about 58 percent of the population was born in Wales. That does not tell the whole story, however, for another 20 percent or so had a Welsh-born spouse or parents. With a total population of 622 inhabitants, at least 80 percent were either Welsh or linked with the Welsh by family. Of the 193 employed outside the home, 147 (76 percent) were coal miners. Thomastown certainly supports the thesis that Welsh miners flocked to coal towns where Welsh owners and superintendents were in charge. Of the six men who were recorded in the 1880 manuscript census as mine bosses, three were "coal operators" (owners), two of whom were born in Wales and married to Welsh women, and the third was born in Ohio but his wife was born in Wales. There were two superintendents, both of whom were born in Wales, and one was a "stable boss" born in England (although he might have been from Monmouthshire) wed to a Welsh spouse. In short, four of the six supervisors were definitely Welsh-born, and the other two were ethnically linked at least by marriage.[29]

Mining communities of the Ohio and Hocking Valleys in the southeastern part of the state had a similar history. Coal had been mined on a relatively small scale along the Ohio River near Pomeroy, Minersville, and Syracuse since antebellum days. Situated about midway between Pittsburgh and Cincinnati, and below the dangerous obstacles to navigation, these mines had an advantage in downstream markets over those in the northern reaches of the Ohio River.[30] Among the pioneer mine operators in the field was Ebenezer Williams, of Llanon, Carmarthenshire. In 1841 he and his wife immigrated to Coshocton, Ohio, and walked to Minersville, arriving on Christmas Day 1841. He became a leading citizen of the area, and for nearly half a century engaged in coal mining.[31] Southeastern Ohio had been a Welsh population center since the 1830s when the Welsh immigrated into adjacent Gallia and Jackson Counties, where they farmed, began a thriving charcoal iron industry, and engaged in some coal mining.[32]

In the early days the mines on the Ohio relied on the river for transportation, but in the years following the Civil War, railroads and innumerable branch lines opened the Hocking Valley region to coal development. The Welsh were well represented in the coal towns that sprang to life along the railroad. In New Straitsville, the *Cambrian* reported, about 800 to 1,000 Welsh lived in this mining town by 1885. Of the thirteen prominent Welshmen who lived there, one was a Baptist pastor, two were storekeepers, and the rest were coal miners, three of whom were bosses.[33]

Although smaller than New Straitsville, Shawnee was another community where the Welsh were influential. The town did not exist in 1870, but in the following year numerous mines were opened in rapid succession along the railroad; by 1880, 2,770 people lived in Shawnee. Including the children born in the United States to Welsh parents, the Welsh population was 769, or nearly 28 percent of the whole.[34]

Shawnee illustrates how coal towns with a minority of Welshmen became known as "Welsh towns" because the Welsh were prominent in all phases of community life. John D. Jenkins, for example, was a miner who emigrated with his wife and two sons in 1865, settling first at Pomeroy, and then moved there in 1873 when the mines opened. Over the years, Mr. Jenkins was one of the founders of the Welsh Congregational Church, served on the County Board of Commissioners, and served as a member of the town council, school board, and township trustees. One of his sons, David C., was a miner until 1888 when he became the operator of the xx Mine, and later president and director of the Shawnee Bank. David's brother Mordecai, also born in Wales, became a coal miner and then partner with his brother in the Jenkins Brothers Department Store. Similarly, John

E. Williams migrated to Shawnee in 1875 where he worked as a coal miner until he opened a hardware store. Also, a disproportionate number of the businessmen and professionals in the town were first-generation Welsh Americans, such as David H. Jones, whose parents were emigrants from Wales. He worked in the mines initially, but entered into a partnership with his brother in the Jones Coal Company, the Jones Brothers Merchandise Company, and other business enterprises.[35]

The coal industry in the area around Cambridge, Ohio, owed its establishment to a large degree to another Welshman, William H. Davis. Born in the mining valleys of South Wales in 1851, he entered the pits at an early age and accompanied his parents when they immigrated to Ohio. Davis mined coal in several Ohio districts prior to 1888, when he opened the Pioneer Mine at Byesville. The Farmer Mine and several others soon followed, and Davis became a prominent businessman of the area. He reorganized his numerous coal mines into the Cambridge Collieries Company in 1907, retaining the position of general superintendent until his death in 1909. At the peak of his career as an operator, Davis employed nearly three thousand coal miners. According to one scholar, Davis "retained much of his Welsh character and upbringing, including his love of Wales, participation in Welsh choral music, deep piety, and dedicated participation in the Welsh Baptist Church."[36]

### Midwest and Far West

Similar patterns prevail with the westward migration of the coal industry during the last decades of the nineteenth century. Experienced Welsh mine managers were hired to open new mines in Indiana, Illinois, Iowa, Missouri, Kansas, and Colorado, and, as they took up new positions, many of their former employees followed them. When the Mahoning Valley field began to fade in the 1880s, a Welsh manager was hired from Trumbull County to open a new mine at Hiteman, Iowa. Of the twelve local Welsh mining families Rev. Owen Thomas mentioned in a series of articles to the *Druid*, three came directly from Wales, seven were from the Mahoning Valley, and two other from Mahoning arrived after a time in Soddy, Tennessee, another mining center established with Welsh managers.[37]

Welsh migrated beyond the Mississippi River, generally to pockets where coal was mined like Missouri and Iowa, but they were comparatively few within the context of the broader industrial migration of the Welsh. The further west, the more scattered they were across the vast open spaces. Even to the isolated pockets of coal mining in the West, however, the Welsh

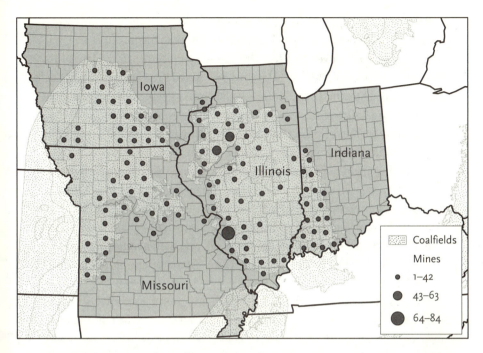

MAP 6. Coal mines in Indiana, Illinois, Iowa, and Missouri, 1880. Map by Sue Bergeron. Source: *Tenth Census of the United States, 1880.*

brought their knowledge of modern mining. Utah provides a unique example of Welsh influence in one of the remotest regions. Utah's coal industry had its origins with the arrival of the Mormon pioneers, and Brigham Young's effort to establish a self-sufficient coal and iron industry. A promising coalfield was located in Sanpete County, about 130 miles southeast of Salt Lake City, and Brigham Young's call for coal miners among the Mormon settlers brought forth two Welshmen: John E. Rees, who first entered the mines back in Wales when he was eight, and John Price, another miner who brought his tools with him to Utah. The two men were joined in the mining venture by several Welsh families, and they were soon shipping coal to Salt Lake City by wagon. More Welsh converts joined the small mine community, and in 1869 it was christened Wales in honor of the homeland. The settlement was handicapped, however, by the lack of capital and inadequate transportation. The mines were purchased by capitalists in 1872, and two hundred miners were hired to expand the works. A large influx of non-Mormon investors, businessmen, and then coal miners gradually assumed the dominant role in the work started by Welsh Mormon converts.[38]

The discovery of coal in Pleasant Valley, Carbon County, Utah, sparked a coal rush in the 1870s. During the winter of 1875–76, the Pleasant Valley Coal Company developed mines in what became the town of Winter Quarters. In 1883 the Denver and Rio Grande Western Railroad, which built a line between Denver and Salt Lake City, purchased the Pleasant Valley Coal Company. By 1887 the Utah Central Coal Company, which connected to the Union Pacific Railroad, also operated several mines in the valley, and major mines were operated by the Utah Fuel Company in the 1890s. These companies produced three quarters of Utah's coal in 1896.[39]

As in other fields, the British held major positions in management, and this pattern was reflected in the Pleasant Valley Coal Company: Thomas J. Parmley, superintendent of the Winter Quarters mine, was English; the Mormon bishop Henry G. Williams, superintendent of the Clear Creek mine, assistant general manager of the PVCC, and then general manager for the Utah Fuel Company, was Welsh; Frank Cameron, superintendent of Castle Gate, was Scottish.[40]

Even as far away as Black Diamond, Washington, being a Welsh miner still carried some weight in 1900. Albert Garrett's father brought his wife and two children to America in 1900. They arrived in New York City, stepped off the boat and onto an "immigrant train" bound for Seattle. After an arduous journey of seven days, and a chance encounter with a cowboy who astounded the Garretts by speaking to them in Welsh, they arrived at Seattle and made straight for the Black Diamond mine office twenty-five miles away. Black Diamond was managed by Welshmen. The superintendent, Morgan Morgan, filled the supervisory positions and all of the best jobs with Welsh miners. According to Albert Garrett, his father found Morgan's son minding the office when he arrived, and Garrett informed him specifically that "he was a Welsh coal miner and would like to have work." Young Morgan responded: "We don't have any work for you. We can't hire you. We have all the men we need." Overhearing the conversation, the senior Morgan emerged from his office and interrupted his son: "You hire that boy. He's a Welsh coal miner."[41]

### Central Appalachia

A map displaying the distribution of the Welsh population would show that the Welsh were not in abundance in all American coalfields. They represented a mere sprinkling in the West, but their absence in the South is striking because of the region's proximity to the eastern coalfields where most Welsh miners congregated. Even though there was no shortage of Welsh mine managers in the southern coalfields, it was no coincidence that the hewers among their countrymen were neither attracted by employment opportunities in the South nor recruited for their superior skills. Part of the reason lies in the timing of the development of the Central Appalachian fields, between 1900 and 1920. Fewer British miners were emigrating, and those who had arrived earlier were either too well established elsewhere or had moved out of the industry into other professions. Moreover, the Welsh were "free labor" republican adherents in practice and ideology throughout the period of greatest influence in the nineteenth century and into the early twentieth century. They refused to compete with oppressed African American labor used by mine operators, with the active support of the state, to maintain an artificially low wage structure. Southern coal operators also used convict labor when possible, which depressed the labor market even more. Finally, while Deep South operators in Alabama and Tennessee preferred blacks to immigrant whites, Central Appalachian operators followed a policy of "judicious mixture," which called for a balance between native whites, African American, and European immigrant workers. Union men need not apply. Consequently, even though Welsh managers and operators were in demand, constructing communities of skilled Welsh miners with a strong sense of craft control was out of the question, and with a few rare exceptions did not happen south of the Mason-Dixon Line.

The Appalachian Coal Basin is one of the richest mineral deposits in the world. A high quality bituminous coal which is low in volatiles (gases) and high in carbon, it has a high BTU rating, is excellent as a stoking coal, and makes the best coke for steel production. Consequently, it was highly sought after for industrial uses in locomotives, steamships, and steel mills. By the early twentieth century, several large railroads acquired hundreds of thousands of acres and leased the mining rights to independent coal operators, most of whom lived and worked on site. Although the point is often belabored, these rugged men carved an industry out of a mountainous wilderness. The principal role of the pioneer operators in the Appalachian coalfields was to assemble a workforce, construct facilities and services for workers and their families, and to initiate coal production. They did this largely on their own, arranged financial backing from third parties, solved daily problems as they arose, and negotiated an independent path between the corporations from whom they leased their lands and the railroads that hauled their coal to market.[42]

Charles K. Sullivan has profiled forty-five of these pioneer operators in the Smokeless Coalfield of southern West Virginia about whom vital information was available. Most of them migrated from Pennsylvania and Virginia, two different worlds for all intents and purposes. The Pennsylvanians came from the anthracite fields and represented "a mature industry in search of new investment opportunities." The Virginians, however, had little or no previous experience with mining, but were aggressive business-men living in towns along the railroads linking the coalfields with tidewater and drawn into the coal industry through businesses or the professions serving the coal industry. Of forty-six operators whose origins could be determined, ten were born in Great Britain, fifteen in Pennsylvania, eight in Virginia, seven in West Virginia, and six in other places; the origins of two others are unknown. All but one of the British operators, Sam Dixon, came to Pennsylvania first before moving to West Virginia. On average they had lived in Pennsylvania for twenty-five years after emigrating from Britain. All were born into mining families; some had entered the pits in Britain, but it was in Pennsylvania where they achieved success as operators or super-visors. Their financial backers were all Pennsylvanians.[43]

Unlike the Virginians, who were from upper- and middle-class origins, all but one of the British-born coal men came from working-class origins, entered the pits as young boys, and succeeded through hard work and personal responsibility. They were proud of their background and believed that it gave them an edge in the industry. The British were also older by an average of fourteen to fifteen years over the Virginia operators and had less formal education. All of the Britons and most of the Pennsylvanians were Republicans, while the Virginians were Democrats. Once the Virginians acquired experience, they adopted the practice of the Britons and Pennsylva-nians of recruiting their own young men into the industry through practical mining experience, technical education, and nepotism.[44] Their class origins do not seem to have been that significant in the coalfields, for the pioneer operators were highly pragmatic men, and the British worked closely with Virginians even before they had gained economic success.

Several of the most successful of the pioneer operators were Welsh. Thomas Phillips Davies, one of the first of the Welsh coal men, seems to have followed the earlier practices of Welsh operators by recruiting a com-munity of his own countrymen. Born in Maesteg, South Wales, in 1849, Davies came to America with his parents when he was fourteen. After the Civil War, the family moved to Coal Creek, Tennessee, where his father held the position of outside superintendent of mines belonging to the Knoxville Iron Company. Like his father, Thomas Davies entered the mines at Coal Creek.

In 1869 Davies moved to West Virginia, where he was employed as boss driver in the mine at Cannelton, across the Kanawha River from present-day Montgomery.[45] Davies organized the Coal Valley Coal Company in 1872, at Montgomery. This was the first coal mine in Fayette County, and the first to ship coal over the newly completed Chesapeake and Ohio Railway. Davies operated the mine until it played out fifteen years later. Like most of the British pioneer operators, Davies worked in the mine himself when he had orders to fill, and, when he did not, worked in other mines in the area. Whether he recruited them or they heard of Davies's mine and came of their own volition, a small Welsh community gathered there. An 1883 report in the *Cambrian* claimed that few Welsh had settled in the Kanawha Valley until recently. Most of them were coal miners, but, carrying the mantra of the working-class movement of the time, the writer hoped that they would soon leave mining, buy land, become farmers, and thereby gain their independence. Few Welsh miners these days "become owners or even partners in any very profitable mines," the writer continued; "these are generally operated by large capitalists and railroad corporations." This was certainly true in Pennsylvania by the 1870s, but the southern Appalachian coalfields were still undeveloped, allowing plenty of room yet for aggressive independents even though they encountered serious disadvantages in dealing with the corporations who leased the land and transported the coal. The *Cambrian* author was not informed of any other Welsh proprietors in the Kanawha Valley "except in the case of Messrs. Thomas P. Davies, of Maesteg, and Evan Evans of Cowbridge, Glamorgan." The two men were partners for several years, but Evans was then managing another mine a few miles distant. The author reported "about 40 families of Welsh at Coal Valley [renamed Montgomery in 1891], but there is no Welsh church there. Many of these families have gone there from Pomeroy and Syracuse, Ohio." According to the 1880 manuscript census, these families lived close to one another, and, as would be expected of an earlier migration, they tended to be older, living in family units, and middle-aged.[46]

Other than a brief venture in 1897 when he went to Alaska to pan for gold, Thomas P. Davies spent the remainder of his days in Montgomery expanding into other businesses, but most of his time was devoted to politics. Called the "Invincible Old War Horse of the Republican Party" by his friends, he served in the West Virginia House of Delegates and in the state senate between 1893 and 1901, served on the city council for six years, and in 1896 was elected mayor of Montgomery. In the legislature he successfully championed the establishment of miners' hospitals. Davies was best known for sponsoring the bill that created the Montgomery Preparatory

School, which eventually became a four-year college.[47] T. P. Davies was also very active in community institutions. He was a "zealous" Baptist and member of fraternal orders including the Masons, Odd Fellows, Knights of Pythias, Owls, Moose, and Red Men. He married Annie Williams, of Monmouthshire, in 1855; she died in 1900, and he followed in 1916.[48]

Like T. P. Davies, many of the pioneer operators worked in their own mines during the early stages of development. But there were Welsh operators like Lord Godwin Powell and his son Lord Evan Powell who had plenty of capital and did not have to do the physical labor. Evan Powell founded the Mount Carbon Company at Powellton, Fayette County, between 1885 and 1888, and his son operated the mines. The estate of over 8,000 acres was acquired in 1860 by a syndicate controlled by Englishman Lord Charles Pelham Clinton. He and his associates leased the land to Lord Powell in 1885, and the final sale was completed in 1901. Godwin Powell and, unlike that of the typical absentee owner, his family spent part of the year in Powellton and took a keen interest in the community. St. David's Episcopal Church was established in 1886, largely through his efforts; the church choir quickly established a reputation for excellence.[49]

The improvement in social relations and quality of coal community life when the owner was on-site rather than an absentee apparently also held true when the ownership was Welsh. This is well illustrated by a comparison, which continues to this day, of Powellton and Elk Ridge, both located on Armstrong Creek. Elk Ridge was operated by the Cardiff Company, headquartered in Cardiff, Wales. The company sent a number of miners to Elk Ridge, but, with only a superintendent to represent the owners, miners recognized the difference between the two communities. One resident claimed that "there was all the difference in the world" between Powellton and its neighbor Elk Ridge, and the difference was Lord Godwin Powell. Even though the town was not incorporated, Powell believed that it needed some form of government, so he organized an election for constable. "Now we know'd that it wasn't legal. But Godwin was nice, so we just went along with it. And it worked out. See that's the main difference. You got somebody who could see with his own eyes what your situation is. And that makes all the difference."[50] The benevolent influence of Powell is credited for establishing a trajectory for Powellton that led to an open community, with its own newspaper, public library, and active intellectual and political life. In 1912, a year when interest in Eugene V. Debs's American Socialist party was peaking in the coalfields, one of the largest Socialist meetings ever held in Fayette

County gathered at Powellton. Elk Ridge, on the other hand, remained an undeveloped aggregation of company houses.[51]

The Welsh mining families of Powellton and Elk Ridge did not remain long, however. There were never a large number of Welsh miners in West Virginia, but one of the unresolved minor questions of Appalachian mining history is when and why the British miners disappeared so suddenly. This exodus is difficult to establish precisely because of the lack of census data, but conventional wisdom is taken from the U.S. Immigration Commission report which claimed that the British left West Virginia to escape the invasion of southern and eastern European immigrants who, they believed, lowered living and working conditions.[52] The growing presence of African American miners arriving from the Deep South must also have stimulated the British departure. It is generally accepted that the biggest decline in British miners came following the failure of strikes in 1902, 1905, and 1907 when the United Mine Workers of America (UMWA) warned union miners to stay away from West Virginia. It would seem that only a few managers remained by 1910, for of the 68,135 miners employed in the state that year, 46,704 of them were foreign-born. Of these only 9 were Welsh, a 92 percent drop from the 118 recorded in 1908. On the other hand, African Americans numbered 11,237 in 1910 and increased to 17,799 by 1920.[53]

The traditional craft structure of skilled miners and laborers began to change when the waves of new immigrants expanded the labor pool in the late nineteenth century. So, too, did the industrial system developed in Pennsylvania and Ohio when it was transported to the newly opening southern coalfields in the late 1870s and northern mine operators confronted the southern caste system. African Americans presented a vast industrial reserve of very cheap labor in the South, and it was in the financial interest of managers to embrace a system that would cost them less money.

A blend of British immigrants, Pennsylvanians, and Virginians, the pioneer operators in southern West Virginia apparently adopted the practice of hiring the cheapest labor available. Consequently, the Welsh pioneer operators who developed the southern West Virginia fields hired Welsh or other British supervisors, but they did not attempt to construct a Welsh ethnic community as their countrymen did above the Mason-Dixon Line. Indeed, even though most came with very little capital, and were born into the lower levels of the working class, they formed one of the most elite communities found anywhere in the American coalfields, the operator town of Bramwell. On the line between Mercer and McDowell Counties,

West Virginia, and just a few miles from Pocahontas, Virginia, Bramwell was a unique town to say the least. Regarded as one of the richest small towns in America, Bramwell was everything the surrounding coal towns and camps were not. It was settled by wealthy coal operators and investors in the Pocahontas coalfield in the last decades of the nineteenth century and never had more than a few hundred residents, but it was home to as many as nineteen millionaires and their families. Norfolk & Western trains stopped at the Bramwell station fourteen times daily. The Bank of Bramwell was reputed to be the richest small bank in the nation, and it served as the financial center for operators of the surrounding coalfields. Other pioneer operators lived just outside of Bramwell but were tied into the town's elite. Tales of the grandeur and opulence of life in Bramwell in its heyday are still a part of local legend.[54]

Among the Bramwell elite lived the steadfast Welshman Jenkin Jones. Born in Glyn Neath, Wales, in 1841, he was eight when the death of his father forced him into the mines as a trapper boy. Working during the day, Jones attended night school long enough to acquire only a rudimentary education, but, like so many socially mobile Welsh miners, he became a self-educated man. In 1863 he migrated to Scranton and later moved to Treverton, Northumberland County, Pennsylvania. In 1872 Jones met Joseph Beury, a mine superintendent from Schuylkill County who assumed management of a new mine at Quinnamont, in the New River Valley, upriver from Montgomery, West Virginia. A number of other anthracite miners from Pennsylvania, including another Welshman, Thomas Davis, and two Englishmen, John Cooper and John Freeman, also came looking for opportunities. The following year Jones, Freeman, and Davis were looking for suitable coal lands to open their own mine, and in 1877 they launched the Fire Creek Coal & Coke Company at Fire Creek, Fayette County. Beury and Cooper found what they regarded as a better investment further downriver. Mining operations were supervised by the three experienced British miners, Davis serving as general superintendent and Jones as mine boss. At Fire Creek, Jones acquired experience with a southern workforce: of the 199 people who lived in Fire Creek in 1880, 99 were recorded in the census as African American; whites numbered 93, only seven of whom were foreign-born, and they were British. All of the Britons came to West Virginia from Pennsylvania. Blacks were found among the skilled miners as well as the laborers, but the workforce at the coke ovens was exclusively African American. By 1883 the mine was well established, but Davis died and the company's financial backer Erskine Miller, a banker from Staunton, Virginia, put one of his relatives in charge.

Pioneer West Virginia coal operator Jenkin B. Jones. Courtesy of Eastern Regional Coal Archives, Craft Memorial Library, Bluefield, West Virginia.

Whether this was a source of friction or not is undetermined, but by 1884 Jenkin Jones and John Freeman had sold their company stock.[55]

Striking out on their own, in 1884 Jenkin Jones and John Freeman leased 1,400 acres of coal land along the Mercer and McDowell County line only a few miles from Virginia, and started the Caswell Creek Coal and Coke Company, the third operation launched in the Flat Top coalfield. Jones was president and general manager. One local old timer, Judge I. C. Herndon, of Welch, McDowell County, informed a reporter in 1930 that he remembered when they opened the mine: "Their equipment was one mule, one mine car and a few picks and shovels. . . . Jenkin Jones and John Freeman both dug coal in that mine in order to get a start." Jones and Freeman invested in other ventures as well, and in 1907 all of these companies were consolidated as the Pocahontas Fuel Company. In 1916, when Jones died, his son James Ellwood Jones assumed his father's role in the company. By 1930, PFC employed 4,000 workers at nine coal mining operations.[56]

Jenkin Jones was proud of being Welsh and he was active in Welsh American societies that promoted cultural identity. He was noted for his appreciation of music and poetry, and he supported the eisteddfod, that uniquely Welsh institution which provided the venue to showcase these gifts. "Should anyone ask you the question: 'who is the most enthusiastic Welshman in America?' you can safely answer, 'Jenkin Jones,'" declared the Welsh American newspaper the *Druid*. "He is one of the most aggressive, energetic and successful Welshmen in this country. He came to America, like many of us, poor; but, unlike many of us, he is today a millionaire."[57] In 1908, Jenkin Jones announced a prize in the *Druid* for fifty dollars at the eisteddfod in Wilkes-Barre to the winning conductor who led the same choir to victory in two successive years. At one of the many Welsh gatherings he attended in Ohio and Pennsylvania over the years, for example, he declared that "love for his native land clings around the Welshman's heart like lichen to the rock, . . . 'cursed be he that hateth his native lan,' he quoted in Welsh, and then concluded: 'but I yield to no man in my fealty to the United States.' "[58]

He went to great lengths to hear music sung in Welsh. On a visit to Wilkes-Barre and Scranton in 1908, the *Druid* reported, Jones attended the *Gymanfa Methodistiaid* held in Scranton on a Sunday, and later that day attended the rehearsal of the Druid Glee Society. Afterward, Jones remarked that he had "not heard better singing in Wales where he attended each year the national eisteddfod."[59] Following the Welsh Day in Scranton, Jenkin Jones was inspired to new heights, devising a plan to organize a musical contest at his home. This story was reported in the *Druid* with a headline proclaiming, "Colored People Hold Eisteddfod." The paper reported that Jones had come to Scranton to make a contract with "the Ladies Choir to appear at his palatial home in West Virginia, where they will give a private concert for Mr. Jones' friends." He wanted to sponsor an eisteddfod in the South, but found that "it was an impossibility as they scarcely know what a Welshman is down there." But he had an idea. One of the "colored maids in my house is an excellent musician, and I offered her five dollars if she would learn 'Aberystwyth', and sing 'Jesus, Lover of My Soul' to the tune." He believed that she more than earned the five dollars, and he offered her another five to teach it to her church choir of which she was also the director. He made the same offer to another African American choir director at another local church. "I have made an offer to give a substantial prize to the choir which gives the best rendition of the tune on these words. So you see that I am going to have a little eisteddfod after all, although all the contestants will be colored folks." His plan was to have them sing for the Welsh Ladies Choir when they visited.[60] It is worth noting that the following month the pastor of a Welsh Baptist church in Edwardsville, Pennsylvania, wrote to the paper that he was pleased with the article about the "colored people" having an eisteddfod. Mr. Jones probably was not amused by the sarcasm, intended or not, that the pastor found "great pleasure to know that the Welsh are interested in the negro brothers," and that they have the right to "every privilege the white man possesses" because they are also "the Incarnation of the Son of God."[61]

Jones lamented that "he never hears the *Hen Iaith* (mother tongue) in his southern home," reported the *Druid*, and yet "he speaks it with wonderful smoothness and accounts for it by stating that he reads more or less Welsh every day." The paper described him as "a poet of no mean ability and delighted the poet laureate of Hyde Park, Cadle, with one of his verses." He also had memorized a "wonderful stock" of old Welsh hymns and entertained the audience by singing a few of them. As a final piece of evidence proving beyond doubt how "thoroughly Cymric" was Jenkin Jones, the writer pointed out that Jones's home in West Virginia was named *"Uwch-Y-Niwl"* (Above the Mist).[62]

Because the outlines of Jones's career as a mine operator are found primarily in public relations accounts, and because he was one of the pioneer operators about whom legends quickly formed, a friendly press always portrayed Jones as a man of the workers. While this may have been an honest assessment, there are some signs that not all of his workers were so contented. The miners of Simmons Creek and Mill Creek near Bramwell went on strike in 1889 because the owners, Jenkin Jones and John Cooper, had increased the size of the coal cars and refused to pay the men for the extra tonnage. The operators apparently telegraphed the governor requesting that troops be sent to control the miners, which he did even though there was no trouble from the 1,000 men at twelve mines who laid down their picks. One of them wrote to the *National Labor Tribune* appealing for the National Progressive Union of Miners to send an organizer. "The operators brought in blacklegs to replace the strikers, and local miners informed the *NLT* that the first men to 'blackleg' were from England and Wales—the last men in the world we thought would blackleg. But it is not the first time they did this."[63]

When Jones's wife died in November 1911, he threw himself headlong into his Welsh heritage. He returned to Wales as often as possible. In July 1912 he was accompanied to Wales by his son and daughter for a six-week holiday at Swansea and Llanwrtyd Wells. Jones supported Welsh causes to the end. The disastrous 1913 mine explosion at Senghennydd, South Wales, which killed 440, prompted Welsh Americans to launch a fund-raising campaign for the survivors. Jones was vice president of the relief committee, which raised close to $5,000.[64] Jenkin Jones died on December 19, 1916, reportedly of tuberculosis, and, according to his instructions, his home was demolished so that no other family could encroach on his friends and relatives, the Bowens and Ellwoods, with whom he shared the hillside. He also left a fortune to his three children, and his son James Ellwood took over his father's business responsibilities.[65]

Another Welshmen instrumental in establishing the southern West Virginia coalfields was William H. Thomas. Born in Carmarthenshire in 1862, he emigrated with his parents to Wilkes-Barre in 1867. Like so many other miners who came to America to improve their chances in life, his father died before he had an opportunity to realize his dream. The family was left in poverty, and William H. was forced to quit school to find employment. His first job was as a newspaper boy, and then he became a clerk in the municipal court of Wilkes-Barre, a position he held for the next twenty-three years. He came to Pocahontas, Virginia, a few miles from Bramwell, West Virginia, and clerked in the first company store established by the Southwest Virginia Improvement Company. In 1887 he married the eldest daughter of John Cooper, and in 1889 he became store manager at the Cooper Company store. Cooper was born in 1842 in South Staffordshire, England, entered the pits at the age of six, and had worked at every non-managerial job in the mine by age twenty. Cooper migrated to Pennsylvania in 1862, and in early 1884 took the first lease in the Pocahontas coalfield. He died in 1898 at the peak of his career, but his son continued his business in close association with his brother-in-law, William H. Thomas.[66]

Although he was not a miner by vocation, Thomas had been around mining his entire life, and with his connections, ambition, and the opportunities presented by the rapid development of the coalfields, not surprisingly he took the plunge. His first mining venture was the Algoma Coal and Coke Company, at Algoma, McDowell County, which shipped its first coal in November 1891. It had a production capacity of 15,000 tons a month and 175 coke ovens; Thomas was general manager and lived in the camp, and his three children were born there. In 1900 Thomas sold his shares in Algoma and moved his family to Columbus, Ohio. But mining was in his blood, and he returned in 1902 to open the Thomas Coal and Coke Company. Thereafter, his businesses grew into a formidable empire including a number of large coal companies, a milling company, and the Bank of Bramwell. Like the other pioneer coal operators of Bramwell, Thomas was actively involved in community affairs. Although he did not aspire to political office himself, he was active in the Republican Party, serving on the staffs of Governors William Glasscock and Henry Hatfield and as a delegate to the party's national convention. Thomas died prematurely on January 11, 1918, at the age of fifty-five, from complications following surgery.[67]

Although there is no evidence Thomas's Welsh identity was particularly strong, he called his Tudor mansion *"Bryn Avon"* ("hill overlooking the river"). Like Jenkin Jones, Thomas did not attempt to reconstruct a Welsh mining community. He hired Welsh managers but relied heavily on African American labor, at least initially. On a visit to Wilkes-Barre in 1895, Thomas met John A. Williams, who had recently arrived from Wales. He was working as a timberman in a local mine, a job for which he was overqualified.[68] Williams had served articles with William Thomas (not to be confused with the West Virginia mine owner), one of the most accomplished professional miners in Wales. Thomas was one of the few self-made managers in the South Wales coalfield, rising from colliery lad to owner and managing director of the Mardy colliery of Merthyr Steam Coal Company. He also operated a mine engineering consulting service from his home, Brynawel, in Aberdare. Few young men were able to pursue this kind of schooling, and the engineers who were qualified enough to offer them articles were the elite of their profession.[69] Williams was well trained and accepted an appointment as assistant mine superintendent at Algoma. Thomas was the general manager, and his brother-in-law, William J. Prichard, was superintendent. According to Williams, Thomas had promised that when he opened his new mine, Williams would be appointed superintendent. Prichard was born in Carmarthenshire in 1863, emigrated in 1881, and settled in Wilkes-Barre. There he married Thomas's sister, who also had been born in South Wales. Pritchard became a mine foreman, and in 1890 joined his brother-in-law in West Virginia as superintendent of the Algoma mine, and subsequently as a full partner in the firm.[70]

There is no evidence that John A. Williams was either promoted or continued to work in the field, but his long letter to his former master, William Thomas of Brynawel, offers a glimpse into how the experienced British miners thought about the labor force in the Appalachian coalfields. Williams reported that two-thirds of the Algoma workforce was African American and the other one-third a mixture of whites. "Before I came here, I was told the niggars were a most treacherous devilish lot of people to deal with, and the only way to manage them was to knock them down with anything at hand at any slight offence on their part, this was told me by several people in Pennsylvania who had had a great deal of experience with them, so when I came here I fully expected to find a jabbering semi-wild lot of people to deal with." Williams was pleasantly surprised to find otherwise, describing them as a "well behaved and enlightened people." He called them "a high breed people, by nature very refined and gentlemanly, such pleasing voices, and unusually well informed and well spoken." Williams declared, "I respect their race, and they appreciate that more than words can tell, for most white people treat them otherwise, which is the greatest mistake a man can commit, as they naturally feel, and resent, any insult given them on account of their race, the same as you or I would resent it, or any other man with a grain of sense. For they are only human nature after all, as we are ourselves." Even though they were not without their faults, he had become "extremely fond" of them.[71]

That was not his opinion of native white men. In fact, Williams declared, he would "rather manage five hundred of them [African Americans] than half a dozen of the white people of this country." The white man of West Virginia and adjoining states "is about the most contemptable person on the face of God's earth, he is unbearably ignorant, and does not know it, he has generally been brought up in the mountains, hog fashion, . . . he is a small ferret eyed fellow, with hollow lanky cheeks, a thin pointed nose, with about 17 hairs on his chin, and thirteen hairs upon his upper lip, which he insultingly calls a moustash, that is the best description I can give you of the native white man of the south," Williams wrote.[72] Perhaps this condescending attitude toward the local white population prompted the British operators to cloister themselves in the respectable confines of Bramwell.

It is difficult to know if this was the perspective of a manager who found the powerless blacks of the Jim Crow South more agreeable than white southerners who were accustomed to thinking of themselves as independent and self-sufficient and therefore were less manageable. One thing is certain: Williams's approach of treating African Americans with respect met with better results in West Virginia—where they were never constitutionally disfranchised, and particularly in McDowell County, where they made up about one-third of the miners—than it would have in the South. In Alabama his breach of the race line would have made him persona non grata.

The Booth-Bowen Coal and Coke Company, founded in 1884 by William Booth and Jonathan P. Bowen, was the fourth coal mine in the Pocahontas-Flat Top field; Bowen and his son Harry took complete control of the mine in 1893. Jonathan was born in Wales in 1830 and was but a few months old when his parents migrated to St. Clair, Schuylkill County, Pennsylvania. He went to work in the mines as a boy, worked his way up the mining hierarchy to superintendent of Reiplier's Colliery at Ashland, Pennsylvania, and in 1871 he resigned and accepted the position of district superintendent of collieries for the Pennsylvania and Reading Railroad, Coal and Iron Company. Harry was born in 1860 in Ashland and left school at sixteen to work in the mines under his father. He joined him in the management of the Booth-Bowen mine when they moved to West Virginia. Three hundred and fifty miners and laborers were employed at the mine, which produced coal for 174 coke ovens.[73]

Little else is known about the mine or Jonathan Bowen, but he probably followed the same practice as the other British and American pioneer operators of the Pocahontas-Flat Top field. They were a cooperating fraternity of businessmen similar in background, of British extraction and Americanized in Pennsylvania, who bonded together in the "wilds of West Virginia." They sat together on the boards of their various companies in a kind of interlocking directorate so common in their day. Their families intermarried and represented a vibrant social circle that the overwhelming majority of people viewed only from a great distance. They helped to create a society based on coal, but they expended not the slightest effort to re-create a Welsh community as did the pioneer Welsh operators of the northern fields. Within their own small circle they might have maintained features of their Welsh heritage; there is a story that several of the women talked by phone every day after their husbands had passed away and exchanged more intimate news in Welsh.[74] The prevailing management strategy of divide and conquer through a judicious mixture of African Americans, foreigners, and native whites that characterized the single industry economy of Central Appalachia militated against the pattern of workforce and community construction practiced by the Welsh in the northern states.

### Deep South

Prior to the Civil War an entire generation of British miners and ironmasters honed their skills in Pennsylvania's developing coal and iron industries. Following the war and to the end of the century, they carried their skills to the newly opened fields farther south and west, where they obtained prominent positions in the mines and mills through informal ethnic networks. No more illustrative case exists in the rising Birmingham coal and iron district than that of Llewellyn W. Johns.

Llewellyn W. Johns (1844–1912), probably the most influential mine manager in the Birmingham, Alabama, coal and iron district, was another Welsh manager who did not recruit Welsh workers. In fact, for one who benefited so much from his Welsh connections, Johns rejected traditional ethnic nepotism as a matter of good company policy. Johns boasted that he was born "atop of a coal mine" in Pontypridd, Wales—a claim all residents

Alabama mine operator and engineer Llewellyn W. Johns. From Ethel Armes, *The Story of Coal and Iron in Alabama* (Birmingham: Birmingham Chamber of Commerce, 1910), facing p. 354.

of that city might have made. His father and mother were natives of South Wales. His father left his engineer's position to speculate in the booming South Wales coalfield during the 1840s by entering the mine provisioning business. Unfortunately, his company went bankrupt after the 1850 strike in the Rhondda, and Llewellyn was forced to leave school at a tender age. After a brief stint at the government chain works in Pontypridd he entered the mines, but in 1863 he departed for the anthracite district of Pennsylvania in search of greater opportunity.[75]

Johns's early years in America reads like a wild-west adventure story; constantly on the move working at a variety of jobs from coast to coast, he prospected for gold, built bridges, mined coal, cut timber, and even fought Indians. He returned to the anthracite field from his first trip west in 1868, quickly found employment in the mines near Scranton, and was soon promoted to the position of mine engineer. He also worked for several members of the David Thomas family, founder of the anthracite iron industry in the United States, including Major William R. Thomas, nephew of Samuel Thomas (David's son). Major Thomas informed Johns that the Thomases were expanding their iron interests into the South, and he induced Johns to try his luck there.

Six months later, in 1872, Johns set out for Rising Faun, Georgia, where Major Thomas promptly appointed him superintendent of the coal mines that supplied the iron furnace. The venture proved to be founded on worthless coal, however, and the business collapsed during the Panic of 1873. Johns again headed west to the Nevada silver mines, where he served as assistant mining engineer, but 1877 found Johns back in Birmingham working for James, one of David Thomas's grandsons, first as the superintendent of the Helena coal mines and then as superintendent of the Pratt Company mines, the largest coal mining complex in the South. Johns benefited from a complex set of acquisitions and mergers of coal and iron companies that occurred during the rapid development of the Birmingham district, managing ever larger operations until he achieved the position of chief mining engineer of the Birmingham district for Republic Iron and Steel Company.[76]

Like Jenkin Jones in West Virginia, and many others referred to in this study, Johns retained a strong Welsh identity throughout his life in America. He returned to Wales several times and remained in close touch with relatives there. His national pride was apparent in 1908 when he responded to a letter in the *Druid* inquiring about Evan James (Ieuan ap Iago), the composer of "Hen Wlad fy Nhadau," the Welsh national anthem. Johns wrote that James was a resident of Pontypridd when Johns was growing up. On a recent trip to Wales, Johns wrote, he had visited James's final resting place. Johns proudly proclaimed that all of his family was "personal friends" of Evan James. In fact, James had composed a poem and given Johns a photograph of himself when Johns emigrated, which he prized to the end of his days. While on an inspection tour of the Panama Canal, he wrote, "I was called on for a song, and on the top of the greatest cut ever undertaken . . . I arose and stepped on top of a boulder and took off my hat to the Atlantic and Pacific Oceans . . . and sang, as I never sang before, that good old song 'Hen Wlad.' " Johns signed the letter with his bardic name "Tragolwyn."[77]

Johns maintained close associations with a small circle of Welsh-born friends who met periodically at his twenty-acre Birmingham estate, The Elms. He attended the Methodist church and was affiliated with the Odd

Fellows, Elks, and Knights of Pythias and was a 32nd degree Mason. A retrospective described him as possessing "a wonderful sense of humor" and as "a great promoter of picnics, excursions, and other entertainment, particularly one in which his Welsh friends could furnish vocal music and band music." He took part in only one political campaign, on behalf of Governor Thomas Jones, to whose staff he was later appointed "colonel." The press reported that he was "the best known and most popular Welsh-American in this part of the country."[78]

When Johns died on February 4, 1912, at age sixty-eight, the local newspapers commented on his civility and generosity. At his funeral, it was reported that "the Welsh singers, of whom he was so fond and a patron always, will render his favorite hymn of his native land—Wales—in the language of that country." The report explained that the singers were a quartet of "special friends" of Johns. Their hymn sung in Welsh was "*Marchog Iesu Yn Llwyddiannus*" (Jesus Is My All in All) and an anthem, "*Ddyddiau Dyn Sydd fel Glaswelltyn*" (Like the Grass All a Man's Day). The report declared that this was his request because "he loved this music better than all other."[79]

In 1912 the local paper reported another meeting of "The Welsh Boys" who spent an evening in song at The Elms. It is not clear if the "Welsh singers" were also "Welsh Boys," a close group of men who held "important positions in the steel mills of the Tennessee Coal, Iron, and Railroad Company at Ensley."[80] Who belonged to this circle of Welsh managers cannot be ascertained with certainty, but Richard Thomas is a likely candidate. He was born in Baglan Parish, Glamorganshire. A relative of Samuel Thomas (David's son), Richard entered the coal business in Wales and had charge of several large mines there. He immigrated to Illinois in 1870 and became the first to make coke in that state. He also patented the Thomas coke oven and loading devices. In 1886 he built the ovens at Coalburg, Alabama, and operated several mines there. In retirement he enjoyed studying the Welsh language and etymology until his death in 1906.[81]

Isaac Price might have been one of the "Welsh Boys" who met at the Johns home as well. He was born in South Wales in 1847 and entered the pits when he was eleven years old. Price emigrated for America in 1869 and worked in a number of Pennsylvania mines. He migrated to New Mexico where he managed a coal mine in 1881, but two years later he was appointed inside manager of mines for the Coalburg Coal and Coke Company, the second largest coal mining operation in Alabama.[82] Another candidate for Llewellyn Johns's round table was Rhymney native John X. Thomas, no apparent relation to any of the previously mentioned Thomases. When he emigrated is uncertain, but he was living in Massillon, Ohio, before moving to Ensley, Alabama, where he rose through the ranks from hewer to mine superintendent and then general manager of the Tennessee Coal and Railroad Company.[83] George A. Davis might also have joined this elite group. A native of Dowlais, he was raised by an uncle in Monmouthshire until 1864, when he embarked for America and settled in St. Clair, Pennsylvania. Moving to Alabama in 1888, he became "one of our most prominent figures in mining circles," according to one observer. While in charge of the Belle Sumter mines, Davis erected a Welsh church, the only one ever built in the state of Alabama. He was unique in another way for, unlike Johns, Davis undoubtedly built the church to serve the Welsh mining community he recruited. Little is known of this community, but, if his obituary is correct, "wherever he lived there would always be found a colony of Welsh miners, for he was never known to turn away a countryman."[84]

Belle Sumter, the large mining operation managed by George A. Davis, was owned by another Welshman, David Roberts, one of the most fascinating Welsh entrepreneurs in the British network developing the Birmingham district. Henry DeBardeleben, the Birmingham coal and iron entrepreneur, convinced Roberts of the great opportunities for investment in the mineral district. Roberts was born on a small farm on the Welsh island of Anglesey, but he decided early in life to seek his fortunes in distant places. Roberts followed the well-trodden road to London, where he planned to leave for Australia but found himself working for a prominent Bond Street banker instead.[85]

Intelligent and ambitious, Roberts discovered financial frontiers worthy of his exploration while working in the bank, and in 1873 he crossed the Atlantic to Charleston, South Carolina. With English businessmen backing him, Roberts was readily accepted into the circle of Charleston's leading businessmen. His position in South Carolina's upper crust was solidified when he married the Charleston socialite Belle Sumter Yates. When Roberts moved to Alabama in 1885, therefore, he brought with him powerful financial backing from both sides of the Atlantic. Pooling their resources, Roberts and DeBardeleben incorporated the DeBardeleben Coal and Iron Company in 1886 with DeBardeleben as president and Roberts as vice-president and general manager, and the board of directors comprised business associates in Charleston and London. As general manager, Roberts was responsible for managing the company on a daily basis, and he worked closely with the company's chief mining engineer, Llewellyn Johns. Bessemer, the company's town, was one of the major centers in the frenzied construction of railroads, coal and iron ore mines, limestone quarries, and iron furnaces that gripped the Birmingham district in the late nineteenth century. In 1892 the DeBardeleben Coal and Iron Company merged into the Tennessee Coal, Iron, and Railroad Company. Roberts retained his office in the new company until 1897, when he sold his stock and organized the Brilliant Coal Company, operating it with his son until the intrepid Welsh developer died in 1909. Two years later, in 1907, TCI was acquired by the even larger United States Steel Corporation.[86]

Writing of Johns in 1887, a biographer declared that Captain Johns was "one of the important factors" in the rise of the Birmingham district. However that may be, he did not extend the ethnic occupational advantage of the Welsh network to others of his nationality. In fact, even though Johns employed some Scots, English, Irish, Cornish, and German miners, he refused to hire Welshmen. In an interview with a newspaper reporter in 1886, Johns explained: "We have no Welsh at the mines. I am a Welshman, and I do not have them because being my countrymen, they would expect favors from me which they could not receive. They are among the best miners in the world," he declared, but he still refused to hire them.[87]

Even though Johns was assertively proud of his Welsh heritage, social, political, and economic imperatives overrode his ethnic impulses when it came to business decisions. Johns played the role of patriarch, but his dependents were African Americans trapped in the nexus of segregation. It is clear that he, like other Welsh managers in southern industry, embraced the southern racial ideology. "The majority of our men are negroes," he explained to a reporter, "who are the best workers and stand heat and cold better. . . . We could not do without negroes. . . . The work does not require brains and they do splendidly." Moreover, Johns publicly declared that "the introduction of negro labor means an end to strikes and labor troubles."[88] Increasingly, convicts were being leased to coal mining companies, and under Johns's direction Pratt Mines became not only the largest coal mining complex in the South but also the largest employer of convict labor in Alabama. One authority estimated that more than 50 percent of the African American coal miners in the Birmingham district learned their trade while employed as convicts. A black convict being interviewed by a Senate committee investigating the conflict between capital and labor was asked if a well-behaved ex-convict could find employment in the mines. He responded: "When he is released he will generally get employment immediately. He generally goes to Mr. Johns here and he will give him a job of some kind."[89]

Although Johns did not employ Welsh coal miners, he certainly continued to think of himself as Welsh, and as a member of the broader British identity which he often reinforced through his personal and professional associates. Johns was not alone in adapting to the South. A number of British-born entrepreneurs, managers, and technical experts played a pivotal role in the initial phases of development of the Birmingham coal and iron district. They constituted a network of men linked by previous experience in Pennsylvania to David Thomas, his son Samuel, and grandson Edwin, who managed the family's affairs in the South. This British cadre also played key roles in founding the largest and most powerful steel corporations in the world, Republic Steel and United States Steel Corporation. Many of the mines in Alabama and Tennessee were captive mines supplying coke to the steel mills.[90]

Giles Edwards, a prominent Welsh ironmaster with career-long membership in the Wales-David Thomas-Pennsylvania network, also was one of the "Johns Boys." Edwards was born in Merthyr Tydfil in 1824, in the shadow of the world-renowned ironworks of Dowlais, Cyfartha, Plymouth, and Penydarren. He received his training in the shops of Dowlais, and became an expert draftsman by 1842 when he emigrated for Carbondale, Pennsylvania, to make the drawings and supervise pattern making for the first mill constructed at Carbondale. Here he met his wife, Salinah Evans, daughter of Welsh immigrants from Tredegar. The quality of his work drew the attention of another influential Welsh immigrant, ironmaster David Thomas, who enticed Edwards to superintend the construction of the Thomas works at Tamaqua, and then manage Thomas's furnace at Catasauqua. While there, David Thomas's famous library on iron-making was available to Edwards, and he took full advantage of the opportunity to further his education. Under the strain of working by day and studying by night, Edwards's health failed. Required to find a warmer climate, Edwards took a position in Chattanooga, Tennessee, in 1859, and built a modern coke-burning, hot blast operation, the first in the southern Appalachians to successfully use coke smelting technology.[91]

Even though the vast majority of his fellow Welshmen were decidedly pro-Union, Giles Edwards cast his fate with the South during the Civil War and after; whether this was out of political sympathy, health reasons, career opportunities, or some portion of all three is a matter of conjecture. Of the early Welsh ironmasters who remained in the South after the war, however, Edwards was the most successful. During the war, he moved from Chattanooga to Alabama to rebuild an ironworks destroyed by the Union army and remained there for the rest of his life. By 1883 Edwards had moved to Oxmoor, then about six miles south of Birmingham, where he was the superintendent of the Eureka Iron Works, which was supplied with coke from Llewellyn Johns's Pratt Mines.[92] Members of the Thomas family were frequent guests at the Edwards home. It was at the invitation of his old friend and fellow countryman Giles Edwards that David, Samuel, and Edwin Thomas came south for the first time to purchase mineral lands.[93]

Salinah and Giles Edwards became southerners and apparently were temperamentally suited to accept slavery and Jim Crow as an insufficient reason to leave the South, as did so many Welsh. Like Llewellyn Johns, the Edwardses retained their Welsh identities too. According to Ethel Armes, writing in 1910, they often spoke Welsh at home. Edwards subscribed to a Welsh paper, probably *Y Drych*, all his life, and Armes claimed that "one of his intimate friends was a Welsh bard." Edwards was described as "a quiet, kindly, deep-hearted man who loved his work." Never in good health, probably from breathing in noxious furnace fumes, Edwards died prematurely in 1893.[94]

Welsh identity aside, Edwards's views on race and labor issues demonstrate just how southern he became. He and Johns both testified before the Senate Committee on Capital and Labor in 1883 that the "unreliability" of labor was the principal problem confronting southern industrialists, and he saw very little possibility of remedying the problem. Edwards explained that "my experience for over twenty years in this State—part of it during slavery, of course—does not lead me to expect to see that evil remedied very soon. You see the bulk of the entire labor here is colored." In other words, he believed that blacks were "shiftless," one of the important building blocks in the ideology of race control upon which the system of segregation was built. Similarly, Johns testified that "colored labor here is very irregular," but he thought it best to train them rather than to import whites. The reason is not difficult to understand when we remember that African American labor was paid one-third less than their white counterparts by legislative edict in Alabama. Johns utilized convict labor extensively, at a cost that was a mere pittance compared with white labor. Consequently, even destitute European immigrants found the South inhospitable to free labor, and most were not attracted by the certainty of competing against a semi-free industrial reserve.[95]

The racial perspective of Johns and Edwards was decidedly southern now. There was nowhere else for the black worker but the bottom of the economic pyramid, for it was "natural to them to submit to the white man," according to Edwards. "You know my ideas and my habits of thought, originally, were formed far away from the Southern States," he stated, but "a great many of my ideas have been changed since I came into this country and have come into contact with the people, both masters and slaves, and, taking a general view of everything in regard to the condition of the colored man." Now "I do not see any hope in the world for them while they are together in large numbers," until "brought in contact generally with the superior race."[96] Obviously Johns and Edwards were in agreement with the southern position on the central issue of race. Welshmen like Johns and Edwards deviated dramatically from the overwhelming majority of Welsh Americans who abhorred the southern race system and refused to venture below the Ohio River.

How do we explain Llewellyn Johns's departure from the practices of the Welsh mining patriarchs in the North who preferred to hire miners of their own nationality? They fused professional management, ethnic progress, and their own personal responsibility, but Johns separated his personal ethnic loyalties from his business practices and elevated cost accounting and regional racial norms in order to succeed. As a result, a Welsh inner circle of managers in the South accepted the moral ambiguities of racism in exchange for personal advancement. With only one known exception, Welsh mining communities were never established in Alabama. In fact, in 1900 only 306 residents in the entire state of Alabama were natives of Wales, 278 of them in the coal and iron district.[97] Most of them had been called there by George A. Davis, the only known Welsh operator to assemble a Welsh coal community in the state. It was a minuscule population for the "Pittsburgh of the South," particularly when compared with the tens of thousands living in the mine and mill regions of Pennsylvania and Ohio.

Welsh industrial immigrants were overwhelmingly miners and iron millhands, yet occupation alone does not fully explain why they were concentrated in particular locations. Although networks and institutions are important in understanding Welsh immigration, it is also clear that individuals often exerted a critical influence on where Welsh communities developed. Welsh nepotism thrived in mining towns, but only where there was a Welsh community, and Welsh mine owners and managers were instrumental in determining whether those communities emerged in the first place. The economic motive goes a long way toward explaining why Johns and Edwards made their choice. Johns himself testified in 1883 that he came to

America because of "the inducements which this country offered," and "if wages were the same here as in Wales, I would have staid [*sic*] in my native land."[98] Johns and Edwards adapted to the labor system they found in the South, and employed oppressed African Americans rather than Welshmen. Therefore, Welsh communities were nearly non-existent below the Ohio River, where the only Welsh nepotism was practiced among elite managers.

# COMMUNITY, REPUBLICANISM, & SOCIAL MOBILITY

When the industrial migration to America began in earnest during the 1850s, the Welsh entered a society that was already long familiar to them because of its deep roots in Welsh culture and the almost continuous migration from Britain since the seventeenth century. Moreover, by the mid-nineteenth century the two economies had become inextricably interconnected through commerce, manufacturing, capital investment, and labor exchange. British immigrants, therefore, were not foreigners, outsiders, or uninvited guests so much as they were "cousins" joining kinsmen who had preceded them and made America part of the Anglo world.

The eminent Welsh historian Glanmor Williams argues in an essay poignantly titled "A Prospect of Paradise?" that the century between 1815 and 1914 represented "a unique chapter in Welsh-American relationships, the like of which can never be repeated. Wales gave America a host of her sons and daughters; America offered them a haven, opportunity and a future. The two countries shared in a religious, political, moral and cultural connexion [sic], which brimmed over with a spirit of confidence and optimism."[1] Beyond the belief that emigrants could elevate their economic position in America, Welsh immigrants also were attracted by the radical social and political ideals of a society that was more equal and democratic, the lack of privileged aristocracy, and the absence of an official state church.

The numerous tracts written by Welsh immigration promoters emphasized these themes over and over again. Benjamin Chidlaw, one of the most influential promoters in the early nineteenth century, claimed that it was hearing his father talk of America as a "free and virtuous country, with neither monarchy nor tithe and where poor people could buy farms," that had prompted him to migrate to America. Henry Davies, an emigrant in Wisconsin, declared that the "feeling of equality" was stronger in America than Wales, and "snobbery and servility were far less evident." Captain David Evans, of Talsarnau, Wales, who found himself seated next to President Ulysses S. Grant in the Metropolitan Methodist Church in Washington, observed that "it does one good to see the chief magistrate of a great nation like another human being, not putting on some artificials to endeavour to make him something above human."[2] Letters to Wales often discouraged workers from emigrating. As one worker warned his countrymen, "America is not all paradise." The level of satisfaction was often determined by the location and experience of the individual worker, and there were many who agreed with David Morgan in Minersville, Ohio, who wrote, "I like the country and the work famously; I wish I had been wise enough to come here years ago."[3]

Welshmen in America were proud of their reputation for religiosity, honesty, sobriety, hard work, and self-improvement, elements closely associated with the Protestant ethic and the cult of success in a country obsessed by it. As one Welshman observed, these qualities placed the Welsh "whether as preachers, farmers, craftsmen, merchants or singers . . . at all times on the top rung of the ladder. We are the leaders . . . and we are recognized as such by other nations."[4]

### Welsh American Coal Communities

Railroad and river transportation expanded dramatically after the Civil War, facilitating both western migration and mining. Beyond the Welsh population centers in Pennsylvania and Ohio, nineteenth-century Welsh industrial immigrants were widely dispersed but likely to be found in colonies scattered, like the mines and mills, along the railroads. The most prominent coal and iron districts, such as Scranton, Pittsburgh, Youngstown, and Birmingham, were often urbanized, but most coal mines were located in relatively isolated small towns, some of which were independent and others company-owned; few provided more than basic social services.

Unlike so many of their agricultural brethren, few miners left Wales with the conscious intention of preserving Welsh culture in a new land. They settled together because miners congregated around coal mines, and settling with kith and kin made the transition to life in America easier, particularly for monoglot Welsh immigrants. Nevertheless, to the degree circumstances allowed, life in the Welsh American settlements was transplanted from Wales. How conscious the immigrants were of this process very much depended on the degree of importance they placed on Welsh national identity before they left their homelands. Large sections of South Wales were heavily Anglicized by the nineteenth century as industrialization drew Wales into the greater commercial and political dynamics of the British Empire. The rise of Wales as an urban industrial society facilitated the development of the verbal and written communications skills required for full participation in the British commercial empire.

The rural migration of monoglot Welsh agrarians into the industrial centers reinforced traditional Welsh culture within the new industrial communities, particularly coal and iron. As with other immigrants who often found their national identity when they became a minority in the American polyglot of peoples, so too did many of the Welsh. The kind of community the immigrant settled in, however, was crucial. In the large cities, like New York or Philadelphia, they could simply disappear. Even in a city like Pittsburgh where the Welsh played an important role in the steel industry, their presence was submerged by the size and great diversity of the population. In rural communities, however, the Welsh language and churches lasted into the twentieth century. In relatively small coal towns of Pennsylvania and Ohio, where they settled in compact Welsh communities, the Welsh language, institutions, and culture might last for several generations.[5]

The cultural background of the Welsh and other British immigrants presented barriers that were far less formidable than those encountered by other foreign immigrants. The majority of the Welsh were fluent in English, shared common legal and political traditions, were devout Protestants and skilled industrial workers, and generally mirrored American middle-class values. As one historian observed, most British immigrants passed almost unnoticed into American life; the "immigrant problem" had nothing to do with the English, Scots, "or even the more clannish and foreign-speaking Welsh." The British generally escaped ridicule from Americans. Opprobrious names such as "micks," "dagoes," and "hunkies" were never attached to British immigrants. The Welsh might object to being called "Taffy" or "goat," but few Americans used these terms at all, and fewer still either understood or intentionally used them as epithets. Welsh immigrants were slightly less inclined to marry native-born Americans than their British counterparts. However, while they generally were inclined to band together in their own communities, they seldom lived apart from Americans and were never segregated by law or custom.[6]

Although one might expect that their language would have served as a hurdle to acquiring American citizenship, a higher proportion of Welsh were fully naturalized citizens than the English or Scots. In fact, only 7 percent of Welsh immigrants had not applied for citizenship in 1900, whereas 13 percent of the English and the Scots had not. The Welsh exhibited a higher proportion of fully naturalized citizens than migrants from any other nation. In 1920, 72.9 percent of the "foreign-born Welsh" were naturalized American citizens, whereas the percentage for all foreign countries combined was 47.2 percent. They were no less attached to their homeland, but they were not equally loyal to the British crown, and were not reluctant to renounce their allegiance to the crown when taking out American citizenship. Measuring return migration with anything like precision is impossible because of the way statistics were, or were not, collected in the nineteenth century, but scholars estimate that only 13 percent of the Welsh and Scottish, and 21 percent of the English, in the United States returned to their homelands between 1908 and 1923. This is an extremely small percentage compared with eastern and southern European groups.[7]

Small, isolated mining towns were fertile incubators of a distinctive work-based culture and a unique perspective on the world. The mining life was reproduced in the nineteenth century by fathers who transferred knowledge of the craft to their sons by taking them into the mines as boys. Mining culture was distinctive, therefore, not only because of the unique bonds formed by the shared dangers of underground toil, but also because it was welded together by inter-generational, inter-familial, and intra-ethnic dependencies. It was very difficult to shift from another occupation to mining without a sponsor. Those who "belonged" in the community were either born there or another community just like it, and probably were acquainted with some of the residents.

Despite these distinguishing cultural features, constructing a prototypical Welsh immigrant coal miner is surprisingly difficult. Popular mythology depicts the coal miner as either the radical, militant "archetypal proletarian," or, paradoxically, the fatalistic, subterranean brute. Both are stereotypes that distort our understanding of the miner as an ordinary human being with an unordinary line of work.[8] Miners themselves left few records, and their organizations concentrated on labor-management relations. There is no "typical" Welsh immigrant coal miner, of course, any more than there is a typical coal mining community. Therefore, some of the most basic aspects of life among Welsh American coal miners remain undifferentiated within generalized descriptions of the mining life. For this study, therefore, Welsh mining communities in Ohio were sampled from the manuscript censuses for 1860, 1870, and 1880 in order to develop a database of personal information containing more than 9,000 individuals. Ohio was chosen because only Pennsylvania had a larger population of Welsh miners. Of the 24,810 Welsh that Rev. R. D. Thomas documented living in Ohio in 1870, 45 percent resided in agricultural communities and 55 percent lived in the coal and iron districts.[9] As a group, Ohio's Welsh mining population was large enough to constitute a significant sample, but small enough to permit quantification. Chosen were Ohio coal communities with a significant Welsh presence in the southeastern counties of Meigs and Perry, and the northeastern counties of Stark, Trumbull, and Mahoning. The database reveals little more than what is already known from standard sources, but provides a greater degree of specificity. Welsh miners did not deviate greatly from either American miners generally or the Welsh immigrant population in particular, but did provide some solid ground for a few important generalizations.[10]

The Welsh communities incorporated in the Ohio database conformed to the standard life cycle of coal towns tracking the influx and decline of the workforce corresponding with the birth, growth, maturity, and decline of the mines themselves. All the communities began to decline toward the end of the century as the coalfields played out, causing the Welsh population to dwindle. The age structure of Welsh-born miners barely changed between 1860 and 1880. Youngsters under eighteen remained fixed between 6 and 8 percent of all Welsh miners in the database, and the next age group of eighteen to thirty, the prime working age, remained between 37 and 32 percent. One intriguing feature that emerged was the difference in the age structure for miners born in the United States to Welsh parents. A larger percentage of this group went to work at an early age. Of the U.S.-born Welsh coal miners in 1880, the under-eighteen group made up one-third of the group (36.6 percent), and the eighteen-to-thirty age group made up 56.9 percent of the group. Of course those born in the United States would be overwhelmingly younger; but they, too, followed dad to the pit at an early age as in Wales. There is a common understanding that Welsh immigrants came to Pennsylvania first, and then moved on to newer fields. While this was a common pattern, those in the Ohio database who were listed in the 1880 enumeration as having been born in the United States were overwhelmingly Ohio-born (76 percent), with Pennsylvania next at 19.9 percent. The Ohio data suggests, therefore, that the primary destination of those immigrants who resided there was Ohio.[11]

Miners in the eighteen-to-thirty age group who were single grew between 1860 and 1880 from 47 to 61 percent. Many no doubt remained at home longer to contribute to the family income, and perhaps it took longer to gain the security required to leave home and strike out on their own because of the economic downturn in the 1870s. Interestingly, an even larger percentage of the U.S.-born Welsh miners waited to leave home; 76 percent of the same age group were still single in 1880. This suggests the financial tenuousness of mining families, even among the Welsh who were the best miners and held the best jobs. Among those thirty-one to fifty, Welsh coal miners were a very married group at about 90 percent.[12] Welsh miners usually married Welsh women. The Ohio database shows that 92 percent of them did so in 1860, 86 percent in 1870, and 77 percent in 1880. Welsh women chose Welsh men as partners even more frequently, with 92 percent doing so in 1860, 95 percent in 1870, and 87 percent in 1880. Single men were much more mobile and frequently came into contact with other nationalities. Many came to the United States as single men and more often than not found no suitable Welsh companion. An average of the marriages represented in the database over all three censuses shows that 16 percent of the women married to Welsh miners were non-Welsh, and only 9 percent of the Welsh women's spouses were non-Welsh. The growing number of non-Welsh spouses from 1860 through 1880 reflects the general assimilation of Welsh miners, and like other immigrant women, a slower pace of assimilation for Welsh women in the coal communities.[13]

Just who the non-Welsh spouses, male and female, were is suggested by the 1890 census data relating to children of "mixed" parentage, that is, either one or both parents born in specified countries. Nationally, for the Welsh, this amounted to 220,540 children, representing 1.07 percent of the American population of 20,519,643. Parentage combinations for Welsh and another nationality show that the vast majority of those non-Welsh spouses were English, Irish, or Scottish, with a smattering of other old-stock northern Europeans. The very few with southern or eastern European spouses were notable only for their rarity. In 1890, 76.3 percent (169,832) of the 222,468 "mixed" Welsh children with Welsh-born fathers also had mothers born in Wales, 7.8 percent (17,425) had mothers of other nationalities, and 15.8 percent (35,211) of the mothers were American-born. The intra-group mating patterns were normal among all immigrant groups during this period, with many of the first generation arriving with their spouses. The marriage data shows Wales with the lowest percentage in fifteen categories of "white persons of foreign parentage."[14] This is probably one of the origins of the idea that the Welsh were "clannish," but marriage within the dominant group also functioned as part of a strategy for success for both parents and their children.

### Labor Republicanism and the Protestant Ethic

The republican ideology of craftsmen also was an integral strategy for success. "All the struggles they have ever had in their native land were but struggles to fit them to be Republicans in America," a Welsh American politician proclaimed to a Welsh crowd in Scranton in 1890. Historian Rowland Berthoff astutely observed that "for the party that had appropriated the traditional name 'Republican' it was a happy if minor circumstance that the Welsh word for republic is *gweriniaeth*: government by the *gwerin*, the people, the folk, the peasantry. To immigrant Welshmen the Republicans were *Gwerinwyr* or *Plaid Werinol*, the folk party."[15] Many Welsh American miners had migrated off the land to take jobs in the South Wales pits. Their life experience rooted them in the *gwerin* even though they had become members of the permanent wage-earning proletariat. In the transition from the land to industry, they substituted customary claims to land with the ideology of labor republicanism that grew out of the industrial revolution.

Belief in the dignity of labor has been one of the cultural underpinnings of American society from the beginning, and by the mid-nineteenth century an affirmation of the north's "free labor" social system as a contrast to slavery in the South. Capitalist values were rooted in Protestantism, but more precisely in the Protestant ethic, which emphasized the notion that each individual had a "calling" for which he was created by God. Achieving success in this calling was, therefore, a service to the Almighty and evidence that the individual was predestined to enter the kingdom of heaven. Thus, the pursuit of wealth became a religious duty; the personal qualities of honesty, frugality, diligence, punctuality, and sobriety required for success were also religious obligations.[16] All these tenets were embraced by Nonconformity, which in turn predestined the Welsh for success in America so long as America was governed by representatives of a free people.

The Protestant ethic carried with it the conservative implication of accepting one's status in a static economy with more or less fixed classes. American political ideology, however, emphasized social mobility and competitive economic growth in a dynamic society with a fluid class structure. The idea of "free labor" rejected the notion of fixed social classes, and embraced a dynamic social hierarchy based on ability. The definition of "labor" was broad, one that included all the "producing classes," incorporating all those who worked, including artisans and shopkeepers; excluded were those who profited from the work of others, such as bankers, lawyers, and speculators.[17]

The economic goal in "labor republicanism" was not great wealth, but rather the middle-class desire for economic security and independence. An ideology articulated most forcefully by the Republican Party during the decades bracketing the Civil War, republicanism generally claimed class conflict had no place in America since all classes benefited from an expanding economy. The ramifications of class conflict, such as strikes, worked against the interests of capital and labor alike because equal opportunity generated the upward mobility that would turn laborers into capitalists. Labor-capital cooperation was what produced long-term upward mobility for laborers.[18]

In an economy dominated by small, privately owned shops and factories, republicans were suspicious of corporations and financial concentration because they limited upward mobility. Nevertheless, republicans believed that an individual's success or failure was largely attributable to one's personal character and adherence to the tenets of frugality, hard work, and sobriety demanded by the Protestant ethic. Even though republicans "glorified labor," they disapproved of those who labored for wages their entire lives because that indicated individual failure. The republican notion that labor created all value (the labor theory of value) was formed prior to the Civil War, an age when craftsmen, yeomen, and indeed all workers could aspire to economic independence. By the eve of the Civil War the republic dominated by craftsmen and yeomen farmers was already being eclipsed by large-scale corporate enterprise. Historian David Montgomery estimates that already by 1860 more than half of American workers were not independent workers.[19] Even though republicanism continued to be a driving force into the postwar decades, and workers could expect a rising standard of living and social mobility in an expanding economy, self-employment and economic independence became increasingly unattainable in the new era of big capital. In late-nineteenth-century America "labor republicanism" increasingly became an outdated roadmap to success. "Free labor" degenerated into the "cult of the self-made man," a mythology that justified the excesses of the "robber barons" and proclaimed personal wealth the measure of moral worth.[20]

Corporate economic and political power became permanently interwoven as America marched into the twentieth century, and it became impossible for the miners to adhere to the republicanism of the nineteenth century. Opposition to the concentration of economic and political power as a perversion of American republican values no longer seemed to be a viable reform strategy. The anti-monopoly platform of labor reformers during the Gilded Age seemed out of step in a society increasingly dominated by large-scale business, a society in which the corporation man was "progressive" and the laborer was "conservative." It seemed obvious that the producing classes could no longer realistically hope to restrain corporate power, so republicanism died the death of spent movements.[21]

Herbert Gutman has argued the common refrains in late-nineteenth-century working-class rhetoric was the "fear of dependence, 'proletarianization', centralization, and the fear that industrial capitalism would transform 'the Great Republic of the West' into a European-style nation." Such men, he notes, had a vision of America as a nation of independent workingmen, and they lamented the loss of Old America in the post–Civil War years. By the 1890s, the New America had fallen under the control of a wealthy, privileged class of capitalists who had reshaped the republic into an "old country" like those of Europe and Great Britain. Workingmen, buoyed by the American ideal of equal opportunity, feared for their future in a country where working-class status was permanent.[22] Ohio Knights of Labor official William A. Davis told those assembled at a miners' reunion in 1880 that, like America, organized labor was a "child of liberty" that had to break away from capitalists who, like the "monarchical governments of Europe," opposed freedom for the workingmen: "The Creator never intended that one man should ride in his gold-mounted carriage with his six in hand, and another to walk barefooted through the mud and mire." Instead of embarking on class warfare, however, Davis argued that the old virtues of republicanism should be resuscitated because they were more "in accordance with the laws of nature."[23]

Nonconformist ministers who embraced labor republicanism turned evangelical religion against the capitalist traducers. The labor press frequently complained that traditional democratic ideals had been compromised by the individualistic materialism of institutional Protestantism. The Baptist minister in an Ohio mining town, J. Thalmus Morgan, warned that "God's laws of right and wrong are ever the same and cannot be changed until God and man's moral nature shall be changed. . . . He shall save the children of the needy, and shall break into pieces the oppressor. Yes, He will do the poor justice." As for "oppressors," on the other hand, "their time of retribution shall come."[24] By the early twentieth century, the optimistic religion of early Welsh Nonconformity had been transformed by activist ministers into the humanistic socialism of Keir Hardie and of the New Theology movement that played an important role in the rise of the Labour Party in Wales. The continuity maintained through labor and Welsh ethnic channels of communication shows up in the Social Gospel movement in America, a movement that turn-of-the-century Welsh immigrants would have readily recognized. In both cases miners were not rejecting religious doctrine, but seeking a broader application to real-life conditions and a broad rather than narrow vision of human potentialities on earth. Those seeking change were translating "socialist ethics into the imagery of evangelical Nonconformity."[25]

Socially conscious Welsh American ministers often supported labor's cause from their pulpits, fusing the democratic ideas of evangelical religion, Welsh Nonconformity, and labor republicanism. In an article entitled "Trusts and Trade Union," Rev. W. R. Evans declared that "every one knows that the profit to the capitalists and manipulators is exceedingly out of proportion to that of the laborer, who is the actual producer of wealth." Even though the courts permitted capitalists to consolidate their enterprises into ever-larger corporations, "from the standpoint of Christian ethics" the minister doubted that "we can sin against God" without His retribution. "Can any act that affect[s] my neighbor inimically, be legally right when the same is morally wrong?" he asked. Operators who owned the mines claimed the right to manage their property as they please, but there are some laws that are greater than the law of nations, "I mean the law of God." Is it, Rev. Evans questioned, "a greater crime to starve a man to death than to freeze him to death?" Altruism, he concluded, "is not a mere sentiment, but a fundamental law—a basic principle upon which rests civics as well as ethics."[26]

Tensions produced by the loss of traditional republican ideals informed artisan and working-class protest and reform during this era, from nativism to labor unions. Gutman claimed that Gilded Age workers coined the pejorative phrase "robber baron" because it encapsulated their concerns about proletarianization. In America, declared the *National Labor Tribune* in 1874, "we have realized the ideal of republican government at least in form." America was "the star of the political Bethlehem which shone radiantly out in the dark night of political misrule in Europe. The masses of the old world gazed upon her as their escape." Men in America could be "their own rulers," and "no one could or should become their masters." But industrialization had created instead a nightmare in which "the working people of this country . . . suddenly find capital as rigid as an absolute monarchy."[27]

### Occupational and Social Mobility

The long-standing scholarly discourse on social mobility in America pivots around identifying the social origins of the American business elite. Determining whether they arose out of the working, middle, or upper social strata would demonstrate conclusively whether the American "rags to riches" myth was verified or just a myth.[28] One of the most influential social mobility studies within the genre was Stephan Thernstrom's book *Poverty and Progress*, which tracked the careers of nearly three hundred unskilled day laborers in Newburyport, Massachusetts, between 1850 and 1880. He found considerable geographic mobility out of the city, while there was substantial improvement in the standard of living among those who remained. However, as working-class people moved from unskilled to semi-skilled and skilled work, not a single worker rose from rags to riches. Warren Van Tine's pioneering attempts to identify common characteristics of union leaders using the collective biography approach also influenced the scholarship on social mobility.[29]

Gutman argued that the problem with these studies was that they profiled nationally prominent figures found in sources like the *Dictionary of National Biography*, but ignored the thousands of local elites. In his classic essay "The Reality of the Rags-to-Riches 'Myth,'" Gutman examined the social origins of the iron, machinery, and locomotive manufacturers of Paterson, New Jersey, between 1830 and 1880. His findings showed that most of the successful proprietors began their careers as apprentices in a skilled trade, often as a machinist, and then opened their own shops and factories. A few became "manufacturers of great wealth," but most acquired modest wealth. Nearly all of them were British immigrants who came from working-class backgrounds. Gutman concluded that, at least in the case of Paterson, the "rags-to-riches" myth was not a myth at all. It is impossible to know to what degree this conclusion is applicable to other industries without systematic study, but Gutman claimed that newly developing industries offered skilled craftsmen and mechanics exceptional opportunities for advancement in the early phases of American industrialization.[30]

The coal industry was largely ignored by scholars of social mobility. Edward Davies's *Anthracite Aristocracy* is an unsurpassed study of the urban leadership in Wilkes-Barre, Pottsville, and several smaller anthracite communities. It demonstrates that the Welsh were represented among the elites and the upper class, but focuses on the elements of change and continuity of the "aristocracy" rather than ethnic groups, and coal mining specifically. The few studies that do focus on mobility within the coal industry are more suggestive than definitive. For example, the social historian Ray Ginger examined the social origins and careers of sixty-five managerial employees in the anthracite industry in 1902. This group of managers, which included corporation presidents down to foremen, appeared before the Anthracite Coal Strike Commission of 1902–3 and provided autobiographical sketches of their careers. Ginger acknowledged that the degree of upward occupational mobility might vary considerably within the region, between cities and rural areas, during periods of war and peace, prosperity and depression, and between small and large firms. He might have added to this list of contingencies the ethnic composition and succession. By 1902 many Welsh of the second generation had left the industry for other employment or professions.[31]

Ginger offers "a crude model" for understanding occupational mobility in the anthracite industry based on the assumption of a random group of two hundred twenty-year-old mine workers in 1865. By 1902 three of them would be inside foremen, and there would be a "fifty-fifty chance" that another miner had advanced to a higher supervisory position. Of the remaining miners, he conjectures, one hundred might have died from natural causes, and another fifteen from injuries sustained on the job. Some would have left anthracite for the bituminous mines farther to the west, or for jobs in other industries, such as steel or the railroad. A few became small businessmen, lawyers, or politicians. Those who remained would still be contract miners who probably received the most favorable treatment from the company. Thus, Ginger concluded, "a man who began life on the lowest socioeconomic level had negligible chances of reaching the highest one." However, many undoubtedly achieved a position that satisfied their own expectations of success. A child laborer of 1860, if he survived to 1902, "has almost certainly climbed above the socioeconomic level of his father, whether by remaining a favored contract miner, rising into management, or leaving the industry for other opportunities."[32]

If we judge "success" by the standards of republicanism, that is, achieving economic security and maintaining an open social class structure, or, as Ginger suggests, whether a miner achieved his own standard of success, then the definition of success should incorporate a broader population than only those who became wealthy elites. Also, social mobility among the Welsh should be compared with other immigrant groups. John E. Bodnar has measured upward mobility among the Welsh and Irish in Scranton, Pennsylvania, using the censuses of 1880.[33] That year, Scranton recorded 16,800 gainfully employed workers, with 8,177 in manufacturing and 3,657 in mining. Of the 15,857 immigrants listed among its 45,850 population, most came from Ireland, England, Wales, Germany, and Scotland. He found significant differences between Welsh and Irish workers. The Welsh had worked in mines in Wales and were similarly employed in the skilled and semi-skilled occupations within mining, whereas the Irish came from agricultural backgrounds and were concentrated in the unskilled occupations. Among Welsh workers only 16 percent were in the unskilled category, while 33 percent were semi-skilled and 45 percent were skilled. Conversely, fully 60 percent of the Irish workers were listed as unskilled, 15 percent semi-skilled, and 15 percent skilled.[34]

The Welsh were generally much more versed in industry than the Irish, and this goes far to explain their superior position in the nineteenth-century workforce. Children usually were sent to the mines with their fathers between the ages of six and ten, and contributed their wages to the family coffers until age seventeen or marriage. Conversely, the Irish immigrants in Scranton were overwhelmingly from rural farm homes, and child labor outside the home was rare. The differences in family structure were carried to America from Ireland and Wales. Whereas 83 percent of the Welsh households were nuclear and only 3 percent were extended family households, 71 percent of the Irish family households were nuclear and 14 percent were extended. Bodnar claims that "the Welsh nuclear family, thoroughly imbued in industrial ways, was a smoothly functioning economic unit by 1880."[35]

Bodnar tracked 423 Welsh and Irish sons during the decade between the 1880 and 1890 censuses by family structure and by ethnicity. He used upward mobility within industrial occupations because skilled manual occupations, such as the contract miner, were among the highest paid of all workers. When ethnicity was used as a variable rather than family structure, the difference was even greater. Among the Welsh sons who remained in Scranton during the decade, 39 percent moved up the scale from unskilled and semi-skilled occupations, while only 21 percent of Irish sons improved. The mobility rates were even more dramatic when family structure was used for comparison: among the Welsh sons from nuclear families only, the upward mobility rate was 45 percent, whereas the rate for Irish sons from nuclear families was only 14 percent.[36]

Ethnic background was a greater determinant than family structure in preparing children for industrial society in nineteenth-century Scranton, but what accounted for their greater success? The answer, Bodnar concludes, lies in the different child labor rates for the Welsh and Irish. Child labor was not only widespread but generally accepted among working-class families, and vital to family survival in the nineteenth century. Parents pushed their children into work and expected them to turn over their wages into the family finances, of which they often made up more than a negligible share. One study undertaken in Pennsylvania by a state agency in 1881 found that, of 142 workers sampled, only in one case did the father's earnings equal the earnings of the rest of the family for that year, and often the father's earnings accounted for less than one-fourth of the family's annual income. "One anthracite miner with five children earned $80 in 1881, yet his total family income exceeded $800." Children had long worked in and about the mines both in Wales and America. In Scranton, Bodnar found that 17 percent of Welsh boys ages six to ten were working, and 100 percent of the boys ages eleven to fifteen; among Irish boys the percentages were 9 and 67 percent, respectively. Child labor was more widespread in Wales than in Ireland, and that practice continued among the Welsh and Irish immigrants in the American coalfields.[37]

The socialization of Welsh boys provided greater exposure to adult occupations, thus giving them valuable industrial skills, whereas keeping children home longer apparently placed Irish youth at a competitive disadvantage in achieving economic success in industrial society. The divergent socialization exhibited by Irish and Welsh families in Scranton reflected their respective historical experiences. The Irish in 1880 Scranton were a premodern people whose family life had been relatively unaffected by industrialization. While they were gradually relinquishing their children to modern economic forces, they were not nearly as disposed to do so as the Welsh.[38]

The common bonds forged in the mines of Britain were strengthened in the United States, according to one scholar, by the need to construct new communities in the coalfields they helped to develop. Social barriers to upward mobility in Britain were absent in America, and there was always the opportunity available to those with the skills required of small shopkeepers, barbers, insurance agents, undertakers, and similar occupations.[39] Such declarations are not uncommon in the literature, but beyond the anecdotal evidence the attempts to quantify social mobility among Welsh Americans are rare. Anne Kelly Knowles's study of the Welsh in Ohio's rural Gallia and Jackson Counties, Ohio, employs a collective biographical approach in an effort to apply measurable values to geographic and upward mobility. What she found reinforces the accepted view that the Welsh, like other British immigrants, achieved success with a minimum of difficulty because of the skills they brought with them to a labor-scarce, expanding economy. The Gallia/Jackson Welsh community, however, was composed primarily of farmers and a smaller number of industrialists instrumental in the development of the Hocking Valley charcoal iron industry. This antebellum settlement was held together through most of the nineteenth century by the Calvinistic Methodist chapel culture, which, along with its rural location, helped to insulate the Gallia/Jackson Welsh from the rigors of capitalism.[40]

For this study of Welsh coal miners, biographies collected from county histories and other sources have been compiled. Although the number is relatively small, they generally reinforce the prevailing interpretation that social mobility was accessible for the Welsh. Henry Bradsby's *History of Luzerne County, Pennsylvania*, published in 1893, is chock full of capsule biographies of respected local residents from all classes, including miners, mine managers, merchants, and local office holders. Bradsby's biographies do not present a valid statistical sampling, but they do provide an insight into the range of occupational and social mobility achieved by first- and second-generation Welsh coal miners. Of the 188 biographies used here, 160 were drawn from Bradsby's history, and another 28 came from a variety of other sources, but primarily from the Welsh American periodicals, the *Cambrian* and the *Druid*. Of the 188 total, 110 (58.5 percent) remained in coal mining throughout their careers, and 78 (41.5 percent) left coal for other careers. That the "Slav Invasion" enabled the Welsh to climb the occupational ladder within the industry is borne out by the biographies of 55 (50 percent) of the 110 who stayed in the industry and moved up the hierarchy into mine management. Only a few slipped from management back to the status of "miner." With the skilled positions dominated by the British miners, a large percentage moving out of mining, and the influx of Slavs and Italians taking the unskilled jobs, the way was open for the older stock to move up into management. Since the Welsh were overly represented in the northern anthracite field in particular, it comes as no surprise that fully one-half of them found their way into management. Their experience may not have reflected the "rags to riches" elevation of American myth, but it certainly illustrates significant economic mobility.[41]

Nearly all of them shared one thing in common with other Welsh Americans: their political and religious affiliation. Of those 103 whose political party was known, 86 (91.5 percent) were Republicans, often qualified as "staunch." Two were identified as supporters of the Greenback-Labor party and four as Prohibitionists, which means that they might also have been Republicans. Only two identified themselves as Democrats. Moreover, they were like other Welshmen in America and in Wales in their religious commitment to Protestant denominations. Of the 76 whose church affiliation was known, there was not a single Catholic, Anglican, nor Episcopalian amongst them, and a majority (41) belonged to the Welsh (language) denominations. Only 75 were affiliated with fraternal orders, most frequently the Knights of Pythias, Independent Order of Odd Fellows, and the Welsh Friendly Society of the Ivorites.[42]

Certainly there were many examples of success within the coal industry for Welsh miners to emulate; some rose through the ranks from breaker boy to superintendent or even owner. Some companies, such as the Lehigh and Wilkes-Barre Coal Company, had an abundance of Welsh bosses who rose through the ranks, undoubtedly with a helping hand from other Welsh managers. Morgan R. Morgans, for example, was born near Llandovery, Carmarthenshire, and emigrated from Wales in 1867 as a teenager. He immediately entered the mines and rose steadily through the managerial ranks. By 1894 he was general superintendent of mines for the largest coal company in the Wyoming Valley, employing over 7,000 men.[43]

Welsh Americans were understandably proud of men such as Morgans, who vindicated their ideal of the self-made man in an open society and reaffirmed their faith in the precepts of hard work, self-improvement, and respectability as the road to success. The sons of Welshmen found even greater success in the mining corporations, few more so than Col. Reese A. Phillips, who entered the pits as a boy and worked his way up from door tender to general manager of the coal department of the Delaware, Lackawanna & Western Railroad, eventually supervising upward of 30,000 employees. There were plenty of others. In 1912, the *Druid* boasted that a "trio of Big Welshmen" had been selected to negotiate a new agreement with the miners by the anthracite corporations: two of them were Morris Williams, president of the Susquehanna Coal Company, and W. J. Richards, general manager of the Philadelphia and Reading Coal Company. These were among the largest coal companies in the nation. Not all of the upwardly mobile miners were managers, however. D. R. Reese began his work life as a breaker boy and mined coal until the age of twenty-nine, when he borrowed money to attend Dickinson Law School. With the support of his wife and two children, he graduated and became corporate council for the DL&W Railroad.[44]

Politics also siphoned off many of the most ambitious miners who wanted to get ahead. David Montgomery has argued that "the capacity of America's political structure to absorb talent from the working class was perhaps the most effective deterrent to the maturing of a revolutionary class consciousness among the nation's workers during the turbulent social conflicts of the late nineteenth century." Similarly, Alan Dawley has suggested that "local politics provided a convincing demonstration to wage earners that men from their ranks could rise to the highest positions of honor in their community, and this experience tended to re-enforce a belief in the legitimacy of the existing system."[45]

## THE CAMBRIAN.

Now, go write it before them in a table, and note it in a book, that it may be for the time to come for ever and ever.

| VOL. VIII. | JUNE, 1888. | No. 6. |

### Biographical Sketches.

WELSH-AMERICAN WORTHIES.

Pennsylvania senator and coal operator Morgan B. Williams. *Cambrian* 8 (June 1888): 161.

From all levels within the occupational hierarchy came examples of miners who entered politics. The Welsh-born John W. Morgan served as an officer in the Workingmen's Benevolent Association during the 1871 strike. He had worked in the mines since boyhood, and in 1873 was elected as a Republican to the first of six years in the state legislature. At the upper end of the hierarchy was Morgan B. Williams, a coal mine operator from Wilkes-Barre. Born in Carmarthenshire, Wales, in 1831, at an early age he was taken into the lead mines by his father, who was a superintendent. When his father became ill, the sixteen-year-old Williams took his place, a position he maintained for years after his father's death. Following a detour through the gold fields of Australia, he migrated to the United States and settled in Wilkes-Barre, where he organized the Red Ash Coal Company. Williams threw himself into civic work, serving on the school board and city council, and in 1884 was elected as a Republican to the state senate. In 1891 he was selected to serve as a commissioner of the Columbia Exposition to be held in

Benjamin Hughes, patriarch of the Scranton Welsh. *Cambrian* 20 (May 1900): 233.

Chicago in 1893. Using his position as a mine owner, Williams expanded his interests into other businesses as well, among them banking, the city's electric railway, and a manufacturing company.[46]

In Scranton, Benjamin Hughes followed a similar career trajectory in business and politics. Born in 1824 near Bryn Mawr, Breconshire, he entered the mines at age ten to assist his father. In 1848, at twenty-four, Hughes emigrated from Wales to Pennsylvania, settled in Scranton, and entered the employ of the Delaware, Lackawanna, and Western in 1853. Hughes rose through the managerial ranks from foreman to superintendent and then general inside superintendent of mines. He was present at the initial stages of the industry's growth in the northern anthracite field; there were five shafts around Scranton when he arrived, and, when he died in 1900, thirty shafts and thirty-one breakers dominated the landscape. Like Williams in Wilkes-Barre, Hughes extended his influence into many directions. He was one of the founders, and served as president, of the West Side Bank; was a founder and president of the Cambrian Mutual Life Insurance Company; and founded and served as president of the Chamberlain Coal

Company after he resigned from the DL&W in 1899. Although he never sought state office like Williams, Hughes also was actively engaged in public service and served as a delegate to the Republican National Convention that nominated Benjamin Harrison for the presidency in 1892. The superintendent served as school director, president of the city council, and member of the state board of examiners for mine inspectors and mine foremen. Hughes helped found the Hyde Park Free Library Association and his own Welsh Baptist church, while innumerable other civic organizations were the recipients of his support. Not the least among these were the Welsh organizations, such as the Order of True Ivorites, which he organized, and the Hyde Park Philosophical Society.[47]

Within the coal industry were specialized vocations indispensable to coal mining, but not part of the production process itself. Shaft sinking and breaker construction, for example, were more akin to engineering and construction than mining, but an integral part of the industry nonetheless. Often the men who worked in these occupations were experienced coal miners or mine laborers who found greater upward mobility within these specialized branches. Newly married John and Margaret Pugh emigrated from South Wales in the late nineteenth century and settled in Kingston, Pennsylvania, near Wilkes-Barre. He was born into a shaft digger family and had come to Kingston because many of the Welsh migrants who settled there were family friends or acquaintances. John went to work as a mine laborer because he needed the money; the superintendent and the foreman were Welshmen who knew his father, so he was hired immediately. Soon the company president proposed that John Pugh organize a crew to sink shafts for the expanding company. Before long, Pugh had organized his own shaft-sinking company, which grew with the industry and even expanded its range of operations to other parts of Pennsylvania. Pugh then branched out into other businesses including rental properties, a pool room, the first automobile dealership in Kingston, and a restaurant. His wealth and community standing made John Pugh one of the leading citizens of the Wyoming Valley.[48]

One of the most accessible routes into the lower middle class was to own a saloon, which was relatively easy to finance and operate, and its provisions were always in high demand in coal-mining communities. The saloon was not merely a place where miners came to "cut the coal dust" in their throats, but it was also one of the few public spaces in coal communities where local miners gathered in their time away from work. In the early days, it was customary in Britain for operators to pay their miners, and they, in turn, settled with their laborers at the saloon. Reformers and the Nonconformist preachers opposed this custom, so it did not survive the passage to America. Nevertheless, the saloon continued to be one of the few recreational centers in the dreary mining villages. "The saloon was the most popular of all institutions" in the mining towns, one contemporary observer reported, and it was patronized by "80% of the adult male population." In Shenandoah, Pennsylvania, there was one saloon for every twenty-six families.[49] There are no statistics that demonstrate the density of saloons in coal towns, although virtually every source that mentions the topic claims that it was high. Nor are there any statistics revealing how many were Welsh-owned, but again the anecdotal evidence indicates that many were.

This was not the case for Ohio's rapidly expanding coal industry. It too was founded by British miners and relied upon them into the twentieth century. Lewis Evans, the Welsh cartographer, recorded the presence of coal in the Hocking Valley in 1755, and, in 1818, another observer noted several mines already in operation along the Ohio River near Steubenville. By the 1830s skilled British miners were sinking deep mine shafts requiring more complex systems of timbering, drainage, ventilation, and haulage. During the 1850s alone, approximately 37,000 British miners immigrated to the United States, and a significant number of them came to Ohio. The 1880 census enumerated a total of 5,575 coal miners in Ohio, of whom 5,047 (90.5 percent) were British, 68 British American, 45 Irish, 41 Americans, 16 Swedish and Norwegian, and 356 listed as "other."[50]

The Welsh were counted among the British, but they played a role in the development of Ohio's coal industry far beyond their actual numbers. Stephen Selway, for example, was representative of many Welshmen with a family tradition in the Glamorgan coal trade who were attracted by opportunities in Ohio. Selway, his wife, and their ten children immigrated directly to Massillon, Ohio, in 1881, where he and his three eldest sons became highly successful mine owners and operators. Directly south of Massillon, in Guernsey County, William H. Davis lent a powerful stimulus to the coal industry of central Ohio. Born in 1851 in the South Wales coalfield, Davis entered the pits at age seven and immigrated to Ohio with his family in 1864. William mined coal in several Ohio fields before opening his own mine near Cambridge in 1888. In short order Davis opened others and became one of Ohio's most successful mine owners, carrying nearly three thousand workers on the payroll. In 1907 he reorganized his mines into the Cambridge Collieries Company. Until his death in 1909, Davis attended the Welsh Baptist Church and participated in Welsh choral music.[51]

In the rising Mahoning Valley industrial center of Youngstown, Ohio, built upon coal, steel, and railroads, the Welsh experience in Scranton and Wilkes-Barre, Pennsylvania, was duplicated on a smaller scale. Local historian Ewing Summers observed in 1903: "No class of foreign born citizens surpasses the Welsh in quick and appreciative adaptability to American institutions. They immediately enter upon the duties of citizenship with a keen, almost juvenile enthusiasm, insisting on their children having the best education that can be obtained, and rearing them to respect their adopted country and participate in its functions." Although slightly patronizing, the qualities Summers attributed to the Welsh are exactly those which other Americans, and the Welsh themselves, believed were essential for success in America. Some sense of occupational and social advancement within the Welsh mining community may be gleaned from several extensive biographical collections for eastern Ohio.[52] Like Bradsby's Luzerne County biographies, these sources do not focus on the rich and famous, but incorporate people from all walks of life.

The number of biographies of Welshmen employed in the Mahoning Valley's rapidly expanding steel industry is far more numerous than those employed in the rapidly declining coal industry of the 1890s. Consequently, the biographies of Welsh-born miners only suggest that the pattern of easy assimilation and social mobility was also at work here. Of the twenty-three miners born in Wales who began their working careers in the mines, only six remained in the coal industry, and they were at the top of the occupational hierarchy: three operators, one shaft sinker, one bookkeeper, and one foreman. Four men remained in mining but had second occupations as well: three were operators who also owned farms, and one was still a miner who also held public service positions for the City of Mineral Ridge. Thirteen of those who began as coal miners left the industry for other work: six became middle-class shopkeepers; three became policemen; and one became a skilled iron puddler. Several of them also had farms. Even though most of these men elevated their status only modestly, three made a dramatic departure from their former lives underground. One quit mining, entered the steel mills, and rose to the position of mill superintendent. Another, H. W. Smith, became a labor organizer, edited a labor newspaper, and then was appointed assistant to the director of the Ohio Bureau of Labor Statistics. Perhaps the most unique story is that of the underground miner who studied at night, saved his money, and graduated from the Baltimore College of Physicians and Surgeons. He returned to Youngstown to set up practice as a dental surgeon. Like their counterparts elsewhere, the twenty-three mining men born in Wales were all Republicans save one Democrat. Similarly, all of them were Baptists, Congregationalists, or Methodists.[53]

The thirty-two sons born in America to Welsh miners in this sample obviously enjoyed greater advantages than did their fathers. Thoroughly Americanized and better educated, they rose higher and faster than their fathers. Of the nine who started their careers as coal miners, seven left the industry: several opened their own businesses, one became a county commissioner, one attended college and founded an oil company, and one became the superintendent of the Brier Hill Steel Company. One of the two who stayed in the coal business managed the family's mine investments, and the other clerked in a mine office and served as postmaster of Girard. None of the thirty-two remained in the industry full-time. A half dozen became small shopkeepers, seven became superintendents or officers in the local steel mills and metal fabrication plants, several held the office of county sheriff, county commissioner, auditor, and treasurer, and several held the position of postmaster while engaged in other businesses. Six of the thirty-two American-born sons of Welsh miners went to college and became professionals: two dentists, one oral surgeon, one physician, and two lawyers.[54]

Ohio also had its second-generation Welsh mine owners who built upon and surpassed the socioeconomic status of their immigrant fathers. One of them, David C. Thomas, was born in Johnstown, Pennsylvania, in 1861. His parents and three of their children had emigrated from Merthyr Tydfil in 1847. From Johnstown the family moved to the Welsh community of Brookfield, Ohio, in the Mahoning Valley, and then to Shawnee, Ohio, in the Hocking Valley in the early 1890s. David attended night school, became a surveyor, and worked his way up to mine superintendent and then chief executive officer of the Continental Coal Company in Athens County. David and his wife lived in Shawnee, a prominent Welsh community. By the first decade of the twentieth century he was an owner of mines in southeastern Ohio; in 1913 he bought coal properties in Blair, West Virginia, at the foot of Blair Mountain, the site in 1921 of one of America's major uprisings between union miners and mine operators. David Thomas sold his mining interests around 1920 and spent the last years of his life in Columbus, Ohio, where he died in 1924.[55] It is impossible to determine how many Welshmen there were like David C. Thomas. References to their lives are scattered through the old county histories and newspaper obituaries, which presents an insurmountable obstacle to quantifying them with any accuracy. They were not nationally prominent or even so well known in their own states to justify biographies in *Who's Who*, but their careers signify how much was accomplished through energy and skill.

By the turn of the twentieth century, second-generation Welsh miners were also finding upward mobility through organized labor. The development of careerism in the United Mine Workers of America is the subject of chapter 9, but it is worth noting here that a number of union officials who never reached the level of national prominence learned their leadership skills in local and state union offices, and then employed them in politics and other vocations. John P. Jones represents a good example of a Welsh-born miner's son who developed career skills within the craft, which led to occupational success within and beyond the union.

Jones was born in 1862, near Youngstown, Ohio, in the Welsh mining community of Mineral Ridge. His parents emigrated from Wales around 1860, worked for a few years in Mineral Ridge, and then settled down in North Lawrence, near Massillon. Here, at the age of eleven, John went to work in the mines with his father.[56]

According to one county history, Jones attended grammar school but was "largely self-educated," devoting "much attention to reading and study, particularly as touching political issues." Early in life he became an "uncompromising advocate" of the Republican Party. North Lawrence was a very small mining village peopled by American and British miners. Although small, it provided Jones with some exemplary mentors for a career that took him out of the mines into labor leadership, politics, and industrial management. Among them was John Pollock, who was born in Ireland but reared in Scotland, and who immigrated and settled in North Lawrence in 1863. Pollock was a pioneer unionist. In Ohio he joined the short-lived American Miners' Association, was a general organizer for the Miners' and Laborers' Benevolent Association, and assisted John Siney in the Miners' National Association. Another of Jones's North Lawrence protégés was Michael D. Ratchford, an Irishman by birth who migrated to North Lawrence with his family in 1860 at age twelve. With the assistance of Jones, Ratchford became president of District 6, and then president of UMWA in 1897.[57]

Although a small village, North Lawrence prepared him well for leadership roles in the labor movement and politics. Already active in local labor organizations at 22, Jones was elected to a three-year term as justice of the peace. Little is known about his early years, but he was one of the leaders in the movement to organize the UMWA. John McBride of Massillon, but a few miles from North Lawrence, greatly facilitated Jones's labor career. McBride had been head of the Amalgamated Miners Association of Ohio, president of the National Progressive Union (NPU), was instrumental in engineering the formation of the UMWA in 1890, and subsequently became head of the American Federation of Labor when Samuel Gompers retired. Jones was president of the Ohio (District 10) NPU by the time of its convention in May 1889, and chaired the convention the following year in Columbus on January 20, 1890, when the UMWA was founded. Following the formation of the UMWA, the Ohio miners met in convention as District 6 of the UMWA; Jones was elected president and then reelected the following year. He declined to stand for reelection in 1892, but agreed to serve on the UMWA's national executive board.[58]

Jones was an ardent supporter of William McKinley in his race for governor. As a young lawyer from Canton, the Stark County seat, McKinley had volunteered to represent the miners during a strike in 1876 and defended several miners who ran afoul of the law. Subsequently, McKinley and the Cleveland industrial magnate Marcus Hanna built a strong Republican base among Ohio's coal miners. Because of his position in the union and his active role in the county's Republican organization, Jones was appointed state inspector of mines when McKinley was elected governor in 1892. In 1898, he resigned to enter the Ohio House of Delegates as a representative from Stark County. Jones held this office only briefly, however, for in May 1898 another newly elected Republican governor, Asa S. Bushnell, appointed him Ohio labor commissioner, a post he held for two years. Jones resigned two years later and he and his wife moved to Canton, where he became a supervisor at the United Alloy Steel Company, a position he held until cancer took his life in 1919.[59] Numerous were the Welsh miners who followed similar routes to success through organized labor, but reconstructing their lives is nearly impossible from the available historical record.

The Ohio database of Welsh coal miners provides data on real and personal wealth for 1860 and 1870, which is another way to measure upward mobility. The published census for 1880 only estimated these figures. Moreover, the following data for 1870 cannot be matched with the 1860 data because the published census did not calculate per capita valuations for the entire state. Nevertheless, the sample still offers a good comparative snapshot of the social and economic stratification of Welsh coal mining communities relative to the average property owner in Ohio. The per capita averages mask some great disparities in the distribution of wealth among Welsh coal miners; they were not a homogeneous group. On average, Welsh miners owned more real and personal property than ten years earlier, and nearly twice as much real property as the average Ohioan.

Based on a sample of 245 miners from sample communities, these valuations seem to show that the Welsh miners in these communities were recent immigrants in America who had arrived with little or very modest means. By 1870, however, they were beginning to stratify with a small number acquiring significant real and personal wealth, while the vast majority languished below the average or owned no wealth at all. Also, there were significant differences among the Welsh coal communities themselves. Some were decidedly poorer than others. In 1860, Syracuse and Minersville were both significantly poorer both in real and personal property. Both were company-owned settlements with little more than general stores, which accounts for low property values, but the residents there are also poor in personal property, and substantially so. It can be surmised that these are newly opened mines in 1860, worked by new arrivals. A few miles away in Pomeroy miners have the highest property and personal values of any of the communities sampled. However, Pomeroy was settled decades earlier, the Welsh had been there longer, and it was not a company town. There seems to be a pattern that miners who live in established urban areas have higher standards of living. Hence, Syracuse has per capita personal property valuation at $22.09 in 1860, while Pomeroy next door has $109.66. In 1870, the disparity was less marked but Pomeroy miners still claimed almost three times more personal wealth than their counterparts in Syracuse.[60]

Each one of these communities has one or two individuals whose real property wealth is vastly greater than the norm, which suggests that they were Welsh mine owners and supervisors who were identified in the census as "coal miner." In 1860, in Youngstown Township, one person with real property valued at $9,000 was far above the other four individuals who claimed $1,000 to $1,500. All the others were far below at zero or a few hundred dollars. Very few, however, claimed substantial personal wealth in 1860. By 1870 this pattern of Welsh owners and superintendents became more pronounced. Pomeroy has three "coal miners" who claimed the highest real property valuations in the total database at $10,000, $9,000, and $7,200. Six others claimed real property from $2,500 to $3,000, located in Youngstown, Minersville, Austintown, and Youngstown Township. Personal property also reflected this pattern, as men possessed $1,200 to $7,000 in all of the sampled communities with the exception of Syracuse. This suggests that the system of Welsh miners following Welsh owners and bosses was at work, but took a while to root itself in the developing Ohio coalfields.[61]

Fewer Welsh miners trekked to coal-mining states farther west than did

TABLE 2. Welsh Coal Miners' Per Capita Wealth, Selected Ohio
Communities, 1860, 1870

|  | 1860 | | 1870 | |
| --- | --- | --- | --- | --- |
| Community | Real Property | Personal Property | Real Property | Personal Property |
| Youngstown Township | $290.91 | $52.57 | $386.84 | $342.45 |
| Austintown | 300.00 | 92.77 | 323.36 | 93.93 |
| Pomeroy | 308.03 | 109.66 | 613.23 | 245.34 |
| Minersville | 195.00 | 46.00 | 403.92 | 273.96 |
| Syracuse | 69.76 | 22.09 | 456.36 | 88.40 |
| Average for database | 243.33 | 67.77 | 460.71 | 200.78 |
| Average for Ohio | — | — | 266.00 | 173.00 |

Source: Compiled from Manuscript Census Schedules, 1860 and 1870, Mahoning,
Trumbull, and Meigs Counties, Ohio (Ohio Database). Manually tabulated.

Scots or Englishmen, and scholars have not studied their social mobility at all. However, John Laslett's study of the northern Illinois coal town of Streator found a significant upward mobility among British miners. Using city directories, he found that, of the 208 miners who changed jobs between 1872 and 1888, 53 (25 percent) moved into skilled positions within the industry. However, at least 117 (56 percent) moved out of the working class altogether. Of these, eight became mine owners and fourteen mine managers. Most became middle-class merchants (37) and saloon owners (13), but others became engineers (11), railroad officials (7), school teachers (6), city officials (6), farmers (5), salesmen or clerks (7), attorneys (2), and clergymen (1). Several of the British migrants attended college.[62] There is little question that upward mobility characterized the British experience in the American coalfields, Welsh included, but quantifying that success is difficult with available evidence.

Coal miners have generally been portrayed as the "archetypal proletarians," members of a subculture of class militancy cemented into a fierce group loyalty by the psychological isolation and occupational dangers of mining.[63] Hence, the popular notion that "once a miner, always a miner" seems to make anomalies of those who left the industry. The evidence is mounting against this interpretation. In fact, many hated coal mining and left at the first opportunity. The high rates of Welsh mobility out of the industry when the opportunities presented themselves belie the commonplace notion of the traditional miner trapped within his own proletarian subculture.

The life of John E. Williams debunks this notion decisively. Born a miner's son in Merthyr Tydfil in 1853, his destiny would seem to have been cast for him. According to his own account, he won the musical competition at the Dowlais Christmas Day eisteddfod in 1860. Williams claimed that he never would be content to think of himself as a miner, for the eisteddfod "stamped in my mind the idea that there were better things in life" than digging coal. John E. Williams sailed with his family for America in 1864 to join relatives in Illinois. At thirteen Williams entered the pits, and for the next fifteen years he labored in the mines of Streator; however, he did so "with reluctance and remained there with a dread at times amounting to loathing, and escaped at the first favorable opportunity."[64]

At nineteen he and eleven other miners organized a self-improvement society. Williams was later described as "the leader of a class of English, Scotch, and Welsh miners who engaged in the study of many subjects, with such success that practically all of its members were called to positions of responsibility as mine managers and mine inspectors." They spent one entire winter working through John Stuart Mill's *Political Economy*, which indicates this was no ordinary book club. The Illinois miners were divided during this period between the "conservatives" who adhered to the republican ideal of labor and management as partners and a "radical" faction who viewed them as two classes with different interests. The former inherited the traditional republican approach of mediation and arbitration rather than resorting to strikes as a way of resolving conflicts with management, while the latter saw the strike as a weapon in class warfare. Williams and the members of his society—their detractors called them the "Twelve Apostles" —supported the cooperative approach.[65]

After the miners lost several disastrous strikes, Williams's influence among them began to increase. He became the secretary of his local, and the first checkweighman at his mine. For fifteen years he also wrote a special column for the local newspaper, the *Streator Daily Independent Times*. Williams directed publicity for a local congressman's campaign and was later rewarded when the politician appointed him manager of his opera house. He also served as city clerk, sold fire insurance, organized the city orchestra and played first violin, was active in the Unitarian church, and served as the Director of the Western Unitarian Conference.[66] Williams eventually rose to national prominence as an industrial mediator and arbitrator, a position for which he was predisposed as a labor republican.

Williams was a pioneer in the art of arbitration who championed the now commonplace idea that successful arbitration will "satisfy both parties and, at least, reconcile their points of difference."[67]

It was a mine disaster in Cherry, Illinois, on November 20, 1909, which brought Williams to national attention. The underground fire killed 259 coal miners and left 615 widows and orphans without visible means of support. At age fifty-six Williams stepped forward to lead the campaign to ameliorate their condition. There was no workmen's compensation law, and the only way the survivors could collect compensation was to prove company negligence in a court of law. But this entailed legal fees and court costs the survivors could not afford. John R. Walker, president of the Illinois district of the United Mine Workers of America, convinced the widows that Williams would faithfully represent their interests in negotiations with the mine owners, the Chicago, Milwaukee and St. Paul Railroad.[68]

The plan devised by Williams was to settle claims with three times the annual wage as indemnity for accidental death, a plan modeled after the British Workmen's Compensation Act of 1906. The disaster gave powerful impetus to the campaign for a method of compensating workers and their families for industrial accidents, and in 1911 Illinois passed legislation creating the Illinois Workmen's Compensation Commission.[69] Williams was credited with the success of this highly visible humanitarian campaign.

In the 1910–11 strike of Chicago garment workers at Hart, Schaffner & Marx, negotiations had reached an impasse, and the final agreement was left to a board of arbitration. After two years they settled on Williams as the independent arbitrator, with the eminent lawyer Clarence Darrow representing the union, and Carl Meyer representing the company. In this atmosphere of suspicion and hostility, Williams created a new model of industrial administration and transformed the role of the arbitrator to one of mediator. Central to his philosophy was the concept that labor and capital were partners in the well-managed industry and that once this was recognized, industrial peace was possible. "It is my opinion that autocratic control of industry by the employer will never permanently prevail in this country," Williams wrote, because "the universally taught idea of democracy in political and social life will not permit it." Workers understood the rights of citizenship in a democratic republic, therefore "the democratization of industry in this country is inevitable," Williams concluded. The first step toward this end was a strong, responsible trade union and on-going collective bargaining.[70]

This was, of course, the foundation of nineteenth-century labor republicanism and the miners' conception of their role as equal partners with capital in the production process. Welshmen were predisposed to this vision by the ideas of "progress" inherent in Welsh Nonconformism. Williams broke with the earlier notion of arbitration as a court of last appeal, and developed an approach that attempted to bring each side in the dispute to understand the position of the other, and then find common areas of agreement to achieve a compromise. He transformed the role of arbitrator from judge to mediator and pioneered the modern method of arbitration.[71]

After a settlement was reached in the Chicago garment industry, Williams stayed on to head a permanent Board of Arbitration that settled disputes between Hart, Schaffner & Marx and the Amalgamated Clothing Workers. In 1917, the Illinois miners' leader John R. Walker secured his appointment as Illinois fuel administrator, an important wartime position overseeing the allocation of coal to the state's military, industrial, and public consumers, but the "great peacemaker" died in 1919.[72] Like countless other Welsh miners who came to America seeking wider opportunities, and psychologically predisposed by religion and ideology to embrace them, Williams grasped his main chance to escape the mines; few miners would have blamed him for doing so.

## Women and the Family Wage

Early in the development of the coalfields, the states prohibited female employment underground. This was one of the reforms British miners transplanted in America. There are few statistics or other information on female colliery workers in Britain prior to 1841, when the Children's Commission launched an investigation into the employment of children in British industry. During these proceedings, the commissioners found deplorable conditions in the mines for children, but seemed to be even more horrified to "discover" that females also labored underground. Even though they had worked there for centuries, the Commission's 1842 Report on Mines shocked the public and generated a movement to restrict women from underground labor. Parliament responded by passing the Mines and Collieries bill doing just that in 1842.[73]

Little effort went into enforcement of the bill, however, and the law was summarily evaded. The Miners' Association of Great Britain and Ireland (founded 1842) was the only organization that officially demanded the law be enforced. Therefore, subsequent scholars have presumed that miners were responsible for driving women from the pits. With little knowledge of the work process in mining, they substituted feminist theory to explain the miners' motives. One scholar, Jane Humphries, explored this issue in depth and concluded that the discourse on the restriction of women in British mines has been "historically underinformed."[74]

In the nineteenth century women were not employed in all British coalfields, but rather were concentrated primarily in East Scotland, Yorkshire, Lancashire, and South and West Wales.[75] Female labor was found underground in these mining districts where the pillar and stall method of mining was utilized. Wherever women were employed underground, they were "drawers." Harnessed by belt and chain to sledges, they dragged coal from the low seams to the pit bottom to be hoisted topside. In Sirhowy district they were called "dragger girls." In Pembrokeshire they were generally found cranking the windless as well, but in North Wales females were employed only on the surface at the pit brow.[76] The highest proportion of female to male workers in Britain occurred in Pembrokeshire where, in 1842, there were 424 adult females per 1,000 males, but only 19 females for 239 males ages thirteen to eighteen, and 19 females for 196 males age thirteen and under. In Glamorgan female employment was much less common, with 19 adult females per 1,000 males, 12 girls between ages thirteen and eighteen compared with 239 boys, and of the children under thirteen only 12 were girls compared with 157 boys.[77]

Boys and girls began work at an early age, and the 1842 Children's Commission heard testimony of girls as young as five tending ventilation doors underground. A girl from Dowlais was carried to work half asleep by her father. At Hirwaun colliers received an extra allowance for taking in young girls. Pembrokeshire girls began on the surface separating coal, but at age twelve were put to work operating the windless below ground, dragging coal up steep inclines, work so hard men refused to do it. Angela John estimates that there were about 150,000 coal miners in Britain at midcentury, and between 5,000 and 6,000 were women working both underground and topside, or about 4 percent of the total. Most women who testified before the commission disliked the work, emphasizing that it was hard, tiring, and frightening, but there were no alternatives.[78]

Hewing was an adult male occupation, and boys progressed according to their age through several stages to become hewers at about seventeen or eighteen. Girls generally left the pits at the age boys became colliers to marry and bare children. Although single women might continue to work underground as adults, only under the rarest of circumstances did they ever become colliers. This clear division of labor developed within the context of a family labor system. Hewers, who won the coal from the face, the strategic point of production in the pillar and stall system, struck an agreement with the mine owners on a fixed rate and were left to hire their own helpers. It was much more economical to employ family members. They were more dependable, easier to discipline, family affection reduced the harshness of the system, and safety would be a greater priority among family members. Moreover, family labor kept the hewer's wage within the family unit. Critics charged that colliers had too much incentive to proletarianize their wives and children in order to maximize the family income.[79]

Colliers themselves contended that their wages were so low that family members had to work in order for the family to survive. Miners increasingly came to insist on a "family wage," that is, one equal to the total earned by all members without women and children working. Colliers did not fear competition from female labor. In fact, they had a vested interest in retaining females and children underground since it seemed unlikely that the "family wage" would ever be achieved. Nevertheless, colliers "almost universally" wanted the state to prohibit women from underground labor even when it contradicted their own economic interests. Apparently, men wanted to abolish a system that worked to their advantage and replace it with another that would require them to work longer and harder.[80]

Why would male colliers do this? Did female underground labor threaten traditional patriarchal privileges by keeping women at work rather than creating comforts at home? Testimony before the 1842 Commission does not bear this out. In fact, colliers' objections were not about their women folk working so much as the lack of other employment opportunities in coal mining districts. Nor did work in the pits liberate any of their family members because they worked directly for the colliers. As Jane Humphries insists, "It is necessary to guard against too instrumentalist an interpretation" of the colliers' apparently ambivalent position on female labor underground.[81] Colliers have been dehumanized, even bestialized, in popular discourse, but if we disregard his long-standing tradition and accept their capacity for human sensitivity, then dual feelings about family labor is easily understandable. Without the supplement to their wages that would make up for the loss of income should women and children be restricted from underground labor, which did not seem forthcoming, family survival would be threatened. On the other hand, as husbands and fathers they certainly were pained to watch members of their own family suffer from such a grueling work regimen. In this dilemma, they favored the ideal of prohibition, but worried about the practical implications. Seeing no immediate resolution they supported both the ideal and the practice, and lamented that there were no other employment options for women.

The movement to restrict women did not arise among the miners, however, but from bourgeois reformers who were shocked by the conditions under which females labored underground. True Victorians, they focused instead on the moral and sexual suggestiveness of innocent girls and half-clad women toiling in the dark with men, rather than on the health implications for women. The testimony of colliers, on the other hand, expressed concern for the health and safety of female "drawers," and also defended their moral integrity. Coal mine owners expressed still different attitudes in the testimony. Like most of the propertied class, they shared concerns about reproducing a pliable labor force, and evidence of undisciplined, independent colliers coming and going as they pleased was disconcerting. The more capital they sunk into the mines the more regularity, predictability, and control was needed to succeed. Prohibiting females and children from working underground would shift the burden for supporting the entire family onto the collier and, consequently, force him into more routinized habits of work. According to the owners, if hewers dug coal more regularly, their wives and children would not have to work at all.[82]

Restoring women to their traditional domestic roles was, therefore, the solution to restoring social harmony. Properly reared children would know their proper place in society as adults. Thus would women the "civilizers" leave the pits and save the nation from "an ignorant, depraved and dangerous population."[83] Restrictive legislation was passed with surprising ease. Miners agreed with the outcome, if not the assessment informing the decision, but they insisted on a "family wage" that would offset the loss. This neither the employers nor the government intended to provide. Neither seemed particularly troubled by the impact restriction would have on families or single women, many of whom were single widows. Everyone wanted to remove females from underground labor, but few of the comfortable flinched from the destitution they inflicted on those who were already poor. In Glamorgan a relatively small proportion of women were affected, but in Pembrokeshire where so many women worked in the mines real privation was rampant. In some mines evasion was common, and as late as the 1860s girls and single women still toiled underground in South Wales.[84]

The most concerted effort to enforce the restriction came from the Miners' Association of Great Britain and Ireland, which agitated the issue through demonstrations, petition drives, and the public exposure of owners who flaunted the law. The union's advocacy did not mean they had adopted middle-class notions about femininity or restoring patriarchy, but rather they embraced a broader working-class movement in nineteenth-century Britain to establish the "male breadwinner" and the "family wage" as social norms and the standard of working-class respectability. Once miners had adjusted to the loss of income and the new division of labor, they became enthusiastic supporters of the new tradition.[85]

By the mid-nineteenth century a maturing industrial capitalism had reconfigured the very idea of compensation from the earlier system when the entire family contributed to the family subsistence to one in which wages were paid to individuals based on their level of contribution to the production process. Not everyone played a central role in the emerging capitalist system; therefore, the presumption took form that the male head of the household, the male "breadwinner," should receive a wage sufficient to support the entire family without the wage labor of his wife and children. This conception of the family wage focused on the point of production, rather than on women's unwaged domestic labor, and rendered women economically dependent on the male breadwinner. Children might be put to work learning the trade, but the wife's place was in the home and "her husband was something of a disgrace if she had to go out to work." Capitalists, of course, paid workers of any age or gender as little as necessary. Therefore, the male breadwinner ideal first became dominant among the British working class during the mid-nineteenth century because of Britain's pioneering position in the Industrial Revolution, and then was embraced by workers throughout the capitalist world, particularly in Europe and the United States.[86]

It was the direct threat that working women posed to skilled male jobs and wages that prompted the labor movement to embrace the male-breadwinner and family-wage ethos to privilege the rights of men over those of women. An extensive body of research on the Industrial Revolution anchors the rise of the family-wage ideal within the skilled trades, the elite segment of the emerging British proletariat. Family hiring arrangements were common in agriculture, mining, textiles, and the cottage industries, where the old custom of family employment still prevailed in the nineteenth century. In the skilled trades, however, the tradition had been established by the end of the eighteenth century of excluding women from entry into those trades.[87]

This artisanal tradition was maintained and further consolidated by their unions in the nineteenth century, the only segment of the working class that could sustain itself without the wages of the wives and children. By segmenting the labor market, that is, by keeping men's and women's jobs separate and restricting the entry of women into a trade, less skilled male workers could also achieve the family wage level. To offset this devaluation of women's economic contribution to the family subsistence, men offered the cult of domesticity and the glorification of motherhood, the sacred duties of the wife and mother in caring for her family, and other related elements of the ideology, such as the woman's proper sphere and maintaining the home as a haven in a heartless world. The male-breadwinner version of the family wage became a powerful ideological weapon for the trade unions in their struggle with capital for more security and higher pay because it enshrined values that were morally unassailable. Only if the employment of women and children was legally curtailed or banned, however, would men's wages ever rise to the level of a living wage. The problem with this ideological brew was that most working women were either single or widowed or they toiled for low wages because their husbands' wages were insufficient to sustain the family.[88]

In America, the male-breadwinner and family-wage ethos emerged in the first half of the nineteenth century almost simultaneously with its ascent in Britain. In fact, British immigrant workers, disproportionately from the skilled trades, were instrumental in transplanting these ideas in receptive American soil. Fearing the erosion of customary craft traditions, a decline in the status of workers, and decreasing wages, workingmen in America agreed that, if the male breadwinner could not earn a living wage, poverty and disintegration of the family would be the inevitable outcome. Many of those American workers were, in fact, British immigrants who transplanted their traditions of work and conceptions about gender divisions of labor to the United States. Mary H. Blewett's studies of families from England who migrated en masse to the New England shoe and textile mills during the nineteenth century demonstrates how "immigrant cultures transferred vital traditions of radical politics to industrializing America." Her examination of labor-management conflicts in the 1870s also reveals how British working-class definitions of masculinity and femininity were transplanted in America, and then modified by local circumstances.[89]

In 1903, the pioneering sociologist Peter Roberts found that in the cities of Scranton and Wilkes-Barre females made up 22.7 percent and 23.6 percent, respectively, of the wage earners. He did not designate how many of these were of coal-mining families, but clearly the employment opportunities for women were greater in the cities than in the rural coal communities where female wage earners did not exceed 5.5 percent of the wage earners. Roberts concluded that "the mining industry is peculiar in this regard, that it casts the entire burden of supporting the family upon the male members." Consequently, boys were sent to work early, but girls remained dependent with no way to relieve family financial pressures, so they tended to marry early, for "few are the avenues open to girls in which they can make a living."[90]

Where possible, Welsh American girls certainly took advantage of employment opportunities. John Bodnar's study of Welsh and Irish patterns of employment in Scranton found that three times the proportion of Welsh girls were working before age ten as Irish girls, 15 and 5 percent, respectively. Between ages eleven and fifteen, 86 percent of the Irish girls were still at home or in school, but 70 percent of the Welsh girls were at home or in school. Even after age sixteen, 38 percent of the Irish girls remained at home or in school, and the respective figure for the Welsh was 20 percent. Bodnar noted that few married women worked outside the home, only 4 percent of the Welsh and 2 percent of the Irish. Wives had more than ample work to do at home, however, and even though it was unwaged their domestic labor certainly contributed to the household finances. In addition to keeping the house cleaned and clothing washed, no mean feat in a coal town, they also gave birth and raised the additional wage earners, cooked, kept the family budget, and often looked after single male boarders.[91]

By the turn of the twentieth century the family wage ideal would be described by American Federation of Labor president Samuel Gompers as "a minimum wage—a living wage—which when expended in an economic manner, shall be sufficient to maintain an average-sized family in a manner consistent with whatever the contemporary civilization recognized as indispensable to physical and mental health."[92] It is clear that Gompers referred to male breadwinners for he declared that a "constantly growing minimum wage" that would be "sufficient to maintain [workers] and those dependent upon them in a manner consistent with their responsibilities as *husbands, fathers, men* and *citizens*."[93] The AFL readily accepted the proposition that men were the family breadwinners and therefore had a stronger claim to economic rights than women. Although the AFL declared its intention to organize working women, there is no evidence that it followed through on this promise. In fact, by 1910 only 1.5 percent of all women workers in the United States belonged to unions. Moreover, most trade unions barred women, and the AFL failed to take action against those union affiliates that excluded women from membership.[94]

Once men adopted the family-wage ideology, and then defined males as the family breadwinners, their identity as males and breadwinners fused into a new masculinity of industrialism. There being only one form of waged labor in most coal communities, this role took on a pronounced importance in the miners' identity. The family was, of course, the primary supportive institution in making the transition to life in America. One contemporary observer claimed that "almost every Welsh family is a tiny little republic in itself, sturdily self-supporting and ambitious—just the sort of a group from which a great man or woman is likely to come."[95]

Marriage to the right person might be the key to survival for ordinary miners, whether their spouses produced great offspring or not. There are no known descriptions of domestic relations among Welsh mining families in Ohio, but Phoebe Gibbons's oft-cited observation on courtship and marriage among the Welsh in Scranton during the 1870s was undoubtedly applicable to the other coalfields as well:

> Courtships are brief and the marriages early and happy. . . . Young women among the Welsh miners marry from eighteen to twenty-two. At the latter age they are joked about as being old maids.
>
> Miners' wives generally hold the purse. As soon as he gets his pay and his fill of beer, the miner hands his wages to his wife, who acts as treasurer with much discretion, making all the purchases of the house and transacting the business of the family. A miner's wife says to me: "My husband is a good workman. He never lost any time by drinking or anything like that. I nearly supported the family by my own sewing and by taking boarders. Ever since I have been married I tried to keep our own table, and could generally do it unless I was sick. I 'most always had a good deal of my own way, but I always consulted him. He always gave me his wages. I think when a man gives his wife his wages she feels more interest. I'd kick up a big fuss if he did not give me his wages. Whenever he was going away, I'd remind him, ' "Charley, haven't you got any money in your pocket?" ' He knew where the money was, you know. We always had one purse. My purse was his, and his was mine. We have always lived in good unity together."
>
> This is not always the way with miners. We have a neighbor who must always go to the office on pay-day to get her husband's money. He'll go and take the pay, and hand it over to her. She says he always

gives it to her. If she did not go and get it, he'd go to the saloon and spend it. "It looks to me as if a man was so weak-minded, to do the like of that!"

The Welsh boys, too, hand their wages over to their mother. . . .

The Welsh woman is ambitious for her husband's shoes to shine, and on every Saturday evening she blacks the shoes of the family (all set in a row), until the girls are old enough to relieve her. Another corrects this statement, saying that by the old Welsh rule Monday is the day for cleaning and putting away the Sunday's shoes.

Mrs.—says that she sets a tub of warm water for her son when he comes home from picking slate at the mine, and gives him soap and woolen cloth, that he may wash all over. To bathe in this manner is almost a universal rule with the men on leaving the mine. . . . Says an acquaintance: "Many think, 'I would not have miners to slop in my beds, they look so black and dirty.' But there is scarcely one in five hundred that does not wash all over when he comes home from his work; the general rule is, before he eats his supper, . . . puts on his clean clothes, and looks more like a clerk in a store than a miner."[96]

Phoebe Gibbons wrote that miners belonged to benevolent societies for the insurance, and depended on credit when times were hard. A local lawyer told her that " 'no Welsh miner ever goes to the poor house. He has a son or daughter, a brother or sister, a nephew or niece, who will not intrust [sic] him to the cold charities of the public. If his wife is industrious, she and the children can take care of him.' Mr. L—says: 'Very seldom does a miner get to the poor house unless he is a drunkard; for if he be sober, his fellow workmen in the mine, in case of accident or long sickness make a collection for him.' "[97]

The drudgeries confronting miners' wives prior to the Great Depression, before the technological modernization of the coal industry, has been described many times and is well known. Most of these are general descriptions, but they suggest a range of household conditions based on how Americanized the family was, and the place of the breadwinner in the mining hierarchy. Thus, while recently arrived Slavs in the anthracite fields lived in small, overcrowded old houses, the skilled miners lived in six- or seven-room houses, comfortable and well furnished like any American home. In the initial stages of development of new bituminous fields to the west, conditions were generally primitive at first, but where a complex social organization developed, so too did the stratification of classes, with the

British and Americans generally occupying the higher rungs of the socio-economic ladder.[98] The shared values of the Welsh and Americans were fostered by Nonconformity, the Protestant ethic, and the ideals of labor republicanism. Their common historical origin and ideals prompted the Welsh to identify themselves as equals of the old natives who rightfully occupied a higher socioeconomic space generally denied to new immigrants.

# WELSH AMERICAN CULTURAL INSTITUTIONS

The Welsh in America adopted an identity constructed in nineteenth-century Wales that incorporated the ideals of a rising nationalism. This national identity embraced, in the words of Welsh historian Dai Smith, "the official or public side of Welshness." Traits regarded as acceptable were a "judicious mixture of national antiquity and conventional morality," and Welsh "nationalists" on both sides of the Atlantic simply dismissed "undesirable" characteristics as "un-Welsh."[1] Exactly what constituted "Welsh-American" was constructed by a lively internal discourse carried on in published essays, speeches, sermons, newspaper editorials, and other written sources. For Welsh Americans, the meaning of "Welshness" was infused by those staunch middle-class Victorian values of sobriety and respectability, as well as pragmatism, rationality, musicality, and poetic sentiment. These traits were manifested in the construction and centrality of Welsh chapels, an expanding literacy, the love of poetry and literature, newspapers, singing festivals (eisteddfodau), self-improvement, industrial skill, business acumen, and upward economic and social mobility. Welsh Americans ignored those "un-Welsh" features found in their communities, such the steady decline in the Welsh language, church attendance, and drunkenness among the working classes.[2]

It is difficult to determine whether ordinary people paid much attention to this social construction of Welsh culture. Plenty of anecdotal evidence suggests otherwise; whether in Wales or America, most people led lives tightly structured by the processes and patterns of work rather than Welshness. According to Smith, "Welsh-America survived as 'Welsh' by ignoring such intrusive reality or by compartmentalizing the occasions of their lives." It seems evident that it was middle-class Welsh Americans who worried about preserving "Welshness." One South Walian who visited his American relatives in 1912 declared them "ten times more Welsh than they were at home. They are Welsh to the core."[3] In rooting themselves in an identity of "respectability" Welsh Americans must have felt vindicated when it appeared that American opinion had embraced this perspective of them. Their upright stature proved that they were worthy of acceptance, unlike Asians, Africans, and those southern and eastern Europeans pouring through the ports of entry at the turn of the century. The "whiteness" of the Welsh was never challenged. Hence, an article on the Welsh in America published in *Munsey's Magazine* in 1906 signified the triumph of the identity leaders sought to construct. "In the matter of morality, no nationality stands higher," the author proclaimed; " 'the truth against the world' is their motto. Their beliefs and feelings have always been more precious to them than wealth." This perception of the Welsh elevated them to a much higher social and moral plane in the American hierarchy of acceptability than other immigrants.[4]

### Literacy and the Welsh Language

The popular image of the Welsh as a literary people elevates the importance of determining the extent to which this idea reflected either the aspirations of the Welsh American middle class or a reality, and for the purpose at hand the degree to which coal miners represented the general experience. Although literary proclivity cannot be measured, the literacy level of miners is an indication that the preconditions existed to support literary interests. Information on literacy from the manuscript census was entered into the Ohio database (see chapter 3, especially note 11). Welsh immigrants who arrived in the United States in the first half of the nineteenth century probably were not as literate as those who came during the last half. Educational opportunities in Wales were limited, but improved dramatically during the second half of the nineteenth century. As historian Rowland Berthoff has observed, "Welsh secular schools might be rudimentary, but the vigorous Nonconformist Sunday Schools taught both child and great grandmother to read the Scripture." After 1887 compulsory universal elementary education in Britain all but eliminated illiteracy in the new generation, and, since Welsh immigrants were generally younger members of the skilled, urban working class, they more likely had a better education than the average Welshmen.[5]

The census collected information on the ability to read and write among the population ten years old and over. Individuals who could not read and write, either in English or some other language, were regarded as illiterate. The published census schedules on literacy break down to the state level, but not to specific groups of people or locations. Therefore, the information on the ability to read and/or write among Welsh miner heads of household born in Wales was also incorporated into the database. Of the 580 miners in four Ohio coal towns with a significant Welsh population in 1870, Austintown, Liberty Township, Weathersfield Township, and Pomeroy, a little more than two-thirds could read, and a little more than half could write (in any language). By 1880 there had been a substantial increase in the ability to read and write in those and two additional Welsh communities. Of the 789 miners sampled in 1880, more than 80 percent could read and three-quarters of them could write in one language.[6]

Although lower, this level of literacy compares favorably with the literacy rates for either Ohio or the nation. Ohio averages were not calculated separately prior to 1870, but of the Ohioans enumerated in 1870, 96.4 percent were able to read and 94.5 percent could write. National data is available for 1880 when 90.6 percent of the native whites and 88 percent of the foreign-born in the United States were literate. Unfortunately, none of this data was calculated by ethnic or occupational group.[7]

Although Welsh miners had a somewhat lower rate of literacy during these years than the norm, a simple comparison hides the more interesting internal dynamic of literacy acquisition among Welsh immigrant coal miners. Most Welsh miners during this period probably were able to speak both Welsh and English, and once in America, with exposure to newspapers and self-improvement efforts, their literacy rates rose dramatically between 1870 and 1880. This progress was not even by any means. For example, in 1870 the ability to read and write among Welsh miners in Pomeroy was well over 90 percent, but in Weathersfield Township near Youngstown fewer than two-thirds could read and a bare majority were able to write. This disparity in literacy between these two Welsh mining communities is directly attributable to the longevity of the miners in America. Even though nearly all Welsh miners came from the South Wales coalfield, their migration was dictated by the expansions and contractions of the coal industry in the United States and in Wales. As new coalfields opened in the United States there was a corresponding demand for skilled miners. Thus, Pomeroy attracted Welsh immigrants during its heyday in the 1850s and 1860s, whereas Weathersfield Township coal was just being commercially developed in the 1870s.[8]

If the opportunity to become more literate was embraced by miners, the change for women was even more dramatic. Recently arrived miners' wives had an astonishingly low rate of literacy in 1870 with nearly 60 percent unable to read and almost 70 percent unable to write. By 1880, however, well over 90 percent could do both. The longevity factor is significant for men and women. In Lawrence Township, Stark County, the mines were opened after the Civil War, and Welsh miners were clustered in the hamlets of North Lawrence and Youngstown Hill. In 1880, 73.5 percent of them

TABLE 3. Literacy among the Welsh-Born in Selected Ohio Coal
Communities

| Community | Welsh-Born Coal Miners | | | | | |
| | 1870 | | | 1880 | | |
| | Number | % Read | % Write | Number | % Read | % Write |
|---|---|---|---|---|---|---|
| Austintown | 104 | 68.3 | 52.9 | 127 | 85 | 69.3 |
| Liberty Township | 109 | 65.1 | 45.9 | 198 | 70.7 | 62.6 |
| Weathersfield Township | 229 | 62 | 50.2 | 96 | 95.8 | 94.8 |
| Pomeroy | 115 | 96.5 | 94.8 | 63 | 98.4 | 92.1 |
| Lawrence Township | — | — | — | 34 | 73.5 | 61.8 |
| Shawnee | — | — | — | 187 | 73.3 | 70.1 |
| | Welsh-Born Miners' Wives | | | | | |
| Austintown | 69 | 46.4 | 24.6 | 96 | 72.9 | 42.7 |
| Liberty Township | 46 | 52.2 | 30.4 | 101 | 60.4 | 52.5 |
| Weathersfield Township | 139 | 40.3 | 30.2 | 57 | 94.7 | 91.2 |
| Pomeroy | 68 | 89.7 | 88.2 | 46 | 97.8 | 89.1 |
| Lawrence Township | — | — | — | 21 | 61.9 | 47.6 |
| Shawnee | — | — | — | 89 | 50.6 | 37.1 |

Source: Compiled from Manuscript Census Schedules, 1870 and 1880, Trumbull, Meigs,
Stark, and Perry Counties, Ohio (Ohio Database). Manually tabulated.

could read English, and only 61.8 percent were able to write. Among the
Welsh-born women, however, 72.5 percent could read and 68.1 percent
were able to write English. Similarly, in the town of Shawnee, Perry County,
which came into existence in the 1870s, the literacy rate in 1880 was significantly higher, with 86.4 percent able to read English and 79 percent able to
write. For Welsh women in Shawnee, however, the rate was abysmal, at 50.6
percent and 37.1 percent, respectively.[9] Why these figures were so much
lower than elsewhere is hidden in the unique personal histories of these
women.

The most distinctively Welsh settlements and institutions in nineteenth-
century America were those in which the Welsh language was the medium
of communication. The number of Welsh speakers in the United States is
impossible to determine because official statistics did not record this figure.
In the 1860s and 1870s, when the first generation had reached significant
proportions, most Welsh people in America spoke their native language,
but most also understood English. How central their native language was to

the preservation of their national or ethnic identity, and how earnestly they tried to cling to this linguistic tradition, is difficult to assess. Welsh Americans were assimilating quickly and there was an inexorable shift to the dominant language of English, although this process was uneven and contingent on local circumstances.

The Welsh language survived longest in the large rural settlements of Ohio and Wisconsin, but also in larger coalfield settlements where traditional Welsh language institutions could be maintained. The largest Welsh mining population was found in the northern anthracite field underlying Carbon, Luzerne, and (after 1878) Lackawanna Counties, Pennsylvania, where 37,000 natives of Wales resided in 1890; 7,500 with at least one parent born in Wales lived in Scranton, and another 4,000 or so lived in Wilkes-Barre. Overwhelmingly, Welsh was the language of conversation among the first generation in these communities.[10]

In smaller Welsh coal towns, such as those in northeastern Ohio near Youngstown and in southern Ohio along the Ohio River from Syracuse to Pomeroy, and in adjacent large Welsh agricultural and rural-industrial communities in Gallia, Jackson, and Perry Counties, the native tongue was also ubiquitous among the first generation. Although the evidence is anecdotal and impressionistic, the numerous Welsh language churches support this conclusion. Welsh mining communities further west were generally much smaller, and the evidence even less reliable, but the language also seemed to survive there at least among the first generation. Again, the number of Welsh churches supports this contention. For example, during the 1870s, Braceville, Illinois, had forty Welsh families, totaling about 200 people, and Oskaloosa Junction, Iowa, had 215 Welsh residents. Bevier, Missouri, had 525 Welsh; nearly all of the heads of household were miners from South Wales who depended on the six coal mines located nearby. All these small communities supported one or more Welsh churches.[11]

### The Press

Welsh American newspapers played a crucial role in the construction of this new identity. One in particular, Y Drych (The Mirror), actively sought to construct an ideology of Welshness for Welsh Americans grounded in the language. Y Drych was one of twenty-one newspapers serving Welsh America between 1832 and the 1920s, among an additional sixty-five journals. Y Drych closely resembled the other Welsh-language newspapers in America, and to a degree the other 1,163 immigrant papers published in America in 1900, but its success was distinctive. The paper's circulation of 12,000 at its peak during the turn of the twentieth century represented approximately 10 percent of the recorded Welsh-born population. What distinguished *Y Drych* was its longevity. The life span of most Welsh American newspapers and periodicals was a few years or less, but *Y Drych* survived for 150 years, from 1851 to 2001, one of the longest-running ethnic newspapers in American history. Most of the Welsh papers accommodated a mixed readership and offered a blend of English and Welsh print, but *Y Drych*'s most distinctive feature was that, for its first seventy or eighty years, it published only in Welsh. Along the way it bought out its competitors: *Baner America* (Banner of America) of Scranton in 1877; *Y Wasg* (The Press), published in Pittsburgh in 1890; and in 1894 *Y Columbia* (The Columbia), a bilingual paper published in Chicago.[12]

The chief competitor of *Y Drych* from 1907 to 1939 was the *Druid*, a popular and widely distributed all-English newspaper that first appeared in Scranton. In 1912 a company of Welshmen, led by James J. Davis, a Welsh iron-puddler who subsequently became the U.S. secretary of labor and a senator from Pennsylvania, brought the paper to Pittsburgh. There were also several religious magazines published in Welsh that became influential organs within their respective denominations. The oldest was *Cyfaill o'r Hen Wlad yn America* (Friend of the Old Country in America), first published in 1838 by one of the most famous Welsh American clergymen, the Calvinistic Methodist minister William Rowlands; it continued publication until 1933. *Y Cenhadwr Americanaidd* (The American Missionary), published between 1840 and 1901, served as the unofficial organ of the Welsh Congregationalists. Less influential and of shorter duration were several Welsh Baptist publications of the nineteenth century.[13]

The most important and successful of the Welsh American magazines was the *Cambrian*. A monthly and later bi-monthly published between 1880 and 1919, the all-English periodical was widely circulated in the Welsh communities throughout the United States. Rev. E. C. Evans, editor of the *Cambrian*, confronted the language issue head-on in a 1893 article outlining the difficulties of confining Welsh nationality to the "narrow limits of the Welsh language." Birth, descent, and speech all bound people together, including the Welsh, but "must a person be able to speak the Welsh language" to be considered Welsh? The *Cambrian* decided that it was not necessary. "The Cornish, Scotch, and Irish people have adopted English, and the children of English, Irish, French, Italian and Jewish parents residing in Wales speak Welsh fluently and identify themselves with national movements without becoming Welsh people." On the other hand, there are many in Wales and America who are "thoroughly Welsh by birth and lineage" but do not understand the Welsh language.[14] A correspondent to the *Druid* observed that Welsh was the language spoken in Aberdare in the 1850s when he went there to work, and "it was almost impossible to get on without being able to speak Welsh. I soon found as an Anglicised Vale of Glamorgan boy that one of the first things I had to do was to tackle and to endeavor to speak the language of which I knew very little before."[15]

National identity, Evans recognized, was a complex matter. Between the extremes of the Welsh language as the only marker of Welsh identity and the complete loss of Welsh lineage and identity were gradations of identity that should be acknowledged. Evans designated several classes: those born in Britain or Wales; American-born Welsh who speak Welsh; American-born Welsh and their descendants who identify themselves as Welsh but do not speak the language; and Welsh descendants in America who have lost their lineage and identity. The census data, therefore, was totally inadequate for establishing the number of Welsh in the United States, and of no value at all in determining how many either spoke the language or shifted to English during this period. Breaking down Welsh Americans into these categories of identity, however, Evans calculated that, of the 400,079 estimated total Welsh and Welsh descendants in the United States, only about one-quarter of them spoke Welsh in 1890, and their numbers were falling.[16]

*Y Drych*, the *Druid*, and the *Cambrian* all had strong readerships throughout the Welsh settlements in America, including the coalfields. It is not possible to determine the readership by communities, much less occupational categories, but the numerous letters from readers located in coal towns strongly suggest that the periodicals were definitely popular among Welsh miners. Similarly, each carried a page listing their agents by community, and a large number of them resided in the coal and iron regions.[17] Correspondents from coal towns in every major coalfield sent news, sometimes on a regular basis over years, concerning their respective Welsh communities to these periodicals, making it possible for the widely scattered mining families to gain information about relatives and friends living elsewhere. The publications named names within the various communities, detailed specific families' migrations from the old country and throughout the new, and explained how one branch was related to another, all in the interests of preserving an insular, if dispersed, Welsh American community. The following story published by the *Druid* in 1911, from a correspondent living in Youngstown, suggests how this might be important for keeping things personal:

I [recently] talked to Mrs. William Davies [and] after a short time I asked her where she hailed from. "South Wales," she said. "What part," I inquired, "Swansea, or Abertawe, as we Welsh call it." "Oh, whereabouts in Abertawe?" I inquired. "Landore or a little place called Plasmarl, near Landore." "Oh, indeed, which of the houses did you live in?" I asked. "Between Rees and Edwards' grocery stores." By this time she found that I was familiar with the locality. We lived within a few yards of each other, and left there within twelve months of each other for the States. . . . The writer ["F. T."] has a father, brother and sisters, and a host of acquaintances scattered all over the United States who will read this little story with a great deal of interest, and will be glad to learn that Mr. and Mrs. William Davies of Plasmarl is still on earth and well and hearty. They desire to be remembered to their old acquaintances.[18]

Thus the Welsh American press served a useful purpose to the incredibly mobile coal miners. The tramping miner could easily lose contact with former family and friends. An announcement of the death of John Savage, "formerly a well known tenor singer of Dowlais," is a case in point. Born in Dowlais, Savage worked in the pits of Cwm Bargoed and Fochriw. In 1870 he came to America and went into the mines at Church Hill, near Youngstown, but in a few years moved to mine towns in Illinois, then Missouri, and on to Kentucky. He came back to the mine at Church Hill in 1881, but, soon after getting married, moved again to Illinois, and then to Iowa. At different times he worked in Cleveland, Ottumwa, and Albia, Iowa, before settling finally in Mystic, Iowa, where he died in 1913 at age sixty-two of an unidentified illness.[19]

Relatives frequently disappeared, intentionally or not. Sara Ann and Connie Jones of Auburn, Washington, posted a request for information in the *Druid* concerning the whereabouts of their father, a native of Glanamman, Carmarthenshire; they included his age and a physical description. Another woman searching for a missing relative asked: "Is he alive or dead?" It would be difficult to know since David Morgan, the relative in question, left Carmarthenshire some twenty-eight years earlier.[20] Among their other important services, *Y Drych* and the *Druid* were "a virtual directory of employment opportunities," carrying job advertisements for a variety of positions including coal miners and managers. In 1868, *Y Drych* carried one of many such notices, announcing Welsh miners were needed in Rock Cabin, Pennsylvania. Again in 1881, Welshmen who had opened a mine in Cadiz, Ohio, stated that they were looking for Welsh miners to come work for them.[21] Similarly, these ethnic publications were boosters of Welsh-owned businesses and volunteered to act as sales offices for some. "The Druid is anxious to help a young Welshman, who some time ago opened an anthracite mine and is desirous of finding a market for his coal."[22]

The three major Welsh American publications were alike in their efforts to shape the cultural definition of Welsh America, and they generally agreed about what they identified as specific traits possessed by real Welshmen. In America Welshness was manifested in support for cultural events, such as eisteddfodau and *gymanfa ganus*, because those activities were manifestations of the underlying poetic and musical character of the Welsh. They supported the Republican Party, which opposed slavery, because they were instinctively democratic and hostile to government oppression. The Welsh were also doggedly patriotic to both Wales and America because loyalty was one of their ingrained character traits. Protestant Nonconformist religion and the centrality of the Bible in Welsh life was said to be a cornerstone of true Welshness because morality was culturally encoded by religious expression and historical experience. A moral life for Welsh men was said to be anchored in the integrity of the family as an institution and as a set of values that were overseen by the "civilizing" influence of women.[23]

Even though the major publications generally agreed on what constituted Welshness, the *Druid* and the *Cambrian* parted company with *Y Drych* on the necessity of the Welsh language in maintaining the Welsh American community. From its beginnings the Welsh American press sought to communicate in both languages, while the *Druid* and the *Cambrian* published only in English. Their position was based on the social reality that the Welsh were in America where English was the lingua franca, and, in order to facilitate their assimilation, the Welsh should accept the inevitable and learn to speak English.[24] On this point *Y Drych* vigorously objected. The paper always promoted the idea that the Welsh should become Americanized in order to take full advantage of the opportunities that came with citizenship. In fact, life was much better in America than in Wales because the opportunities were greater, and the social structure was much more open and egalitarian. However, becoming American did not require the abandonment of their language and customs.[25]

The language embodied the very essence of being Welsh, according to *Y Drych*, which editorialized that "in accordance with an unwritten but inflexible law, a man cannot be a Welshman without knowledge of Welsh. His veins can be full of the reddest purest blood in the world; but if his tongue cannot speak the old language he is nothing but an excommunicate in our midst. . . . The Welsh will surely lose themselves in and melt into the American nation when the language is lost. The only hope of maintaining alive the Welsh character and separateness is through adherence to the language. Be it wise or foolish, Welsh life in America is concealed in the language."[26] Sociologists call attempts to define ethnicity in essential traits, which understands culture as static, fixed, and immutable rather than dynamic, interactive, and changing, "ethnic absolutism." The predominant voices speaking from the Welsh ethnic papers reflected this understanding of culture, but *Y Drych* took that step beyond to enshrine the Welsh language as the dominant marker of Welshness in Wales and the United States.[27]

The particular kind of American that these ethnic papers wanted the Welsh to become was not available to all immigrants. All three drew a line on the "new" immigration from eastern and southern Europe but especially *Y Drych*. In an 1888 article, entitled *"Peryglon Ymfudiaeth"* (The Perils of Immigration), the paper stressed that America must be kept for Americans, which could be achieved by excluding people of Asian, African, or southern and eastern European origin. Ironically, the July 4, 1893, issue carried an article declaring that the Welsh were entitled to be part of the great American nation, but warned that "it would be futile and foolish to argue that all the tribes and nations of our Republic should melt into each other. Would it be appropriate for Gomer's race to mix with the black Negro and the red Indian, or the bloody Dago?"[28]

The perennial immigrant conundrum also faced the press that served them: pluralism allowed ethnic groups to retain their ethnic identity and gave the press a reason to exist; assimilation offered the greatest opportunities for the social and economic advancement that the group presumably came to America to find, but it undermined the purpose served by the press. Published in English, the *Cambrian* and the *Druid* avoided the pitfalls by unambiguously embracing the major distinction that marked a group as "unassimilated." *Y Drych*, on the other hand, advocated that the key reason for assimilation and loyalty to the United States was that this country offered them the opportunity to remain Welsh in language, religion, and culture. As historian William Jones argues, those readers, writers, and editors of the Welsh press were searching for ways to become Americans without surrendering their own culture.[29]

Aled Jones and William Jones argue that *Y Drych* was in many respects not so much a "Welsh American newspaper as a Welsh newspaper in America." For sixty or seventy years, beginning in the 1860s, Welsh newspaper editors openly copied stories from abroad and inserted them in their own papers. *Y Drych* and Welsh language newspapers in Wales exchanged copy freely, and they used each other's newspapers like a news exchange to form part of "one transatlantic Welsh newspaper economy." But over time *Y Drych* became progressively American in tone and content, even as it continued to publish in Welsh. Jones and Jones have shown that 34 percent of *Y Drych*'s news coverage in 1856 originated in Wales, but by 1950 this had fallen to only 2 percent, and the ratio of news coverage of Welsh activities in the United States increased from 15 percent in 1851 to 98 percent in 1950.[30]

The Welsh press in America, therefore, had undertaken a project to construct a distinctive moral and cultural Welsh American identity signified by key markers. The three major publications agreed on the form and content of these cultural characteristics, although *Y Drych* believed that the Welsh language was the key marker, whereas the *Druid* and the *Cambrian* regarded the language as only one element. Nevertheless, they demonstrate that Welsh American leaders were, like those of other ethnic groups, searching for a way to become Americans on their own terms, although the Welsh were in a much better position to achieve that goal than other nationalities. The official, public elements of this effort are reflected by the Welsh periodicals, but the great unanswerable question remaining is to what degree their readers agreed with, and acted upon, the remonstrations of these cultural opinion makers. We can never know, but the immigration historian Rudolph Vecoli's observation on the Italian immigrant press must equally apply to the Welsh: readers' minds were not "simply a tabula rasa upon which print culture impressed its definitions of social reality. Rather, they filtered media messages through the sieve of their own experience. Finally, they decided what was reality—and its meaning."[31]

Lamentations published in the press over backsliding from these standards of Welshness is evidence that many ignored them. Hence, in 1884 a correspondent complained that among the thousands of Welsh residing in the northern anthracite field of Pennsylvania were "many fellow Welsh" who were mired in alcohol and drunkenness. The Germans and Polish know no better than to spend the Sabbath drinking and getting drunk, he opined, but the Welsh sinned voluntarily. "Yes, there are hundreds of our nation throughout the coalfields and quarrying districts who are heavy weights . . . pulling us down in the eyes of society." He would rather "relate the history of the honourable, wealthy and religious Welsh I see and meet on my way, yet it is incumbent upon me, even though anxiously, to relate that such thorns and brambles are on my path."[32]

Welsh periodicals certainly filtered reality. Reliance upon the Welsh language screened out those who did not read it, and the Welsh press took no notice of social and labor problems in the coalfields, filling their pages instead with biographical treatments of successful coal mine operators and managers. Little or no news beyond the Welsh community networks of churchgoers, merchants, and professionals cluttered their pages. Bill Jones has characterized *Y Drych* as the paper of the "Welsh language elite" who represented a "thin layer of immigrant intellectuals" managing a "White-Anglo-Saxon-Protestant newspaper in Welsh," whose project was constructing the "whiteness," and therefore the "Americanness," of the Welsh.[33]

### Religious Denominations

The Welsh language exerted its greatest influence through the cultural institutions and societies that the Welsh immigrants established in the United States. If the Welsh mine superintendent was most responsible for attracting a Welsh workforce, the Welsh chapel was not long in arriving to serve their spiritual needs in the good old mother tongue.

The evangelical camp meetings that swept colonial and antebellum America in the first and second "Great Awakenings" were initially a British form of Methodism brought to the colonies by the revivalist preacher George Whitfield. The camp meetings were Americanized on the frontier, and then reexported to Britain in the early nineteenth century by American revivalists. In Britain, Wesleyan Methodists were expelled for holding American-styled camp meetings because church authorities regarded them as excessively emotional. The evangelists who believed in predestination, the Calvinists, were far more successful in converting the Welsh during the great revival meetings than were the Armenian Methodists, who did not. By the 1850s half of the Welsh population had adopted a Calvinistic form of Methodism and rejected the established Church of England, a noteworthy circumstance because Nonconformists were much more likely to emigrate. The religious census conducted in England and Wales in 1851 demonstrates this outcome very clearly. The religious preferences of British immigrants to the United States between 1845 and 1855 break down as follows: Church of England / Episcopal, 12.6 percent; Presbyterian, 19.7 percent; Nonconformist, 67.7 percent. Of the latter, 44.7 percent were Methodist; 10.2 percent were Congregational; 4.6 percent were Baptist; and 8.2 percent were other (Catholics, Mormons, Independents, Unitarians, Quakers, Universalists, and others).[34]

Calvinistic Methodism opposed emigration during the late eighteenth and early nineteenth centuries. Having accepted John Calvin's doctrine of predestination, efforts to improve one's personal welfare and satisfaction by emigrating struck the Welsh Methodists as going against God's will. By the 1830s respected theologians had resolved this issue by concluding that as long as Welshmen continued to live modest, respectable lives and adhered to the discipline they would not defy the will of God by migrating to America. Certain features of Methodist Nonconformity itself prepared its adherents for emigration. They were less encumbered by central organizational structure than the continental denominations and thus could function independently. These independent congregations found ready acceptance in America and wide latitude toward religious practice. Among the Nonconformists, Methodism had a particularly dramatic behavioral impact on believers. The momentous conversion and the charismatic revivals exhorted converts to greater diligence at work, frugality, and ambition for upward social mobility in order to fulfill God's grand plan. The poor and the working class, particularly coal miners, were receptive to Methodism and found in its teachings a way out of poverty. That road often led to America. Moreover, Nonconformists already regarded themselves as political and social outsiders even though the laws barring them from political office and the universities were repealed in 1828. Finally, social, political, and intellectual traditions oscillated in reciprocal waves between America and Britain through revolutionary ideologies dating back into the eighteenth century rather than official church channels. Institutional and intellectual links between Methodism in America and Britain were far more dynamic than those between the Church of England and the Episcopal Church in America.[35]

The preeminent Welsh American community institution was the chapel, and their distribution mirrors the dispersal of the Welsh American population in the nineteenth century. Among the immigrants were adherents of the Church of England, Quakers, and Mormons, but they were decidedly in the minority. As many as 85 percent of those who attended church in nineteenth-century Wales were Nonconformists, as were the vast majority of nineteenth-century immigrants. Nearly all the immigrants to America were associated with three organizations: the Calvinistic Methodists (or Welsh Presbyterians), the Congregationalists, or the Baptists. Exact figures are not available, but Rev. R. D. Thomas's generally reliable survey of Welsh church distribution and attendance in the United States buttresses the contention that the immigrants were overwhelmingly Nonconformists. He counted 384 Welsh churches in the United States in 1871 with a total attendance of 50,053 distributed as follows: 20,200 (40.2 percent) attended 152 Calvinistic Methodist churches; 20,828 (41.6 percent) attended 154 Congregationalist churches; 8,595 (17.2 percent) attended seventy-one Baptist churches; and 430 (0.08

percent) attended seven Wesleyan churches. These churches were led by Welsh clergymen who were conscious of their national identity, preached in Welsh, and maintained communication with their native land.[36]

The Calvinistic Methodists tended to be stronger in the agricultural communities and the Midwest, particularly Ohio, Wisconsin, and Minnesota, reflecting church preference in western Wales where many of these immigrants originated. Of the 152 churches in existence in 1871, only 24 were located in Pennsylvania and 30 in Ohio, but most of the latter were in the Welsh agricultural communities. Relatively few Calvinistic Methodists resided in the mining states in 1871. The Congregationalists, on the other hand, were most numerous in South Wales, and, therefore, had a stronger showing in the mining states than in the agricultural states. Of their 154 churches, 43 were in Pennsylvania and 40 in Ohio. The Baptists were a smaller denomination, but they were disproportionately concentrated in the mining states of Pennsylvania and Ohio, where 53 of the 71 Baptist churches were located in 1871. Of the entire first generation Welsh population and their children, Rev. R. D. Thomas estimated a total attendance in all churches of 50,053 in 1871. The mining communities that can be identified among these church communities and states are numerous, and in states like Pennsylvania and Ohio where Welsh miners were a larger presence, perhaps a majority of the Welsh churches were in coal communities.[37]

The first Welsh immigrants were not numerous enough to transplant their own churches, so they worshiped together in "union churches" composed of all three churches with governing policies worked out amongst themselves. As their numbers grew, the Baptists and Calvinistic Methodists withdrew to form their own churches and left the "union" churches in control of the Congregationalists. The Welsh disagreed over issues such as church organization, Calvinism, and infant baptism. The Calvinistic Methodists adopted a more formal church organization with a hierarchical structure. But others did not support a strong organizational structure, preferring instead, as did the Congregationalists and Baptists, to rely on a decentralized organization with decision-making powers residing in the individual churches. While the Baptists favored adult baptism, the Congregationalists did not. But the three major Welsh churches shared the basic tenets of Calvinism over Armenianism, although there were some Baptists and Congregationalists who took exception to this doctrine. Also, they all were "fundamentalist" in their understanding of religion and the primacy of the Bible. And they generally conformed to a similar style of religious expression and ritual that historian Edward Hartmann ambiguously called "the Welsh way of life."[38]

The church was the undisputed center of the Welsh community and therefore the defining element of the "Welsh way of life," whether in the rural agricultural or in the industrial settlements. The Welsh way was definitely puritanical. It demanded a rigid observance of the Sabbath, temperance and preferably abstinence, and austerity in church and daily life. Ideally, most of one's leisure time was taken up by the church. Sunday from 9:00 A.M. to 8:00 P.M. was taken up by activities at the church, and all secular activities were to be avoided. In addition to Sunday services, two meetings run by lay members were held during the week, usually one on Tuesday night devoted to prayers and singing, and another on Thursday night devoted to the affirmation of faith.[39]

Preaching was the most important part of Sunday for adults. Welsh preachers became known for dynamic preaching and Welsh *hwyl*. This distinctively Welsh characteristic was often the subject of comment. One writer described it this way: "The best description I can give of this peculiarity is this: it is the application of sentences in a chanting style to portions of the minor scale. The minister is never at a loss how to apply the words to the melody; they appear to run together as by mutual attraction. The sentence is started, for instance, on E minor. The minister has his own peculiar melody. It ranges here and there from the first to the fifth, often reaching the octave, and then descending and ending in sweet cadence on the keynote. I am sure that in the genuine *hwyl* the intonations are always in the minor mode. The introduction and the deliberative parts are in the major, and the voice continues thus until the emotional point is reached; then it glides triumphantly into a thrilling minor, which generally continues to the close."[40]

Sunday school was a Welsh invention and fundamentally important to their religion. It also played a vital role in bringing literacy to the Welsh, providing an elementary education at a time when it was not generally available. Classes were organized by age, with topics of study appropriate for the level. The topic was known in advance, and the scholar studied the Welsh Bible and the commentaries carefully prior to Sunday school until a clear argument could be presented for one's point of view. One learned to read from the Welsh Bible, grew up learning it backward and forward, and used it in understanding the world. The Sunday school, therefore, not only taught church members to read but prepared them to be biblical scholars capable of reciting long passages by heart, and so produced the next generation of Welsh spiritual leaders in a distinctively Welsh mold. As a result Welsh ministers could count on preaching to a congregation well-versed in the Bible, and one which measured the minister's oratorical skill and Biblical knowledge by a lofty standard.[41]

Innumerable Welsh ministers began their lives in coal communities and grew up in these churches. Gradually the larger congregations demanded college-trained ministers, but throughout the nineteenth century few of the Welsh American ministers were college trained. Most were well-informed, even well-educated men who obtained their knowledge through self-discipline, diligent determination, having been schooled in experience and most emphatically in the Welsh Bible and the commentaries. They all served a long apprenticeship, were carefully examined by committees in their denominations, and finally ordained if found worthy. Many worked as miners to earn a living while following the call to preach.[42]

The example of the Calvinistic Methodist Reverend Howell Powell is by no means exceptional. Born in 1819, in Ystradgynlais, he was orphaned at age eight, reared by relatives in Tredegar, Monmouthshire, and entered the mines at twelve. The Sabbath School provided him with most of his education, and he became a teacher himself. At age sixteen he experienced a conversion and was urged to prepare for the ministry. Powell married in 1842 and emigrated from Tredegar with his wife and her parents to Brady's Bend, Pennsylvania, where he worked in the coal mines and became an active worker in the Calvinistic Methodist chapel. He was ordained in 1846 in Pittsburgh, continuing to mine coal as well as preach until he finally was able to "live by the gospel." He trod a familiar path for ministers to this point, but was unique in being the first Welsh American minister to live primarily by preaching. In 1851 Powell assumed a pastorate in Cincinnati and held that post for nearly twenty years before accepting a pastorate in New York in 1870, where he died five years later. A minister respected for his intellect, piety, and *hwyl*, Powell became a well-known figure of the Welsh church in America. No one could have predicted it, much less himself, and it was possible in the first instance because of the Sunday school. Many such stories appeared in the Welsh American press.[43] One observer illustrated the difference between the English and Welsh pulpit. The English, he wrote, were "high platform men wearing high vests and standing much upon their dignity," whereas Welsh ministers were "low platform men," self-respecting and yet "always in sympathy with the people."[44] Nothing less would do in a Welsh coal community.

The Welsh church was vital to preserving the old language (*Cymraeg*) in the new American settlements. It also provided the venue for the congregational singing that Americans associated so closely with the Welsh that it was thought to be innate to them. Sung in four-part harmony from hymnals using the tonic-sol-fa musical notation, the hymns were drawn from a large storehouse of hymns written and composed by Welsh musicians. One of the greatest hymn writers ever, William Williams of Pantycelyn, wrote over one thousand hymns. Although hymn singing has deep roots in Wales, it was the great Methodist revival of the eighteenth century that enshrined the practice in Welsh religious expression.[45] Welsh churches often met during the middle of the week for congregational singing, and from the generations brought up in this culture emerged the famous Welsh choirs, male choruses, and musical competitions that so many think of as distinctively Welsh.

The editor of the *Cambrian* estimated in 1893 that there were 150,000 Welsh speakers in the United States, of whom 61,500 were adherents of the Welsh churches and 88,500 attended non-Welsh churches. The figures show clearly, he wrote, that "the great majority of the Welsh people in America are connected with the various American churches, and that only a small number comparatively are connected with the Welsh churches," and the number continued to fall as the Welsh became Americanized.[46] Similarly, according to Rev. R. D. Thomas's figures, 43.3 of Welsh Americans attended Welsh churches, which is probably a generous estimate. It is also highly unlikely that all those Welsh and Welsh speakers who did not attend the Welsh chapels actually attended American churches; most likely there were a large number who did not attend at all.

Declaring the centrality of the church in Welsh culture and institutional life is not to claim that its teachings were universally followed. In the religious census taken in England and Wales in 1851, nearly half (47.7 percent) of the population of Wales claimed no denomination at all.[47] Industrial emigrants bound for the United States, therefore, were as likely to be unchurched as they were to be safe in the "fold of the lamb." The constant refrain against "demon rum" in the Welsh American press suggests that the underside of Welsh culture was not as respectable as the church would like. Clergymen worried that the widespread dispersion of the flocks might mean that they were neglected, but in other cases the clergy were simply rejected by migrants who saw America as an opportunity to break away from a suffocating religion they found overbearing.[48]

For Methodists and other Nonconformists, religion was the basis for living moral lives, and temperance was essential to that end. Britain and America shared a transatlantic temperance movement that originated in the American evangelical movement and then spread to Britain, another linkage that facilitated Nonconformist emigration and eased its way into American life. Immigrants did not support temperance wholeheartedly, however, and coal communities were notoriously committed to the saloon and the miners to their beer.[49]

The "lack of morality" among the Welsh was one of the great concerns expressed publicly by "respectable" Welsh Americans. As early as 1851, when H. Seymour Tremenheere, a British mining commissioner, made a trip to the United States to visit coal communities near Pottsville and Pittsburgh, he noted the miners' penchant to live for the moment. He observed that the Welsh and Irish predominated, along with a few Scots and Englishmen, and that they made excellent wages and could "afford the opportunity of acquiring an independence in the course of a few years." Some were taking advantage of the opportunity, but "the majority were described as retaining the habits contracted by the worst specimens of the colliery population in Great Britain—of great extravagance in eating and drinking, and making no provision for the future."[50] An article published in 1870 under the pseudonym "Huw o'r Ddol" declared that morality in the Hyde Park section of Scranton was "second to those of Sodom, and the equal of Gomorrah." Saloons were "as numerous as the frogs of Egypt" there, and one could find men and women alike "forever half-drunk, fooling, idling around and singing in Welsh until they are a disgrace even to the half-civilized Irish." The "language of the fiends of hell" poured out of the saloons, and the Sabbath enjoyed no respect there at all. Responsibility for this state of affairs, according to "Huw o'r Ddol," fell upon the shoulders of Welsh men and women from Tredegar, Rhymney, Dowlais, Merthyr, and Aberdare, "those who have recently arrived from there or within the last two years. The scum of the works of Wales has been shipped to Hyde Park." What should be done about this deplorable state of affairs? The answer was that ministers from Wales should serve as temperance missionaries among the nonabstemious of Hyde Park.[51]

The Welsh American press pounded out a constant drumbeat of abstinence for decades and stood foursquare behind the temperance movement. There may have been some exaggeration in articles such as those cited above, but there is also an abundance of evidence that popular culture among Welsh coal miners was something quite different from what the official shapers of Welsh culture had in mind. Although the pietistic platitudes and preachments from the respectable elements probably bordered on self-aggrandizement, there is no doubt that drunkenness and disorder and other social problems provided sustenance for the temperance movement. Nineteenth-century America was a rough-and-tumble society, and mining towns often bordered on lawlessness. Drinking was as prevalent in the Welsh mining communities as it was in coal-mining towns generally. The saloon and church vied for the coal miners' loyalty both in Wales and in America, and this competition turned into a struggle between the Devil himself and Nonconformist church leaders. Campaigns for temperance faced an uphill struggle as unrelenting as that facing Sisyphus. Still, Welsh prohibitionists continued their fight for decades, right up to passage of the Volstead Act and later the Nineteenth Amendment, which ushered in prohibition in 1919.[52]

Miners generally understood the problem of drunkenness but did not see a conflict between drinking alcohol and religion, making the prohibitionists' mission a formidable one indeed. The anecdote repeated by a Welsh Congregationalist minister illustrates how impervious the popular culture was to the pressures of the churchmen, and why miners regarded the position of the teetotalers as unreasonable. The story was told of William Maxey, a Welsh miner from Monmouthshire who had lived for a long time in Carbondale. He was described as a church stalwart who was a regular in the "amen corner" every Sunday. His church hosted a local preaching *gymanfa*, and one of the preachers was the Rev. Morris Roberts of Remsen, New York, who attempted to convince the members of his congregation to join the temperance society. The minister was invited to dinner afterward at Maxey's home, and Roberts asked him why he had shaken his head in disagreement when the minister had spoken of the temperance society's struggle to end the evil traffic in alcohol and stated that men would be better off without drink. Maxey responded that he did not believe it. "When I am drilling in the mines and the coal dust almost choking me, a drink of beer is very refreshing, and when I come home in the evening after a hard day's work it is very satisfying to have a drink of it." Rev. Roberts's rejoinder was that Maxey must join the temperance society or the church would disown him. In New York, he said, "we have a powerful machine now to pull out stumps," and we need something like this to pull the drunks out of the church. Maxey was unperturbed: "You can't do it my boy, I was a member of the church before you were born. . . . As for the old engine you have in New York State to pull the stumps out; our way down here in Pennsylvania is to leave them rot in the ground, and it is quite as well for you to leave me alone."[53]

While the Welsh churches served as the principal transitional institution for the first generation of immigrants and the single-most unifying cultural institution in Welsh American communities, they did not initiate communities so much as follow them. This state of affairs represented a major difficulty for the churches, for no sooner were they established than the Welsh superintendent moved to another location, taking his workforce and leaving the ministers to follow or face deserted pews.[54]

### Societies and Eisteddfodau

The Welsh were as deeply influenced by the popularity of fraternal and social orders as were other Americans in the nineteenth century. Miners, including the Welsh, belonged to benevolent societies as a protection against misfortune from serious accident, protracted illness, or death. The most popular of these American organizations among Welsh miners were the Odd Fellows, the Order of Foresters (Welsh origin), and the Knights of Pythias. According to one reporter who examined the subject in 1877, very few miners joined the Freemasons.[55]

Most prolific of the Welsh societies were the cultural societies that sponsored programs such as concerts, banquets, speakers, and readings. Most important, they led celebrations on March 1 for St. David, the patron saint of Wales, and sponsored Welsh Days at community parks. These were major events where the Welsh were numerous, and miners generally stopped work to enjoy them. "None of the big companies will expect a Welshman to work that day in Lackawanna or Wyoming valleys," declared the *Druid* in 1908. "Cymro" [Welshman] had written an editorial urging Welshmen to work that day, but the Welsh newspaper could not support such a message, pointing out that Cymro was a mine foreman, which apparently was sufficient explanation. Every Welsh American community had its St. David's Society or Cambrian Club, which took the lead in remembrance celebrations of their Welsh heritage. Edward Hartmann claimed that over one hundred such societies existed at one time or another. There were, of course, numerous choral societies organized in the communities, and they often competed with one another. Some of them were well known, even famous in their day, among them the Cymrodorion Choral Society of Scranton, led by the famous composer Daniel Protheroe. Perhaps the most famous of them all was the Orpheus Glee Club of Wilkes-Barre, which won national renown.[56]

Choruses from Wales frequently toured the Welsh American settlements. In 1914 the Gwent Glee Singers, "the best aggregation of singers that Wales has sent over in the past twenty years," came to America on their second tour. Local Welsh societies sponsored each stop on the tour. After performances in Welsh communities of the northern anthracite coalfield, the Gwent Glee Singers were scheduled to appear in a variety of Welsh towns in Iowa including those in the coalfield, such as Hiteman. The tour caught the interest of the UMWA, which reported in its own newspaper that the singers from Gwent were all coal miners, and mused that the singing might be fostered by the solitude of the mine, with the song of hammer on drill providing a solid sense of rhythm.[57]

Touring Welsh choirs from Wales became common in Welsh American communities by the 1890s. Hazleton, Pennsylvania, was looking forward to a performance of the Welsh Prize Singers in October of 1897. The Welsh Prize Singers of Cardiff stopped for a concert at the opera house in the small northern Illinois coal town of Braceville in 1889. The local Welsh community numbered only a few hundred, but Welsh people from the entire region undoubtedly attended the concert for "a rare musical treat." A choir from Llanelli, Wales, touring in the United States in 1909 and sponsored by local Welsh societies, gave seventeen concerts in the month of December on its Ohio leg of the tour, nearly all of them either in or near the coalfields. The tour had already taken them to large cities, such as Chicago, Milwaukee, and Pittsburgh, and from Ohio the choir was headed for Scranton. The local Welsh society of Morgantown, West Virginia, sponsored a "grand concert" of the Cambrian National Glee Singers in 1911. In Alliance, Ohio, "the first number of the winter series of entertainments was given in the Welsh C.M. church" on December 30, 1914, the *Druid* announced. "These entertainments are anxiously looked forward to and are well attended."[58] Touring singers were amazed by the enthusiasm that greeted them in America. On returning to Wales, one recounted to the *Merthyr Express* how the émigrés were "ten times more Welsh than they were at home. They are Welsh to the core and will travel hundreds of miles to hear anything Welsh."[59]

Coal-mining communities were generally too small to support the benevolent societies found in the urban centers. The Welsh Society of Philadelphia, the oldest of such societies, founded in 1727 and still in existence, aided Welsh immigrants who found themselves desperate in a strange city by helping them with food, clothing, lodging, finding work, or reaching their destination. Others with similar benevolent missions included the Welsh Benevolent Society of Utica and Vicinity, founded in 1849, and the Cambrian Benevolent Society of Chicago, founded in 1854. Many coal communities had chapters of the Independent Order of True Ivorites, however, which often provided similar functions for Welshmen. It was founded in Wrexham, Wales, in 1836, and named for Ivor Hael (Ivor, the Liberal), a fourteenth-century Welshman whose generosity and deeds of kindness elevated him into legend. The Ivorites had a secret ritual and ceremonies that celebrate the great leaders in Welsh history, such as St. David, Howell the Good, Llewellyn the Great, and Owen Glendower. The American Order of True Ivorites was founded in Pittsburgh in 1848 by immigrants who had been members in Wales. Chapters soon sprang up throughout the Welsh American settlements. In the coal communities, the Ivorites were noted for providing health and death benefits for members and assistance to other Welsh families in times of need. Cultural and social activities were also sponsored by the Ivorites, and sometimes took the place of the St. David's Society or Cambrian Club. The Ivorite lodge in Hyde Park, which was established in 1867 as a self-improvement and benevolent order, also functioned as a cultural society sponsoring eisteddfodau and concerts.[60]

The Welsh Philosophical Society was the most influential organization in Scranton, the largest concentration of Welsh coal miners in America. It was founded in Hyde Park in 1857 by some of the most prominent mining men of the community, including Benjamin Hughes, Thomas D. Davies, and Thomas Phillips. The society was established "to enable the Welsh working men of Hyde Park to meet at least once a week to investigate and debate questions relating more particularly to mines, mining, geology, natural philosophy and other kindred subjects." Its intended goal was to help its members to get ahead, and apparently it succeeded. According to one contemporary writer, "a large number of the members of this society are now filling positions of profit and responsibility in the management of the mines. Some have become mine inspectors, others have become superintendents of mines, and many others mine foremen. The society has been the best possible preparatory school for its members, preparing them for higher and better positions."[61]

The Welsh Philosophical Society sponsored concerts, excursions, and the annual eisteddfod on Christmas Day, high points on the Welsh social calendar. The origin of the eisteddfod, the uniquely Welsh gathering to observe poets, writers, and musicians as they compete for prizes, dates back many centuries. The first such competitions to be called by that name began in the fifteenth century, but declined in popularity as the gentry who had sponsored them became Anglicized and lost interest in the sixteenth and seventeenth centuries. Interest was revived in the eighteenth century with the embryonic movement that would lead to the full-blown cultural nationalism of the nineteenth century. By the end of the nineteenth century, the Royal National Eisteddfod had become institutionalized in Wales, and the tradition continues today.[62]

The Welsh who immigrated to America transplanted the eisteddfod with them as a way of regenerating Welsh culture, and it became second only to the chapel as the most important Welsh institution. The first recorded eisteddfod in the United States occurred in Carbondale, Pennsylvania, on Christmas Day, 1850. Others soon followed during the 1850s in Pittston and Scranton, Pennsylvania, and elsewhere. From the 1860s eisteddfodau of various scales were held throughout the Welsh American communities, usually on Christmas Day and New Years Day. As the nineteenth century waned, these events gradually shifted away from primarily poetry and literary competitions in the Welsh language and began to emphasize choral music, particularly the great choir competitions. The coal and iron districts of Pennsylvania from Nanticoke to Carbondale, and in Ohio's Mahoning Valley settlements from Warren and Youngstown to New Castle, Pennsylvania, were the great centers of eisteddfodic enthusiasm. Eisteddfodau in these centers were magnets for Welsh miners from all the smaller towns linked to the centers by railroads.[63]

The eisteddfod served several important social functions in the Welsh community. It nurtured local literary and musical talent by providing a competitive venue and a purposeful goal for Welsh writers and choirs whose ambition was to win the eisteddfod. It also provided intellectually rewarding activities for the community, performers and audience alike, and was often referred to as the "university of the poor." Since the event was not segregated by sex or class, the entire community was served, and unified by, the eisteddfod. The popularity of these events is evident in the attendance and the number of them, especially in the larger Welsh centers. In 1877 Luzerne County, Pennsylvania, hosted three large eisteddfodau within eight days of each other, all of them well attended. One observer compared Luzerne County with Glamorgan County in Wales, and the eisteddfodau at Hyde Park, Plymouth, and Pittston with their counterparts in Wales at Aberdare, Pontypridd, and Mountain Ash. Commenting on the local eisteddfod in 1871, the *Scranton Republican* reported that Welshmen of every stripe were present, but "mostly those with brains, religious and non religious, rich and poor, sober and a sprinkling of jesters."[64]

The first of a long series of national eisteddfodau, which carried into the late twentieth century, was sponsored by the Welsh Philosophical Society of Hyde Park in 1875. Over six thousand people crowded under the large tent where the events were held. They came from near and far, and numerous notable Welsh Americans with reputations as speakers, adjudicators, and conductors were in attendance. It was a day on which the Welsh proclaimed the significance of their presence in America. Phoebe Gibbons, a writer for *Harper's New Monthly*, was probably referring to this event when she wrote in 1877 that eisteddfodau were "very generally attended by the Welsh, and are held in some large public hall, the greater part of the performances being in the Welsh language." A miner explained to Gibbons that church choirs attending the eisteddfodau would select a difficult piece of music to sing and compete for the choir prize, as would trios of singers and then solo singers. Poets, essay recitations, and sight singing also were important parts of the general program.[65]

The large size of these gatherings, and their cultural distinctiveness, caught the attention of the non-Welsh population. Commenting on a forthcoming eisteddfod in 1875, the *Scranton Republican* poked gentle fun at the Welsh, announcing that a "polysyllabic tournament" was scheduled in which they would be overcome by an "orthographic epidemic." If the local paper had a bit of fun with the Welsh, it was not lacking in respect for their culture. Several weeks later the paper announced that the national eisteddfod to be held in Hyde Park that year "will be a great credit not only to the Welsh people; it will reflect honor on this city. There is no class of people who place a higher estimate upon the advantages of intellectual culture than the Welsh and however limited the opportunities of a community composed of this nationality, it will abound in organisations and societies for music, literature, oratory and the lesser sciences. They are a reading people and one who has not mastered English is a rarity."[66]

The 1875 eisteddfod packed a message that reinforced the construction of a Welsh American identity built on respectability, religiosity, and intellectual attainment manifested in literary and musical sophistication. Despite clinging to its distinctively Welsh cultural practices, the eisteddfod highlighted the similarities between white Anglo-Saxon Protestantism and the middle-class foundations of Welsh culture, thereby demonstrating that the Welsh were worthy of acceptance as valued and respected Americans. But the eisteddfod was so popular in Scranton that it became the city's festival and subsequently would be open to all musical talent without regard to ethnic identity or even language. Hence, this uniquely Welsh institution became not only a vehicle for cultural reinforcement, but also an instrument for achieving Welsh assimilation.[67]

The *gymanfa ganu*, loosely translated as "singing festival," was another uniquely Welsh institution. The first known *gymanfa ganu* (pronounced ga-mán-va gán-nee) as an independent singing festival took place in Aberdare, Wales, in 1859, and quickly grew in popularity in Wales and in the United States. As Americanization progressed, English replaced Welsh as the language of the eisteddfod, and hence some of the original cultural significance of the eisteddfod was lost. This opened the way for the musical portion of the festival to take preeminence, and for the *gymanfa ganu* to replace the eisteddfod in the early twentieth century as the most popular cultural festival in Welsh American communities. As mentioned above, Welsh churches traditionally gathered to sing at a host church, which rotated annually for multiple congregational singing. The idea caught on and spread so that communities in a district would gather to sing hymns. This was greatly facilitated because the "tonic-sol-fa" method of music reading, so useful to laymen for part-singing, was taught to children in Welsh Sunday schools. In 1929 the first National *Gymanfa Ganu* Association was founded in Niagara Falls, New York, led by officers of the St. David's Society of Youngstown. The movement grew in the twentieth century, and by 1942 ninety-four different Welsh societies were members. The NGGA continues today, and the community singing that grew out of it is embodied in the annual North American Festival of Wales.[68]

The *gymanfa ganu* was popular in the small towns widely scattered across the American coalfields. Like the eisteddfod, it not only reinforced cultural identity but also provided important leisure-time activities for miners and their families in places where cultural opportunities were limited. Also like the eisteddfod, it was open to men, women, and children alike, and, in bringing people of like interests together from outside the community, they also expanded the social world of mining families. Unlike the eisteddfod, however, the *gamanfa ganu* was not competitive at all. Its sole purpose was to congregate and sing hymns, and eventually a mix of secular music written for chorus was added to the event.

Reinforced by the church, eisteddfod, and *gymanfa ganu*, choral singing became a significant part of the daily life of Welsh Americans in the coalfields. The awe-inspiring exhibitions of four-part harmony delivered by Welsh choirs attracted so much native comment that they became indelibly linked in the American mind with the Welsh. In the 1830s, it was reported, residents of the anthracite field near Carbondale, upon "hearing the strong minor chords of Welsh hymns on the frosty night air for the first time, got out of bed to listen." Another observer declared that "one of the grandest rehearsals it was ever my good fortune to listen to was the singing of 'Coronation' by the miners a mile under ground."[69] A retired Welsh miner who worked in a Pennsylvania mine during the 1870s remembered that "while waiting for a car to come so that they could load the coal they had 'shot down', someone would produce a piece of chalk or pick up a fragment of slate and write a four-part tune on the broad face of the wall of coal still standing. Then those in the room gathered around and soon the deep caverns underground re-echoed with men's voices singing an old Welsh hymn."[70]

It is in the nature of memory to be nostalgic about the past, and nostalgia was common among immigrants whose enthusiasm for their strange new world was tempered by their loss of the familiar old one. Welsh American cultural institutions were vehicles for preserving and expressing these contradictory impulses. Welsh American identity emerged from this dialogue between what it meant to be Welsh and American, from the dynamic interaction across class and gender lines within Welsh immigrant communities as well as between those communities and the dominant culture. A distinctive Welsh American identity emerged based on Nonconformist Protestantism, Republicanism, the Welsh language, sobriety, and ethic of work, respectability, self-improvement, and social mobility. These values were celebrated in Welsh American newspapers, chapels, and cultural festivals in a way that not only preserved their version of "Welshness," but also prepared the way for full assimilation on their own terms. Their experience underscores one of the dominant themes in current historiography by demonstrating how immigrants transferred homeland practices and adapted them with advantage to "hostland" conditions.

## PROFESSIONAL INSPECTORS
## FOR A DISASTER-PRONE
## INDUSTRY

British miners generally came to America to improve their condition, but they frequently confronted unanticipated obstacles. Not the least of these were the dangers of the mines themselves, which, in fact, were among the most dangerous in the nineteenth-century world. Prior to the establishment of mine inspections in Pennsylvania in 1870, the data on casualties from mining accidents was unsystematically reported in coalfield newspapers. One authority calculates that the 1870 statistics for the four southern counties of the Pennsylvania anthracite field (Schuylkill, Northumberland, Columbia, and Dauphin) show that casualties were much more frequent than in Great Britain: 172 deaths and 396 injured, a death rate of one per 36,875 tons, a rate three times higher than in Britain. The figures were much worse in Schuylkill County, where most of the deep mining was located: 149 killed and 335 injured, and 3,938,429 tons of coal mined, a tonnage-per-fatality ratio of one per 26,432. In short, a miner was four times more likely to be killed on the job in Schuylkill County than in Great Britain.[1]

Earlier, the rate might well have been even worse had accurate data been available. A Tamaqua correspondent in the *Pottsville Miners' Journal* in 1858, arguing in support of a Miners Hospital and Relief Association, claimed that 2,140 accidents each year among the 12,000 miners who toiled in Schuylkill County was a low estimate. He calculated that one-third (721) of these men were permanently disabled, and another third killed, leaving 700 widows and 1,400 orphans annually "with no provision for their support." A modern scholar of the Schuylkill coalfield claims that "a colliery employee had a less than even chance of surviving for twelve years; he could expect to be killed or crippled for life in six." The death rate for underground miners came close to 10 percent a year, comparable to military losses in combat.[2] The miners might not have had a command of the casualty statistics, but they knew all too well the dangers, and the politics of safety were articulated in popular culture such as the folk ballad "Down in a Coal Mine":

How little the great ones care,
who sit at home secure,
What hidden dangers colliers dare,
what hardships they endure;
The very fires their mansions boast,
to cheer themselves and wives,
Mayhap were kindled at the cost
of jovial colliers' lives.[3]

Pennsylvania was the major coal-producing state throughout the nine-teenth century, and it was to Pennsylvania that most of the British colliers came first. They transplanted not only their skills, but also the political culture of mine-safety reform.

### The Mine Safety Reform Movement

Among the most historically significant benchmarks in the struggle for amelioration of the miners in Great Britain was the Children's Employment Commission appointed by Parliament in 1840. The commission's 1841 re-port exposed in a comprehensive way the deplorable conditions under which children and women were employed in the nation's mines and facto-ries. As we have seen, testimony taken by agents in the coalfields of Scot-land, England, and Wales revealed the deleterious effects of underground labor on children, some as young as six years old, and women working like horses, carrying and pulling coal for twelve or more hours a day. The report, which was the subject of extensive public comment, recommended the abolition of female and child labor in the mines. That same year a bill was introduced that advanced specific regulations abolishing female labor, limit-ing the age of employment for boys to thirteen and above, and other sought-after reforms. British coal miners bombarded Parliament with petitions for the bill's passage, but it met with stiff resistance, particularly in the upper house, on the same grounds that mine owners have always argued against reforms—that the cost would result in the closing of coal mines and hurt the nation's economy. Conservatives joined the industrialists' representatives in opposing the measure as an intrusion of government into the relations between employer and employee. The bill was not killed, however, and an important precedent was set with the passage of an amended bill that changed the minimum age of boys to ten, abolished female employment underground, and provided that an inspector might be chosen "when nec-essary" to inspect any mine and report on the conditions found there.[4]

Britain continued to endure preventable disasters on a major scale, and the Miners' National Association of Great Britain grew apace to over 60,000 by the mid-1840s. A bill for the inspection of mines, introduced in Parliament in 1850, called for the improvement of ventilation and the appointment of inspectors to see that the regulations were enforced. Owners, of course, opposed the measure again, arguing that their business and property interests would be injured. The final version of the bill provided for the appointment of only four government inspectors, made the health and safety regulations recommendations rather than requirements, and limited the act to a five-year term.[5]

Reliance on four mine inspectors for all of Great Britain was, of course, totally inadequate for the mission. It would have taken hundreds of inspectors to routinely inspect the more than two thousand mines operating in Britain at the time. In addition to the scale of the problem, they struggled against a lack of scientific knowledge about the complexity of natural forces involved in deep mining, and against the entrenched resistance of powerful industrialists who opposed government intrusion into their affairs. Nevertheless, the inspectorate became an important force for reform because by sheer will and superior knowledge it transformed itself from an advisory service into an "executive corps" with the coercive powers to ensure compliance with the laws. The inspectorate drew strong public support from the resulting decline in the fatality rate among miners. In 1851 the colliery death rate was 19.4 deaths per million tons of coal mined; in 1861 the figure was 10.0, and in 1871 it was 9.2. Similarly, the accident rate declined dramatically, from 1 per 245 employed during the years 1851–60, to 1 per 430 during the years 1871–75. Even though mining accidents were always a present reality, killing one miner every six hours between 1868 and 1919, the likelihood that a miner would be killed at work decreased three and a half times during that same period.[6] This pattern would be mirrored in the United States.

British miners succeeded in electing Alexander MacDonald, president of the Scottish miners' union, to Parliament in 1855. MacDonald was an able advocate of the miners' cause in Parliament, and he defended demands for improvements in health and safety against the politically powerful mine owners. When the 1850 law came before Parliament for renewal in 1855, miners petitioned for its renewal and an increase in the number of inspectors, establishment of a mine boss examination board, and the education of boys before they entered the mines. The legislation was renewed with only minor revisions, but MacDonald kept up the pressure, adding an additional provision requiring that coal mines have two separate openings. These demands were incorporated in a new bill presented in 1860, and a large delegation of miners lobbied Parliament for its passage.[7]

Although initially Parliament ignored the miners' demand for reforms for a second opening, public pressure following the Hartley Colliery disaster of 1862 soon forced members to act. A fire in the single shaft mine had closed off the only means of escape, and 205 miners suffocated to death; shortly thereafter, the mining law was amended to require two openings for each mine. The miners' union continued to gather strength and members became active in district elections, demanding that candidates for Parliament promise to support mining reforms. Then in December 1866, the Oak Colliery exploded, killing 362 miners, the largest loss of life in a mine disaster recorded up to that time. By 1872, sufficient pressure had been exerted to finally prompt Parliament to pass a mining code containing nearly all the safety regulations demanded by Great Britain's coal miners.[8]

The migration of British miners to America began in earnest in the 1860s and 1870s, and they brought with them the sense that change was indeed possible through organization and political action. The safety reform movement in the United States mirrored that in Britain, which supplied not only the political consciousness but also the activists in the form of immigrant miners who educated their coworkers about the advances in safety and mining methods in Britain. In the Pennsylvania coalfields British miners at first were active at the grassroots level, stirring up the issue of safety in the newspapers. In 1854, for example, John Morris, a Welsh miner in Schuylkill County, wrote in the *Pottsville Miners' Journal* that, even as the industry became prosperous, life for the miners became ever more dangerous because the operators did not take the appropriate measures to provide for the safety of the miners, particularly proper ventilation. He declared that the most effective recourse for miners was to approach their state representatives to pass safety legislation.[9]

The most important newspaper serving coal miners during this period was the *Pottsville Miners' Journal*, the newspaper for independent mine operators edited by a scientific miner of Welsh parentage, Benjamin Bannan. British safety legislation was followed with keen interest in the paper and provides strong evidence that miners in Pennsylvania were abreast of mining reform in Britain. For example, the *Pottsville Miners' Journal* reproduced the British Mine Inspection Act of 1855 and editorialized that a similar system of improved ventilation would have salutary effects on American mining. It also supported various efforts of the miners to pursue safety measures through the legislature, such as the mine ventilation bill introduced in 1861, and urged Americans to follow the British model.[10]

In March 1866, "an act for the protection of miners and laborers in the collieries of Schuylkill County" was introduced in the legislature, calling for a provision to permit mine inspectors to fine owners for infractions and shut down unsafe mines. The bill was killed on the second reading in the Pennsylvania senate, but support was growing as the death toll continued to increase. In February 1869, a bill that would become the Schuylkill County Ventilation Act of 1869 was introduced into the lower house of the Pennsylvania legislature. Thousands of Schuylkill petitioners supported the bill, and petitions came in from Luzerne County seeking similar legislation. When a senator proposed that the bill be applied to the entire commonwealth, Senator Samuel G. Turner, a Democrat from Luzerne County, opposed the measure, arguing that there was no need for the law in Luzerne because the mines were not gaseous. Turner was a coal dealer, raised among the Welsh and English coal miners of Plymouth, Pennsylvania, who had been elected by them to represent Luzerne in the state senate. Claiming to be unaware of a single methane, or "firedamp," explosion in his county, even though there had been at least three during the 1860s, he must have seemed transparently self-serving. Other senators did not press the issue, however, noting that "important interests" were involved. Consequently, the final legislation applied only to Schuylkill, but it set the precedent for subsequent legislation. Modeled after the British mining law, the act contained several important provisions: it placed responsibility for safety on the mine owners and bosses; it stipulated penalties for failure to comply; and it created the office of mine inspector.[11]

### Avondale, the Welsh Disaster

Although the miners of Luzerne had been active in trying to secure safety legislation, the Schuylkill Ventilation Act applied only to that county, thanks to Senator Turner. Unfortunately, the passage of this limited legislation preceded by less than five months the worst mining disaster in American history to this time. It occurred in Luzerne County, in the Steuben shaft at Avondale, near Plymouth, on the western bank of the Susquehanna River, and killed 110 miners. The mine was constructed in 1868 by the Nanticoke Coal Company, a subsidiary of the Delaware, Lackawanna and Western Railroad, one of the largest integrated coal, iron, and rail corporations in the northern anthracite district. For the previous three and a half months the miners were on strike, but they had returned to work on September 3 and 4, just before that fateful Monday morning of September 6, 1869.[12]

When the colliery started operation Monday morning, an underground workforce of 108 men was on the job, and they soon began to raise coal up the shaft from more than 300 feet below. About eight o'clock in the morning the stable boss had taken a load of hay down the shaft for the hauling mules and at the bottom discovered the fire. As he gave the alarm, a cloud of smoke followed by a column of flames shot up the ventilator shaft and set fire to the breaker and engine room built directly over the shaft topside. The heat was so intense that the engineer was unable to do anything but escape with his life. It seemed but an instant before the entire wooden structure was engulfed in flames, which rose like a torch for more than one hundred feet above the head house. The men and boys working in the breaker were forced to jump for their lives, some from high elevations. The shaft was ten by sixteen feet, over three hundred feet deep, and bisected by a wooden partition forming a ventilation flue. All the gear above that would not burn fell crashing into the shaft among the burning shaft timbers and other debris clogging the shaft for forty feet.[13]

Recognizing that there was no means of escape for the men working in the chambers below, the men on top looked on in horror. The mine had no fire equipment of its own, but the news spread throughout the coalfield in a flash, with fire departments from Wilkes-Barre, Scranton, Plymouth, Kingston, and nearby towns soon converging on the scene. Other than putting out the surface fires, however, there was little that could be done. As always with mine disasters, people flocked to the scene; by noon they numbered "many thousands," which included relatives and would-be rescuers, but mostly concerned and curious spectators. The onlookers became such an impediment to the rescue efforts that at one point it became necessary to turn a fire hose on them to drive them back to a safe distance.[14]

The most authoritative source of information on the Avondale tragedy was written by H. W. Chase, city editor for the *Scranton Morning Republican*, who compiled reports from the scene and subsequent official documents into a single publication. Chase recorded the rescue efforts in great detail. Not only were the entrapped miners overwhelmingly Welsh, so too were the rescuers. Once quiet was achieved, calls were made down the shaft but none were answered. As always, the agony of death was over for the men below. "Now piercing shrieks proceeding from heart-broken women were heard, as the horrid truth began to dawn upon their minds that they were in fact bereaved," Chase wrote.[15]

Rescue efforts began by lowering a small dog with a lighted lantern into the mineshaft, to determine if the air was foul enough to kill the animal or to extinguish the light. Then Charles Vartue stepped forward to make the first descent. He ascended shortly after to report that about half-way down the shaft was choked with obstructions that would need to be cleared to finish the descent to the bottom. Two Welshmen, Charles Jones and Stephen Evans, volunteered and descended the shaft. When the men returned topside they reported that they had found a closed door and assumed that the miners had barricaded themselves from the noxious gases, although pounding on the door brought no response. Most people hearing this news understood that there was little hope for the entrapped men now, and "the shrieks of women and the cries of children rent the evening air. No words can describe the scene. It continued far into the silent watches of the night," Chase reported.[16]

A request was made for two more volunteers to search for the miners. Thomas W. Williams and David Jones stepped forward, but this trip to the bottom would be their last. When no contact was received from them, two additional men descended to discover Williams and Jones lying insensible. They brought out Williams but, when another party went after Jones, one of them was prostrated by the gases and resuscitated only with great difficulty. Now Thomas L. Williams went down for the body of Jones, but he, too, was overcome and had to be drawn up. John W. and Isaac Thomas made another effort and finally retrieved the unconscious rescuer.[17]

James George, president of the Plymouth miners' union, convened a meeting to organize a company of fifty experienced miners from whom rescue squads would be formed. Thomas J. Phillips, superintendent of the Jersey mines, also attended to facilitate cooperation between operators and miners in the rescue efforts. The miners elected George as superintendent, Henry W. Evans and George Morgan as foremen, and Thomas E. Davies and John H. Powell as advisors to direct rescue operations. Nearly all the rescuers were Welshmen. The first squad to reenter the mine found carbonic acid gas (black damp) three feet thick covering the bottom of the mine but returned safely, as did the second squad. The third squad returned in fifteen minutes, two of them so overcome by black damp that it took an hour for three physicians to revive them.[18]

To rid the mine of deadly gas, the rescuers made what turned out to be a serious mistake when they decided to pump air into the mine. They believed that the coal in the ventilating furnace had been extinguished the night before. Sadly, that was not the case, and, when the air sent into the mine swept over the burning furnace, it carried the gases and smoke into the deepest recesses of the mine. If the men had survived until that point, this action alone would have been sufficient to cause their deaths. Squad after squad went down at great risk to their lives. Finally, R. Williams, D. W. Evans, John Williams, and William Thomas went down and reached a closed brattice that the men had built to protect themselves from the gases. When they broke through, the rescuers found sixty-seven men and boys who appeared as if they had fallen asleep. William R. Evans was stretched out holding a son in each arm, and a third lying between his legs with his head resting on his father's breast. Evan Hughes, the inside boss and brother of Benjamin Hughes, the famous Welsh superintendent of mines for the DL&W Railroad, was found sitting with his head bent forward and hands clasped in front of him.[19]

Six relief squads were formed to carry the dead men to the top, but, before they came out, acting coroners E. C. Wadhams and J. W. Eno, both justices of the peace, impaneled a jury to identify the bodies as they were brought to the surface. As each miner was identified, his name was announced to the crowd and the body conveyed to the dead-house to be cleansed and claimed by relatives or friends. With each announcement shrieks of agony went up from the thousands anxiously waiting and watching. The county sheriff appointed deputies and Scranton officials sent a special police force to preserve order because the crowd was now so large that it was difficult to control.[20] Over the course of four days, life stood suspended as forty-one more bodies were given up by the pit. Each dead miner was identified in the jury report with heart-wrenching brevity. Some of the men still had families in Wales: "William D. Johns, Welsh Hill; boarded with Samuel Howell. Mouth open; hand closed. Wife and four children in Aberdare, South Wales"; "William R. Rees; boarded with Kirk Owens, Avondale; very bloody about the nose; hands clinched. Wife and children in Neath, South Wales"; "William D. Jones. Face bloated, and arms extended over his head. Wife in Merthyr Tydfil, South Wales." There were others with loved ones in Wales waiting for the passage money that would never come.[21]

The bodies of the 110 dead miners were delivered to surviving relatives and friends and prepared for burial. A Scranton reporter observed that the village of Avondale itself was "nearly depopulated, the head of nearly every family has been taken to the tomb." But Scranton was hit hard by the tragedy as well, for 61 of the 110 victims were either residents of or closely associated with the city. Trains bearing thousands of passengers accompanying the caskets slowly bore their burden to Scranton on September 9 and 10, where seventy men had been busy digging graves in Washburn, the Welsh cemetery in Hyde Park. Fifteen hundred people escorted the coffins to their burial site, and church bells tolled throughout the city.[22]

The Avondale disaster story was spread throughout the United States and Europe by the large newspapers, such as the *New York Times* and the *Philadelphia Ledger,* as well as the widely circulated popular periodicals, such as *Harper's Weekly* and *Frank Leslie's Illustrated Newspaper,* which published a special edition filled with illustrations sketched at the scene. Avondale was the worst American mining disaster to that time, and the testimony taken at the coroner's inquest, which convened on September 11, pointed to the dangers of mines with only one means of egress. But the jury's investigation of the tragedy was marred by ugly rumors and intimations that Irish arsonists had set the fire because of the intense antagonism that clouded their relations with the Welsh. A special report to the *New York Times* noted that "it is generally sincerely believed that the shaft was fired, but no miner is so unjust now as to charge the crime upon any nationality." The Welsh miners, however, were loath to admit publicly even the possibility of such depravity. Acrimonious feeling existed between the Welsh and the Irish, the *New York Times* reported, but even though some of the Welsh believed the shaft was intentionally set on fire, none believed that it was "with the intention to take life."[23]

Several Welshmen testified at the coroner's jury that they believed the fire was the work of arsonists. A mine owner who operated the properties next to Avondale discounted the notion that relations between the Welsh and Irish were so bad at Avondale that death was the result of revenge. While he acknowledged that there might have been some "clannish feeling" and harsh words exchanged on occasion, he rejected the idea that "warm-hearted" Irishmen would have committed so diabolical an act. The Avondale operators made no attempt to either prove or disprove the incendiary theory, but they "studiously kept it in the background" and were at great pains to show that the mine had been worked with "care and prudence" to avoid legal responsibility.[24]

The exact cause of the fire was not an immediate concern to the 72 widows and at least 153 orphans, nor was it the main issue confronting the coroner's jury. The real issue was why the law did not require mines to have a second opening. The political clamor for an appropriate safety law began

The Avondale disaster: miners volunteering to search for victims. *Frank Leslie's Illustrated Newspaper* 29 (September 25, 1869): 37. Courtesy of Paterno Library, Pennsylvania State University.

in earnest the day after the Avondale disaster when John Siney addressed the miners of Avondale. Terence V. Powderly, who became the leader of the Knights of Labor, heard Siney speak and claims he told the crowd: "Men, if you must die with your boots on, die for your families, your homes, your country, but do not longer consent to die like rats in a trap for those who take no more interest in you than in the pick you dig with." Would there be a second means of escape if the owners went into the pits everyday, Siney asked rhetorically. Yes, there would, and "what they would do for themselves they must be compelled by law to do for their workmen."[25]

Petitions flooded Harrisburg, newspapers almost universally demanded improvements in the law, and miners held mass meetings to press the point. Siney founded the Workingmen's Benevolent Association (wba) in 1868, and as president he and Secretary of the General Council Thomas M. Williams headed a committee sent to Harrisburg to lobby for improved safety legislation. In January 1870, Governor John W. Geary presented the

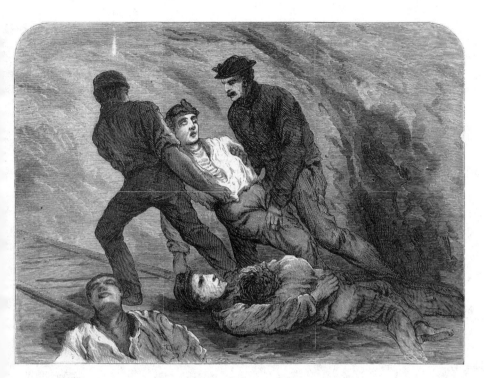

The Avondale disaster: removing the victims from the mine. *Frank Leslie's Illustrated Newspaper* 29 (September 25, 1869): 36. Courtesy of Paterno Library, Pennsylvania State University.

legislature with the desired bill, and Senator Turner, now fighting for his political life, took the lead in the effort to secure its passage. By March 3 the bill had passed both houses and the governor signed it into law.[26]

The mine law of 1870 adopted the provisions of the 1869 act and applied them to all of Pennsylvania. For that reason it is regarded as the first significant mining code passed in the commonwealth. The 1870 bill incorporated numerous additional provisions, such as complete maps showing the progress of the workings, a prohibition against boys under the age of twelve working underground, and a prohibition against construction of the breaker and engine house directly over the furnace shaft in furnace-ventilated mines. The measure also required at least two outlets and provided for six mine inspectors for the anthracite counties.[27]

Candidates for the office of inspector were required to be citizens of Pennsylvania, at least thirty years old, have five years' experience in anthracite mining, working experience in the ventilation of coal mines where firedamp and other noxious gases were present, and knowledge of the

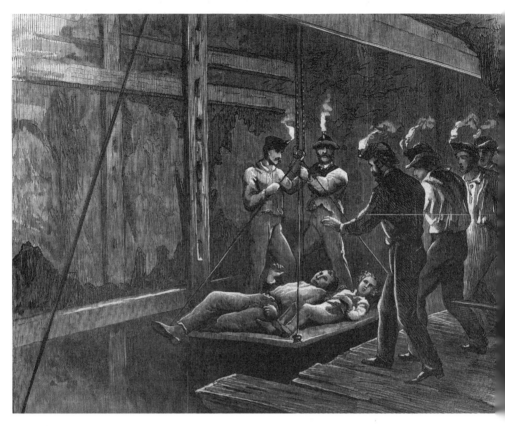

The Avondale disaster: hoisting the victims to the surface. *Frank Leslie's Illustrated Newspaper* 29 (September 25, 1869): 36. Courtesy of Paterno Library, Pennsylvania State University.

various systems for underground mining. A board of examiners reviewed the qualifications of each candidate, and the governor appointed the most qualified to terms of five years. No person who had a financial interest in coal mines was to be appointed. Inspectors were charged with examining the mines in their districts as often as practicable, keeping records of their inspections and investigating accidents. Since safety of the miners was their primary duty, inspectors were authorized to enter the mines at any time, and, in case of violations, had the authority to apply to the courts to shut down a mine until it complied with the law. When investigating accidents, the inspector also had a coroner's power to compel people to attend hearings and testify under oath if necessary.[28] The Avondale disaster, therefore, had important historical repercussions, and it was British and Welsh immigrants who were at the forefront in pushing for new mine safety legislation,

The Avondale disaster: widows identifying victims. *Frank Leslie's Illustrated Newspaper* 29 (September 25, 1869): 1. Courtesy of Paterno Library, Pennsylvania State University.

modeled after the British law. The tragedy was that it took the deaths of 110 men for the law to pass.

### Professional Inspectorate and the Second Avondale

From the beginning Welshmen were the predominant ethnic group represented among the Pennsylvania inspectorate. In the first decade the inspectors served only the anthracite fields. All the first appointees under the 1870 law were foreign-born; three were Welsh (Thomas M. Williams, John T. Evans, and David Edmunds), Frank Schmeltzer was German, and John Eltringham was English. For the next fifteen years a similar ethnic representation prevailed: three Welsh, one English (Samuel Gay replaced Eltringham), and two of undetermined ethnicity (Robert Mauchline and James Ryan). In 1886 the anthracite inspectorate was increased to seven, and the number of Welsh remained at three and the English at one. Three others were of undetermined origins, but their names suggest their ancestry: H. McDonald (Scottish), James Ryan (Irish), and William Stein (German).[29]

A force of eight inspectors was appointed to serve the western Pennsylvania bituminous mines in 1888. The Welsh were not so highly represented either among the mining population of the Pennsylvania bituminous fields or among the inspectors. Even though their origins have not been determined, three of them, William Jenkins, J. J. Davis, and T. T. Evans, were probably of Welsh origin. The number of inspectors in both fields crept higher over the years, and by 1900 there were eight anthracite inspectors, half of whom were definitely Welsh-born (James Edward Roderick, H. O. Prytherch, Gwilym M. Williams, and William H. Davis). Among the ten bituminous inspectors in 1900 two were definitely Welsh-born (Elias Phillips and J. T. Evans). By 1910 the inspectorate in both fields had grown substantially to twenty anthracite and twenty-one bituminous inspectors. Interestingly, the number of Welsh anthracite inspectors had also grown to eleven of the twenty, although a few of them were born in Pennsylvania to Welsh parents. Among the bituminous inspectors only four had Welsh names, although two were definitely of Welsh birth (Elias Phillips and Thomas D. Williams). The number of inspectors grew as the industry expanded and, by the year 1920, a similar percentage prevailed with twelve of the twenty-five anthracite inspectors being Welsh, but only four among the now thirty bituminous inspectors with typically Welsh names, even fewer than before.[30]

The difficulty of enforcing the safety regulations mandated by the 1870 Mine Ventilation Law became apparent a year after its passage in what many called the "Second Avondale." This catastrophe occurred on May 27, 1871, when the breaker caught fire at West Pittston Shaft. The fire apparently was caused by overheated journals in the hoisting wheel at the top of the shaft. As at Avondale, the breaker was built directly over the shaft, and again the debris fell into the shaft. Construction of a second opening had been carried on intermittently but had not been completed. Moreover, the mine had no water supply or any firefighting equipment. Knowing this, "the agony of those having loved ones in the mines is beyond description. Their screams and moans fill the air, while they swing their hands and tear their hair in grief," reported the *Scranton Morning Republican*. The very first news report raised the question on everybody's mind: "Why was there no second opening to this shaft?" The mine ventilation law had been in place for many months, and stipulated that a second opening must be completed in working mines within four months of the bill's passage.[31]

The rescue effort began immediately. Eight thousand people concerned about the fate of the thirty-eight men trapped below soon congregated around the shaft. A dog was first sent down the shaft to test the air, and then teams of volunteer miners went down to explore the workings for victims. They found the first miner, Andrew Morgan, lying in the gangway alive but unconscious, and the rescuers then realized that others might be alive as well. Most of the miners were found behind a barricade of trimmed lumps of coal. Reports conflict, but at least eighteen men were dead or died soon after reaching the surface, while most of the other nineteen men who were rescued alive lived to tell of the ordeal. W. R. Davies, the only miner brought out of the mine who retained consciousness, said the barricaded men believed they would never leave the pit alive when some of them began to feel drowsy from the gases. "We afterwards resigned ourselves to die, and made preparations accordingly. We had prayer meetings, singing, and we finally caressed and kissed each other, bidding one another an affectionate farewell, hoping to meet each other in Heaven," Davies informed an interviewer.[32]

There were heroes who entered mining lore. Phillip Jones, one of the volunteers, was so overcome that he was not expected to live. His father, brother, and another relative had died in the Avondale disaster. Another was Martin Crane, a twelve-year-old driver boy, who stepped off the last cage trip up the shaft to warn the working miners that the breaker was on fire. He returned to the bottom of the shaft but left to search for the other men. By then the barricade had been constructed. Crane begged "in the most piteous manner" to be taken into the barricaded chamber, but the miners would not risk the lives of the group to save one. The boy then went to the stable where he wrote down the names of his father, mother, and cousin, before lying down beside his mule. There the rescuers found his body next to the mule. Another hero was the hoisting engineer who stayed at his post at the top of the shaft as long as the wire rope was attached to the cage. Although his arms and face were burned and his hair scorched from his body as the flames surrounded him, he continued to hoist men out of the mine until the rope finally snapped on the fourth trip and he jumped to safety.[33]

Welshmen were among the victims and heroes, but one was also a coward. Thomas Phillips, the weighmaster at the bottom of the shaft, received the danger signal, but instead of warning the miners he jumped aboard the carriage and went up the shaft. According to the *Scranton Morning Republican*, he testified that "he did not know it was his duty to give the men the alarm," to which the newspaper opined, "What miner or laborer could be safe in a mine with such an idiot and coward at the foot of the shaft to give the alarm in case of danger?" The report contrasted Phillips's cowardly behavior with the bravery of young Martin Crane and with that of the engineer who, "had he been one of the Phillips class of men[,] not a soul would have been hoisted."[34]

Mine disasters are tragedies for the living as well as the dead, especially the families. William James died after he was brought out of the mine. A Welshman, he had been in the United States for only seven months. His wife related a story that has its counterpart in most coal-mining disasters. On the morning of that fateful day, James was in a state of "deep melancholy" staring into space. When it was time to go to work, he kissed his wife and children several times, started off and returned several times, reluctant to go. Pressing family necessity, his wife urged him to go and he did so reluctantly. When the alarm was given, she screamed, "The breaker is on fire and my husband is lost!" Her grief magnified by guilt, "the poor woman has been in a state of frenzy ever since," according to a reporter, and "the unfortunate little ones have been suffering the most acute pangs of hunger, and with no hope of relief only in the sympathy and aid of a humane public."[35]

The position of mine inspector required extensive technical and administrative skill, but the West Pittston disaster demonstrated very early that their duties were carried out in a hostile political arena of competing interests. Of all the company men and coal miners who could be blamed for this catastrophe, therefore, the person both groups attacked was the mine inspector, Thomas M. Williams, a former Workingmen's Benevolent Association official with indisputable credentials. The smoke had hardly cleared from the shaft when the *Scranton Morning Republican* declared that Williams must bear the burden of blame. Williams knew that more than sixty men had entered the West Pittston shaft that day, the paper editorialized, and, therefore, the inspector should have shut down the mine immediately. The newspaper demanded that, along with some of the mine bosses, Williams should be removed from office.[36]

At the coroner's inquest, William Kendrick, the mine superintendent, who had recently emigrated from Denbyshire, North Wales, testified that Williams had been through the mine with him and had not informed him that too many men were working there. At this point Williams remonstrated so vigorously that he was asked to leave the room. A few hours later Williams himself took the stand and directly refuted the superintendent's testimony claiming that too many men were underground, and he expected the superintendent to correct the violation. Called back to the stand the following day, Kendrick again claimed that "Inspector Williams never gave me any official instructions as to the number of men I should employ; I understand that we can employ as many men as we please if the inspector does not object."[37]

It would seem self-evident in legal proceedings that the superintendent of the mine would be responsible for conducting operations, and held liable for understanding the laws under which his mine operated, but the inquest and the newspapers completely exonerated him. The coroner's inquest effectively accepted the operator's word over the inspector's and laid the blame for the accident on Williams, accusing him of dereliction of duty. The union leader was undoubtedly accustomed to fighting against officialdom, but he was obviously angry that the company had not complied with his directive, and that he alone was being wrongly blamed for the tragedy. Williams dismissed the coroner's inquest as a sham, charging that the coroner was not qualified to conduct such an investigation and launched his own inquiry into the disaster. Williams's objections and his investigating committee were dismissed by the press as vehicles for "whitewashing himself."[38]

The quickness to blame the inspector, the vehemence of the denunciation, the lack of criticism of the mine superintendent, and the willingness to accept the word of someone who might well be criminally negligent should raise serious questions from an objective observer. The Workingmen's Benevolent Association, for example, did not hold Williams responsible. But the *Scranton Morning Republican* editorialized that it had uncovered the reason for the union's support of Williams, despite what it called "his negligence of duty." The answer was found, the paper declared, in the fact that "Mr. Mine Inspector Williams is a member of the W.B.A. while all the men who were killed in the West Pittston shaft are of that persecuted wronged class of miners stigmatized by the W.B.A. as 'Blacklegs' [non-union]!" William Scranton, owner of the *Morning Republican*, was adamantly hostile to labor unions, and his faction of the Republican Party was fighting the Welsh faction for control over the local organization. Inspector Williams, who was Welsh, active in local politics, and also a union official, was, therefore, subjected to a scurrilous campaign in the paper that tarnished his reputation for the rest of his illustrious career.[39]

Thomas M. Williams, John T. Evans, and Patrick Blewitt were three Welsh-born Pennsylvania mine inspectors of the first six appointed to office. Like their counterparts in Britain, they established the proper methods and procedures for inspectors in the service as they interpreted and enforced the safety law as best they could. The inspectors were fully aware of, and interested in, the experience and knowledge of the British mine inspectors, and this is evidenced by the frequent references to British accident investigations, experiments in ventilation, and other technical knowledge gained by their counterparts in Great Britain.[40]

Opposition to the interference of Pennsylvania mine inspectors came from every direction and, without the determined professionalism of inspectors like Thomas M. Williams, the inspectorate would not have achieved the respect it needed to promote safety in the industry. There is also little doubt that the criticisms from the miners, whose lives they were trying to protect, pained the former union official. He wrote of unreasonable letters of complaint he received from miners in his annual report for 1877. A large portion of the letters "were not worthy of any attention, from the coarseness of language employed, the insinuations and personal abuse, and threats that they contained, and being invariably anonymous," Williams wrote. But even these "undeserved insults" were given his attention "for fear that there were some worthy persons suffering." Some miners always had a grievance against another worker, a boss, or the rules, but "these are the most inferior of all the workmen, yet they are the ones that have all the complaints to make."[41]

There has always been suspicion among miners that inspectors informed the operators of pending inspections, and that inspectors informed the operators of miners who lodged complaints. Sensitive to these suspicions, Williams reiterated on a number of occasions that he engaged in neither practice. He always told the miners in the presence of the managers that it was not a privilege but a duty to bring to the inspector's attention any imminent danger to the health of miners. The miners responded that they did not dare to reveal dangerous conditions for fear of persecution from the company, and Williams acknowledged that "the majority of our mine officers" would think sending complaints to the inspector was sufficient cause to rid themselves of such employees.[42]

The miners leveled a broad range of complaints against the inspectors about which they had neither the knowledge nor the power to control. Williams responded that "when an inspector has over one hundred openings, and when they extend for a distance of twenty-six miles in length, by a width of three to four miles, covering an area of over one hundred square miles, and, where an aggregate number of fifteen thousand workmen are employed, two thirds of the same being employed inside the mines, then, I say, he cannot make frequent visits." The miners believed the inspectors had nothing else to do but visit mines when in fact they spent considerable time in court, writing reports, and investigating accidents, among other duties. Additional complaints included long hours, stolen clothing, the absence of a carriage to ascend at the end of a shift, and lack of pay for non-coal-producing work. All these complaints might have been legitimate, but the inspectors had no power to address them.[43]

Where the miners saw inaction or collusion with the companies, the operators constantly protested against the "dictations of the inspector." The miners could only complain, but the operators often took legal recourse against the inspectors, charging them with being "biased and prejudiced" and "favoring the workmen too much." The inspectors did take operators to court for violations of the law. On one occasion, Thomas Williams wrote, he had a court case against an operator who had failed to make a second opening. The operator accused Williams in open court of "persecuting" the company because their mine was a "black-leg operation," or operating non-union. In fact, "an inspector that will do his duty . . . is continually a target for both sides." Williams served in the position for ten years before resigning to escape both the constant resistance from operators and "the senseless opposition of the miners."[44]

Another Welsh mine inspector from the eastern district of Luzerne and Carbon Counties, William S. Jones, also complained in 1877 about a suit he brought against a miner and a mine boss for gross negligence of duty in which a laborer lost his life. Even though the manager was a friend, the inspector had them both arrested because he was sworn to uphold the law. When the case came to trial, however, it was "unceremoniously" thrown out of court, and Jones "barely escaped being saddled with the costs." His inability to impose the penalty of law, Jones was convinced, "accounts, in a great measure, for the heavy mortality from falls of roof and coal in my present report."[45]

The first mine inspectors were forced to overcome resistance from both capital and labor, but their persistence was instrumental in establishing a professional inspectorate. The disproportionate number of Welshmen who became mine inspectors played a major role in establishing that tradition, and the profession itself was attractive to ambitious Welsh mining men with a desire to advance in the world.

There is no secret to the disproportionate influence the Welsh exerted on the development and continued expansion of the anthracite inspectorate. They had been recruited to the anthracite fields to develop and then manage the industry because of their extensive knowledge and experience. Their skills and the timing of their arrival during the expansion of the industry ensured that they would hold a privileged position within the industry. As managers of the industry, they attempted to assure the success of operations by recruiting other miners from Wales who also came to find secure employment at high wages and the potential for upward mobility. Many rose from the ranks of miners to become managers and operators, and not surprisingly the same process occurred with the inspectorate. Welsh miners seeking upward social and economic mobility found the position of state mine inspector open to them because the technical requirements to hold this position were similar to those required for certification of mine managers.

Even though they were a diverse group, and it is not feasible to systematically identify the nativity of all mine inspectors, a sampling of their biographies suggests some common threads. Most of them had acquired at least the rudiments of an education that facilitated the additional study necessary for passing the rigorous examination taken by all would-be managers and inspectors. The knowledge required, and selectivity of the process leading to appointment, is suggested by the number of miners who took the test and passed it, especially in light of the fact that a score of 90 percent or lower disqualified a candidate. For example, in 1899, fifty-two applicants took the examination for bituminous mine inspector, but only eight positions were open and only eleven had passed.[46] Experience and knowledge were a prerequisite, therefore, and Welsh miners raised within a mining family and culture held an obvious advantage over others without that experience.

The Welsh tradition of self-improvement reasserted itself in America and merged with a self-help movement among skilled workers and the ethos of the self-made man. Among the Welsh, self-improvement was facilitated within their own unique community institutions as well as those found in society generally. Welsh institutions, such as the eisteddfod, the Welsh churches, and learned and fraternal societies exerted a distinctively Welsh influence within the community in defining "success" and "progress," in addition to enriching life generally. The biographies available for the Welsh inspectors all pay homage to the influence of the Welsh self-improvement tradition. Many found even higher positions in the coal industry upon leaving the inspectorate than they had held when they were appointed.

The few biographies of Welsh inspectors show that each followed a unique path to the profession, but all were motivated by a strong desire for upward mobility. Thomas D. Jones exemplified the younger Welsh immigrant who came to America with his parents as a youth. Born in South Wales in 1842, he emigrated in 1850, became an assistant engineer, and then rose to the position of superintendent of collieries with the Lehigh Coal and Navigation Company. In 1875 he was appointed state mine inspector, a post he held until 1881 when he resigned to accept more lucrative company positions as superintendent and general manager. Biographical sketches describe him as a learned man who was active in the civic life of Hazleton, his hometown. Reflecting the great admiration for those who elevated themselves through their own efforts, a biography rhymed: "Long may he live, self-tutored son of Wales, Whose life reflects the beauty of her vales."[47]

Similarly, David H. Thomas was born in the Rhondda Valley in 1857 and emigrated with his family in 1870 to Clearfield, Pennsylvania. Like most miners' sons, he entered work early, but he was persistent in improving his education. He studied the science of mining and passed the mine foreman's examination, and in 1886 became a foreman for Berwind-White Coal Company. Thomas passed the inspector's examination with the highest percentage in his class (98½), and was commissioned mine inspector in 1888. Like other strivers of his day, he was active in community affairs and in numerous benevolent societies. Unfortunately, he died prematurely of acute Bright's disease in 1895. A biographer heaped praise on him as "the son of a poor Welsh miner, with few educational advantages," but a man "determined to rise to something above the pick and drill."[48]

The career of Isaac M. Davies, like many prominent Welsh American miners, followed the path of youthful adventure. Born in Cwmafon, South Wales, in 1854, he crossed the Atlantic for the first time as a cabin boy at age sixteen. Looking for adventure rather than a home in the new world, after a brief stay in Pennsylvania he set sail for South America, where he lived the life of a plainsman in Uruguay and Argentina for two years before returning to Wales to work in the coal mines. The second trip to America was in company with his brother, William H. Davies, who became division superintendent of the Lehigh Valley Coal Company in Hazleton, Pennsylvania, while Isaac went to work in the mines. At age twenty-five he set sail again, this time for Australia, where he mined coal and gold for more than a decade before returning to Pennsylvania in 1890 and setting down roots at Lansford. In 1907 he became mine foreman for the Lehigh Coal and Navigation Company, and in the same year was appointed mine inspector.[49]

Gwilym M. Williams represented those who migrated to America as young men without a family. Born in Breconshire, South Wales, in 1841, he came to America in 1859 and entered the mines of Carbon and Luzerne Counties, married a Welsh woman, and made Wilkes-Barre his home. Appointed inside foreman of Oxford Colliery in 1873, he held this position until 1880 when he was appointed mine inspector. After ten years of service, Williams resigned his commission in 1890 to accept the position of general manager of the Kingston Coal Company. Gwilym Williams was, like many Welsh mining leaders, also a well-known figure as a choir director, trustee in the Welsh Presbyterian Church, member of ethnic organizations like the Cambro-American society, and an active member of the Republican Party.[50]

### Ohio

The Welsh Disaster at Avondale in September 1869 prompted miners to demand mining reform in other coal-producing states as well, particularly that coal companies be required to construct two means of egress and to appoint inspectors to regulate underground safety. Expert miners in Ohio took up reform almost simultaneously with Pennsylvania. These two states had the largest proportion of British miners. In Ohio the agitation initially came from the most established of the state's coalfields in the Tuscarawas Valley near Massillon and the Mahoning Valley near Youngstown. A series of letters appeared in 1868 and 1869 in the *Miners' Journal*, the official organ of the Mahoning miners, under the nom de plume of "Jock Pittbreeks." Written by Andrew Roy, a prominent Scottish miner living in Church Hill, Trumbull County, the letters called on the Ohio general assembly to enact safety legislation for the protection of coal miners.[51] The Mahoning miners had a strong organization, and at their 1870 convention in Youngstown, a committee including William Thomson, a Scottish engineer, and David Owens, a Welshman, proposed a resolution that would become the basis for a bill. Andrew Roy and John B. Lewis, the Welsh-born president of the Miners and Laborers Benevolent Association in the Mahoning Valley, drafted the resolutions into a bill that was introduced by Senator Michael Daugherty, who represented the Hocking Valley. The bill's principal features required two openings for all mines and the appointment of state mine inspectors, and Thomson and Lewis remained in the capital to lobby for its passage.[52]

Coal operators immediately dispatched a delegation to testify against its passage at committee hearings. Their arguments were similar to those long-standing among operators who opposed state regulations of any sort, on the grounds that mining was inherently dangerous, that two openings and professional inspectors would not make the mines any safer, and that legislation would only injure a growing industry. To counter the influence of the operators, miners in the Mahoning Valley held a mass meeting in Youngstown in support of the bill. On the given day, Roy writes, "every miner in the Valley laid down his tools and marched into Youngstown, dressed in holiday attire and carrying United States flags and banners." As the 3,400 miners reached the city limits, numerous Civil War veterans appeared in uniform along with several bands to escort the parade to an overflowing meeting where a petition demanding passage of the bill was approved. Miners throughout Ohio filled their local papers with resolutions of support and flooded the legislature with petitions.[53]

Nevertheless, the Ohio senate voted down the safety bill in April 1871, but Senator Lauren D. Woodworth of Mahoning Valley succeeded in establishing a mining commission to ascertain the condition of the mines and recommend legislation. Governor Rutherford B. Hayes appointed a commission consisting of two businessmen with little knowledge of mining, Charles Reemelin of Cincinnati and Benjamin M. Skinner of Meigs County, with Andrew Roy representing the "practical miners." The commission was supposed to inspect the mines, take testimony in the coal-producing sections of the state, and then prepare a report on its findings.[54]

The results were predictable. The majority report from the two businessmen saw little reason for alarm about safety and health conditions in the coal mines and blamed the miners themselves for accidents. In his minority report, Andrew Roy strenuously objected, laying out the case for state regulation and inspection of the industry and claiming that neither of the other commissioners had actually inspected the mines.[55]

Even though there seemed to be public support for the mine safety bill, and the Senate voted for it, the House of Delegates balked. The opposition was led by Reemelin, who headed the commission, and Joseph Conrad, a mine operator and delegate from Portage County. The conference committee was deadlocked on the provision of an inspector, and a compromise emasculated the final bill that passed on April 27, 1872. As in Pennsylvania, where the Avondale disaster prepared the way for the Ventilation Law of 1869, a tragedy dramatically changed the political atmosphere. In this case it came at the Atwater slope in Conrad's home of Portage County, where the mine had only one opening. On July 3, 1872, fire from the ventilating furnace spread to the timbers in the slope. A young boy at the top observed the fire and ran down the slope through the burning timbers to warn the twenty-one miners working inside. They made a dash up the slope, and, while eleven of them escaped, ten died a miserable death, including the boy who gave the alarm.[56]

The constitutional convention, which met in the summer of 1873, presented the next opportunity for miners to enact legislation for the inspection of mines. Delegates inserted the position of mine inspector into the new constitution, but voters defeated the constitution in 1874. By then, however, a new governor and a legislature aware of the disaster supplied the necessary political support for creating the office of state mine inspector. Andrew Roy was appointed to the post in April 1874, and was surprised that the new governor, William Allen, had read the reports of the British Houses of Lords and Commons "of the monstrous abuses as practiced on miners."[57]

Although Roy believed that the inspector's responsibility was to educate operators and miners about safe mining practices, he was not reluctant to take operators who ignored the law before the court. When Chauncy Andrews, a powerful coal operator from Youngstown, refused to sink a second shaft, Roy took him to court and forced him to comply with the law. However, Roy's close association with the miners' organizations, his willingness to bring legal action against recalcitrant operators, and his Greenback-Labor Party affiliation ensured that he would be replaced when the political circumstances changed. It was probably powerful opponents in the industry and the Democratic Party, however, who opposed reappointment. State Treasurer Anthony Howells, a prominent Welsh businessman and coal operator from Canton, turned against Roy because he was a "one-sided man."[58] Roy was replaced in 1878, but in 1880 a new governor reappointed him to a four-year term as state inspector of mines. In 1882, Roy successfully won passage of legislation requiring that all inspectors and mine managers be certified by a board of examiners, and in 1883 the state increased the number of inspectors to four.[59]

It is clear that the mining legislation passed in Ohio was based on the British model. The vast majority of Ohio coal miners during the last half of the nineteenth century were British, and whether miners, managers, operators, or inspectors, they followed methods of work and organization rooted in the homeland. Andrew Roy himself cited British legislation and mining reports as his authority. Looking to precedents also prompted Roy to consult Pennsylvania inspectors on methods and technical information. For example, he became acquainted with Thomas M. Williams when the latter shared information with Roy regarding the size of speaking tubes used in Pennsylvania to communicate between the top and bottom of the shaft. Roy stated that T. M. Williams was "the most intelligent of the Pennsylvania mine inspectors," and he cited Williams's 1875 report on the superiority of the fan over the furnace for ventilation.[60]

Little information about Ohio's inspectors has survived other than for Roy, who left an important paper trail. In fact, it is possible to identify the ethnicity of only a few of the inspectors. Seven chief mine inspectors held the post between 1874 and 1908, and only one, David Owens of Trumbull

County, who held the position in 1879–80, was definitely born in Wales. Roy was born in Scotland, and Robert M. Haseltine was an Ohio native. The nativity of the other four chief inspectors remains unknown. The record also is spotty for the thirty-five district inspectors who held the post between 1881 and 1907. Three were definitely Welsh-born, and eight others were either born in Wales or were the children of Welsh parents. Of the remainder, one was Scottish, one German, and one was an Irishman who had worked in the mines of England before coming to America. The nativity of the remainder has been lost to history.[61] Some of these men certainly used the office as a stepping stone on the rocky road to self-improvement.

### Illinois

As in Pennsylvania and Ohio, British immigrants transplanted their standards of mining, community, culture, and political action for mining safety in the coalfields of Illinois. In Illinois they carried on a vigorous exchange of information with their colleagues back home concerning the science and politics of mine safety. According to the authority on the subject, leaders of the British miners in Illinois "prepared bills and made requests for legislation related to the regulation of the mines at almost every session of the General Assembly between 1863 and 1911."[62]

As early as 1870 the miners secured an amendment to the state constitution requiring the General Assembly to pass legislation "as may be necessary for the safety of the miners." Alexander McDonald, the Scottish mine leader and member of Parliament, arrived in America one month after the 1869 Avondale disaster. He proceeded directly to the mining town of Braidwood, Illinois, where Scottish miners predominated. He had visited once before in 1867. Strong circumstantial evidence indicates that his unrecorded discussions with miners in the northern Illinois coalfield centered on the passage of mine safety legislation, a project in which McDonald played an important role in Britain. On both visits, McDonald was accompanied to the northern coalfield by Andrew Carr Cameron, editor of the *Workingman's Advocate*, and regarded by at least one authority as "the greatest labor editor of his time." Born in Northumberland, Cameron emigrated in 1851 to settle in Cook County, Illinois, and brought his Chartist ideas with him.[63]

Shortly after McDonald's second visit, the British miners decided to push for an amendment to the Illinois constitution mandating regulatory legislation. Andrew Cameron's brother, Daniel Cameron, who served as a delegate to the constitutional convention that met in January 1870, agreed to sponsor the miners' request for the amendment. In impassioned speeches on behalf of the measure, Cameron referred to Parliamentary regulations and the duty of Americans to follow their lead. He succeeded in convincing the other delegates, but the measure carried the vague language "as may be necessary" and "when the same may be required." Operators and legislators simply ignored the measure.[64]

In 1870, John Hinchcliffe of Saint Clair County was elected to the House of Delegates. A friend of the miners, Hinchcliffe was born in Yorkshire, England, and had edited the *Weekly Miner*, official organ of the American Miners' Association, and served as its second president. The miners' new organization, the Miners' Benevolent and Protective Association, drew up a bill providing for the health and safety of coal miners, which Hinchcliffe sponsored in the house. The major provisions of the bill derived almost entirely from the regulatory measures passed by Parliament in 1860 and 1862, which called for two openings and the appointment of state mine inspectors with the power to prosecute operators for noncompliance. The bill itself was patterned after that introduced by the Ohio miners, but caused such a negative reaction among house members that it was withdrawn.[65]

A revised version of the bill was prepared by the Miners' Benevolent and Protective Association between sessions and was introduced by Hinchcliffe when the legislature convened in November 1871. Although supported by the governor, the measure was vigorously opposed by sixteen coal-mining companies that lobbied fiercely against it as detrimental to the business. As in other states, operators opposed legislation that would involve significant capital outlays, but finally an amendment relegating enforcement of safety in the mines to the counties was adopted. The opponents obviously believed that placing enforcement in the hands of county officials rendered the regulation meaningless since they were susceptible to company influence. Those in favor hoped to salvage something from defeat, so the measure was passed and signed into law by the governor. The miners understood that the bill had been emasculated, and they did not give up. At each legislative session following 1872, miners attempted to secure an inspectorate under state rather than county control. While the counties had been given authority to enforce safety, the paltry salaries offered were so low that it was difficult to attract competent miners. Most of them were dependent on the very same coal companies they inspected for employment. Moreover, without police powers backed by the state, county inspectors who did stand up to the companies were no match for them in local politics or the courts.[66]

In subsequent years safety legislation was advanced by a myriad of state agencies, such as the Bureau of Labor Statistics (established 1879), reformers, and the press. The next major piece of legislation regulating mine safety was enacted in 1883. Based on the Coal Mines Regulation Act passed by Parliament in 1872, the statute finally created a corps of technically competent mine inspectors appointed by the state. As in other states, legislators were not convinced that this was necessary until the political climate forced them to act: in Pennsylvania it had been the Avondale disaster of 1869; in Ohio the Atwater disaster of 1872; in Wyoming two disasters at Almy, in March 1881 and January 1886, killing 56 miners; in Virginia nine disasters that killed 329 men, the worst at Pocahontas in March 1884 in which 112 were killed; in Missouri at Rich Hill in March 1888, killing 24; and in Oklahoma at Krebs Number 11 mine, where 100 miners lost their lives.[67]

In Illinois the opportune political climate was created by the Diamond No. 2 Mine disaster on February 16, 1883, at Braidwood, which took the lives of 67 miners and left 39 widows and 93 children fatherless. The mine had two shafts; otherwise all the miners would have died in the worst disaster in America since Avondale. In this mine, as in most others, the main shaft was located at the low point of the coal, so that the water drained into a cistern and was then pumped to the outside. Unseasonably warm weather caused the ice and snow to thaw, swelling the amount of groundwater from heavy rain. The water rose and cascaded into the underground opening in such volume that a whirlpool was created. Miners working near the air shaft managed to climb to safety, but within a few minutes the inundation blocked the escape of 67 miners. The inundation was so complete that thirty-eight days of pumping were required to lower the water level sufficiently to recover the bodies. The property was abandoned and allowed to fill again with water. Two rescuers also died, bringing the total to 69, all immigrants. The ethnic composition of the dead reflected the composition of immigrant miners living in the area: 3 English, 21 Scottish, 2 Welsh, 7 Irish, 25 Germans, 10 Polish, and 1 Swede.[68]

The disaster shocked the people, and an outraged press criticized the resistance of legislators to government-mandated safety regulations. Following the disaster, the political atmosphere changed dramatically, and new legislation based on the 1872 Coal Mines Regulation Act of Parliament passed, which established five district mine inspectors within the Illinois Bureau of Labor Statistics. Among other credentials required for the post were ten years of practical mining experience and passing an examination of technical competency as judged by a state examining board composed of two miners, two operators, and a mining engineer appointed by the governor. Illinois inspectors, like their colleagues in other states, often found themselves caught between recalcitrant operators and the sniping of the miners they were bound to protect.[69]

British immigrants were the chief agents for bringing safety regulations up to British standards in Illinois and other states. Nor surprisingly, therefore, they dominated the office of district mine inspector in Illinois. The ethnic makeup of the inspectorate between 1883 and 1911 roughly reflected the nationalities within the British Isles. Thirty-five inspectors between these years can be identified: 25 were born in Britain: Scotland (11), England (10), Wales (3), and Ireland (1). Only six of the inspectors were born in America, but several of them were of British parentage. Fifty-seven British immigrant miners who played important roles in advancing mine safety regulation in Illinois to 1911 have been identified: 26 were born in Scotland, 23 in England, 5 in Wales, and 3 in Ireland.[70]

Even though the Welsh represented a much smaller proportion of the British immigrant miners in nineteenth-century Illinois, Amy Gottlieb has identified five men born in Wales who played key roles in the state's mine safety legislation. Their career trajectories differ from other British immigrant miners only in the level of achievement. Ebenezer Howells was born in Tredegar, Monmouthshire, in 1843, the son of a miner. He emigrated in 1880 and eventually settled in Braceville, where he worked as a miner, was elected secretary-treasurer of District 12 United Mine Workers of America, became part owner of a cooperative mine in 1892, and was appointed to the State Mining Board in 1897.[71] Evan David John was born in Maesteg, Glamorganshire, in 1861, also the son of a miner. John entered the mine at eight, and at nineteen emigrated from Wales to join his father who had already relocated to Illinois in the 1870s. John rose to the position of mine superintendent, and in 1897 was appointed state mine inspector. He resigned in 1904 to become superintendent of another coal company, was appointed to the State Mining Board, and, in 1917, was appointed director of the newly created Department of Mines and Minerals.[72] Harry W. Smith was born at an unknown location in Wales in 1854, another son of a miner. He too began work in the mines as a boy of eight, and with his family emigrated from Wales in 1866, settling in Trumbull County, Ohio. In 1877, he moved to Illinois as an organizer for the Knights of Labor and helped to establish the *Western Advance*, the official organ of the k of l in Illinois. In 1886 and 1887 he was elected vice president and then president of the Illinois Miners' Protective Association and lobbied effectively in the state capital for mining legislation.[73] William W. Williams, born in Caerphilly, Glamorganshire, in 1846, entered the mines at age ten. In 1866 he and his wife migrated to Ohio and then Illinois. He became secretary of the Streator Institute of Mining in 1883, was mine manager for several coal companies, and then served as a state mine inspector between 1905 and 1913.[74]

Although far less influential than their counterparts in Pennsylvania and Ohio, Welsh miners in Illinois seem to have advanced themselves through self-study and application in order to acquire the technical or political skills which elevated them to positions of leadership.

### The West

By the 1890s, even the smallest and most isolated mining states had taken at least some tentative steps toward improving mine safety. Utah coalfields were slow to develop, but federal legislation in 1891 required the appointment of a mine inspector in each territory with coal mines. The position of mine inspector was retained when Utah became a state in 1896. The first inspector served only briefly, but his replacement, Welshman Gomer Thomas, persisted long enough to turn an ineffectual office into one respected for its professionalism.[75] It was a long, uphill battle the conclusion of which Thomas would not live to witness. The first miners in Utah were Welsh Mormons, but by 1900 large numbers of European immigrants and native Americans had surpassed the Welsh and other British miners in the workforce. Nevertheless, the influence of the Welsh as skilled miners, managers, and tradesmen in the coalfield communities, many of them former miners, remained significant. As in other coalfields, the daily injuries and fatalities failed to attract public attention until an explosion ripped through the Winter Quarters mine on May 1, 1900, taking at least two hundred lives.

Winter Quarters was the worst mine disaster in American history to that time, and still stands as the fourth worst ever. Located one mile west of Scofield, Carbon County, in a remote canyon eight thousand feet above sea level, the Winter Quarters disaster sent shock waves reverberating throughout the nation. Just forty days earlier, the general assumption that Pleasant Valley Coal Company mines were non-gaseous and, therefore, would not explode was challenged by a near disaster not far away in its Castle Gate mine. Fortunately, company policy at Castle Gate required all miners to leave the mine when the electric blasting mechanism was triggered. Therefore, when a major explosion was ignited by remote blasting on March 22, all two hundred miners who worked in the pit had safely evacuated. This precaution was not followed at the Winter Quarters mine.[76] More than three hundred miners entered the Winter Quarters mine on that fateful morning in May when, at 10:25 A.M., a ferocious explosion shook the mountain. One hundred and three managed to scramble to the surface, but two hundred were killed directly by the explosion or by the after damp (carbon monoxide). Unofficial sources—miners who counted the bodies as they were carried out of the slopes—placed the number even higher, at 246; the discrepancy was due to the era's common practice of contract miners hiring additional laborers, including children.

Mine explosions are amazing in their randomness, and the Winter Quarters disaster, sometimes referred to as the Scofield because so many of the victims lived there, was no exception. James Naylor, a young Welsh boy, was blown two hundred feet away but made a soft landing and miraculously survived to assist in the rescue effort. Evan Williams was blown through a door but survived and walked out. Fifteen-year-old Tom Pugh bit down on his hat and then ran one and a half miles to fresh air; he fainted but remained safe. Amazingly, he had no light. His father, with whom he worked, was not so fortunate. Another Welshman, Roderick Davis, escaped the explosion, but reentered the mine to assist with the rescue and fell unconscious from after damp. He was then placed in a row of bodies at the rooming house being used as a temporary morgue, but when he was being washed Davis regained consciousness and walked out of the room on his own strength.[77]

With two hundred dead, and hundreds of widows and orphans without a breadwinner, the scale of the personal tragedy is hard to imagine. For "one of the Evans brothers," Winter Quarters brought back depressing memories as he "gazed at the mangled bodies" waiting to be prepared for burial: "I went through the Abercarn horror in Wales in 1878, when 240 were killed," he exclaimed, "but the scenes were tame compared with these." Two of the six Evans brothers at work in the mine that morning were killed. They were described as "professional musicians, and natives of Wales. They have taken prizes at all musical events in this locality." Richard T. Evans was praised by a local writer as "the sweetest singer in Israel," the name given to Utah by the Mormons.[78]

Most of the bereaved families faced significant practical problems. Welshman John T. Davis migrated to the United States in 1875 and lived in Scofield for twenty years; all his children had been born there. The deaths of J. T. Davis and his two sons, ages nineteen and twenty-one, left Mrs. Davis a widow with eight children to support. Many of the children suffered not just from lack of food and clothing, but because so many grief-stricken mothers could not properly care for their children. A local writer thought the grief was so widespread that it threatened "the disorganization of the community."[79]

It is unclear how many of the victims were Welsh, but Welsh, English, and Scottish families represented a large percentage of the mining community in and around Scofield, most of them Mormon converts. The official list of the two hundred killed in the explosion does not identify the place of birth, but at least one quarter of them have traditional Welsh surnames, and, given the history of the field, a large percentage were bound to be either Welsh or born to Welsh parents. Some of the Welsh had moved out of mining and into other occupations. John L. Price, for example, was born in South Wales in 1854. For seventeen years he worked in the mines of Pleasant Valley Coal Company and thirteen years for the Union Pacific mine, which was idle by 1900. At the time of the explosion Price had become town marshal. Bedlington E. Lewis was also a native of Wales and worked as a miner at Winter Quarters for six years. One year before the disaster he made a fortunate career decision by abandoning mining to become a professional photographer. Lewis documented the disaster with his photographs, and his work illustrates the pages of the only comprehensive, contemporary account of the disaster, James W. Dilley's *History of the Scofield Mine Disaster*. Dilley himself was born to Welsh parents in Wilkes-Barre, Pennsylvania, in 1861. A graduate of Bloomsburg (Pa.) State Normal School, Dilley became a teacher, principal of the Scofield Public School, and also the town clerk. The book chronicling the disaster was published to raise money for the survivors.[80]

The Winter Quarters disaster received media attention far and wide. Regrets came in from foreign governments, and President William McKinley sent his condolences. Neither state nor federal governments lent any financial assistance, but private relief collections totaled $110,000, according to Dilley's account. Welsh Latter Day Saints played a leading role in raising funds for the relief of widows and orphans left by the disaster. A. L. Thomas served as treasurer of the Salt Lake Relief Committee, which raised $20,000. The Cambrian Society of Salt Lake City also organized a concert in the Tabernacle, which was described as "the great popular concert of the year."[81]

Determining the cause of the explosion fell primarily on the shoulders of the Utah's lone mine inspector, Gomer Thomas. His 1893 report indicated how haphazardly the industry had developed in these remote mountains, claiming that with a few exceptions the mines were worked in a "primitive and incompetent manner." Mine managers were often chosen not because of their expertise but because of their connections with prominent share-holders. Unsafe practices were widespread. When Gomer Thomas accepted the position of state mine inspector in 1897, the only resources at his disposal were his own knowledge and experience. Fortunately, Thomas was a professional miner who had spent his entire life in the industry. Born in Wales in 1843, he emigrated in 1864 and worked in the mines of Pennsylvania and Ohio before settling in Utah in 1878. He held various positions with the Union Pacific Coal Company prior to his appointment as state coal mine inspector in 1897, including mine superintendent.[82]

Thomas's reports prior to the explosion indicate that he went to work immediately to correct the problems, focusing on the state's three largest mines, all of which were owned by the Pleasant Valley Coal Company. Winter Quarters was the largest by far in 1899, employing 342 men and producing 438,107 tons that year, 87 percent of the state's total production. Thomas inspected Winter Quarters seven times in 1899, reporting that superintendent William Parmley ran his mine professionally and attempted to correct the defects identified by Thomas.[83]

Thomas arrived at the scene shortly after the explosion, and worked tirelessly for two weeks as rescue crews searched for bodies. Then Thomas launched an investigation into the cause of the explosion. He took testimony from eight survivors, all of them highly experienced miners from Great Britain. Assisted by a team of company managers, Thomas Parmley, H. G. Williams, Robert Forrester, and George W. Snow, the inspector conducted a thorough analysis of all known factors pertaining to the explosion and reestablished the ventilation system that enabled the mine to reopen. Thomas concluded that "some person accidentally ignited a keg of powder which caused the dust to rise and ignited the same." Ten kegs of powder exploded in one place, twenty kegs in another, and fifty-six sticks of dynamite elsewhere, generating enough heat to ignite the coal dust. Storing explosives underground eased the workload but was a dangerous practice known to both miners and managers, and Thomas recommended limits on how much powder could be taken into the mines.[84]

Like most mine inspectors, Gomer Thomas was a lightning rod in the conflict between capital and labor and drew criticism from both sides. At the coroner's inquest he declared that the explosion was "either due to carelessness in handling explosives or to a windy or blown-out shot, thus igniting the dust, in air free from fire-damp." He also publicly defended the mine owners, pointing to the willingness of the managers to comply with his suggestions. This was not entirely correct because many changes recommended by the inspector, both before and after the explosion, were implemented only after persistent badgering or legal filings. Moreover, he seemed to blame the "careless miner" again when he pointed out that the miners had taken in too much powder and used dynamite, without mentioning that it was the manager's responsibility to prevent such practices. A Carbon County grand jury investigated the case for three days and concluded that no liability could be charged against the company. Many survivors disagreed and sued Pleasant Valley Coal Company, but it won each case. A few days after the coroner's inquest, where the inspector seemed to blame the miners and exonerated the company, Thomas was quoted in the *Salt lake Herald* as accusing Pleasant Valley of negligence. Later that day, Thomas issued a signed statement through the *Salt Lake Tribune*, a competing paper, declaring that the statement in the *Herald* was false, and that he was not in a position to lay the blame on any particular party.[85]

Largely as the result of Thomas's insistence, when the legislature met in 1901 it passed a law mandating measures to improve dust-control, ventilation, the use of explosives, and other safety improvements. Thomas continued to serve as the state's chief mine-safety advocate and encouraged the adoption of new inventions that reduced the dangers of mining, like the safety blasting cartridge used successfully in Pennsylvania in 1902. Although he continued to press for improved mine-safety measures, a divisive strike in 1903–4 largely diverted public attention to immediate concerns. His 1906 report notes that the law requiring explosives to be fired electronically when the mine was empty of men still languished in the legislature; the bill was not passed until 1924.[86]

By 1906, however, Gomer Thomas had reached the end of his professional life. As with most inspectors properly performing their duties, he made enemies among some employers as well as some miners. Although he still had political support in the governor's office, a Carbon County editorial declared that "Thomas has simply outlived his usefulness, if he ever had any."[87] Thomas's health was failing by then and he retired from the inspector's office in 1907. He died on September 1, 1912. His obituary stated: "He had not been well since the Winter Quarters Coal Mine disaster eleven years ago, when two hundred and one miners were killed." He was not injured by the explosion, but "inhaling the poisonous smoke and gases" had permanently affected his health. "One of the best informed men in Utah on coal and coal mines. . . . He belonged to no church, but was broad in his religious views and tolerant of the views and beliefs of others."[88]

Gomer Thomas was a professional mining man who attempted to institutionalize modern mine-safety procedures in Utah. He understood the lessons of Winter Quarters and tried to teach them to others, a function characteristic of all good mine inspectors. Whatever the industrial scale, large as in Pennsylvania, medium as in Ohio, or small as in Utah, it took decades to develop a professional corps of mine inspectors. The traditions they drew on were rooted in British experience and put into practice by British miners who immigrated to America. Many Welsh found an avenue of upward mobility in mine safety, and served a cause that improved the lives of their colleagues as well as those who lived and worked in these transnational spaces.

# ETHNIC CONFLICT THE WELSH & IRISH IN ANTHRACITE COUNTRY

6

The experience of ethnic miners in the coal regions of nineteenth-century America was contingent on their nationality and the timing of their arrival. English and Welsh miners were preferred for most of the century because of their experience, skills, and cultural compatibility with Americans. The Scots found a similar welcome, but their industrial migration began later in the century when the coalfields further west were being opened. The Germans, too, found a ready acceptance, but coal mining in Germany was not as technologically advanced as it was in Britain, so they were viewed as less skilled. While individuals within these groups encountered resistance from natives, they generated the kind of conflict triggered by outsiders elbowing their way into the local economy and community. Violent resistance to the Welsh as a group was almost unheard of. In addition to their perceived cultural compatibility, the Welsh arrived in the coalfields to build the industry, which the natives could not have accomplished on their own. The Americans needed the Welsh and they were treated accordingly.

The Irish, on the other hand, experienced a magnitude of hostility unlike any other immigrant group before them. They were viewed as a threat by many Americans because of their Catholicism, and because they arrived in numbers that aroused the anxiety of an overwhelmingly Protestant nation. In the nativist clamor to restrict their entry, the staunchly Nonconformist Welsh allied with the Americans. The Irish migration between 1845 and 1860 coincided with the dramatic expansion of the anthracite coalfields. Only a handful of the Irish had any mining experience, and most of them were chronically poor after suffering through years of famine in Ireland. Labor scarcity prompted companies to welcome the Irish, but British and American miners viewed them as an undesirable addition to their communities and as a threat to high wages.[1]

Nineteenth-century American coalfields were a patchwork of ethnic groups bound together only by the common occupational culture of coal mining, which organized their lives both inside and outside the mines. The

TABLE 4. Ethnic Composition of the Pennsylvania Anthracite
Coalfields, 1860, 1870

| County | 1860 | | 1870 | | | | |
|--------|------|------|------|------|------|------|------|
| | Native | Foreign | Total | Foreign | Irish | Welsh | German |
| Carbon | 21,033 | 5,324 | 28,144 | 6,964 | 3,577 | 1,456 | 1,651 |
| Columbia | 25,065 | 1,607 | 28,766 | 2,153 | 1,050 | 708 | 303 |
| Luzerne | 90,244 | 23,486 | 160,915 | 54,688 | 24,610 | 17,910 | 8,749 |
| Northumberland | 28,922 | 1,718 | 41,444 | 4,325 | 1,420 | 1,378 | 1,006 |
| Schuylkill | 89,510 | 26,267 | 116,428 | 30,856 | 13,465 | 9,333 | 6,701 |
| Totals | 254,774 | 58,402 | 375,697 | 98,986 | 44,122 | 30,785 | 18,410 |

Source: *Ninth Census of the United States, 1870: Population*, 1:369–70.

same should be said for Irish miners, such as John Siney, who came to America after years of working in Britain. This common culture developed within a shared technology, material culture, and social organization of British coal mining brought over by the English, Welsh, and Scottish miners. Whatever their national origin, all ethnic miners and their families lived out their lives on the monochromatic cultural landscape dominated by the same gray towns and houses, hovered around indistinguishable mine breakers and tipples, a regional organization determined by canals, roads, and railroads that linked the mines to the markets. They all knew the social roles, occupational ranks, and class structure within the industry, and recognized that there were great inequalities of wealth and power. Even though they shared the same physical and cultural landscape, they also understood that some would climb the ladder of success and others would not.[2]

Prior to the arrival of the eastern and southern Europeans in the late nineteenth century, the English language was also the medium of communication within anthracite culture. Welsh and German families continued to speak in their native tongues at home, clubs, churches, and newspapers for many years after their arrival. Nevertheless, nearly all of them developed a degree of facility in English, the language of American society and its institutions. Moreover, as Anthony Wallace found in his study of St. Clair, Pennsylvania, religious differences were generally "more conspicuous than important to working people, certainly less threatening to them than to the more evangelistic middle-class businessmen." Considerable social latitude was conceded for ethnic differences among mineworkers because no single ethnic group could physically dominate the cultural landscape or restrict the access of newcomers. People were acutely aware of what differentiated them from the others, but their personal lives were carried out within their own groups.[3]

Games, entertainment, and ethnic food preferences also provided the opportunity for notice. In a letter home, one Welsh miner expressed his bemused annoyance with his Irish neighbor's love for potatoes: "I know a man from near Merthyr who is laboring for an Irishman in these works and, from his appearance, I suspect that he did nothing but plant and pull up potatoes before coming to this country. This old sinner lives near where I stay and he thinks so much of the potatoes that one gets no peace from him even on the Lord's Day and he is continually busy with his hoe and his rake."[4] Cultural attitudes often collided in America even among the English speakers. The English generally thought Americans were rambunctious and vulgar, while the Americans thought the English were stiff and arrogant. The Scots regarded the Americans as too indecorous and informal, and the Americans thought the Scots were overly dour and humorless. Americans did not construct powerful negative stereotypes of the British immigrants, and while they caricatured the Welsh as "Taffy" or "Goat," these names did not pack much pejorative punch. Americans and British alike regarded the Irish as deprived, troublesome, even inferior members of the species; grotesque cartoon caricatures in the popular press portrayed the Irish as ignorant simians.[5]

### Roots of Animosity

By the mid-1840s about one-third of the population of Ireland was dependent on the potato for subsistence, and, as the world now knows, the potato famine of the forties cast most of them into destitution and outright starvation. Ireland was still overwhelmingly a rural agrarian society, one with a population growth of geometric proportions and natural energy supplies too scarce to sustain industrialization beyond small-scale factories and shops. Therefore, the famine resulted in a great migration and a transatlantic diaspora, beginning in the 1840s and continuing into the twentieth century. On the other hand, Wales in the 1840s was on the leading edge of industrialization in Britain, and South Wales in particular became a powerful magnet for Irish farmers who could no longer sustain themselves on the land.[6]

Trade had carried people back and forth across the Irish Sea between Wales and Ireland since ancient times, but industrialization in Wales gave a new and different impetus to trade between the two nations. Ireland was a major supplier of copper ore and tin plate to the industrial district of Swansea and Llanelli. Early in the nineteenth century, Welsh bar iron also was an important item of trade with Dublin and Belfast, but coal played a far more significant role in shaping the patterns of Irish migration to Wales than either copper or iron.[7]

The earliest industrial laborers migrating from Ireland were often found in the manual occupations, such as navvying, which the Welsh were not inclined to accept. By midcentury, however, most Irish workers came to work in the industrial centers of Swansea, Cardiff, Newport, and the coalfield valleys. Almost from the beginning, the Irish industrial migration prompted Welsh worries that the Irish immigrants would reduce wages and the standard of living. It was a commonsense reaction, and even the philosopher Thomas Malthus argued that Irish immigrants increased the labor supply and, consequently, depressed wages. In the coal and iron industries, therefore, the Irish confronted a determined resistance from the resident workforce. By controlling entry and knowledge of the craft, and by restricting the Irish to manual labor, Welsh miners maintained cultural as well as employment barriers to the newcomers, which natives perceived as maintaining the local standard of living but the Irish regarded as unjust discrimination.[8] The barriers confronted by the Irish in the anthracite fields of Pennsylvania, therefore, were an extension of the cultural patterns transplanted by Welsh immigrants.

Attempts by Welsh miners to drive potential Irish competitors out of the South Wales coalfield in order to preserve control over the local labor supply occurred simultaneously with their migration to the Pennsylvania anthracite coalfields. As in the United States, the virulence of the inevitable ethnic clashes was aggravated by the stresses imposed by strikes and economic downturns. As early as 1826, following the importation of sixty or seventy Irish laborers, several hundred Welsh workers responded by stoning the Irish and besieging them in their shelter for three days until a detachment of troops arrived to save them. Although some historians have claimed that the cause of the rumpus was wages, the leading authority on the Irish in Wales, Paul O'Leary, quoting official correspondence, states that the Welsh were "dissatisfied that any people but their own Countrymen should be employed." The notion that the Irish intruders had violated the customary rights of resident Welsh workers is one found everywhere in the industrializing world, and often resulted in what Eric J. Hobsbawm called "collective bargaining by riot." These spontaneous reactions took on unique local features shaped by the culture that gave them form, and is clearly seen in the enforced social justice of the Scotch Cattle movement and its more ancient cultural precursor, the *ceffyl pren*, or ritualistic mock trial of the folk.[9]

The material and cultural basis for the hostile reception of the Irish in Wales was greatly aggravated by the huge influx resulting from the potato famine. Between 1845 and 1850 hundreds of thousands of Irish left their native land to escape starvation, and thousands of them went to Wales. Between 1841 and 1851 the Irish-born population in Wales mushroomed by 153 percent while the overall population grew only 11 percent. This dramatic influx of destitute people created the perception of the Irish as a "social problem." In Wales the Famine Irish were regarded as tramps and beggars who overloaded the public relief system, people with poor health who were carriers of disease, lived in squalid housing, and compounded their poverty by excessive consumption of alcohol. These appalling conditions might have produced sympathy for the Irish, but the Welsh associated them with chaos and violent behavior. "Faction fighting" in pre-famine Ireland involved clashes between feuding families or villages, or simply boisterous bravado. The practice was transmitted with the Irish emigrants to Wales (and America), where faction fights frequently erupted between immigrants from different regions or towns.[10]

Given this attitude toward the Irish and the fact that they sometimes entered the coalfield as strikebreakers, conflicts were inevitable. In South Wales, however, miners and ironworkers went a step further and virtually drove the Irish out of the valleys. Mobs attempted to expel the Irish from Beaufort, Ebbw Vale, and Brynmawr in the 1850s. In 1869 a crowd of over one thousand attacked Irish homes in Pontlottyn (near Rhymney), causing severe damage and killing one Irishman. Reportedly, the Irish had undercut wages, but a deep-seated hostility had existed between the Welsh and Irish of Pontlottyn for forty years. The Welsh workers channeled their deep-seated animosities through efforts to protect their customary rights reinforced by the self-serving theory that an Irishman was constitutionally incapable of replacing a Welshman. While Welsh miners sought to protect the value of their labor by controlling entry into the craft, employers increasingly assumed the right to employ whomsoever they pleased, and to pay the lowest wages the market would bear. Workers still observed customary rights, but employers increasingly played by the rules of capitalism.[11]

Until the mid-nineteenth century, the main points of conflict were in the iron industry, but thereafter the focus of ethnic clashes shifted to the coal mines, where a sharp division prevailed in status and pay between skilled hewers at the coal face and unskilled outside labor. More than twenty years after the famine migrants arrived, they were still largely absent from the coal face. By the late 1860s, the small mines worked by recent migrants from the countryside were eclipsed by large-scale industrial operations. Thereafter, much deeper shafts were sunk into the middle of the South Wales coalfield, which required greater capital investment. A larger and more diversified labor force was massed, and communities therefore became larger and more diverse. These new towns bore no resemblance to the earlier mine villages, and old deferential class relations gave way to the rise of a working-class consciousness. In this larger context of dramatic change, ethnic relations between the Welsh and Irish immigrants became intertwined with class warfare.[12]

Anti-Irish episodes may be divided into two broad categories: those which emanated from the workplace, such as strikebreaking and undercutting wages, and those disturbances that arose within the mine community, such as pub brawls, ethnic gang assaults, or anti-Catholic bigotry. They were not mutually exclusive categories, and often the two were intertwined. Anti-Irish hostility succeeded in preventing a major penetration of the Irish into the South Wales coalfield. During the last half of the nineteenth century, when the population of the Rhondda virtually exploded to more than 150,000 by 1911, fewer than one thousand Irish resided there. The Tredegar riots of 1882 demonstrate the reason. The press reported on July 11, 1882, that "the houses of at least sixty Irishmen were gutted and that all the furniture in those houses was burnt to the public streets; and that not only men but women and children were attacked by the mob."[13] The Welsh and English had been throwing stones and fighting with the Irish for some time prior to the riot, and, while the Irish had tried to avoid an all-out battle, this time they fought back. Eventually, two hundred Royal Welsh Fusileers were sent to Tredegar to quell the riots; when it was over, sixty Irish houses had been destroyed and another one hundred gutted by the mob. During the disturbance the Irish fled en masse. Wild rumors circulated about the causes, mostly of purporting Irish atrocities about to be committed. However, the causes were more correctly analyzed by the Reverend William Williams, the local Catholic priest, who claimed that the riots were triggered by the Irish taking jobs Welshmen regarded as rightfully their own. According to Father Williams, "There has always been a grudge rumbling in the minds of the Welsh people in the iron and coal districts in consequence of employing Irish. Our works are being converted from iron works to steel works, and it is certain that many men who found employment here before would not be able to find it in the future because steel works employ far fewer men than iron works and because puddling is not required. Most of the puddlers here are Welshmen[;] they might be able to cut coal in collieries but the collieries are already overmanned and wages in consequence low, so the colliers object."[14]

As so frequently is the case, native Welsh found absolution for their violence against the Irish interlopers in religion (as discussed in Chapter 3). In reaction to the 1847 "Treachery of the Blue Books," Welsh Nonconformity constructed a populist concept of Welsh nationality in which they defined themselves as chaste, church-going, and law-abiding people. Blaming the Irish for criminality and lax morals conveniently deflected the criticism of the "Blue Books" away from the Welsh. Similarly, charging the Irish with depressing wages undermined community and was, therefore, an obvious way to blame the anti-Irish riots on the victims themselves without tarnishing the image of a "virtuous nation."[15]

Linking the Irish with immorality persisted long after the debate over the Blue Books had subsided. The views contained in a paper read at the National Eisteddfod at Merthyr Tydfil in 1881 claimed that the "ignorant and dissipated habits" of the Irish in the Rhondda mining districts inflated the crime statistics and gave a "misleading impression of Welsh criminality." Nonconformists regarded intemperance as the chief obstacle to achieving the ideals of thrift, self-help, and self-reliance that marked men as "respectable." The Welsh saw themselves continuously striving to achieve the ideal, and the Irish as their binary opposites. Sunday closing of the pubs in Wales after 1881 was regarded by many as the harbinger of Welsh nationhood. Working people in the mining and agricultural districts supported the act, but it initiated a growing estrangement between the ideals of the temperance movement and the actual behavior of the people. Ultimately it was the Catholic Church that defined the Irish identity by providing the religious and institutional cohesion for the Irish, but also a focus for the Welsh opposition. It is generally agreed that the Catholic Church hampered assimilation and galvanized the Welsh Nonconformists who were sustained by their opposition to the established Church of England; the Catholic Church it grew out of was simply anathema.[16]

This history of Welsh-Irish conflict in Wales was transported across the Atlantic by the emigrants. In America the first-generation Welsh continued to condemn the Irish for their uncleanliness, ungodliness, insobriety, general bellicosity, and rowdiness, constant themes in Welsh emigrants' letters home in the nineteenth century.[17] And, as in Wales, in no sphere of life was this traditional animosity more pronounced than in work relations.

## Welsh "Bossism"

The Welsh assimilated relatively easily into American society, but the ethnic conflict they did encounter emanated from their dominant position in the coal industry and with their old-world antagonists, the Irish. Welsh miners dominated the skilled and managerial positions in the anthracite coalfields. In fact, they enjoyed a near monopoly over positions of power and responsibility, such as superintendent, inside and outside foreman, and fire boss. Upward mobility in the coal industry was very competitive because there were relatively few supervisory positions. In Schuylkill County, for example, between June 1869 and June 1870, there were 91 collieries in operation with 15,778 total employees who were managed by 91 mine bosses, 91 assistant mining bosses, and 91 breaker bosses.[18]

With so few managerial positions, the success rate for the Welsh, particularly in the northern anthracite field around Wilkes-Barre and Scranton, is all the more remarkable. Welsh preponderance in the supervisory roles was a notable feature of the anthracite industry, but it was also common throughout the coal industry prior to World War I. The extent of their influence is examined in chapters 2 and 3 but is well illustrated in the case of the mines owned by the Delaware, Lackawanna and Western Railroad Company, the most powerful company in the northern anthracite field. Welsh supervisors were ubiquitous in the organization from the pit bottom to the central office throughout the late nineteenth century: Benjamin F. Hughes, general inside superintendent of mines; Hughes's assistant between 1872 and 1889, Thomas D. Davies; the company's chief engineer, Henry D. Phillips; and Phillips's assistant, Richard Evans—all were Welsh. When Thomas D. Davies resigned to run the New York and Scranton Coal Company's properties, his replacement was another Welshman, Thomas H. Phillips, who had been the Jermyne Coal Company's superintendent of mines. In 1898 Colonel Reese A. Phillips, the inside foreman at Oxford mine, became Benjamin F. Hughes's assistant and succeeded Hughes as inside general superintendent following the latter's death in 1900. This was a spectacular rise for one who had started life as a trapper boy. All these men rose through the ranks into management. They were, however, only the most visible of the company's "Welsh dynasty."[19]

There is no question that knowledge and previous experience in coal mining was the single most important asset that Welsh immigrants brought with them to America. Nearly all of them hailed from South Wales, where they acquired mining experience unrivaled by any other ethnic group. Without this experience and knowledge, they would not have been recruited to build the industry in the first place. Maintaining that dominant position, however, called for an approach utilized by many immigrant groups struggling to secure a rung on nineteenth-century America's economic ladder— ethnic nepotism. The Welsh took advantage of their privileged position not only to maintain their own dominance, but also to further the interests of their own nationality. This was very well understood at the time by everybody in the industry, from mine owners down to mine laborers. If concerned at all, the owners looked the other way because they believed that Welshmen were the best judges of how to run coal mines. The overwhelmingly Irish mine laborers, however, were convinced that the owners colluded with the Welsh to prevent the Irish from securing skilled positions.[20]

Allan Pinkerton, founder of the Pinkerton Detective Agency that was used extensively by the coal companies to spy on the anthracite miners, claimed that "Welsh bosses discharged all the Irishmen under them in order to make way for fellow countrymen just arrived from Wales."[21] Welsh underground foremen were widely criticized for granting the best places to miners of their own nationality, as well as a whole host of common practices that might be considered abuses of power. The inequities embedded in the system created tensions among the Welsh themselves when, for example, Welsh bosses pushed them to increase production, thus pitting the miners' ethnic loyalties against their class interests. Welsh foremen were often caught between their ethnic brethren who worked for them and the managerial middle class to which they aspired. Historian William Jones has concluded that the weight of the evidence suggests that the "unenviable popular reputation of Welsh mine foremen was deserved." Welshmen found foremen of their own nationality every bit as domineering toward Welsh miners as they were toward others. Welsh American newspapers often carried letters and stories complaining of Welsh foremen who acted like "tyrants." The Welsh American community acknowledged the foremen among them were competent, hardworking, and "respectable," and conceded that this intra-ethnic class antagonism might be the product of envy. Yet it was also admitted that Welsh mine managers often forgot "the rock from which they had been hewn" and took advantage of their position to further their own interests at the expense of others.[22] "Hen Golier" (Old Miner or Collier) of Ashland, Pennsylvania, complained in Y Drych in 1885 that Welsh bosses generated hostility from all ethnic groups who worked under them; citing a common charge of miners everywhere, "Hen Golier" claimed that the attitude among foremen was that mules were more important than miners. If a miner was hurt or killed he was easily replaced at no cost, but another mule cost the company money. Above ground, Welsh bosses might have been respectable citizens who attended chapel regularly, but underground they became crude tyrants who ruled corrupt regimes. What the Welsh mining community found most irritating, however, was the demeanor of Welsh bosses who strutted about full of their own importance. "*Hen Golier*" complained that these bosses "must be in the forefront in the chapel, in every committee, in every donation, in every festival and the better of every minister; and they are, of course, so knowledgeable, and so capable in their criticism that they can discuss, measure and weigh them all up. They do this at work, surrounded by a lot of men who must smile in appreciation, even though they are poking fun of their [the bosses'] behaviour in their hearts. I have had to listen to a boss in this way but there was no point in my saying anything derogatory, otherwise I would surely feel his displeasure in my work." "*Hen Golier*" concluded that bosses should "remember that it was their duty to be respectful and gentlemanly towards the workers, who after all were the source of the wealth and success of the mining companies and who deserved as much consideration as the investors."[23]

Similarly, "*Mwnwr*" (Miner) observed that life in Hyde Park was no less oppressive in America than it had been in South Wales. Bosses still ruled community institutions as they did the pits. They might have hired Welsh miners before other ethnic groups, but within the group they also favored those miners who belonged to their own chapels. Consequently, a mine might be filled with Welsh miners, but they recognized that the mine bosses favored men of their own denomination. It was obligatory for bosses to be Masons as well, and those who aspired to rise took note of the fact. Even the cultural activities of the Welsh community were taken from the people by the managers, complained "*Mwnwr*." The 1872 Scranton eisteddfod had failed, he observed, because the mine bosses had taken control of the event, and the Welsh Philosophical Society had become a mutual admiration society where Welsh bosses met to honor each other. Worse still, the Welsh workers had become servile in the face of "bossism." Even the purchasing habits of the Welsh community was shaped by the fact that many bosses either operated or were partners in stores, and they were assured of patronage because "we are so slavish in our spirit and so very careful to keep the boss happy, and our wives, who get what the family needs from the store, are more careful than we are to keep him and his wife happy; the boss knows this as well as we do . . . a worker [will] change the store he shops in because . . . 'that's where the boss trades now.' " "*Mwnwr*" exclaimed, "This is the freedom of America, or the freedom of the Welsh Athens of America! . . . freedom for the boss to rule over us in work and in the town, and freedom for us to make him rich. . . . This is not fair, legal, and just. . . . I prefer the Company Store which is open to the world in its dealings, like our shop in Scranton, than the screws and the underhand, secret, cunning oppression we get in Hyde Park."[24]

Again, it is difficult to know if the attitudes expressed in these and other letters published in Welsh and Welsh American publications were accurate assessments of Welsh bosses; there were those who denied these accusations. Most likely, Welsh foremen used their power to further their own interests in the style that became traditionally associated with mine bosses generally, before the large modern corporation and a powerful miners' union protected miners from such abuses. "Screwing," or wringing money from the workers by "applying the screw," was a particular irritant. Bosses often coerced their workers to give to charities, subscribe to papers, deal at stores, or otherwise financially support enterprises in which they had a personal interest. In fact, this became an entrenched practice in the industry that extended to union officials as well. John Mitchell, the legendary president of the United Mine Workers of America during the first decade of the twentieth century, used his office and the union newspaper to promote scores of products (from soap to tobacco) in which he had a personal financial interest.[25]

Miners of every ethnic origin complained about foremen and managers, but Irish laborers encountered real occupational discrimination in the anthracite coal districts even lower down in the working-class hierarchy. They usually arrived without mining experience, but the lack of experience alone does not explain why the Irish found it so difficult to rise above laborer. In a study of St. Clair, Pennsylvania, one scholar claimed that, according to the 1850 census, experience had not benefited the Irish as much as the English, Welsh, or Germans, and they were concentrated in the status of mine laborer even though they also represented old immigrant stock. Of those listed as miners and laborers in 1850 St. Clair, 167 Irish were laborers and only 24 were miners (12.6 percent). Among the English, however, 10 were laborers and 73 were miners (88 percent), and among the Welsh only 6 were laborers and 73 were miners (92.4 percent). Even among the newest of the immigrants, the Germans, 36 were laborers, and 45 (55.6 percent) were miners. By 1870, the Irish had improved their status in St. Clair; there were 58 laborers and now 78 (57.4 percent) miners. Among the English, 22 were laborers and 180 (89.1 percent) were miners, and among the Welsh 42 were laborers while 134 miners (80 percent) were miners. Of the smaller German group, 17 were laborers and 40 (70.2 percent) were miners.[26]

Ethnicity as a marker of who rose within the mining hierarchy stirred great resentment among the Irish laborers trapped in the hard, low-paying status of laborer. As skilled men, miners did not perform the menial tasks; these were left to the laborers they hired. In the northern anthracite field, the miners hired and paid their own laborers. Elsewhere in the anthracite fields, the company assigned the laborers and deducted their wages from the miners' gross earnings, and in 1902 this became the universal system throughout the region. The rule from at least the 1860s to 1902 was that the laborer received one-third of the miners' gross earnings.[27]

In the late 1860s a Welsh American miner reported to a newspaper back in Wales that "the laborer's work is fairly hard and this is the first work a stranger gets when first coming here and it has become the custom for a man to labor first of all wherever he comes from. Most labor for six to nine months before they get a place of their own. The laborer's wage is one third of that earned by the miner."[28] In the 1870s a laborer complained that "we often hear of the injustice of the coal operators toward the miners," but few of the operators "treated the miners so bad as the miners have treated the laborers."[29] Some Welshmen recognized the legitimacy of these complaints. Writing home, one miner reviled:

> The unfairness of the system to the laborer who has to fill from six to seven cars a day with coal and he gets but one third of the wages of the miner. . . . The miner and laborer go to work at seven o'clock in the morning and [the miner] probably will go out leaving the [laborer to] fill three or four cars with coal after the gentleman had left. He will wash, put on a shirt, and white collar and will go to dinner boasting that he has cut enough coal for the laborer. After he has had enough, he calls for his cigarbox and enjoys himself for an hour or two and because he is a religious man he says that it is nearly time for him to go to a prayermeeting. Between five and six o'clock the laborer, poor thing, arrives home as wet as a fish and after eating his supper, in spite of his weariness, goes to the prayermeeting and who should be praying at the time but the man he works for. These are the words he uses. "May our peace be like the river our justice like the waves of the sea." Oh! Terrible hypocrite![30]

Although this Welshman was complaining for the benefit of his compatriots who might be planning to work in American mines, the letter demonstrates the inequities of the system. Rather than improve the opportunities for advancement, the miners marshaled a political campaign for legislation to protect their privileged position. In 1889 they finally succeeded in persuading the Pennsylvania legislature to incorporate a certification requirement for miners in the Mine Safety Act. To be certified, the miner had to prove that he had worked two years as a miner's laborer, and was required to pass an examination demonstrating his technical expertise to a board of nine skilled miners. In 1895 an attempt to repeal the law providing for the certification of miners was introduced in the Pennsylvania legislature on grounds that the law did not work as intended. Rather than keep out unskilled laborers, it deterred skilled British miners who would not work the required two years as a laborer in order to obtain a certificate. The bill did not pass, but did point to an undesirable, and unintended, consequence of the reform.[31]

Experience was presumed to be the determinant of qualifications, but the concentration of the Irish in the laborer classification well into the 1880s cannot be explained by inexperience when they had been in America for decades. It is more likely that Welsh miners, managers, and operators sought to protect Welsh control of the craft and camouflaged it with stereotypes about Irish suitability only for unskilled labor. The linkage between ethnicity and occupational status constructed in South Wales became a deepening fault line between Welsh miners and Irish laborers in the American coalfields.

Since job classification was drawn along ethnic lines, the privileged position of the Welsh further magnified ethnic differences and diminished the common bond between all mineworkers. In 1871, an Irishman, "J. C." of Pittston, Pennsylvania, formerly a laborer in Hyde Park, described how he came to the conclusion that the Welsh miners were, in his words, "tyrannical":

When I worked in Hyde Park, I was not only obliged to do my own work but the greater part of that miner that hired me. It was John or Pat or Jacob or Hans "give me the drill, the scraper, the needle, the wedge; go get some tamping and then help me tamp the hole." This I was expected to do after drilling four out of five feet of hole, while we poor devils innocently believed him to be preparing a cartridge to be put in the hole that we had to drill, and when there was enough coal cut, no matter how hard or how long the labourer had to work, Mr. Welshman put on his coat and went home to enjoy himself in the bosom of his family, cultivate his mind if he felt so disposed or engage in any other amusement.

And we get a nominal one-third of the sum total, whilst we performed nine-tenths of the sum total of work.[32]

## The Welsh Strike of 1871

The Welsh strike of 1871 released the pent-up grievances of the Irish laborers against the Workingmen's Benevolent Association in the northern anthracite district, which was dominated by the Welsh miners even though Irish laborers were also members. In November 1870, miners in the northern field carried their tools out of the mines rather than accept a 30 percent wage reduction. They convinced the leadership of the WBA to call a general anthracite strike, but their counterparts in the southern and middle fields failed to respond, in part because the northern miners had failed to support their strike two years earlier. The strike resulted in extensive property damage, beatings, and the death of several miners and strike breakers, and required the presence of the Pennsylvania National Guard for several months to restore order.[33]

The strike was confined primarily to the northern field against the Scranton companies, particularly the Delaware, Lackawanna & Western Railroad Company (DL&W), the Delaware and Hudson, and the Pennsylvania Coal Company. The stoppage was intended to prevent further erosion of their wages and to maintain the system that linked wages to the price of coal, known as "the basis" in America, and the "sliding scale" in Britain. According to reporter Phoebe Gibbons, the "leading Welshmen" preferred compromise to striking, but they were outnumbered by "the more reckless of their own nation." Although initially reluctant, the Welsh put up a determined fight once they had taken up the cause.[34]

The strike commenced; many of the Welsh miners migrated to the Schuylkill field, others went further west to the opening bituminous fields, and some undoubtedly returned to Wales. Most stayed, however, and survived on financial reserves that their relatively high incomes allowed them to put aside for the periodic disruptions miners expected. The Welsh also dominated leadership of the Scranton local of the Workingmen's Benevolent Association; the president, John P. Lewis, and secretary, Watkin H. Williams, headed the local strike committee. The prominent role of the Welsh as protagonists prompted the public to refer to the stoppage as the "Welsh strike," highlighting another set of tensions inherent in the Welsh position of dominance. On the one hand, the owners regarded them as clannish and radical unionists, while on the other the Irish perceived the Welsh as a privileged, managerial group. This perception was enhanced, perhaps unwittingly, by "H.P.M.," who wrote several letters to the *Morning Republican* editor justifying the strike. One letter claimed that the companies had caused the strike by paying starvation wages and "intimidating our bosses by arousing the spirit of nationalities against them just because they happen to be (a majority of them) Welsh."[35]

The perception of Welsh domination was further reinforced by the cohesive support the miners received from local Welsh merchants and Welsh ministers who publicly advocated the miners' cause from their pulpits. Welsh mine supervisors found themselves in the uncomfortable position of choosing between loyalty to their company or their ethnic community. Most chose the latter. In fact, even some Welsh foremen demonstrated the primacy of their ethnic loyalty by quietly assisting the miners' struggle. The *Scranton Morning Republican* reported that one Welsh foreman, Enoch Davis, "made haste to inform his clansmen, the Welsh," when he learned that the German laborers at his pit had decided to return to work. The editor questioned whether "the aforesaid bosses living in Hyde Park lifted a finger to point out the fallacies into which the workmen have fallen?" He thought it "strange that the little dependency of Wales should have a patent for exclusive manufacture of mining bosses."[36]

While actions such as Davis's were applauded in the Welsh community, they prompted some owners to reappraise their commitment to Welsh managers. Following this particular episode, W. R. Storrs, the general agent of the DL&W in Scranton, reported to company headquarters that "our intentions are to make all foremen for some time to come out of other material than Welshmen if we can find them." Benjamin Hughes, the superintendent at the DL&W's Diamond mine in Hyde Park, attempted to avoid making a public choice between loyalty to his countrymen and to the company. For his effort, Hughes was immediately distrusted by the business and industrial elites because he was Welsh, and his silence prompted distrust among the Welsh because of his prominence as a manager.[37]

When destitute Irish laborers approached the companies about reopening the mines, the owners saw their opportunity for breaking the union by firing a number of Welsh miners and hiring Irish and German laborers to take their places. In response to this divide-and-conquer strategy, Welsh miners resorted to a strategy of intimidation, or "Ku Klux" methods according to a local newspaper, which precipitated violent confrontations. Miners who went down in Tripp's Slope confronted nearly one thousand strikers when they came up at the end of the shift and were greeted by a shower of stones; some were beaten and several were shot. Roving bands of strikers broke up meetings of laborers, damaged strikebreakers' homes, burned down a coal breaker, attacked foremen, and assaulted Irishmen. Acts of violence and retribution were aimed in both directions, however. Early on the morning of March 4, shots were fired into the house of WBA leader David Williams, resulting in the death of a man named Hoffman when a shot exploded a keg of black powder stored in the house. The situation deteriorated to the point where the governor felt compelled to declare martial law in Scranton, and the Pennsylvania National Guard patrolled the area for several months.[38]

The miners ignored the laborers' demands that the strike be called off, which led to an inevitable split in the Workingmen's Benevolent Association along ethnic lines. During the last week of the strike, ethnic acrimony prompted Irish laborers to organize their own Laborers' Association, leaving no doubt that their action was in response to Welsh domination of the chambers. "Laborers" wrote that it was time for the "miners' slaves (for that is what we are)" to ask the companies if the laborers could "have and retain the chambers, if we will mine coal at the price named by the company." While the miners went on strike because they could not live on their wages, "Laborer" continued, they tell the laborer that "we must live on one third less. . . . Now is our time . . . let the company reply, and we will organize." In another letter to the editor the following day, "One of the Oppressed" sought assurances that if the laborers did return and take the places of the Welsh miners, the companies would not permit their bosses to fire the laborers turned miners "on some pretext of incompetency, when their real motive is merely to get him out of the way to enable them to give his place to one of their own 'cousins.'" The depth of distrust was illustrated in the conspiracy theory "One of the Oppressed" advanced, which claimed that the Welsh miners' strike "is to protect suspension, starve the laborer, force him to seek work elsewhere, so that in the event of resumption they could employ green hands, and pocket the proceeds of their labor."[39]

This conspiracy theory must have been common among the Irish laborers and rooted in historical experience. "A Doomed Laborer" charged that the Welsh, who were "as rich as the companies," would sustain the strike until the companies came to terms. At the same time they would starve the Irish out of the coalfield and then they would "do as they have done in Wales—to hunt down the Irishman as they have done from Aberdare to Mountain Ash. How many a poor Irishman, looking for honest bread and labor in that principality, has fell victim to those selfish butchers?" The laborers could not afford to wait any longer for justice, he continued, for they had "never got anything but drudgery from the Welsh foremen." He warned the laborers to "put no faith in the Welsh miners, they have too often betrayed you; they have too long been your task masters."[40]

The laborers apparently followed this advice, for they began holding meetings to form their own Laborers' Association. The Welsh miners correspondingly stepped up pressure to hold the laborers in line, and events began to spiral out of control. At a meeting on May 9, it was reported that "a crowd of frenzied Welsh females" and twenty or thirty Welshmen stormed in, "throwing stones at the laborers, and calling them 'blacklegs' and every opprobrious epithet their filthy tongues could utter." Not wanting to confront them, the laborers withdrew, "but they were immediately followed by the infuriated Amazons, who continued to shower stones on them." The laborers moved again and the Welsh moved up to the front. A general riot ensued with several shots fired, one lodging in the thigh of a laborer. During the melee, men, women, and boys all joined in and a number were injured, including some of the Welsh women. The Welsh pulled back, but hundreds of reinforcements soon arrived to join in the assault upon the laborers. The authority on the Scranton Welsh, William D. (Bill) Jones, writes that the women's attack is "strikingly reminiscent of similar actions by women in resisting strikebreakers in the Welsh coalfields and the manner they were reported in the press." The following day two dead laborers were found in the swamp near the riot. They had been beaten and kicked to death.[41]

On May 10 the laborers met and officially withdrew from the Workingmen's Benevolent Association. The New York Times reported that the strike had "resolved itself into a war of races, the Welsh against the Irish and Germans." Father Hennessey, a priest who attended the meeting, advised the laborers "to stand together as Catholics, with Irishmen and Germans, and to forever ignore the Welsh miners' union, and free themselves from bondage." The laborers then passed resolutions denouncing the "premeditated assassination of Irishmen," the Scranton paper reported, and declared that "we Irishmen, laborers and miners throughout the district, dissever and stand aloof from having any connection respecting union and fraternity with the Welshmen in the future."[42]

The Irish turned out en masse the following day at a large meeting of the laborers and voted to return to work. They also resolved that they had "no animosity to the Welsh as a class," but they did harbor a "deep sense of the wrongs which have been inflicted on us by the inside foremen for the last quarter of a century." Moreover, the Welsh miners had been subjecting the Irish laborers "to a tyranny which was no longer tolerable," and the circum-

The Welsh strike, 1871: strikebreakers attacked at Tripp's Slope. *Frank Leslie's Illustrated Magazine* 32 (April 29, 1871): 108.

stances that found "laborers working in this district for ten or twelve years, [and] they have not been able to get a chamber." By May the strike had taken on the form of a "race war" according to the *New York Times*, and the "Welsh banditti," as the press called them, ultimately found themselves pitted against all of the laborers whatever their ethnicity. The papers were filled with reports of violent episodes perpetrated by persons unknown, including beatings, shootings, explosions at railroad tracks and mine openings, and incendiary attacks.[43]

The final episode occurred on May 17 when a group of Irish strikebreakers were being escorted home from work at the Briggs Shaft by the state militia, accompanied by coal operator William Scranton. In addition to the military detachment that marched in the rear, ten laborers on the flanks were armed with Remington rifles. As they marched down the street through Hyde Park, they were hazed by a crowd lining the street, and at the end of the street another crowd of 200 Welshmen blocked their passage. Intimidated by the

The Welsh strike, 1871: laborers' meeting broken up by Welsh miners and their wives.
*Frank Leslie's Illustrated Magazine* 32 (May 27, 1871): 177.

crowd, one of the strikebreakers, Michael Cairns ("Fenian"), fired his rifle
and killed Benjamin Davis and Daniel Jones. Both were Welsh-born miners,
members of the Workingmen's Benevolent Association, and respected
members of the Hyde Park community. The crowd scattered for cover but
soon regrouped into a still larger crowd and, according to the local newspaper, the Welsh women were "giving full vent to the force of their lungs in
the most terrific howls."[44]

The shootings outraged the Welsh, and they prevailed upon Alderman
D. M. Jones, a Welshman, to arrest Michael Cairns, William Garrety, president of the Laborer's Association, and William W. Scranton for ordering the
shots that killed Davis and Jones. A Welsh witness testified at the coroner's
inquest that, when he encountered the Welsh crowd, Scranton had shouted,
"We'll give them the price of labor," convincing many that he had played a
direct role in the killings. The men were taken to Wilkes-Barre for their own
safety and released on bail. The deaths produced an explosion of indignation from the Welsh, but also released the last air out of the strike. The men

charged with their deaths were released, and charges against them were dropped. With the streets quiet again, the militia was withdrawn from Scranton on May 25.[45]

The strike was over by June, but the hostility between the Welsh and Irish continued to fester long afterward. The *New York Times* noted six months later that "differences of race and religion have apparently proved more powerful than the common interests of labor. The Welsh miners distrust the Irish, and the Irish refuse to be guided by any propositions save those emanating from their own countrymen." Consequently, the miners' organization in the northern field "appears to be practically broken up," the *Times* noted.[46]

The deaths of Davis and Jones reinforced Welsh solidarity, but it also revealed how isolated the Welsh had become. The strike highlighted the relationship between the Welsh concentration in coal mining and the strong sense of cohesion that allowed them to reproduce their own distinct ethnic identity. In fact, the ability of the Welsh miners to sustain a long strike, even though they were almost completely isolated, was possible only because of the strength derived from the fusion of their ethnic and occupational identities.[47]

There were some reprisals against the Welsh by their employers, but most of the miners returned to their old jobs, which reemphasized the importance of their skills and further frustrated Irish hopes of replacing the Welsh at the work face. The Workingmen's Benevolent Association in Scranton was destroyed. Some unsympathetic merchants found their businesses boycotted by the Welsh, and community meetings continued in the effort to raise money and support for the prosecution of Scranton and Cairns. This persistent hostility was seen as counterproductive by some, particularly the heads of industry who wanted nothing more than a return to normalcy. The DL&W's chief agent in Scranton, W. R. Storrs, wrote to his superior in New York, Sam Sloan, on May 23 informing him that "our Welch [sic] friends are holding exclusive meetings which excite Irish jealousy and some fear may lead to trouble," particularly since the purpose of these gatherings was "to prevent trade or intercourse with any but Welshmen."[48]

The Welsh also sought retribution against the *Scranton Morning Republican*, which represented the city's middle-class Anglo-Saxon Republicans and generally was favorably disposed to the Welsh, who seemed so solidly part of this group. Once it was clear that the Welsh were leading the strike, the *Scranton Republican* turned on them, and the Welsh were deeply offended. In June a large general assembly of Welsh passed a resolution condemning the *Republican*. "Whereas, the Welsh miners and laborers of Luzerne County, as well as the Welsh people in general," the resolution began, "have been misrepresented by the press and declared to be an element of danger in the community, of malicious and riotous disposition, unworthy of social recognition and other wise slandered and vilified." The *Republican* was condemned for its biased editorials, its subservience to the corporations, and attempts to "divide the people into nationalities, and put them one against the other." Because the Republican Party had remained silent while the paper slandered them, the Welsh resolved, therefore, to "form ourselves into an association independent of political parties." The *Scranton Republican* denied the charges in an adjoining editorial, noting that "people know that there has never been any love lost between the Welsh and Irish." The Welsh could join any party it chose, but the editor warned that they should avoid the anti-Irish Know-Nothingism of the past.[49]

With Welsh preachers and bosses taking the lead, a campaign was conducted to boycott the *Scranton Republican*. At "weekly indignation meetings," the paper reported, the "Taffys" hurled abuse at the paper, and their community leaders canvassed Luzerne County looking for support for a boycott of the paper. But what else could be expected from Hyde Park, the editor opined, that "headquarters of ignorance and obstinacy." Whether under community pressure or for some other reason, the late-night editor at the *Scranton Republican*, Welshman Ellis R. Williams, left the paper in June 1871 to become city editor for the *Scranton Daily Democrat*.[50]

Another important consequence of the strike for Welsh miners was a reassessment of their allegiance to the Republican Party. Welsh miners in Scranton were loyal Republicans, at least in part because the Irish and Germans exercised considerable influence in the Democratic Party. In fact, ethnicity was the dominant motif of political life in Scranton during the late nineteenth century among both the Republicans and the Democrats, and political campaigns in the city were organized upon and around ethnic antagonisms. Their isolation from the broader community and the Republican Party during the strike prompted Welsh miners to undertake independent political action in 1871 and 1872 and paved the way for more independent campaigns in 1877 and 1878, another period of bitter labor unrest locally in Scranton as well as nationally.[51]

For a brief period, loss of the 1871 strike prompted many Welsh miners to opt for independent political rather than industrial action to protect their interests. In Hyde Park, Welsh leaders held a meeting on February 27, 1871, where a new political party was announced, the Workingman's Political

Party. Resolutions declared that the coal and railroad companies had combined to "deprive workingmen of their lawful rights" as citizens, and, whereas both houses of the legislature as well as the two major parties were dominated by capital and monopoly, the Workingman's Political Party was organized "to defend the fundamental principles of our Republic." In the summer of 1871 the first defection took place when they rallied to the support of the wpp, now renamed the Labor Reform Union of Luzerne County (lru). The popularity of the lru grew rapidly among Welsh voters generally, not just the miners. The Welsh language newspaper *Baner America*, published in Scranton, encouraged Welsh voters to support the party. Republicans countered through the *Scranton Morning Republican* in an attempt to divide the Welsh electorate between the disaffected Welsh workers and the Republican faithful, like mine managers Benjamin Hughes and Henry D. Davies.[52]

No lru candidates ran in the Luzerne County elections in October 1871, but, rather than vote for the Republicans, a significant number of the Welsh voted for Democrats, leading to a clean Democratic sweep. The full extent of the Welsh defection became more apparent in the spring of 1872 when an lru candidate lost to the Democratic candidate by a narrow margin, although he had claimed 75 percent of the votes in the Hyde Park and Providence wards that were traditional Welsh mining neighborhoods. Even more significantly, the Republican candidate who came in third was a Welshman, Lewis Pughe. As the hard feelings toward the Republican Party healed, however, the lru waned in popularity among the Welsh. By the fall elections in 1872 the Scranton Welsh fell solidly behind the reelection of Republican presidential candidate Ulysses S. Grant.[53]

Following the violent conflicts between labor and capital nationwide, initiated by the general strike against the railroads in 1877 and bloody confrontations in Scranton, the Welsh miners again took up independent politics by supporting the new Greenback-Labor Party (glp) and its successful candidate for mayor, Terence V. Powderly, in 1878. This was an interesting turn of events because Powderly was an Irish machinist who helped to found the Knights of Labor among the railroad workers of Scranton in 1875 and later became its Grand Master Workman. It looked like the first step in a reconciliation of Welsh and Irish ethnic differences in favor of common class interests, particularly when lodges were organized for the coal miners in 1876 and Welsh and Irish miners and laborers joined en masse. The miners' lodges had been organized primarily by former members of the now defunct Workingmen's Benevolent Association, and two Welshmen were prominent among them, John F. Williams and John H. Powell. A miner from Aberdare who immigrated to America in 1866, Powell became a prominent union leader in Scranton and respected member of the Welsh community. He became chairman of the miners' central committee during the strike of 1877 when, after a series of wage cuts, the DL&W miners struck for a wage increase.[54]

The Scranton miners' strike coincided with the national railroad strike that began in the summer of 1877, and, although the railroad workers capitulated after a violent few months, the miners remained on strike until October. The strike culminated on August 1 when a large crowd of mixed ethnicity attempted to lynch the mayor, and the Scranton City Guard fired into the crowd, killing four Irishmen and wounding twenty-five others. Following these disturbances, an interest in independent political action was rekindled among the Welsh miners by the GLP, founded a year earlier by Powderly. Several Welsh served as GLP committee members and John H. Powell became editor of the party's newspaper, the *Industrial Advocate*, which also had a "Welsh Department." The Welsh vote went to the GLP in the fall elections of 1877, and some Irish voters defected from the Democrats as well. Consequently, the GLP candidates made a clean sweep of the offices.[55]

Even though both Welsh and Irish mineworkers chose cooperation over antipathy in the fall of 1877, a series of events threatened Welsh involvement in both the Knights of Labor and the Greenback-Labor Party. Welsh and Irish hostility welled up again at the Greenback-Labor Party's convention when it failed to nominate any Welsh candidates. To make matters worse, Powderly defeated Powell in the primary race to be the party's candidate for mayor. Powell then refused to support the GLP and resigned as editor of the *Industrial Advocate*. The probable reason for Powell's departure from the newspaper was, according to one historian, "a coup by the Irish faction on the newspaper's board of managers which disfranchised nearly all its Welsh members and replaced them with Irishmen." Undoubtedly, the growing Irish dominance of the Knights and the Greenback-Labor Party resulted in a heightened ambivalence among Welsh miners toward both organizations.[56]

Ethnicity played a major role among the Welsh miners during the 1878 mayoral election. Local Republicans and Democrats decided to mount a united assault against the GLP by splitting away the Welsh vote, which was generally the swing vote in Scranton elections. They did this by creating a fusion party, the Citizen Party, and nominating D. M. Jones, a popular

Welsh figure who was active in the Workingman's Party of 1871–72 to lure the Welsh vote away from the Greenbackers. The Citizen Party claimed that the Irish would soon take over the police force if the GLP won. Powderly garnered the most votes and won the election, but the Welsh wards in Hyde Park voted for Jones.[57]

The Welsh abandoned the Greenback-Labor Party in 1878 because it was dominated by the Irish, and they defected from the Knights of Labor for similar reasons. The Knights were completely controlled by the Irish in Scranton, so during the late seventies the Welsh became active in alternative unions. The most important of these organizations was the Miners and Laborers' Amalgamated Association, which drew considerable support from Welsh and English miners throughout the anthracite region after 1885. It collapsed after the failure of the 1887 strike, and the refusal of the Knights to support this strike generated acrimony between the two organizations. In January 1887, W. R. Storrs, the DL&W agent in Scranton, informed headquarters that "some effort is being made to get the miners to join the Knights. So far our Welshmen keep out of it."[58] The United Mine Workers of America, which was founded in 1890, eventually succeeded in organizing the anthracite fields. The Welsh played a more limited leadership role in the formation of the UMWA in the Scranton area than they did in the bituminous fields because, as one historian concluded, "the Welsh had difficulty in gaining credibility at the union leadership level when so many of their countrymen were increasingly occupying managerial positions in the industry."[59]

### Ethnic Gangs and Retributive Justice

Class and ethnic conflicts were not easily distinguished in the anthracite fields of the 1870s. An Irish laborer's attack on a Welsh mine boss might be sparked by ethnic and class animosities simultaneously. The context of ethnic conflict is obscured by the complexity and scale of the changes underway throughout the anthracite fields during the 1870s, but is particularly visible in the southern field of Schuylkill County where the rise of the first modern corporation, the Philadelphia and Reading Railroad, was the harbinger of things to come. While small operators and contract miners believed that it was their responsibility to set the price of their own labor and control the supply of coal to raise the market price, emerging corporation managers sought to sell coal as cheaply as possible and thereby expand the market.[60]

Franklin B. Gowen was the chief architect of the new approach. He was the district attorney for Schuylkill County from 1862 to 1864, a failed coal operator who became the acting president of the Philadelphia & Reading Railroad in 1869 and president in 1870. By 1875, the Reading had gained a monopoly over coal transportation in the county, acquired 100,000 acres of land, and controlled 85 percent of the collieries in Schuylkill and Northumberland Counties. The Reading controlled coal properties, mining, transportation, and sales in the marketplace, a complete vertical integration. The strikes that wracked the anthracite coalfields throughout the 1870s were all about the growing power of the Reading and its determination to reduce labor costs. During the "Long Strike" of 1875, the Philadelphia & Reading Coal and Iron Company locked out the miners and hired gunmen and strikebreakers. The miners responded by burning coal breakers, dynamiting railroad tracks, and attacking locomotives and railroad cars. The violence played into the company's hands, however, allowing the Reading to virtually starve them into submission and turning the public against them. One superintendent required emergency provisions before he could restart the mines because the miners were too weak to work. It also resulted in the virtual destruction of the Workingmen's Benevolent Association, the only voice of moderation in the industry and between the ethnic groups.[61]

In this tumultuous social context in which the miners' freedom and the values of republicanism were under attack by the "hydra-headed" monopoly, the distinction between ethnic and class conflict became blurred beyond recognition in the now well-chronicled Molly Maguire killings. The first public mention of an Irish secret society called the Molly Maguires probably appeared in 1857 in Benjamin Bannan's *Miners' Journal*, published in Pottsville. Born to Welsh parents, Bannan was outrageously anti–Irish Catholic as well as anti-monopoly, an expert on mining geology, and an advocate of the independent operator and traditional republicanism.[62] While Bannan blamed the turmoil on a Molly Maguire conspiracy, Franklin Gowen claimed it was the work of the Workingmen's Benevolent Association. Gowen accused the WBA of being responsible for sabotage and killings before the Pennsylvania legislature in 1871. The head of the WBA, John Siney, vehemently rejected this charge, but this was an association that Gowen made repeatedly in order to stigmatize the organization he would eventually destroy. Gowen contracted the Pinkerton Detective Agency in 1873 for undercover operatives to infiltrate the secret society and uncover the assassins and saboteurs. The first agent was P. M. Cummings, an Illinois miner, who found no evidence of a secret society. Another agent, James McParlan, alias James McKenna, was sent in and took up residence in Shenandoah. McParlan succeeded in infiltrating an inner circle of the Ancient Order of Hibernians who called themselves the Molly Maguires. Although many questions surround the character and honesty of McParlan, it was largely on his reports and testimony that twenty Irishmen were tried, convicted, and hanged in 1876 and 1877 all the while protesting their innocence.[63]

The stronghold of the fabled Molly Maguires, Schuylkill County, had grown from a population of 11,311 in 1820 to 116,428 in 1870. That year, 30,856 (26.5 percent) of the county's residents were foreign-born: 630 of them from Scotland, 6,709 from Germany, 9,333 from England and Wales, and 13,465 from Ireland. The foreign-born Irish made up 43.5 percent of the immigrant population and 11.5 percent of the county's total population. The vast majority of them worked in the mines, and, therefore, represented at least half of the population in most mining townships. The Molly Maguire strongholds of Shenandoah and Mahanoy City, where most of the violence occurred, were disproportionately made up of young, single males. Mahanoy City, Pinkerton undercover agent McParlan reported, was the most "Godforsaken" place he had ever seen. The town was one long street running down a narrow valley in the 1870s. Half the town was Irish, and the other half Welsh, English, and German. Main Street was the dividing line between the Irish section and the others, and it was unhealthy to cross the line at night. As in the northern field, a complicated mix of ethnic and class conflict was always simmering below the surface in Schuylkill County, which frequently boiled up because of the occupational division separating the Welsh miners and Irish laborers. These tensions often spilled over into warfare between rival street gangs, the Welsh "Modocs," the Irish "Sheet Iron Gang," and the "Molly Maguires." In segregated Mahanoy City, for example, ethnic gangs frequently found themselves locked in street warfare. The Molly Maguires generally were pitted against both the Welsh Modocs and the Sheet Iron Gang, which was composed of Irishmen from the county of Kilkenny, Ireland. Sometimes they allied with the Modocs against the Molly Maguires, a fact that is not so exceptional considering that Kilkenny was the one county in Ireland where a limited amount of coal mining occurred. Catholic Irishmen called the Kilkennymen "soupers," or "soup drinkers," a derisive term for Protestant converts. Many were Protestants, although not converts, and some had immigrated to Britain where they acquired experience in South Wales or Lancashire coalfields prior to their arrival in America. Others were descendants of British miners who had settled in Kilkenny and worked in the pits.[64]

The Modocs in Mahanoy City, according to Munsell's *History of Schuylkill*

*County*, published in 1881, were "a body of Welsh and English roughs" led by a man named John Hurd. While they occasionally teamed up with the Sheet Iron Boys against the Molly Maguires, they were so prejudiced against the Irish that they preferred to stand alone and fight both Irish gangs. Both the Modocs and Mollies had friends in city government, but the Mollies had become so adept at phony alibis to protect their comrades from jail that the Modocs preferred "to trust their own arms to defend themselves," a contemporary local historian wrote. In this manner was laid "the foundation for a series of vendettas, the account of which reads more like a chapter from the history of the Dark Ages than a recital of events occurring in a civilized community, within the last quarter of a century."[65]

Volunteer fire departments were enabling institutions for interethnic group clashes in the nineteenth century. Mahanoy City had two fire companies in 1870, the Humane Fire Company No. 1 and the "Citizen's Fire Company" No. 2, composed primarily of Irishmen and Welshmen, respectively. Each company served its own side of the town, but, when both companies answered the same alarm, a brawl generally ensued. At midnight, on October 30, 1874, a major fight broke out when both companies reached the fire and gunshots were exchanged. When George Major, a burgess and the foreman of the second company, attempted to restore order, he was shot by someone in the crowd. Daniel Dougherty, an Irishman, was charged with Major's murder on the presumption that Major must have fired in self-defense. Dougherty was acquitted, however, because the bullet that killed Major did not match the pistol fired by the Irishman. Nevertheless, the killing of George Major erupted in something bordering on mass hysteria against the Molly Maguires, and was further aggravated by the Long Strike of 1875, then entering its fifth month of violent and bitter class and ethnic violence.[66]

Much of the Molly Maguire violence of the 1870s involved the enforcement of a specific type of retributive justice. The victims included Welsh gang members, miners, mine superintendents, and public officials, but most of the violent acts were connected to labor relations generally, and discrimination at the mines specifically. Since this discrimination was aimed against the Irish laborers because they were Irish, clashes between the Welsh and Irish erupted along the fault lines of ethnicity rather than class. The collapse of the Workingmen's Benevolent Association in June 1875 brought an end to the one organization that encouraged the Welsh miners and Irish laborers of Schuylkill County to overcome their craft and ethnic differences and fight together in a common cause. The Working-

men's Benevolent Association discouraged the use of violence in labor disputes, and evidence of its success is found in the fact that Molly Maguire
violence occurred primarily before and after the WBA, the 1871 Welsh strike
notwithstanding. The union sought to dampen ethnic and labor violence,
but it also attempted to protect its members from oppressive employers,
particularly the Reading Railroad and its brutal Coal and Iron Police. Without the restraining influence of the WBA, ethnic and labor conflict spiked in
the anthracite fields.[67]

The absence of mine owners among the Molly's victims resembled agrar-
ian violence in Ireland that rarely touched the absentee landlords directly.
Instead, violence was deflected onto the nearest available targets, such as
middlemen, land agents, and local authorities in Ireland, and toward mine
superintendents and foremen, contract miners, and local authorities in
Pennsylvania who for whatever reason incurred the wrath of the Molly
Maguires. Intimidation was used, as was the ultimate penalty of retribution.
For example, James McParlan, the Pinkerton spy who broke the Molly
Maguire cases, reported to the head of the agency that a Welsh superintendent at a mine near Shenandoah "had been discharging all the Irishmen
operating under him and putting his countrymen in their places." The
Mollies informed the superintendent that he must leave the area or suffer
the consequences, but the Welsh boss refused to take the warning. As a
result, Pinkerton wrote, a group of Molly Maguires "went to his house, at
the dead hour of night, broke up his furniture, ill-treated his family, and
taking the stubborn fellow into the yard, in his night garments, beat him
with clubs until he was nearly dead." The Welshman decided from that
experience, Pinkerton observed, that "the colliery was not exactly a healthy
place of residence or refuge for him, and, as soon as able to do so, removed
to Pottsville."[68]

The Mollies did not confine their retribution to the Welsh, but, of the
sixteen killings attributed to the Molly Maguires between 1862 and 1875
whose ethnicity can be identified, four were Welsh, two were Welsh Americans, and a seventh victim who survived almost certainly was Welsh. The
Mollies were also implicated in the killing of William Williams in 1865, but
this murder did not play a part in the infamous Molly Maguire trials of the
mid-1870s. Morgan Powell, a native of Wales and a skilled miner, was killed
at Summit Hill, Carbon County, on December 2, 1871. He had risen through
the ranks to become a superintendent at the Lehigh & Wilkes-Barre Coal
Company, and reportedly was assassinated for refusing to give Alexander
Campbell his own coal face at the mine, favoring his Welsh compatriots

instead. George Major was killed on October 31, 1874, as described above, during a drunken brawl between Welsh and Irish fire companies in Mahanoy City. The pattern of ethnic-labor killings continued after Daniel Dougherty was acquitted of shooting George Major in April 1874. In this case, however, the Welsh wanted revenge. The Welsh "Modocs" were thought to be behind an attempted assassination of Dougherty who escaped death because the bullets passed through his clothing. The Molly Maguires met on June 1, 1875, and three Welshmen were singled out for revenge: contract miners William and Jesse Major, two kinsmen of George Major, and local Welsh thug William M. "Bully Bill" Thomas. Plans to kill the Major brothers were thwarted by the arrival of the national guard, but assassins found "Bully Bill" on the morning of June 28, 1875, in a stable and fired a dozen bullets at the Welshman. Tough he was, though, for even though he was shot in the chest, neck, and fingers, and a horse killed in the barrage fell on him, "Bully Bill" survived to identify his would-be assassins. One of them he claimed also slashed the throat of Welsh miner James Johns, who was not included among those the Molly Maguires were convicted of killing.[69]

The next victim, Gomer James, was not as fortunate as "Bully Bill." James was born in America to Welsh parents. The two oldest of their seven children were also born in Wales, but Gomer was born in Pennsylvania in 1847. One evening in August 1873, James was drinking at a Shenandoah saloon when he heard a ruckus on Main Street. Going to investigate, he found Edward Cosgrove and Thomas James giving Tom Jones, a Welsh friend of James, a savage beating. Gomer James rushed into the street to help Jones, who lay unconscious in the street, while Cosgrove and James took flight. Pulling his pistol, James fired several shots, killing Cosgrove. James was taken into custody the next morning but was released on bail and acquitted of murder by a jury. He may have been free of the law, but not from Molly justice, and Thomas Hurley, a miner from Shenandoah, accepted the assignment of killing James. On August 14, 1875, as James was tending bar at a fire company picnic just outside of Shenandoah, Hurley shot James at point-blank range and then escaped into the crowd. The Molly Maguires provided Hurley with a reward for the murder and enough money to escape to Colorado.[70]

The day Gomer James was assassinated was a bloody day indeed in Schuylkill County. In Girardville, gangs of armed men roamed the streets looking for trouble. The losers of a tavern brawl went to the office of Thomas Gwyther, the local justice of the peace, and swore out a warrant for the arrest

Molly Maguires attempt to murder William "Bully Bill" Thomas. From Alan Pinkerton, *The Molly Maguires and the Detectives* (New York: G. W. Dillingham, 1887), facing p. 324. Courtesy of West Virginia and Regional History Collection, West Virginia University Libraries.

of an assailant. No sooner had Gwyther stepped out of his office onto the porch when he was shot dead. The murderer, William Love, pulled the trigger and fled for parts unknown. Another incident on "Bloody Saturday" once again involved the Welsh tough William "Bully Bill" Thomas, who exchanged gunfire with Irishman James Dugan on the main street of Mahanoy City, and a stray bullet killed an innocent German bystander. Thomas was arrested for the death but no charges were brought against him, presumably because he cooperated with the Coal & Iron Police by providing evidence against the Molly Maguires.[71]

The final assassination of a Welshman attributed to the Molly Maguires was that of John P. Jones, of Lansford, Carbon County, on September 3, 1875. Jones was born at South Wales, in 1832, emigrated with his parents in 1852, and settled in Tamaqua, Schuylkill County. He first worked as a mine laborer for his brother-in-law, became a miner, rose through the ranks, and was promoted to mine superintendent at the Lehigh & Wilkes-Barre Coal

Molly Maguires murder Gomer James. From Alan Pinkerton, *The Molly Maguires and the Detectives* (New York: G. W. Dillingham, 1887), facing p. 422. Courtesy of West Virginia and Regional History Collection, West Virginia University Libraries.

Company—the same position held by Morgan Powell when he was assassinated four years earlier. Both managers were assassinated for discriminating against Irish workers. Morgan Powell allegedly favored a Welshman over an Irishman who took revenge, and Jones blacklisted Hugh McGehan, who then arranged for the Tamaqua Mollies to assassinate Jones. Officially, the last of the Molly Maguire assassinations was committed in September 1875, but interethnic violence continued unabated in Schuylkill County for the rest of the year. In just one "night of terror" in Shenandoah, an Irishman named John Heffron attempted to shoot Daniel Williams, a Welsh bartender at the National Hotel; another Irishman, Richard Finnen, was shot by an unknown assailant in Couch's Saloon; and at eleven o'clock a Welshman named Reese Thomas was arrested and jailed for firing his revolver in public, even though shots were heard all over town. James Johns, another Welshman, was shot and had his throat slit by Thomas Hurley, the same man who killed Gomer James; at midnight fifteen shots were fired into the tavern of "Muff" Lawler, a noted Molly. The following night one hundred special policemen patrolled the streets to restore order.[72]

The Molly Maguire trials took place from January 1876 to November 1877, and resulted in the hanging of twenty men on weak and contradictory evidence. In retrospect, most scholars of this well-documented episode agree that the public hysteria, the ambiguous motives and slanted testimony of

Molly Maguires murder mine superintendent John P. Jones. From Alan Pinkerton, *The Molly Maguires and the Detectives* (New York: G. W. Dillingham, 1887), facing p. 445. Courtesy of West Virginia and Regional History Collection, West Virginia University Libraries.

James McParlan-alias McKenna, and Franklin Gowen's efforts to crush any and all opposition to the Reading Railroad cast a pall over the fairness of the trials. The capacity of McParlan and Gowen to bend the truth challenges the credibility of the documentation upon which most accounts are written. One thing is certain, and more pertinent for this study: the ethnic antagonism between the Welsh and Irish during the nineteenth century was a significant feature of life in the Pennsylvania coalfields. It is also clear that the attitudes of miners in Wales toward the Irish were transplanted and took root in Pennsylvania, where they continued to serve the same exclusionist social function. By the end of the nineteenth century, however, circumstances had changed dramatically in the American coalfields.

The winds of change were, as usual, felt first in the anthracite fields of Pennsylvania. Coal operators learned to appreciate the value of surplus labor in depressing wages and deflecting the demands of organized miners. They accomplished this goal by recruiting much more labor than they needed, and from those parts of Europe that were non-industrial—southern and eastern Europe. Usually these immigrants had no mining experience; therefore, they had no work traditions to protect, no preconceived ideas about how coal mining should be conducted, and no opposition to the new machines that began to enter the mines by the end of the nineteenth century. The "Slav Invasion," as the new immigration was referred to by anxious Americans, not only allowed the coal operators to change the rules of work, but the work process itself, and this had a dramatic impact on the role of the Welsh coal miner in America.

## THE SLAV "INVASION"
## AND THE WELSH "EXODUS"

Barely had the Irish conflicts diminished when the American coalfields were gripped by a new series of ethnic tensions. The British and northern European immigration to the United States altogether contributed nearly 13,000,000 of the total 15,428,000 immigrants entering the country prior to 1890. They were quickly assimilated, blending with the native-born Americans to become what a contemporary observer referred to as the "English-speaking races."[1] Between 1890 and 1900, however, a noticeable shift in the origins of immigrants occurred, with 2,147,938 of the 3,687,564, or three-fifths of the immigrants, entering the United States from eastern and southern Europe. The 1910 census recorded 5.8 million born in Austria-Hungary, Italy, and Russia residing in the United States. Nervous Americans called the massive migration that followed the "Slav invasion," a pejorative phrase that suggests the degree of fear and apprehension the influx generated among natives. As one hostile critic declared with alarm, "hordes" of these foreigners were descending on American communities, which were being "denationalized by the scum of the continent."[2]

The rising tide of immigrants from eastern Europe carried Germans, Russians, Lithuanians, Poles, Czechs, Slovaks, Ruthenians, Ukrainians, Magyars, Rumanians, Serbs, Croats, Slovenes, Bulgarians, and Macedonians to American shores. Ignorant of the cultural and national differences among these diverse people, Americans simply called them "Slavs." After 1900, several million Italians joined the flow of emigration from Europe to America. As late as 1870, less than 1 percent of the foreign-born in the United States were from Italy, Russia, and Austria-Hungary. That trend took a marked turn in the 1880s, when 16 percent of the immigrants emanated from southern and eastern Europe; during the following decade more than 60 percent (614,500) of the immigrants were Slavs; during the first decade of the twentieth century 65 percent of all immigrants were Slavs. Most of them settled in the major cities, but relatively large numbers found their way into the coalfields. By 1903, 40 percent of the 93,508 miners surveyed in Pennsylvania were of southern and eastern European origin, and Americans and British immigrants resented sharing the work with a class of people they regarded as antithetical to their traditions and interests.[3]

It is difficult to know exactly when the first Slavs entered the Pennsylvania anthracite region (Carbon, Columbia, Dauphin, Lackawanna, Luzerne, Northumberland, Schuylkill, and Susquehanna Counties), but in 1880 they numbered only 1,925 of a total 108,827 immigrants there. By 1900, however, their numbers reached 89,328 out of a total 193,692 immigrants. At the same time, between 1880 and 1900, the percentage of foreign-born English-speaking groups in the anthracite counties fell from 94 percent to less than 52 percent, while the percentage of eastern and southern Europeans rose from less than 2 percent to over 46 percent during the same period.[4] The impact of this shift in the workforce at the mine level is illustrated by the Philadelphia & Reading Coal & Iron Company. In 1892, the company operated sixty-one collieries and employed 24,754 employees. The birth or parentage of the total was distributed in the following manner: 4,718 American, 6,887 Irish, 4,287 Polish, 3,709 German, 2,089 English, 1,466 Hungarian, 1,282 Welsh, 210 Scottish, 86 Italian, and 20 French. By 1896, the Reading Company employed more Polish-born workers than any other group of people.[5]

In 1900 the Pennsylvania Bureau of Mines counted 147,651 employed in and about the state's mines, and questions of ethnic ancestry were part of the Bureau's mine-by-mine survey that year to ascertain the number of each nationality working in the mines. Only 232 of the 375 collieries responded, but they employed 96,077 mine workers (about two-thirds of the total mine workers in Pennsylvania). Of these, 55,426 were of English-speaking ethnicity, and 40,651 were non-English-speaking. By 1915, the southern and eastern European immigrants clearly dominated the mine force totaling 98,142 (56.4 percent) of the 173,907 anthracite mine workers. The Americans came in second at 58,284 (33.5 percent), the British third at 8,690 (5 percent), and the fourth at 5,411 (3.1 percent). The Welsh had shrunk to only 4,292 (2.5 percent).[6]

### Slav Settlements and Conditions

Most of the new arrivals had been agricultural workers attracted by the lure of jobs they learned about through word of mouth or correspondence from other emigrants in the United States. Their principal motivation was economic. In Poland, where agriculture was the primary occupation of eight out of every ten inhabitants, misery was widespread because of soil exhaustion and an inefficient land system unable to support a population that doubled during the last half of the nineteenth century. The increasing likelihood of sinking into a landless state was unbearable to contemplate, and, while most Poles migrated to other European countries, the prospect of high wages in America was irresistible. While unskilled workers in Russia earned thirty cents a day in 1900, their equivalents in the anthracite coalfields of Pennsylvania earned $1.15 a day. It was the hope of earning enough money to reestablish themselves as landholders, at least in the early days, which motivated them to immigrate to the United States. Initially, Slavs perceived their emigration as a temporary expedient, a sojourn to America that would restore their status in the old country. Americans generally believed that these "new immigrants" were not just impoverished, but lived by such low standards that they were convinced that the Slavs were inassimilable and, therefore, favored restricting their entry. Of course, time proved the restrictionists wrong.[7]

Miners who favored restriction were motivated by self-interest, but mine operators who rolled out the welcome mats were too. The first Slav immigrant communities were founded in mining towns such as Mt. Carmel, Mahanoy City, Minersville, and Hazleton, in the southern anthracite coal district centered in Schuylkill County, but soon the migration was directed to the middle and northern coalfield towns such as Nanticoke, Shamokin, Pittston, Plymouth, Wilkes-Barre, and Scranton. Shenandoah, in Schuylkill County, was the most ethnically diverse town in all the anthracite fields, although in most of these relatively small towns English, Irish, Welsh, and Germans lived in close proximity to the Polish, Lithuanian, Ukrainian, and Slovaks.[8]

Each of the Slav groups had its own distinctive culture; the Slovaks, Ruthenians, Poles, and Lithuanians understood each other's language and worked and worshiped together. The Americans made no distinctions between them, however, and discriminated against them as though they were a homogeneous group; it was their collective resistance to discrimination that provided the impetus for their unification as "Slavs," which would never have occurred in Europe. The Slav "ghetto" was usually in the poorest section of town, where squalor was common and privacy unknown. Overcrowding was ubiquitous because households took in lodgers, often several bachelors per room, in order to reduce the cost of living and to maximize their income.[9]

Custom and the drive to economize forced Slav women into the role of servants to the men. They increased the family income in a way that the

English-speaking working class regarded as "unrespectable," because their women were "debased" by dirty and heavy manual labor. Americans and British immigrants saw Slavic wives in their bare feet, chopping wood, gathering coal from the culm banks in their skirts, and in a few cases they were known to have worked as mine laborers. They had large numbers of children who were generally put to work: girls in the textile mills and boys in the mines to contribute to the family income. Historically, the family and social characteristics of coal miners followed a common reproductive pattern with others in the trade, and that should provide the basis for comparisons rather than nationalities. In the United States, Great Britain, Germany, and France, large families were common to coal-mining communities. The charge that the Slavs were unnaturally fecund, therefore, was a bit disingenuous and reflected prejudice toward a particular nationality rather than a markedly different reality. The birth rate in Ashland, Pennsylvania, where virtually the entire population in the 1890s was of American, British, or German parentage, was 24.9 per 1,000; in Hazleton, with a large population of Slavs and Italians, the average birth rate was 31.9 per 1,000 population. The "old stock" English, Welsh, and Irish anthracite miners married thirty years or more were no strangers to large families either; their wives gave birth to an average of 10.6, 8.9, and 8.3 children, respectively.[10]

Neither of the institutions at the center of the Slavic communities, the church and the saloon, was regarded by the Welsh as "respectable." Their hostility toward the Catholic Church and disdain for imbibing alcohol were linked by a hyper-Protestantism (see chapter 3). Respectable Americans and British immigrants tended to decry the drinking practices of the Slavs as degenerate. Most disturbing was the custom of the men to head for the saloon after Sunday mass. Uninfluenced by the Protestant Reformation, or its secular reformist legacy, Slav immigrants unabashedly enjoyed their liquor. The Reverend Peter Roberts quoted a Protestant minister's characterization of this desecration of the Sabbath: "It was terrible; saloons full blast; singing and dancing and drinking everywhere; it was Sodom and Gomorrah revived; the judgment of God, sir, will fall upon us."[11] Wild times at weddings and christenings were likewise rebuked by the Calvinistic Welsh, who voiced their hostility toward Slavic drunkenness and ignorance. Respectable people railed against the saloons where "the worst specimens of humanity" could be found. Those who frequented them were "the off-scourings of Europe—brigands of the Carpathian Mountains, and the murderers of rural Hungary and the Russian steppes" and were "no farther along in human progress than were their ancestors, the hordes of Attila, when he led them howling up to the gates of Rome."[12] Even the social workers who attempted to help the Slav immigrants regarded them as having "brought over to this country the manners and customs of a lower civilization than ours." Beside themselves with self-righteous indignation, the guardians of respectability were uninterested in the important community functions performed by these institutions for newly arrived Slavs, particularly single men or those separated from their families.[13]

For many years Slavs worked at unskilled jobs, primarily as miners' laborers or even breaker boys, but seldom as miners or skilled men. They were restricted to the hardest, worst-paying jobs, but they were determined to save their money and suffered a lower standard of living for greater security. Most authorities agree that the Slavs saved at least half of their earnings to build a cash stake toward returning home to buy land, or to build their own house in America; many sent money orders back home to support their families. Whatever their motives, saving half of their pay, even if it meant living at a very low standard, became a recognized Slavic trait.[14]

### Labor-Capital Conflict

The image of crafty operators marching hordes of docile, ignorant Slavs and Italians into the coalfields to break strikes is an old one but nonetheless erroneous. The Slav presence in the anthracite fields during the decade of turmoil that characterized capital-labor relations in the 1870s was too insignificant for mention by contemporaries. Strikes in the 1870s failed because the anthracite miners were fragmented by coalfield geography, ethnic conflicts, destitution, and the crushing power of the Reading Railroad. Unionization also failed in the anthracite fields during the last third of the nineteenth century because of the conservatism of the British-inspired union leadership and ideology. Both the Workingmen's Benevolent Association and its successor, the Miners' National Association, adhered to the philosophy that the greatest threat to organized labor was the overproduction of coal, which drove down the price and cast men out of work. The operators and the miners were partners in production; one could not do without the other. Hence, the miners' union assumed the responsibility for controlling the coal supply and preferred arbitrating their grievances with operators rather than pursuing a class action. This was unionism shaped by the British labor movement and transplanted to America by the British miners. Its failure to produce results during the 1860s and 1870s had nothing to do with a "Slav invasion," the leading edge of which did not become noticeable until the mid-1880s. Instead, strikes failed because the unions did not have the power to impose their will. The issue for contemporaries, therefore, was whether the Slavs would support or undermine the efforts to organize a strong miners' union.

Even though the reasons for their failure to organize lay at their own doorsteps, the British and American miners blamed their problems on the wage-debasing "Hun." Frank Warne summarized this point of view: "When the competition of the Slav . . . became too strong, the English-speaking miner-worker resorted to various methods of defense. Race prejudice, manifested in innumerable ways, was directed to keeping the Slavs out of the mines."[15] The English-speaking miners had a stake in the contract system that protected their own higher-paying jobs and had generated a measure of prosperity for them during the preceding twenty years. But the Slav laborers had no cause to support a system that did not benefit them unless they could count on similar opportunities for advancement in the future. In fact, English-speaking miners themselves bore some responsibility for employing the Europeans. Rather than hire English laborers at the regular wage rate, "the miner would employ a big Slav or Hun cheaply, increasing his own pay check quite an amount," a lesson that was not lost on his comrades.[16]

When an anti-immigrant petition circulated through the coalfields in 1884, an Irishman reminded his fellow miners that they brought this problem on themselves when they employed Slavs as laborers. The "Irish and Welsh emigrants began to quit the area on the advice of friends," he concluded, and, because the Hungarians were willing to replace them, "we hire their labor and are glad to get it." A Welshman agreed and added that the anti-immigrant petition had originated in the bituminous districts: "Few anthracite-district workmen had wanted such legislation."[17] The Welsh mine inspector, Gwilym M. Williams, lent his expert opinion that, even though the miners complained, they had only themselves to blame. "Many more than half" of the contract miners "prefer Huns and Poles for laborers," he declared, because the miner found that "he can get more work out of a Hun than he can out of one of his own class." Moreover, Inspector Williams continued, "The Hun is anxious to learn, and the miner, in letting him drill for blasting and do other work that the ordinary laborer would not do, teaches him as much as he knows himself. The consequence is that after this kind of training the Pole or the Hun comes out a full-fledged miner and takes his place at the same rate of wages paid his other brethren."[18]

Native and British immigrants expected the Slavs to undermine the labor movement, but they were wrong. Although many early Slav immigrants were transported to America by the coal companies and became completely dependent on the companies for survival, circumstances changed quickly as they were socialized to life in America and provided ethnic leadership for newcomers. The first sign of labor consciousness among the Slavs was the strike of 1887–88 when they not only quit work sooner and stayed out longer than their American and British counterparts, but also pushed them to action. The Slavs threatened to shut down the William Penn Colliery, Superintendent William H. Lewis testified before a U.S. House of Representatives investigating committee, but his contract miners had resisted the strike and continued to work. "We have about 18 percent of Irish, and the rest of them are made up of Welsh, English, German, and Americans," he declared. When the miners rallied to the defense of the company, Lewis provided them with arms because the Slavs "said they were going to kill us, and so we went out with sixty carbines, and when they saw them they did not come any farther."[19]

Although some mines were American and British bastions that resisted foreign penetration, most became highly mixed work sites, like those of Eckley B. Coxe, a large independent operator in the Lehigh field, who employed more than 3,500 men and boys in 1888. Coxe testified before the same House committee that his workforce was a mixture of nationalities: "We have, I suppose, a larger number of Irishmen than any other [group]. We have Englishmen, Welsh, a good many Americans, Pennsylvania Germans, Hungarians, and Poles, and quite a number of Italians, Tyrolese, and Austrians." As in the 1870s, however, fragmentation within the workforce, rather than ethnic tensions, explains their failure to organize. The miners were split in their union loyalties between the Knights of Labor and the Amalgamated Association of Miners (AAM) and Mine Laborers of Pennsylvania, the ideological successor to the Workingmen's Benevolent Association of the 1870s. Both organizations preferred arbitration over strikes, and the AAM's president, George Harris, an Englishman in the model of John Siney, continued the conservative labor strategy that was transplanted to America by British migrants.[20]

The House of Representatives committee taking testimony into the labor troubles of 1887–88 heard from John H. Davis, chairman of the joint committee representing the coal miners, mine laborers, and others who worked about the mines. Davis was born in Hirwaun, in Glamorganshire, South Wales, the son of a miner, and came to the United States in 1869, settling in Mt. Carmel, Pennsylvania. He worked most of his life in America for the Philadelphia and Reading Mining Company and was elected by the employees to present their demands for higher wages to the company in September 1887. The miners presented a new wage scale, but the company refused to negotiate and the union men set a strike date of January 1, 1888.[21]

Although money was the central issue, a whole cluster of grievances stood in the background. Thomas A. Buckley, a naturalized citizen serving as a justice of the peace, also testified before the House committee. At age forty-four, he had worked his entire life in the mines of both Wales and America. Buckley was a member of the Knights of Labor, and initially did not approve of the strike because he regarded it as "premature," but he also thought there was "sufficient cause" for the miners to go out. Buckley claimed that the operator of his company wanted the miners to sign an agreement that would permit the company to deduct debts from the men's wages, but miners refused to pay their bills in that manner, considering it "an imposition on their manhood." The congressman responded that the men were "right in objecting to that contract."[22]

Unfortunately, the union attitude toward the Slavs in the 1880s was ambivalent at best, and occasionally hostile. While foreign speakers were used at some rallies, at primarily English-speaking rallies they denounced the Huns as inferiors who were undermining the American standard of living that Anglo-American miners hoped to maintain. Some labor leaders, like Terence Powderly of the Knights of Labor, were sympathetic to the plight of the Slavs but did not try to win them over to the cause. The only active ethnic factor in the 1887–88 strike, however, was the split found among the English-speaking unions: the K of L attracted the Irish, while the AAM appealed primarily to the English, Welsh, and German skilled mine workers. This split was amplified during the strike when William T. Lewis, a Welshman from Ohio, and Master Workman of the K of L Trades Assembly 135 for miners, called the men back to work after discussions with Powderly. The major split among the K of L miners was whether their interests were better served by organizing along trade lines, like the AAM, or to follow the Knights' "one big union" approach. Lewis favored the trade-union approach, and losing the 1887 strike probably reinforced his conviction, for he would be instrumental in leading many miners out of National Trade Assembly 135 and into the United Mine Workers of America in 1890 (see chapter 9).[23]

### The Lattimer Massacre
Although the 1887–88 strike failed, it was the first labor conflict in which the entire Slav community participated. By 1897 there were a host of new reasons for labor unrest among the Slavs: for a decade new immigrants

augmented their ranks; a cadre of socialized American Slavs had emerged; festering grievances surfaced over discrimination at the mine and in society; the American economy took a sharp downturn during the 1890s; and a massive shift in economic power to the barons of industrial capitalism posed a threat to American republican ideals. The strike that broke out in 1897 demonstrated that a great transition had occurred from a British- to a Slav-dominated workforce. The decline of British miners was more than matched by a corresponding increase among the Slavs, and by 1897 the British miners who remained were either skilled men or bosses. The strike of 1897 was almost entirely a Slav event, and the resulting Lattimer Massacre revealed the scale of the discrimination confronting Slavs in the anthracite fields. At the center of the conflict was the very caricature of the overbearing Welsh superintendent in Gomer Jones.

On April 24, 1897, Gomer E. Jones was forty-two. He had already worked thirty-five years in the mines, having entered the pits back in his native Wales as a child of seven. In 1868, at age thirteen, he migrated to Pennsylvania with his parents. Jones worked at nearly every position in the mines as he rose through the ranks. In 1878 he became a mine foreman for the Upper Lehigh Coal Company, and by August 1891 had become the general foreman responsible for six mines. In 1897 he was serving as division superintendent of the Lehigh and Wilkes-Barre Coal Company near McAdoo.[24]

Like many Welshmen, Jones reportedly had little use for Irishmen and was openly disrespectful toward the Slavs and Italians. They "moved too slow," he told one reporter, and he was so unpopular with those mine workers that their hostility toward Jones was frequently reported in the newspapers. Jones told a Wilkes-Barre reporter in 1897: "When I came here a year ago, I came to restore discipline in the mines and to operate them in such a manner that the company could continue in business. The discipline was certainly lax. The two superintendents who were here then associated with the men and drank with the men. I'm not a drinking man, and did not practice hobnobbing with the men, but when I give orders I expect them to be obeyed. I dismissed a good many men," presumably because they did not obey his orders or moved too slowly.[25]

Clearly, ethnic tensions within the company's workforce were high a year earlier. Griffith G. Roberts, the assistant superintendent of the Lehigh and Wilkes-Barre Coal Company, was found dead by the railroad tracks in Hazleton in May 1896. From the large gash on his head, and with no apparent motive, it was suspected that he had been the victim of foul play, perhaps retribution from a disgruntled employee. Roberts was born in Dolwyddelan, Caernarfonshire, North Wales, in 1854, and came to America with his parents in 1869. He entered the mines of Luzerne County and rose through the ranks. In 1892 he was appointed assistant superintendent of the Honey Brook division, the same division to which Gomer Jones was appointed after Roberts's death. Roberts probably had some help from his wife, who was the daughter of Walter Phillips, general superintendent of the Delaware and Lackawanna Coal Company in Scranton, and sister of Thomas W. Phillips, the general superintendent of the DL&W Railroad, also of Scranton, a very powerful duo of Welsh managers.[26]

Like many coal companies, the Lehigh and Wilkes-Barre Coal Company employed Welshmen disproportionately at management levels, which probably solidified the general association of the Welsh, not only with management but also "bossism." This might have aggravated and focused Slav irritation at bosses, especially Gomer Jones, as it did the Irish decades earlier. The Welsh were impediments to their rise in the workforce hierarchy. The hiring of Jones fit into a broader set of labor-management issues. In 1889, when William T. Smith retired as general inside superintendent of the company, "a great revolution" saw nearly all of the mine foremen and their assistants changed and men from other districts took their places. The moves probably indicated that upper management thought the foremen, who typically emerged from the miners, were too close to their men and were not driving them hard enough. In 1891, the company's new general manager, E. H. Lawall, appointed Morgan R. Morgan to the position of general inside superintendent over all the company's collieries in Wilkes-Barre, Ashly, Sugar Notch, Wanamie, and Plymouth. Morgan saw immediately that instability had been created by all the changes.[27]

Morgan R. Morgan was born near Llandovery, Carmarthenshire, South Wales, in 1849, migrated to America in 1867, and settled in Wilkes-Barre. He worked his way up the ranks in the Lehigh and Wilkes-Barre Coal Company to fire boss and mine foreman, and in 1887 was appointed assistant superintendent under William Smith. Morgan replaced Smith as general inside superintendent when the latter retired in 1891. The largest coal company in the Wyoming Valley, the Lehigh and Wilkes-Barre employed more than seven thousand men and boys in thirteen operations, including the Nottingham No. 15 at Plymouth, the largest anthracite mine in the world. Like other Welsh bosses, Morgan was no doubt helped along in his career by inside connections. He married the daughter of Thomas M. Williams, a Welshman who served as a state mine inspector and then as superintendent of the Lykens Valley Coal Company. Upon assuming control of the mines, Morgan replaced many of the foremen and appointed "men of ability and experience to take charge of each of the collieries."[28] Gomer Jones was probably hired by Morgan at this time because of his experience and reputation as a tough, high production company man.

Jones attempted to impose a sterner discipline and dismissed those who resisted him. As a result the men hated him, and other mine managers faulted his methods.[29] A headline in the *Ashland Advocate* undoubtedly captured the feelings of mine laborers toward their boss: "Gomer Jones, Slave Driver." The paper explained that Jones "was once a poor miner; in fact, until quite recently. Power suddenly thrust upon him made the fellow a cruel master. It is generally the case. Put a beggar on horseback and nine times out of ten he makes an ass of himself. A prominent Shamokin mining official says of Jones that he is the worst slave-driver who ever set foot in the coal region."[30] Jones was characterized as a strict, religious, and self-righteous man with a violent temper who treated his men with contempt. The *Hazleton Daily Standard* reported that the miners who worked for Jones "tried to become accustomed to the despotic methods. Not only in the lowering of wages did he make himself odious, but by his frequent boisterous expressions about the workers."[31]

Jones was hired to improve profitability, and he examined each of the company's mines for ways to boost production and cut costs. The miners usually worked in teams, and Pennsylvania law dictated that only citizens could become miners; foreigners needed a two-year apprenticeship and some knowledge of English even to become a miner's helper. But there were other entry-level jobs in which foreigners could begin, such as air-boys, breaker boys, carpenters, blacksmiths, and mule driver. Jones decided that he could save the company money by cutting back on the number of mule drivers. If he built a central stable instead of one for each mine, only one crew would be necessary for watering and feeding the animals. The men would have to go further for their mules, but the burden would be on them because pay did not start until they entered the mines. The foreign workers were already in a bad mood because the mines were only working about half time. Also, United Mine Workers of America district president John Fahy, who had supported passage of the anti-immigrant Miners' Certificate Law of 1889, now led a delegation of union men to Harrisburg and secured passage of the Campbell Act in 1897, which imposed a tax of three cents per day on each adult immigrant on company payrolls. Employers immediately docked workers' paychecks by that amount, and, even though the courts subsequently declared the act unconstitutional, the measure aggravated the foreigners considerably. To add insult to injury, the legislature also reaffirmed the law restricting work as miners' assistants to American citizens. Even though the law was not rigorously enforced, the restriction cost them money, was insulting, and effectively barred them from access to knowledge of the miner's craft. Moreover, there were numerous other miners' grievances, such as not receiving biweekly cash payments as required by law and the system of deducting costs from trade at the company store for rents, medical expenses, and other fees. For the Slavs, withholding paydays undermined their ability to save money, the opportunity for which they had immigrated to Pennsylvania in the first place.[32]

Jones announced his plan to the mule drivers, and, when they complained that they should be paid for the extra two hours of work that was entailed, he rejected their demands. At Honey Brook Colliery, Jones agreed to a meeting with the mule drivers outside the superintendent's shed on August 12. Jones stood before the men with a crowbar in hand, explained the order again, and walked back into the shed. The drivers who understood English informed the others that the new policy would add two more hours to the workday, walking to and from the central stable. The men became angry as they discussed the directive and decided to strike until the order was rescinded. The next morning, August 13, they set up a picket line preventing others from entering the mine. In a fury, Jones stormed out of the superintendent's office with a crowbar and clubbed the first striker in reach, a young man named John Bodan. He buckled but recovered and lunged for Jones, pulled the bar from the superintendent's hands, and hit him several times on the back. Others jumped into the fray, but fortunately for Jones, Oliver Welsh, a mine foreman, was able to free the general foreman before he was seriously injured. Bodan swore out a warrant for the superintendent's arrest; Jones was arrested the next day and released on bail. In Michael Novak's narrative of the strike, a young Slav miner recounted the fight, and an Irish breaker boy remarked that even the name Gomer Jones "sounded like a superintendent's name."[33] True or not, the anecdote suggests how Jones, by far the most common Welsh surname, had become synonymous with "Welsh," and how the Welsh had become synonymous with "mine boss."

The indiscriminate physical attack on Bodan became symbolic of a larger set of issues for the foreigners. As the story about Jones's clubbing of Bodan circulated among Slavs, Hungarians, and Italians, their resolve to fight back against further indignities stiffened. By Monday morning, August 16, they were tramping from mine to mine, and soon more than three thousand other mine workers in the Lehigh and Wilkes-Barre mines had decided to throw down their tools. The strikers demanded first a wage increase, and second the removal of Jones for "tyrannical methods of ruling."[34] The foreigners had the grievances and they called the strike, while many of the Welsh, Germans, Irish, and Americans refused to participate because the measures that aggrieved the Slavs protected their economic interests and social standing.

With thousands of foreign mine workers now idle, a grievance committee composed of representatives of the English-speaking and the Slav and Italian miners waited on the general superintendent, Elmer H. Lawall, at the Lehigh and Wilkes-Barre offices in Hazleton. Wisely, two representatives of each nationality were represented, including two Americans. Lawall agreed to revoke Jones's original work rule that had sparked the revolt, but he refused to punish the superintendent and urged the men to return to work, at which time he would consider a wage increase. The English-speaking miners wanted to go back, but the foreigners refused and became even more determined to resist. On August 20, the grievance committee again met with Lawall. The 10 percent raise was affected, and he promised the men that Jones's conduct would be scrutinized. The English-speaking miners again favored conciliation, while the foreigners decided to halt direct action pending the outcome of the promised investigation into the superintendent's conduct.[35]

After the men returned to work, the second phase of the strike broke out at the Coleraine mine of A. S. Van Wickle's collieries near Hazleton. On August 21 the first paychecks with the new alien tax deductions were distributed, and the next Monday the outside men walked out at Coleraine. Finally, the general superintendent, James E. Roderick, arrived to hear their grievances, but, when they could not articulate their concerns, Roderick suggested that they form a committee to present their grievances the next morning in English. The *Hazleton Daily Standard* reported their grievances: "The men are dissatisfied since receiving their pay on Saturday when the alien tax was retained for the first time." The miners decided to strike if wages were not advanced enough to cover the tax, and Roderick increased the wages for some of the workers. After another meeting with Roderick the men remained dissatisfied, and on August 27 five hundred Coleraine strikers began to "march the mines" to bring the other miners out with them. The *Hazleton Daily Standard* reported that the foreign men outnumbered the English speakers three to one, and even though the alien tax was instrumental in arousing the ire of the foreigners and prompted the strike, it was but one of a multitude of other grievances.[36]

In Superintendent James E. Roderick, the Slav strikers encountered another Welsh boss, but there all similarities with Gomer Jones ended. Like most caricatures, "the Welsh boss" was a multifaceted social construction, and, if Jones represented the tyrant, Roderick embodied that of the respected master of the mines. Roderick was born in 1841, in Cardiganshire, South Wales, and in 1864 joined his parents in migrating to Pennsylvania. Roderick settled briefly in Pittston, where he mined coal for the Pennsylvania Coal Company, but soon moved to Wilkes-Barre, where he became mine foreman for the Lehigh and Wilkes-Barre Coal Company. In 1870, Roderick accepted the position of general superintendent for A. J. Davis & Company in Warrior Run, but resigned in 1881 to assume the post of mine inspector for the fourth district. He served a full five-year term, and was in his third year of a second term when he accepted the position of general superintendent for the Linderman and Skeer collieries. After another brief stint as mine inspector, he resigned in 1896 to take the position of general superintendent of A. S. Van Wickle's collieries.[37]

Unlike Gomer Jones, Roderick was liked and respected by all segments of the industry. When he became superintendent for Van Wickle, a trade magazine observed that "the state loses the services of an inspector who ranks in ability and general mining knowledge with any inspector of mines in the world, and Mr. Van Wickle secures one of the most competent mine managers in America."[38] The Luzerne County historian declared that "among the men who have had vast experience in the anthracite coal regions of Pennsylvania, none are more prominent" than J. E. Roderick. Although he had been a candidate for county treasurer on the Greenback-Labor Party ticket in 1879, like most Welshmen, Roderick was a loyal Republican. A contemporary described Roderick as "a shrewd political worker, nevertheless one of those who believe that hard-fought political battles can be won without resort to unfair methods. With this principle for a foundation, Mr. Roderick has a very large following in this county, and his influence is of vast importance to the party which he represents."[39] In 1887 mine inspector Roderick induced the legislature to construct a state miners' hospital at Hazleton. Inspector Roderick's report for 1882 called attention to the suffering of disabled miners: "Humanity demands that something be done to relieve them, and that as speedily as possible."[40]

Undoubtedly, his political connections helped him to get ahead, and in

1899 he was appointed chief inspector of mines for the state of Pennsylvania. He had been chief inspector for fourteen years in 1913 when the *Druid*, a Welsh American paper published in Pennsylvania, crowed that Roderick had "the distinction of being the only Welshman in charge of a state department in the commonwealth, in fact, the only Welshman who has presided over an official department in Pennsylvania in many years." Roderick was "more instrumental than any other man in codifying and improving the mine laws of the state especially for the protection of human life in this hazardous calling." The inspector resided in Hazleton, where, according to the paper, he was a "Cymric pillar of strength and a leader in all movements for the welfare of his people."[41]

The industry's technicians and engineers, as well as the mine workers, managers, and owners, all held Roderick in high esteem. He treated the workers with respect, and they appreciated that, but, whether it was Roderick's velvet glove or Gomer Jones's clinched fist, the foreigners felt their progress was hedged in all too often by Welsh managers. Nevertheless, Roderick was not immune from the potential dangers that emerge during a strike. Early in the morning of August 30 police officers observed four men lurking outside Roderick's home in Hazleton, but they fled upon spotting the policemen. "They had every appearance of being Huns and Italians," the newspaper reported, "and their mission evidently was for no good purpose."[42]

The Lehigh and Wilkes-Barre Coal Company released its investigation of Gomer Jones on September 1, but to the strikers' great disappointment it rejected a pay raise and only promised fair treatment in the future without even mentioning Jones. At the same time, Van Wickle permitted Roderick to raise the wages of the foreigners. The men of Milnesville readily accepted the raises as well as Roderick's promise that, if the Coleraine men did not accept the offer and marched on Milnesville, Roderick would protect them. They expected trouble, but they had no idea that the next morning 1,500 strikers would gather at McAdoo, the site of Jones's intemperate assault that had ignited the strike, and that along the march to Milnesville another 1,500 from Coleraine would join them. On their return to McAdoo that evening, the two thousand remaining marchers passed the house of Jones. The superintendent cautiously hid in the nearby woods and watched as the marchers stoned his house, breaking every window and door in the process.[43]

By the weekend of September 4 and 5, 1897, Roderick had convinced all his men to return to work at both Coleraine and Milnesville. Demonstrating flexibility in dealing with them, Roderick informed a reporter: "Our men seem to be perfectly satisfied, there will positively be no compulsion for any man to deal with the company butcher and the company store, nor will any intimidation in this direction be permitted by any of the subordinates." Mr. Roderick declared that "the alien tax withheld last week would be repaid to the men next pay day." They may not have known it, but the courts had just ruled that Pennsylvania's alien tax law was unconstitutional.[44]

Although the period of quiet would not last, the Welsh of Hazleton found an opportunity in the lull for their eisteddfod in Hazle Park. "A very respectable crowd" reportedly gathered under the large tent erected for the event. The vocal music presented by local and visiting choirs, glee clubs, trios, duets, and soloists was greatly appreciated. In the evening a concert by a chorus of two hundred was a "grand success" and thrilled "a very large crowd."[45] Harmony was not to prevail on the industrial front, however.

By Monday, September 6, the coal operators had reached a joint decision to reject the immigrant workers' demands and to pay for armed deputies to supplement the Coal and Iron Police. John Fahy, the United Mine Workers of America district president who had spent considerable energy resisting the use of immigrants, now entered the field to convince those same workers that joining the union rather than staging independent marches was the most effective long-term strategy. In the end, the men were determined to "march the mines" to bring out the entire field. On September 8 Jones telephoned Sheriff Scott in Pottsville to tell him that the main body of strikers was in Audenried. They had prevented the firemen at colliery Number Four from tending the boiler fires and, consequently, the mine lost power. Jones demanded that the sheriff send a posse immediately, but the sheriff refused without some guarantee that the company would pay the expense. By now ten to fifteen thousand discontented men were idle and appeared ever more menacing to the county's English-speaking residents.[46]

On "Black" or "Bloody Friday," September 10, 1897, the strikers prepared to march on Hazleton, the Schuylkill County seat, where they intended to press their grievances. Four hundred men assembled at Harwood, and falling in behind the protection of the American flag they began the march in hopes of gathering strength as they trooped along the road. After several tense encounters with officials along the way, the column arrived at Lattimer, where county sheriff James F. Martin and a force of armed deputies stopped them in the middle of the road. Lattimer, established in 1869 by the Pardee Coal Company, was one of those undifferentiated coal towns found throughout the region dedicated to the mining of anthracite. The first residents were primarily Welsh, and in 1897, when ethnicity was a key social marker, Welshmen made up the management personnel who lived in big houses on "Quality Row." Very few Slavs or Hungarians lived in Lattimer, but, when coal company deputies killed at least nineteen Slav strikers in cold blood there on September 10, 1897, the town instantly became a memorial site for Slavs and a benchmark in the development of the American labor movement. The sheriff stepped forward to speak to the leaders, and, although there are differing accounts about what transpired, the deputies commenced firing into the unarmed marchers. Many of the marchers were shot in the back as they ran away, and some had multiple gunshot wounds as though they had been targeted. At least nineteen marchers, all foreigners, died, and thirty more were wounded on that day. The event immediately became known as the "Lattimer Massacre."[47]

The entire region was shocked by the events that transpired that day, and fear was widespread that the foreigners would go on a general rampage. This fear seemed verified when later that night a mob attacked Jones's house. Indeed, the "tyrannical" Welsh manager personified all the grievances that weighed on the recent immigrants in anthracite country. In the immediate aftermath of the massacre, Jones saw the wisdom of staying out of sight. On the night of September 12, it was reported, strikers searched in vain for the hated superintendent, and he was presumed to have taken refuge in an old slope. From this vantage point Jones and his men crouched in the darkness with Winchesters at the ready, and watched as several dozen men destroyed his house as completely as if "a cyclone hit it." Jones later claimed that the strikers also stole $200 worth of silverware from the house, an amount that equaled two-thirds of the average annual wage of a miner's laborer.[48]

In the immediate aftermath of the massacre, Slav community leaders attempted to bring about some order by organizing rallies and meetings. At a meeting on September 11, 1897, in which the crowd was addressed in English, Slovak, Italian, and Hungarian, Roderick again distinguished himself as the antithesis of Jones when he declared to the crowd: "A great calamity which will go down in history as the greatest crime of the Christian era has befallen this peaceful community, and the rights of people to assemble for a redress of grievance has been attacked in an unwarranted manner." By voice vote the assemblage then approved a resolution that condemned the shooting, objected to the presence of the recently mustered National Guard, called on Sheriff Martin to resign, and demanded the prosecution of the sheriff and deputies "for disgracing American citizenship." At the same meeting Roderick also contributed one hundred dollars to the newly formed

Committee for Prosecution and Charity. Approximately 250 contributions were received, by far the most of them for $5.00 or less; only ten reached $100 or more.[49]

Meanwhile, the strike resumed even stronger than before with the English and Welsh miners now joining the walkout. UMWA organizer John Fahy increased union membership by over 30 percent, or 10,000 new members, in August and September 1897, and ensured that the foreigners were represented in the offices and committees of the new locals. By September 20 Jones had been forced to resign. A few months later, the *United Mine Workers Journal* reported that Jones, who was infamous long before the recent strike for his "tyrannical methods as a mine boss," was still as "overbearing as ever." The miners' paper opined that the rebellion sparked by his attack on Bodan had taught Jones the lesson that "a man is a man even if he is a Hungarian."[50] It is unclear how the episode affected Roderick, but in 1899, as previously mentioned, he was appointed to the position of chief mine inspector for Pennsylvania and remained at that post until his retirement in 1919. Apparently, he had tired of managing coal mines.

In the end, and to the outrage of Slavs and Italians everywhere, the jury acquitted the deputies in a legal process that coal miners everywhere realized was stacked against them. The Lattimer Massacre dramatically illustrated how class and ethnicity were inextricably bound together in the coalfields.[51] The Lattimer Massacre also demonstrated just how different the anthracite country was in 1897 from what it had been in the 1870s, when mine workers were overwhelmingly English speakers of British Isles extraction. The strike of 1887 was the first indication that the tides of immigration were changing, but the 1897 strike confirmed that a sea change had occurred and mine owners preferred Slavs over British mine workers. Ironically, John Fahy, who initially believed that Slavs were unorganizable, was sent by the United Mine Workers of America to bring them into the union, for which the Slavs regarded Fahy as a hero. All the more ironically, it was the Slavs who initiated the movement that resulted in the UMWA's successful campaign to organize all the anthracite fields for the first time. In fighting back against the arbitrary Jones, and the shooting at Lattimer, all the mine workers acquired a class solidarity that replaced ethnic fragmentation and elevated the union above cultural animosities.[52]

### Welsh Miners Abandon the Industry

A closer look at the Welsh population clearly shows that as the Slavs came in the Welsh departed the industry. The Slav invasion was not the only reason for their departure, but many Welsh and their contemporaries certainly were of that opinion. A Welsh miner in Pottsville, Pennsylvania, wrote home in 1888 that "competition is strong and the companies are taking advantage of this to employ Poles, Hungarians, Negroes, and foreigners unused to that kind of work and in this way making the old workmen idle. It is a good thing that Welshmen understand every kind of work better than they do, so that the Welsh get the jobs of foremen because they must have some experienced men whom they can trust as many accidents have taken place because some workman was not careful enough or did not know enough to avoid such occurrences. Hundreds of lives were lost because of this."[53]

Similarly, in 1895 the same John R. Williams described in chapter 2 wrote to his former mine engineering teacher in Aberdare that labor was so much in oversupply that "operators can do just what they please." Pennsylvania, he wrote, "is swarming with foreigners—Poles, Hungarians, Slavish, Swedes, and Italians, etc.—who are fast driving the English, Welsh, and Scotch miners out of competition." Before the influx of the foreigners into the American coalfields, "the Welsh had the best show in the mines here, but in consequence of their foolhardy and unreasonable impositions in pretty well everything, they at length became perfectly unmanageable and the operators had no alternative but to send and get whole cargoes of the foreigners I have named, who now practically monopolize the business, and no longer will America hold out a friendly hand to the British miner who must stay at home and do the best he can there or come here and starve. There are in America today and especially in the west, thousands upon thousands of our countrymen who would gladly return to England and Wales if they could only do so, but they cannot find the money."[54] Williams, who was an assistant foreman at the time, reveals the management perspective in blaming the Welsh for putting the operators into the position of hiring the more tractable eastern and southern European immigrants instead of British mine workers by their obstreperous behavior.

Unlike Welsh letters home from the agricultural regions that praised America and the opportunities available for farmers here, letters from Welsh coal miners and other industrial workers during the last decades of the nineteenth century almost universally discouraged compatriots from immigrating to America. In America and Wales most strikes came about to prevent wage reductions, and while generally they were at best only partially successful, labor militancy in America was weakened by the loss of labor power. In Wales, however, labor found a new unity, and in the Welsh mining industry it became more attractive than the industry in the United States. According to Alan Conway, "faced with the choice between strengthening their national position with new immigrants from Wales or that of weakening the owner's powers by discouraging immigrants, the Welsh coalminer chose the latter."[55] Contrary to Conway's contention, the letters discouraging miners back home in Wales from immigrating to America were not merely self-serving attempts to preserve jobs in America for themselves. A government study comparing wages and productivity in Pennsylvania, Great Britain, and Germany in the 1880s found that the wages paid per ton of coal in Pennsylvania were 25 to 40 percent lower than in Europe even though production was higher.[56]

Explanation for why the Welsh abandoned the industry they had dominated for so long has typically followed a class and cultural differences model. With the exception of scholars sympathetic to the Slavs, the standard interpretation adopted by historians has followed that presented in *The Slav Invasion*, a 1904 study by a contemporary social scientist, Frank Warne. Two general classes of employees could be found in and about the mines, Warne wrote, the skilled and the unskilled. The skilled included occupations such as blacksmiths, carpenters, engineers, firemen, miners, and the foremen and fire-bosses. The unskilled groups included slate-pickers, door-boys, helpers, drivers and runners, and the laborers who composed the majority of the inside employees. Within each classification was a wide variation in the degrees of skill, and as individuals acquired more skill they climbed the occupational ladder. Consequently, miners were not only constantly passing out of the unskilled into the skilled ranks, but skilled men were also moving up to become fire-bosses, foremen, and superintendents. Some left the coal industry entirely to take better jobs outside of the coal industry, while others were killed or incapacitated by injuries. In this dynamic labor pool, therefore, mine laborers were always qualifying by experience for passage into the ranks of the skilled miner. Immediately upon entering the industry the Slavs began acquiring experience as mine laborers, and then pushed for entry into the position of miner. As the Slav immigration grew into an "invasion," they became competitors with English speakers for jobs as miners. According to Warne, "the Slav was willing to work for longer hours than the English-speaking laborer, to perform heavier work, to ply his pick in more dangerous places, and stolidly to put up with inconveniences that his English-speaking competitor would not brook. But, more than all, he had a lower standard of living; he could produce his labor at a lower cost and sell it at a lower rate. He was a cheap man; and it was to the interest of the mining companies . . . to secure and give employment to cheap men."[57]

Under the contract system skilled miners as well as the operators gained advantages from cheaper Slav laborers. As their numbers multiplied the English-speaking laborer was forced to either "work more cheaply or withdraw from the competition; and in a market usually over-supplied with mine-labor, owing, among other things, to the lack of regular employment the year round, there could be but one result. In a short while the English-speaking laborer was being forced out of that position." The English-speaking miners saw their mistake too late as the Slavs acquired the skills to become full-fledged miners. Unfortunately, Warne wrote, "as he had been a cheaper laborer, so was he a cheaper miner." He was willing to accept lower living standards, and his indifference to harsh working conditions which had made him a useful laborer also led him to work in more dangerous seams than the English-speaking miner. Therefore, according to Warne, "as he had driven out the laborer of the older industrial group, he now began as surely to drive out the English-speaking miner."[58]

The major problem confronting the English-speaking miner, wrote Warne, did not lay in a reduction of the wage rate, which remained practically unchanged from 1880 to 1900, but rather in his declining net earnings. The miners' tools grew in number and cost; poorer seams now yielded less for the effort; allowances for extra work were withdrawn; insurance became a necessity and at the same time more costly because of the increase in the number of accidents involving unskilled men; the number of pounds to a ton and the size of the mine car increased; and miners were docked for impurities in the coal sent out. If the English-speaking miner was to maintain his standard of living, these cost-cutting arrangements had to be offset by compensation that did not occur. As a result, many voluntarily abandoned the mines. "The pressure on some mine-workers was so great as to force their boys of tender years into the breaker and their girl children into the silk-mill, in order that their pittance might add to the family income," Warne wrote.[59]

"Progress" and "rising expectations" also prompted the English-speaking miners to leave the anthracite industry, Warne wrote. These motivating forces inspired the Welsh, and other English-speaking miners, to desire a better life for their families, Warne believed, and they found that mining no longer provided those desired improvements, so they sought other options. The mine camp was similarly restrictive, and greater opportunities were found in the larger cities. If they remained, they strove to become fire-bosses, foremen, or superintendents. "Practically all the best-paying positions about the collieries today are filled by English-speaking mineworkers," Warne observed, but these positions were relatively few in number, so many Welsh mineworkers left for other employment that offered greater opportunity and mobility. By the turn of the twentieth century the sons of Welsh miners no longer followed their fathers into the pits. As an illustration, Warne pointed to the town of Shenandoah, where the Slavs had displaced the older immigrants as the predominant element in the population. There, "four once flourishing and largely attended Welsh churches are now so weak that their disbandment seems to be only a question of a very short time. (2 Baptist; 1 Congregational; 1 Presby)."[60]

The same year that Warne published his sociological study of the "Slav invasion," 1904, another scholar published his own assessment of social conditions in the anthracite fields of Pennsylvania. Peter Roberts's *Anthracite Coal Communities* followed a somewhat different line of inquiry, but his conclusions were similar to Warne's, that the desire for upward mobility among English-speaking miners prompted them to leave the coal industry in search of greater economic opportunity and that left the door open for Slavs to take their places. The "Anglo-Saxon mine employees" had attempted to thwart the Slav competition, Roberts claimed, but they failed, and the coal-mining towns once inhabited by miners from the British Isles had passed into the hands of the Slavs. Roberts agreed with Warne in his claim that the Slav standard of living was lower than the English-speaking miners would accept, making them willing to work for lower wages.

The pessimistic opinion of these contemporary scholars was proven wrong during the course of the twentieth century by the assimilation of the eastern and southern European immigrants into American society, and by their support of the labor movement and its ideals.[61] Nevertheless, the arrival of the "new" immigrants did indeed coalesce with the departure of the "old" immigrants from the British Isles. Certainly this was the case for the Welsh. William D. Jones concludes that Scranton "experienced a profound and irrevocable occupational transformation" when, by the turn of the twentieth century, the Welsh began an "exodus en masse" from the mines. Far more than an occupational shift, the abandonment "took away one of the strongest bonds which had kept the Welsh community together and given it a distinctive identity." As the coalfield cities diversified, and economic opportunities opened up, the Welsh were in a position to take advantage of them.[62] But this transformation of the social structure went far beyond Welsh Scranton or the anthracite region and affected the older bituminous coalfields in western Pennsylvania and Ohio as well.

Like the anthracite fields, the bituminous regions of western Pennsylvania grew phenomenally. In 1870, bituminous production in the state was 7.8 million tons, but by 1909 annual production soared to 150 million tons. The workforce in bituminous mining reflected this growth, rising from under 17,000 in 1870 to 185,921 in 1909. Demand far outstripped the local labor force, and employers recruited mine workers from others states and in Europe. The U.S. Industrial Commission published a comprehensive study in 1911 that reported that immigrants in the Pennsylvania bituminous fields from England, Scotland, Wales, and Germany were being displaced by workers from southern and eastern Europe without prior mining, or even industrial, experience.[63]

The commission's report demonstrated that the bituminous fields of Pennsylvania were not a major destination of the Welsh or other older immigrant groups displaced by the Slavs, Hungarians, and Italians. According to the Industrial Commission, of the 53,793 coal-mine workers whose ethnicity could be determined by state officials in 1903, only 411 were Welsh, the smallest group reported. That number remained relatively constant each year through 1907 when 409 Welsh-born miners were among the total 47,908 bituminous mine workers reported. The Welsh who left the anthracite fields, therefore, did not migrate to the bituminous fields of Pennsylvania, probably because the "invasion" of Slavs, Hungarians, and Italians overwhelmed both the hard and soft coalfields of Pennsylvania. Based on the same study, the eastern and southern European immigrants substantially and consistently outnumbered the native and older immigrant groups between 1903 (53,793 versus 39,793) and 1907 (47,908 versus 31,325). The commission concluded that, for the bituminous region of Pennsylvania as a whole, the immigration of British and northern Europeans was "proportionately very small since 1890, and at the present time has practically ceased."[64]

The commission took as the "most representative" case study the Connellsville coke region, a sixty-mile-long area between Point Marion and Brownsville northeast to Greensburg and Latrobe, where development of the coal resources was extensive and foreign immigration was massive. During the early years of coal mining in western Pennsylvania, before the Civil War, the Americans, Irish, and Germans were the pioneers of the industry; the number of English, Scots, and Welsh was negligible. After the war there was a minor increase in the number of British immigrants, but by 1893 they had stopped coming altogether. Desperate for labor, a few operators employed some Slovaks and Poles from a New York employment agency and found that they performed satisfactorily in unskilled positions. Several companies retained agents in Europe to hire more of them, and from that point the immigration of southern and eastern immigrants into the region rose rapidly.[65]

The commission's figures on the length of time each group was employed in the bituminous industry substantiated the ascent of the new and decline of the old immigrants. Of the 37,016 bituminous mine employees included in the Immigration Commission's study, only 191 were Welsh, 73.3 percent of whom had been in the United States twenty or more years. All the British and northern Europeans had similar lengths of residency, whereas the southern and eastern Europeans who made up the vast majority of the study had resided in America only a few years. Nor were many American-born children of Welsh fathers moving into western Pennsylvania bituminous mining since only 210, or .4 percent of the sample, were reported by the commission. Those Welsh who did come at the turn of the twentieth century were disproportionately found in the managerial and skilled positions. In another sample of 45,052 foreign-born bituminous mine workers in Pennsylvania, the Scots, Swedes, English, and Welsh averaged the highest daily wages, between $2.35 and $2.27, indicating that the men in this small ethnic cluster were skilled workers. Of this same study group, 9,954 were native-born sons of fathers born in Austria, Germany, Ireland, England, Scotland, and Wales. The data show that the native sons of Welsh-born fathers represented the elite among the mine workforce from the standpoint of average daily wages, earning the highest wage of $2.43; the Scottish sons second at $2.30. The British, Irish, and German immigrants came to the bituminous fields prior to the great expansion of the industry. They and their sons were, therefore, prepared to assume positions of responsibility and higher pay when the industry grew.[66]

◆ Of course, it is well understood that Americans, mine owners among them, were prejudiced against the non-English-speaking and Catholic Slavs, Hungarians, and Italians. After surveying the opinions of coal operators about the progress the new immigrants were making, the Immigration Commission concluded that the general feeling among operators toward recent immigrants "seems tinged with the conviction that they are inferior intellectually to Americans, English, Scotch, Irish, and Welsh, and not adapted to supervisory work." All the operators were in agreement that the new immigrants were less ambitious, relatively uneducated, generally inexperienced, and hampered in communicating effectively with their bosses due to an inability to speak English. As a result, the operators employed only Americans or old-stock immigrants as supervisors and in positions of responsibility. In rank-and-file positions, however, operators regarded the recent arrivals as more industrious and more tractable than the British, who insisted on proper ventilation and timbering in the mines when the superintendents were generally attempting to reduce costs by cutting corners.[67]

The Immigration Commission's investigation mirrored Warne's analysis of ethnic succession with "new" replacing the "old" immigrants because they were "cheaper." The commission reported that the use of cheaper immigrant labor also stimulated the use of mining machinery because recent immigrants would "work after these machines with less objection than persons of native birth or immigrants from Great Britain, who seem to prefer pick to machine work."[68] In other words, the British miner's control over the craft was undermined by the shift to machine mining. The shift was enabled by the operators' employment of the new immigrants in the unskilled laboring jobs that multiplied as machines displaced the miners' traditional craft skills. As the traditional miners lost control of the craft, they also lost leverage within the system.

Ethnic succession not only prompted the departure of the Welsh miners, but also the refusal of their sons to enter the industry. Significantly, Welsh parents frequently discouraged their sons from entering the mines by the turn of the twentieth century, even though they themselves had found success because their fathers had taken them into the pits at an early age. The commission concluded that the relatively small number of sons of Welsh-born fathers was accounted for by the fact that their children were "steadily leaving the industry for more attractive vocations." Almost all the native-born Welsh youths attended school, became Americanized, and sought employment in industries where the work and wages were better. On the other hand, most foreign-born Slav youths "do not know English, and do not attend school, but go into the mines as soon as possible and remain there."[69]

Ethnic groups were not segregated at work because company officials believed that segmentation fostered a clannishness that would hamper production. In the more intimate spheres of housing, boarding, and sleeping places, however, each group was more or less segregated unto itself. In her 1908 survey of the Pennsylvania coalfields, Annie MacLean found that "in the better parts of the towns quite apart from these [Slav] immigrants live the Americans and the immigrants of Anglo-Saxon and Celtic origin, holding the best positions and frequently scorning the Slavs. Socially they will have nothing to do with them; many of them have the strongest dislike, even contempt, for the Slavs."[70] Similarly, the Immigration Commission reported that "this clannishness is carried to such an extent that it is seldom that families of different races will occupy the same double house." Among the second generation, however, social barriers were less rigid, in part because of the familiarity stimulated by the public school system. At least for the first generation or two, the pattern established in the anthracite region was replicated, as described by Peter Roberts, in the bituminous fields. He noted that "in large towns, where the mine employees live, the various races form colonies and generally keep within the limits of the section appropriated by them. Hence we have 'Scotch Road,' 'Murphy's Patch', 'Welsh Hill', 'Hun Town', 'Little Germany', 'Little Italy', etc. where ethnic customs continued to shape life."[71]

Finally, prejudice against the recent immigrants prompted the Welsh to leave the industry. The Immigration Commission, and many other contemporary sources, reported the aversion of the Welsh to the eastern and southern foreigners. The commission observed that the "Welsh did not and do not desire to be associated in the mines with the recent immigrant." English-speaking miners regarded working alongside the recent immigrants as degrading, the commissioners reported, and that was "one of the strongest forces toward the displacement of the older employees." Instead, they left mining and "entered other work which, in the popular phrase of the coal regions, is not 'a Hunkey's job.'" Some of the displaced miners were promoted to higher positions that opened as the industry expanded. Their numbers were relatively small, however, and the majority found new employment in the region's steel mills and metal manufacturing shops, or went into business for themselves. Some of them migrated to the bituminous fields further west that were coming into production. The commissioners also found it noteworthy that the greatest number of English-speaking miners became employees in those plants nearest to cities, "where the workmen are free to live and trade where they please, and where they do not have to accept the immigrants' standards beyond wages, hours, and conditions of work."[72] It would seem that most of the Welsh finally achieved upward mobility by leaving coal mining behind to follow the path that led directly into middle-class America.

The upward mobility of the Welsh miners and the corresponding influx of southern and eastern European immigrants had a dramatic impact on the composition of the mining force. British miners were neither able to retain their control over the production process nor were they able to re-produce class leadership grounded in the traditional ideology of labor re-publicanism. The Slavs and Italians accepted the mechanization of the mines that deskilled the traditional craft miner. The 1890s was a hiatus in the political ideology of miners between the nineteenth-century republican reform ideology as expressed by the Knights of Labor, and the bread-and-butter industrial unionism of the twentieth century embraced by the United Mine Workers of America. It was a decade when the ethnic composition of the mine workforce was reconstituted, and a political economy emerged that was dominated by the growing power of corporations.[73] It was a period before the new immigrants were organized by the labor movement and Anglo-American miners succumbed to the grip of nativism and individual-ism.[74] By 1906, a Pennsylvania mine inspector confirmed the trend that had been underway for more than a decade when he observed that "it would seem that the old standbys of the anthracite region, the English, Welsh, and Scotch, Irish, and Germans are going elsewhere."[75] To the Welsh, the ideals enshrined in the gospel of success and labor republicanism seemed to be passing away with the nineteenth century. Their opportunities for social mobility had given way to their darkest fears—permanent proletarianiza-tion. One writer traveling the coalfields summed up the lack of organization and commitment to collective action among miners: "One who studies the condition of coal miners in America will feel as if he has descended a ladder, the lowest rung of which is in the east and highest in the west." The coal miner of Pennsylvania, in fact, seemed to this observer to be "a different creature from the coal miner of Illinois, Missouri, and Colorado."[76] With a multitude of nationalities, languages, and traditions now present in Penn-sylvania, there seemed to be little continuity with the British and American mining culture and its supporting ideology. A new mining culture emerged that rejected republicanism and built unity upon common class values rather than ethnic origin.

# WELSH AMERICAN
# UNION LEADERSHIP

Some Welsh American coal miners achieved upward mobility within the industry by rising into the ranks of industry management, and others became technical experts such as engineers and mine inspectors. Many more, and practically all the Welsh-born in America, abandoned mining to enter other professions. There were some, however, who found career opportunities within organized labor. With the founding of the United Mine Workers of America (UMWA) in 1890, ambitious union officials had a national organization in which to learn valuable leadership skills and a springboard for launching careers in politics or management. By the 1920s the UMWA had grown into a national organization with a bureaucratic structure operated by union professionals. Primed with the ideology of progress and success, Welshmen were strategically positioned within the industry and the union to personally benefit from the opportunities presented as well as to shape the direction of the labor movement.

In his study of union leadership in the United States between 1870 and 1920, Warren R. Van Tine examined the careers of 350 unionists and broke them into two distinctive leadership models: traditional "reform unionism" and, after the mid-1890s, the new "business unionism." By the 1890s the reform-minded Knights of Labor (K of L) had failed in their effort to unite producers into one big union and to replace the wage system with cooperative associations as a way of elevating the condition of all workers. The American Federation of Labor (AFL) replaced the K of L, and with the acceptance of industrial capitalism it abandoned the reformist vision of turning workers into owners, to concentrate instead on the bread-and-butter issues of improving their conditions, hours, and wages.[1] Of the old-school leaders, nearly one-half were foreign-born with the vast majority originating in the British Isles. Similarly, the new-school leaders were either second generation or immigrants (42 percent), mostly of British Isles origin. Although the number of foreign-born leaders declined over time, their places were taken by their American-born sons, who were raised in families and communities that esteemed unionism. As John Brophy, the son of an English-born miner, noted, "Everybody belonged to unions" in the Pennsylvania coal town where he grew up; unionism was simply "taken for granted." British immigrants brought with them not only the skills developed in British mines, Brophy observed, "but also, like my father, the experience of British unions."[2]

Van Tine found that the traditional labor leader in the period before 1920 typically began his work life at fourteen, joined the union, rose through the ranks quickly to become a national officer by thirty-five, remained in office a few years, and then returned to the rank and file in his previous line of work. Relatively few traditional unionists escaped labor by entering business, politics, or the professions after leaving office. By 1920, a major shift in this pattern had occurred as a new generation of leaders had gained social advancement by becoming "corporate executives within the union structure." The differences between the two groups evolved not from their sociological origins, but rather from "the institutionalization of the union, and the simultaneous professionalization of union leadership." Adapting to modernization transformed their organizations from a loose confederation of semi-autonomous locals into centralized organizations with managerial subdivisions.[3]

Unions struggled against powerful trends that restructured the American economy between 1890 and 1920 as the national market system dissolved local labor markets, severe competition undermined wages and conditions, and large industries demanded control over their own workforce. Against these pressures labor unions were forced to organize nationally in order to exert counterforce and to standardize labor conditions. Centralization, standardization, and increasing bureaucratization of organized labor resulted in a growing gap between the leaders and the led. An editorial in the *United Mine Workers' Journal* noted that "the miners will need, as never before, a solid organization headed by able men who can present convincingly the miners' side of any controversy that may arise on prices or working conditions." By 1920 the role of the national labor leader had changed dramatically from one that was largely informal, reflecting the decentralized nature of unionism, to one requiring the skills of a chief executive officer of a corporation.[4] Reformers and radicals, like Socialist Eugene V. Debs and Communist William Z. Foster, denounced the new business unionists for succumbing to capitalist "embourgeoisement" by embracing middle-class values, social striving, and the acquisition of property and wealth. The rank and file themselves, however, generally regarded the advancement of their leaders to prominent positions in government and industry favorably. As one miner commented in 1905, a successful career "should be an object lesson to every man" because it indicates "by honesty, devotion to his ambition, hard work and determination what a man may accomplish."[5]

The UMWA reflected a mirror image of these larger trends in organized labor. The national union evolved out of local organizations that emerged after the Civil War to become regional associations. Then, in 1890, the UMWA was founded, and by 1920 had grown into the largest labor union in the United States. Like the leaders of other national unions, leadership in the centralized UMWA sought to maintain order, discourage rank-and-file spontaneity, negate local control, and proceed cautiously in matters of politics. These developments encountered opposition from local and district officers whose resistance had to be overcome. Centralization did make the UMWA less democratic, but also led to a qualified social acceptance of career unionists as "embourgeoisement" softened radicalism.[6] Welsh union men occupied pivotal positions at strategic moments to make a profound impact on the evolution of organized labor among American coal miners.

## Reform Unionism: David R. Jones

David R. Jones is an excellent example of the strengths and limitations of the reformer as labor leader. He was born in 1853 near Swansea, Wales, and immigrated as a young man to Wilkes-Barre, Pennsylvania, where he worked in the mines. In 1874, at age eighteen, he left the mines and attended Mount Union College in Alliance, Ohio, graduating four years later. Jones took up residence in Six Mile Ferry, a Welsh settlement near Homestead, Pennsylvania, where he taught school, and began the study of law in Pittsburgh. As a former miner himself, Jones empathized with the coal miners who lived around him and whose children he taught in school. His identity with the local miners was solidified when, shortly after his arrival at Six Mile Ferry, he closed the school and joined the miners on the picket line. Because of his education, experience as a miner, and his demonstrated solidarity with them, the miners accepted him into the K of L Assembly 860 and employed him as their checkweighman.[7]

The Monongahela strike of 1879 was a district-wide success, and the miners credited Jones for the outcome. Jones attributed the success to a conversation he overheard at the Pittsburgh Coal Exchange from which he learned that a growing number of orders were piling up on the mine owners' desks, and that they were on the verge of conceding to the miners' demands for a pay increase. Jones encouraged the miners to hold out for a few weeks more and, when the owners caved in to their demands, the miners credited him with uncanny ability. During the course of the next three years Jones served as the executive secretary of the Miners Association in the Pittsburgh district, which was also K of L District Assembly 9.[8]

The Pittsburgh district miners gave Jones their complete confidence by appointing him general secretary and then president. There was no vice president, secretary, treasurer, or executive board to advise or oversee his performance. Each miner who belonged to the association paid him five cents a month as his salary. Because of the general economic prosperity, and the rising orders for coal at higher prices, Jones was able to exercise considerable influence on the regional economy. Andrew Roy observed that Jones "wore a broad-brimmed hat and was known to every business man in Pittsburgh."[9] Jones himself was fully aware of the unusual confidence placed in his charge. In "An Address to the Miners of the Pittsburgh District," he noted that "we had no written constitution and by-laws defining and enjoining our reciprocal duties. . . . What I should or should not do, so far as any written rule went, was left entirely to my judgment and honesty. At first glance this looks as though I was vested with imperial powers over your affairs; but the second glance will dispel the appearance." Jones recognized that he was functioning within the realm of customary rights and privileges rather than a governing document. "Long before I came here you had certain usages based on your notions of honor, justice and equity. These were well known to you, and had I been disposed I could not have dared to violate them" without being "at once adjudged totally unfit for the office and quickly ousted."[10]

If Jones's influence and unprecedented power over the Miners Association was confidently given by the members, it also brought out the "backbiters" among other leaders and aspirants. Andrew Roy noted that Jones was "as much of an autocrat as the Czar of Russia." David R. Jones acknowledged the limits of his power, but his obvious ambition made other labor leaders wary of him. Even at the height of his popularity he was criticized for "authoritarian tactics and the relentless pursuit of his own power." Thomas Armstrong, the editor of the *National Labor Tribune* who also served as treasurer of the Miners Association, wrote to Terence Powderly in 1880 that Jones should be closely monitored because of what Armstrong regarded as Jones's egotistical drive for personal advancement. "He is very ambitious. . . . He is an indiscreet talker so far as saying I, 'Big I' at that." Armstrong suggested that, if Jones did anything improper, Powderly should "sit down on him." One miner lodged an alliterative complaint in the *National Labor Tribune* that Jones's "lucrative love of loquacity" was overbearing.[11]

In a field with limited opportunities for leadership, Jones's ambition pitted him against every other would-be leader. How threatening he was is demonstrated in his attempt to create a national organization to restrict coal production when the markets were glutted and the price could not sustain a living wage. In 1879 Jones attempted to organize a national conference on restriction. He sent notices to "the miners at every pit in Ohio, West Virginia, Kentucky, Indiana, Illinois, Iowa, Missouri, and other states" to provide him with the name of every pit secretary with whom he would communicate about the national restriction convention to be held the following spring. "Restriction is our only salvation, but if all miners, everywhere, will not restrict universally and unanimously together, individual pits or even regions cannot, and it would be suicidal for them to try."[12] A man with big ideas must also have big ambitions, and that established Jones as a competitor.

D. R. Jones also successfully established a system of regional arbitration as a way to quell industrial conflict. "A strike, like the right of a people to rebel when their rights are ruthlessly violated, is a right that should be preserved, but never used when by other means the desired end can be substantially obtained. Nothing so embitters our industrial relations, nothing so widens the chasm between Capital and Labor, and there is nothing so baneful to the community and so destructive to the comfort, happiness, and elevation of workingmen and their families, as hasty and unnecessary strikes."[13] Jones proposed that miners in western Pennsylvania adopt the approach of Alexander McDonald's Miners' National Association of Great Britain, which was to establish a board of arbitration to settle disputes through cooperation with the operators. He formulated the principles governing such a board of arbitration, published them in the *National Labor Tribune*, and gave the miners the opportunity to vote on the idea. His language was not that of a tyrant: "This board of arbitration is a creation of your collective feelings and minds, not of any one else. I am merely your servant, your clerk, hired and 'bossed' by the miners, and as such it is my duty to paint to you the dark as well as the bright side of the question." Jones successfully used the arbitration board to win wage concessions for the miners, further bolstering his popularity.[14]

Jones favored arbitration over strikes, but he also believed that only through labor solidarity could the workers protect their interests. He was not advocating strikes, but rather "system, unity and uniformity." Jones carried the labor unity theme further than most labor leaders of the day by encouraging miners to ignore racial and ethnic differences and to include African Americans and immigrants: "Let no creed, color, or race pollute its sacred shrines. Protestantism has nothing to do with bread and butter, and Catholicism has nothing to do with clothing. . . . The Germans, Irish, Welsh, French and Americans all have stomachs; they must have clothing, and a slice of beef is just as delicious to one as another."[15]

Like other reform labor leaders of the period, Jones learned the hard way that separating politics from labor union formation made little sense when the law was written to serve the interests of capital. Employers fighting the fledgling labor movement in Pennsylvania found support in the state's anti-conspiracy laws, as well as the common-law tradition, which defined a conspiracy as any combination of two or more persons seeking to commit a criminal act. Unions confronted similar anti-conspiracy and anti-monopoly laws throughout the United States until well into the twentieth century. It was Pennsylvania's 1876 conspiracy law that Thomas Mellon, an owner of the Waverly Coal Company just west of Pittsburgh, charged Jones with breaching by urging Waverly miners, who were working for less than the miners' scale, to go out on strike. Mellon's lawyers argued that Jones was a revolutionary Communist, conspiring against the American system. According to Jones's own account, on November 18, 1880, he was on a train en route to a meeting with the Waverly miners when he was arrested and held under $1,000 bail to appear at the February 1881 term of court. Jones argued that his arrest on public property was a "flagrant outrage upon your and my constitutional rights as men and citizens of a free country." The judge's charge to the jury, however, called for a hard-line interpretation of the anti-conspiracy law. In the end, he was sentenced to twenty-four hours in jail and a $100 fine, which his lawyer promptly appealed to the state supreme court. At the time, Jones was studying law under the sponsorship of George W. Guthrie, one of Pittsburgh's most prominent attorneys, and the public knowledge that he would soon leave the miners' union to become a lawyer probably explains the light sentence.[16]

The arrest and trial of David R. Jones only confirmed to the miners that he was on their side. In June 1882, when it was already known that he intended to step aside as head of the Miners Association in order to practice law, Jones was asked to preside as Chief Marshal of the Labor Day parade in Pittsburgh. Approximately six thousand marchers led by Jones wended their way through the streets between thousands of onlookers. In October 1882, Jones resigned his position as head of the Miners Association in an open letter published in the *National Labor Tribune*. Jones's "embourgeoisement" did not mean that he stored his sympathy for the working class in the closet. Even though he turned down the nomination to become a Union

Labor Party candidate in 1882, he continued to concern himself with the conditions of labor.[17] Indeed, workers admired his personal achievement and social advancement. The *National Labor Tribune* proclaimed: "We are proud to see a coworker, by his own exertions and diligence, the possessor of an enviable fame and an independent profession." He made a tour of England and Wales during July and August 1883, and published a series of eighteen articles chronicling his travels under the title "Ex-President Jones' Jaunt" in the *National Labor Tribune*.[18] His ship docked in Liverpool where he boarded the train for Wales, and traversed Monmouth and Glamorgan counties on his way to his birthplace in Swansea. He was struck by the expansion of South Wales's coal and iron industries that extended "nearly continuous for nearly thirty miles." Jones spent the next three weeks "visiting scenes of my childhood, mingling with the workmen." It had been thirteen years since he left, but great changes had occurred in his absence: "New mines opened, new tin, steel and other works built, with new towns and suburbs and a strange population in them. Parents grown gray-haired; those small when I left now men and women, unrecognizable; of companions of former years, some were soberly settled with families, some in America, some in Australia, and not a few had been buried in the old crowded churchyard."[19]

Like so many immigrants who return to their homeland after a long absence, Jones encountered the uncomfortable reality that his memory of the homeplace was fixed in an earlier time that social change had altered irretrievably. During his visit Jones made detailed observations on working-class life, conditions, and politics in England and Wales, which he shared with American readers of the *National Labor Tribune*. In the end, Jones was happy to step ashore in Philadelphia on August 30, "having on our two months 'jaunt' discovered no place as sweet as home and no country as good as this."[20]

By the mid-1880s Jones was keeping up with the respectable middle class of Homestead, where he bought a house and enjoyed a flourishing legal practice. In 1886 he was elected burgess of Homestead and reelected in 1887, winning by large majorities. "The miners and mill men nearly all voted for him, which was a deserved compliment," declared the *National Labor Tribune*. Jones relinquished the position in 1888 when he was elected to serve in the Pennsylvania legislature. No doubt remembering his own experience with the conspiracy laws, Jones sponsored legislation in Harrisburg to protect the right of labor unions to incorporate just like corporations.[21]

During the tumultuous events surrounding the Homestead Lockout of

William T. Lewis, Grand Master Workman, Knights of Labor Assembly 135. *Cambrian* 29 (May 15, 1909): 10. Courtesy of West Virginia and Regional History Collection, West Virginia University Libraries.

1892, David R. Jones, now a former legislator, was called on to defend James Holleran, who, along with others, was charged with resisting arrest and disorderly conduct. At the hearing before the squire, Jones argued that "the person under arrest and all others not only exercised a right but performed a sacred duty in resisting unless the officer had a warrant for the arrest." The sheriff appealed to the judge, contending that the disorderly element had been incited to further disorderly conduct by Jones, and the lawyer should be called to account for his utterances. Jones's explanation that his comments were misunderstood and not aimed at incitement was accepted by the judge and the matter was dropped.[22]

The historian of the Homestead Lockout, Paul Krause, notes that, while Jones supported labor's cause, "he continued to aspire to the kind of respectability enjoyed by his mentor, George Guthrie, a man destined to become Pittsburgh's leading reform mayor and hero in the polite world of liberal Progressivism." There was "a world of difference [that] separated apparent reformers such as David Jones" from labor activists of the working class. In fact, Krause concludes, "Jones seemed to have more in common with his ostensible antagonists—Mellon, Frick, Carnegie, and the like."[23] Surely this assessment is too harsh within the context of Jones's own time and circumstance, as well as a romanticized view of labor leadership that, if accepted, would impose on the old adage "once a miner always a miner" a permanency that Welsh miners and their colleagues would have rejected. Jones was more of a worker who became a reformer, rather than the traditional union leader who returned to the pits after his term in office was over. Both the traditional and reform union leader, however, stunted the growth of organized labor by depriving the union of continuity in experienced leadership however noble their motives. But the movement that they hindered had yet to come into existence.

### Transition from Reform to Business Unionism: William T. and Thomas L. Lewis

W. T. Lewis was a transitional figure, a reformer turned strong national trade unionist by bitter experience. He found himself in a strategic position to strengthen the labor movement for coal miners, and he sacrificed his own career within the movement to achieve that goal. Nevertheless, like David R. Jones, Lewis was an ambitious man who used the union as a springboard to success in law and politics. His younger brother, Thomas L., was a professional trade unionist who used the union movement as a way to advance his own career in industry once he had reached the limits of advancement within the UMWA. Unlike Jones, or his brother, Thomas Lewis did not continue to support labor's cause after he left his UMWA office.

Most major leaders among the coal miners came from small, unstimulating hamlets that might be regarded as unlikely incubators of leadership. Shawnee in southern Ohio was no exception. Arguably the most influential organization in Shawnee during the 1880s was the Knights of Labor. The local assembly built its own two-story meeting hall where members attended weekly meetings and original essays were read, discussions were held on industrial subjects, and lessons were offered to prepare members for citizenship. Books and newspapers were also provided for members. When not in use, the building served as the local opera house. The first floor was rented out to stores. The K of L certainly had a profound influence on the sons of Thomas and Mary Lewis, who emigrated from the Dowlais district of South Wales to Pennsylvania in 1866. Thomas and Mary first came to Northumberland County, Pennsylvania, to work in the anthracite mines and became acquainted with John Siney and other early pioneer unionists of the Workingmen's Benevolent Association; he remained an ardent union man for the rest of his life. The family moved to the western Pennsylvania bituminous mines in the Clearfield district, and to Shawnee, Ohio, in 1879. Thomas died prematurely from "consumption," probably pneumoconiosis ("Black Lung"), at age forty-six. His death left Mary a widow at forty-one with eleven children to support, so they all went to work at an early age.[24]

Even though Thomas J. and Mary Lewis led an all too common life of hardship and tragedy, the efforts of their children to elevate their condition led to exceptional success stories. Four of the sons went to work in the mines and iron mills and used working-class organizations to elevate their status. The oldest, William T. Lewis, was born in Dowlais, South Wales, in 1860, and accompanied his parents when they immigrated to the United States in 1866. He entered the coal breaker at age six and went down in the mines at age nine. At twenty-three he became the main support for nine surviving brothers and sisters. Nevertheless, he worked during the day and studied at night, and managed to save enough money to attend a term at the Normal School in Lebanon, Ohio, during the 1884 Hocking strike. While still in Lebanon, the executive board of the Knights of Labor sent him to Indiana to manage a Knights' cooperative mine in Cannelburg. Lewis advised the board that market conditions would not justify the additional expenditures required to operate the mine economically; thus, the board decided to cut its losses, and Lewis returned to Shawnee.[25]

Back home, Lewis worked in the mines during the day and opened a night school, more out of a desire to elevate the children of fellow miners than pecuniary advantage according to one source. During his leisure hours he studied surveying and higher mathematics with "an old and erudite scholar." In his history of the American miners, Andrew Roy, a contemporary of Lewis, observed that Lewis was "a young man of commanding presence, and possessed a fairly good education." Roy also observed that Lewis was "ambitious to make a career in the labor movement."[26] One local biography states that from an early age he became a leader among the miners because of his advocacy skills and commitment. Also, he was early on an adherent of the Republican Party, believing that "capital and labor should work in harmony and on terms of equality—that neither should oppress the other—that both are essential in the full and complete development of the country."[27] Like most Welsh miners of the period, he articulated the ideology of labor republicanism.

To the extent that William T. Lewis is remembered in history at all, it is as a labor leader. Unfortunately, his reputation has been sullied by historians who have accepted the characterizations of his opponents, such as Knights of Labor's Grand Master Workman Terence V. Powderly and Secretary-Treasurer Robert Watchorn. Their acrimony toward Lewis was so intense because he committed the heresy of switching sides. In the beginning the Knights' leadership saw in W. T. Lewis a star in the making. In his mid-twenties Shawnee Knights elected him Master Workman of Local Assembly 169, one of the strongest assemblies in Ohio. At the second convention of Knights National Trade Assembly (NTA) 135 in June 1877, William H. Bailey, also a member of the Shawnee assembly, declined to stand for a second term as master workman, and Lewis was elected to replace him.[28] It was during his brief tenure of two years as head of the Knights' NTA 135 that Lewis made his most lasting contribution to the coal miners of America, and also made him vulnerable for the most virulent attacks against his character.

To understand the vindictiveness against Lewis, we must understand his role in the ideological struggle between the social reformers and the national trade unionists. The Knights of Labor grew out of a pre–Civil War reform movement that attempted to organize all producers of wealth into a coalition that would then abolish the wage system and usher in a new society. The Executive Board announced before the General Assembly in 1884 that "the essential difference is that our Order contemplates a radical change in the existing industrial system, and labors to bring about that change, while Trade Unions and other orders accept the industrial system as it is, and endeavor to adapt themselves to it. The attitude of our Order to the existing industrial system is antagonistic, and is necessarily one of war."[29]

The problem with defining the labor union as a reform organization of producers was that the Knights accepted all producers, which excluded only speculators and lawyers. The assemblies were, therefore, composed of a variety of people and occupations, and could become little more than political discussion groups. The trade unions rejected the broad-based reform thrust of the Knights in favor of focusing on higher wages, shorter hours, job control, and working conditions. Instead of the mixed assemblies preferred by the Knights, trade unions organized along craft or industrial lines from the local to the national levels. The rapidly expanding economy and relative scarcity of labor in America during the late nineteenth century provided trade unionism fertile ground for growth.[30]

The conflict also pulled the Knights apart from within as the leadership clung to reform while a growing number of tradesmen within the organization demanded immediate amelioration of conditions. Therefore, in 1879 the K of L General Assembly authorized the establishment of national trade districts within the Knights' organization. There was strong philosophical opposition to homogeneous assemblies composed of members of the same craft, like coal miners, but the Knights were forced to affirm them in order to prevent the various tradesmen from abandoning the K of L for affiliation with the American Federation of Labor (AFL). In 1886 this internal struggle between trade unionists and reformers culminated in an open rupture.[31]

The split was not predestined because many Knights belonged to trade unions and many trade unionists belonged to the K of L. Trouble ensued, however, when the Knights attempted to organize workers who already belonged to national unions into competing trade assemblies, which resulted in jurisdictional disputes that undermined the negotiating power of the trade unions within their respective industries. Following the formation of the American Federation of Labor in 1886, the umbrella organization of trade unions, the Knights launched a campaign to induce the national unions to affiliate with the K of L rather than the AFL. What followed was a titanic struggle within the ranks over philosophical and jurisdictional issues of fundamental importance. In few trades was the battle so fierce as among the coal miners.[32]

National union organization among American coal miners preceded the formation of the Knights of Labor. The American Miners' Association, founded in 1861, was the prototype miners' union organized along industrial lines with federated state level organizations. It failed in the early 1870s, and many coal miners joined the K of L. The Knights proved inadequate to the task of serving the immediate concerns of miners, however, and the failure of the Hocking strike of 1874–75 convinced many of them that a national trade organization was vital. In Ohio, John McBride of the Massillon district, himself a Knight, organized the Ohio Miners' Amalgamated Association. One of his first moves was to call for a convention to meet in Indianapolis in September 1885 to form a national organization. Out of this convention emerged the National Federation of Miners and Mine Laborers (NFM).[33]

At the same time that McBride was organizing the NFM in 1885, miners within the K of L were seeking to organize a national assembly of miners. In May 1886, NTA 135 was empowered to organize miners and mine laborers nationally. Now the miners found themselves with two trade organizations, and relations between the two deteriorated rapidly. Organized on the heels of the NFM, unionists were convinced that the Knights' intention was hostile. Therefore, the NFM responded at its 1886 convention by flatly refusing to merge with the Knights and denying them representation. The NFM leadership also issued a circular claiming exclusive jurisdiction over coal mining, and cursed those "selfish individuals that are bent upon the destruction of our National Trades' Union."[34]

Several meetings were arranged during the spring and summer of 1887 between the executive boards of the NFM and NTA 135 in an effort to iron out the differences. William T. Lewis attended these conferences as the secretary of the Ohio district of NTA 135. President McBride of the Ohio Amalgamated Miners and his vice president, N. R. Hysell, represented the NFM. Finally, the executive boards of the NFM and NTA 135 met in November 1887 for talks. McBride led the NFM delegation, and W. T. Lewis, who had been elected master workman of NTA 135 in June 1887, led the delegation of Knights. Lewis was elected chairman and presided, but he disappointed the NFM delegates, who attended under the assumption that NTA 135 had accepted the principle of joining forces, by informing them that he was not authorized to discuss a merger. At this point reconstruction of these and subsequent events leading up to a new national miners' union becomes muddled, particularly the role of W. T. Lewis, who allegedly conspired to lead his miners into the NFM.[35]

In his often quoted history of American coal miners published in 1903, Andrew Roy, himself a loyal Knight, claimed that Lewis was less than honest as a leader of the miners. Roy pointed to a speech Lewis delivered at the third annual convention of NTA 135, affirming the worthiness of the Knights' cause, but he reversed himself and "suddenly reached the conclusion that the Knights' NTA 135 had proved a failure, and undertook without the knowledge or consent of his associates, to turn it over to the management and control of the National Federation of Miners." When NTA 135 Secretary-Treasurer Robert Watchorn learned of the plot, Roy writes, he issued a circular urging that Lewis be deposed as master workman of the organization. Both organizations met simultaneously in convention in Columbus, Ohio, on December 5, 1888, to discuss a new amalgamated organization. According to Roy's account, Lewis learned that there was little support for his "scheme" to merge NTA 135 into the NFM, but he nevertheless determined to work for the new union "regardless of what the convention would do."[36] In other words, Lewis was a traitor to the K of L, which had elected him to serve its interests.

Real life, and historical reconstruction, is generally more complicated, and this case is no exception. For one thing, W. T. Lewis was always a trade unionist and he represented that point of view in the internal struggle for influence within the Knights. He had not suddenly changed his mind, and far from acting stealthily his views were publicly expressed long before the fateful convention of December 1889. For example, John McBride, president of the Ohio Amalgamated and the NFM, reported in the *National Labor Tribune* in May 1887, when Lewis was still head of the K of L miners in Ohio and prior to his election as master workman of NTA 135, that the two of them had discussed unification of the two organizations. McBride proposed a merger, and Lewis agreed to consult the head of NTA 135. McBride then wrote personal letters seeking a response to his proposal from the NTA 135 executive board without much success. McBride clearly laid the failure to make progress at the door of the Knights of Labor.[37]

A few months later in 1887, Lewis wrote a letter to the *National Labor Tribune*, the official organ of the miners, which sounded like a response to McBride's charge that the K of L was not really interested in unification, and the widespread belief that NTA 135 was founded to oppose the NFM. Lewis wrote that he was proud to have been at the NTA 135 founding convention. Its stated purpose was to organize all miners who belonged to the Knights into one trades district, and not to counter the work of the NFM. In fact, he was "ready and willing to do anything that is honorable to unite the two forces" in service of the entire craft, and if there were leaders who "were making a fight for personal reasons, let them be the sufferers—and remove them from the positions they hold and put men in their places who will work for the good of the craft at large."[38]

W. T. Lewis's experience as leader of NTA 135 provided him with ample evidence that the miners would be successful only with a single, unified trade union. In Schuylkill County, the Amalgamated Association of Miners and Mine Laborers of Pennsylvania emerged to replace the defunct Workingmen's Benevolent Association. In 1886, the AAM and the Knights agreed to form a joint committee to coordinate their actions, but they were never able to reconcile their differences. The animosity between the two organizations in the summer of 1887, when Lewis was elected master workman of NTA 135, had reached the breaking point, but the rank and file of both unions walked out in protest over the influx of the Slavs. W. T. Lewis arrived to assume command of a strike that involved the two antagonistic unions, but fragmentation doomed the stoppage from the beginning. After meeting with Powderly in February 1888, Lewis ordered the miners to return to work on company terms. Although dismayed by the sudden capitulation, most local assemblies complied, but other locals were so angry that they returned their founding charters.[39]

The problems Lewis experienced with the Knights during this period were formative. The basic problem was the old split between the AAM's trade unionist, bread-and-butter approach versus the Knights' "all-for-one" policy. This lesson was driven home by John L. Lee, the head of the railroaders, who in typical Knights' fashion tried to take advantage of the miners' stoppage by leading the railroaders in their own strike for higher wages. When Lewis called an end to the strike, therefore, Lee was angry and blamed Lewis for hanging the railroad men out to dry. AAM miners regarded Lee's attitude as evidence of the Knights' misguided philosophy, and the plea for unity still more of the K of L "utopianism." A letter castigating Lewis for calling off the strike prompted the *Irish World* to editorialize that "the general executive board, K. of L., shifted 'the unwelcome responsibility [of management of the strike] upon the shoulders of W. T. Lewis.' . . . We cannot, therefore, agree with our correspondent that Mr. Lewis was in any way untrue to the trust reposed in him."[40] The lesson Lewis learned from this experience was that fragmented loyalties and internal conflict led to demoralization among rank-and-file miners who were simply looking for redress of immediate, practical grievances. He also might well have concluded that Powderly and the Knights' executive board were scheming against him and could not be trusted.

Lewis became convinced that the Knights' leadership rather than the NFM was blocking unification of the miners, a view he did not conceal. Following a joint meeting of NTA 135 and NFM in December 1888, Powderly confirmed Lewis's conviction by charging in an open letter that Lewis was misrepresenting his own organization and members. If Lewis "had labored as earnestly to build up and strengthen NTA 135 as he did to destroy it, there would be a far different story to tell today," Powderly declared. He questioned whether miners should "follow in the new organization a man who did not know how to lead in the old? . . . Can a man who proves untrue to the Knights of Labor be true to the Miners National Progressive Union?"[41]

The split was now open and Lewis's course was set. He responded directly to Powderly, charging him with driving miners out of NTA 135. In the letter, Lewis declared that he was "not surprised, but sorry," that Powderly was "confirming what you are frequently accused of—being the principal cause of the discord and turmoil in the ranks of labor." Powderly knew that the miners left NTA 135 "individually, silently, as they came in," but he did nothing to keep them from leaving. While the Knights were trying to organize the miners, Lewis complained, why did Powderly proclaim "God forbid that we return to trade unionism?" when he ought to have known that "a trades district is nothing more nor less than a trades union." Now there were two rival organizations of miners, when "there is no room for more than one organization of miners in this country," Lewis wrote, and "I will advise them to have but one organization, call it what they may."[42]

General accounts of the joint convention of the NFM and the Knights' NTA 135 are strikingly devoid of the passion that actually prevailed on the floor. The real difficulty lay with the division among the Knights. Lewis represented the labor-union faction, but as master workman of NTA 135 he was strategically positioned to influence the outcome. On December 4, 1888, the Knights met to prepare for the meeting and political wrangling began immediately. According to a press report, W. T. Lewis made "a fierce onslaught on the General Board, not sparing [Grand] Master Workman Powderly, who arrived during the day, and who sat quietly taking notes of the remarks. He then fiercely attacked Secretary Watchorn." Miners were leaving the K of L in droves, he declared, and bungling by national administration was to blame. Lewis then delivered "a strong plea in favor of one organization and declared, no matter what this convention should do, he would work in the interest of the new organization."[43] Robert Watchorn, secretary-treasurer of NTA 135, launched a vigorous reply to Lewis. Avoiding the central issues, Watchorn countered that Lewis was derelict in his duties; this, rather than miners abandoning the Order, accounted for the financial disorder of NTA 135. Lewis demanded a thorough investigation, a committee of three was chosen to conduct the inquiry, and the meeting adjourned.[44]

The next morning, December 5, 1888, the joint convention assembled in Druid Hall. John McBride called the convention to order, and Lewis was elected chairman. "The objects of the convention will be to decide upon the form of organization to govern our organized craftsmen in the future," Lewis declared, and "to determine upon a policy that will more effectually protect and promote the interests of our craft." The time given for discussion was set for two hours, and the convention recessed until that evening when the meeting was again called to order. Illinois, Ohio, Indiana, West Virginia, and Pennsylvania sent NFM delegates; reflecting its central role in the one-union movement within the K of L, Lewis's hometown sent four of the seventeen delegates. All the Knights' delegates were from Ohio and Pennsylvania. The Welsh delegates were much more in favor of the single trade union approach rather than the secret fraternal order represented by the Knights. Among the NFM delegates, Ohio miners clearly dominated, and at least five of the twenty-one were Welsh. In anthracite country, the Protestant English, Welsh, and German miners were more likely to join the NFM while the Irish Catholics favored the K of L; Powderly himself was Catholic.[45]

According to Andrew Roy's account, the K of L delegates were sent to the convention to discuss conciliation and cooperation but not unification. When the joint convention reconvened in the evening of December 5, it soon became apparent that the Knights were unprepared to relinquish their identity. The atmosphere became so poisoned that, upon the reading of an NFM resolution calling for the union to abrogate all previous agreements with the Knights, many of the Knights walked out of the convention. According to Andrew Roy's account, "all the Knights of Labor delegates, with the exception of Lewis and a few others, walked out of the convention and returned to their own hall." The delegates representing the NFM continued in session after the withdrawal of the Knights, and with the rump Knights adopted a new constitution for a new union, the National Progressive Union of Miners and Mine Laborers, or NPU. John McBride was elected president and W. T. Lewis general secretary. The NTA 135 delegates who returned to their own hall replaced Lewis with John B. Rae as master workman, and elected Robert Watchorn as secretary-treasurer. Shawnee Local Assembly 169, home local of W. T. Lewis and W. H. Bailey, withdrew from the K of L and divided its $2,500 treasury among its members "to escape the vengeance which Powderly has sworn against all who withdraw from National Assembly 135." Local Assembly 2620, also of Shawnee, returned its charter.[46]

Creation of the NPU had failed to unify all coal miners into one national organization, even though official pronouncements and proceedings suggested it was a fait accompli. In fact, open hostility flared up between competing locals within individual mines. In addition to the chaos came the collapse of the joint conference system founded by the operators and miners' unions to negotiate a standard wage scale. As a result, each labor organization negotiated separate local agreements, and the operators took full advantage by playing one union against the other. Each union refused to support the other's strikes.[47]

The last straw for Lewis was the charge of corruption leveled against him by the Knights' top officials. The story first surfaced at the joint convention in 1888 when a K of L delegate reported in the *National Labor Tribune* that an episode occurred on the convention floor that was not recorded in the proceedings but should be known by readers of the *National Labor Tribune*. W. W. Rae, who replaced Lewis as master workman of NTA 135, was in "earnest conversation" when W. T. Lewis was informed that he was the subject of their discussion. Lewis admonished Rae straightaway that he should be careful about diminishing the character of another. Rae asked

Lewis if it was true that he, Lewis, had worked in the interest of a railway, and charged the railway company and NTA 135 both for his time and expenses. Lewis emphatically denied the charge, and replied that " 'I make you and your friend Watchorn the proposition to refer the whole matter to an independent committee; if their verdict is against me I will retire from the labor movement. Will you and Watchorn retire if I am vindicated?' " Rae declined the challenge.[48]

A December 1888 circular distributed by Robert Watchorn to members of the local assemblies of District 135 presented similar charges of corruption against Lewis, and Lewis wrote a public letter to Powderly declaring that he would meet Powderly and Watchorn in the courts, adding: "Let me say in plain, unvarnished English that you are a liar."[49] Lewis was apparently genuinely offended by this charge as a slur against his character. Lewis wrote to John McBride requesting that an investigation be conducted immediately into the charges to "preserve the purity and integrity of our association." He recommended that a committee of inquiry be appointed, one by himself, one by Watchorn, and a third member agreeable to both parties. Watchorn and Lewis agreed that sworn testimony before a notary public would be taken verbatim by a stenographer, and that the expenses of the investigation would be borne by the losing party.[50] The episode is an excellent insight into the temper of the times and the ambitions of labor leaders and other "progressive" men of the day.

Watchorn based his charges on the statements of F. L. Patrick, a real estate agent who had offices in the same building as NTA 135, who made the statement to Knights officials that with $10 he could get rich by starting a railroad. NTA 135 officials recognized the scheme as a joke playing along with the agent and even went so far as to map out a good route for the railroad. W. T. Lewis, then master workman of NTA 135, at first declined to participate, but agreed to lend his name to secure the charter. The road was named the Indianapolis, Chattanooga and Southern Railroad. All those present subscribed $10, making $90 total, and the charter was successfully procured. Watchorn claimed Lewis was paid by the railroad and NTA 135 for expenses incurred while conducting railroad business. However, Patrick, the president of the supposed railroad, swore that the company had no books. In the end, the committee completely vindicated W. T. Lewis of all charges. It was proven that Lewis severed his connection with the railroad a few days after the charter was obtained, and the report concluded that "the honesty of Lewis has been established."[51]

The news of Lewis's vindication prompted many letters of approval from readers of the *National Labor Tribune*, such as one from Phil Penna of Indiana, future president of the UMWA, which began: "Glory to God in the highest!"[52] Even though his union lost the case, Watchorn continued in the role of K of L attack dog. Responding to charges of misuse of funds during a strike in Illinois, Lewis reprinted a full financial disclosure in the *National Labor Tribune*. He commented that, if Watchorn paid more attention to the financial records, and less to making "slanderous attacks" against Lewis, the K of L would be in better condition. But, if he insisted on venting his "malicious spleen" about NTA 135 finances, Lewis wrote, "they will find me *at home*."[53]

Actually, the vindictiveness of Watchorn and Powderly had followed Lewis even into his retirement as general secretary of the NPU. On July 15, 1889, Lewis submitted a letter of resignation to union president John Mc-Bride. "This step I am compelled to take because of the continued quarreling that is going on in the miners' ranks," Lewis explained. At no time has a single organization been needed more, he wrote, but instead, the miners were "in the ridiculous position of paying you and I and our associates to look after their interests, and then paying another set of men to prevent us from carrying out any plans for their benefit. An employer who took such a course would be a miserable failure, and our employers (the miners) will be no exception."[54]

McBride had the letter printed in the *National Labor Tribune* and announced that W. T. Lewis would soon travel to Europe as the miners' delegate with the Scripps League Commission, which consisted of delegates of several crafts, to investigate and report on labor conditions in European industries. Upon his return from Europe, Lewis completed his study of the law, was admitted to the Ohio bar in December 1889, and went into practice with Reuben Butler of New Lexington. William Scaife, secretary-treasurer of District 12 NPU (Illinois), posted a card in the *National Labor Tribune* congratulating Lewis on his admission to the Ohio bar. "If the miners expect to keep good men they will have to use them better than they did W.T.," Scaife wrote. In the same issue, Chris Evans, president of NPU District 10 (Ohio), congratulated Lewis as well. "Such evidences of ability go to show the marked progress that is being made among the young coal miners of America," Evans declared.[55]

While the Knights' leadership vilified Lewis as a deceitful traitor, other miners judged him a man of foresight who sacrificed his own career for the good of the craft. Lewis left the labor movement to practice law, but he also understood that, while he was an officer in the NPU, rapprochement with the Knights would be difficult, and he indicated that in his letter of resigna-tion. He also must have known that another effort to unite the NPU and NTA 135 into a single miners' union was underway, and his presence repre-sented a barrier to achieving that objective. In January 1890, the two organi-zations met again in Columbus, and this time succeeded in organizing the UMWA, which has continued to represent miners for more than a hundred years. Following the formation of the UMWA, Rae, who became the union's first president, and Watchorn, who became the first secretary-treasurer, ceased their attacks against W. T. Lewis. Whether this was for unity's sake or because the chief competitor in their own ambitions was removed is unclear.

The Republican Party regarded W. T. Lewis as an up-and-coming political leader, and in 1890 southeastern Ohio Republicans nominated him as a candidate for Congress from the thirteenth district. They received the support of numerous labor leaders, including Chris Evans, N. R. Hysell, Richard L. Davis, John Nugent from the Hocking Valley, and John McBride, Andrew Roy, Patrick McBryde, and John B. Rae at the national level. The three Knights of Labor assemblies at Shawnee, totaling hundreds of mem-bers, as well as assemblies in Rendville and Coalton, endorsed him as well. Local Republican papers printed many letters and editorials in his support, most of them noting that he had raised himself up by his own bootstraps. Lewis was presented as "a true representative of labor," a candidate who showed what "a poor boy can do in this great land of freedom," where, through "indomitable pluck and manly perseverance," he demonstrated "what a man can be, no matter how obscure his beginnings."[56] This charac-terization of Lewis was the very personification of the Welsh American Dream.

As might be expected, the local Democratic newspapers were not kind to candidate Lewis. The *New Lexington Herald* dredged up all the old allega-tions against him in an effort to tarnish his image as a labor leader. The paper reprinted correspondence between a local Knight and Grand Master Workman Terence V. Powderly in which Powderly again denounced Lewis as a man without honor and unworthy of a seat in Congress. John B. Rae and Robert Watchorn, now officers in the newly formed UMWA, released their own statements to the press, unconditionally declaring that Lewis had been completely exonerated of the charges of misuse of union funds by the investigation. Watchorn characterized the attack on Lewis's character as "a malicious pack of lies." John Rae concurred. Three impartial men of integ-rity had investigated the charges against Lewis and exonerated him, Rae declared. "W. T. Lewis was the victim of others' wrongdoing," and he hoped that workingmen would "refuse to be the playthings of scheming politicians while they profit by our stupidity."[57] After leading such a vitriolic campaign against Lewis, it is interesting to note that in his autobiography Robert Watchorn included W. T. Lewis in a chapter devoted to "friends I made in America." W. T. Lewis of Shawnee, Ohio, Watchorn wrote, was "a very forceful and persuasive personality, to whom the miners of America owe a debt of gratitude for his tireless and effective efforts in their behalf."[58]

Republicans did not fare well in southeastern Ohio that year, and no doubt the opposition of Powderly and other embittered Knights must have cost Lewis some votes. When the ballots were cast, Lewis lost by a significant margin of 712 votes, 2,256 to 1,544. He carried the Shawnee area by a margin of two to one, and won Perry County by a slim margin. Elsewhere in the thirteenth district, however, he was less competitive and probably a long shot at best in a Democratic district. After the November election W. T. Lewis moved to Bridgeport, Belmont County, where he continued to practice law. In 1892 Governor William McKinley appointed Lewis to a term as Ohio labor commissioner; he was reappointed in 1908. In that position he served as a liaison between the state government and labor unions in Ohio, and became one of "the right-hand lieutenants" of U.S. Senator Mark Hanna.[59]

What W. T. Lewis might have achieved had he lived longer will never be known; he died suddenly on April 28, 1909, at the Gilsey Hotel in Cleveland. He had gone to Cleveland on official business, was "caught in the cyclone" that hit the city on April 23, and gave up his shelter in a doorway to a "storm-driven woman struggling against the gale in the street." Exposure resulted in pneumonia, and five days later, with his wife and their only child, Irene, at his bedside, W. T. Lewis passed away at the age of "about 48."[60] He had proven to be a man of vision and commitment to the miners he led, yet he moved aside to facilitate the formation of the UMWA.

Thomas Llewellyn Lewis, W. T.'s younger brother by five years, also became a prominent Welsh American leader of the miners. Like his brother, he too was upwardly mobile and worked hard to achieve social "respectability," an unquestionable ideal of the American middle class and a defining feature of Welsh Americans. Both used the union as a stepping stone, W. T. into politics, and T. L. into a career as a coal industry executive, and yet their motivations were quite different. Born in Locust Gap, Pennsylvania, in 1866, shortly after his parents arrived from Wales, Tom Lewis went to work in the coal breakers at Wanamie, Luzerne County, at seven, became a trapper boy in the Pittsburgh district at nine, and worked with his father under-

United Mine Workers president Thomas L. Lewis. From Andrew Roy, *History of the Coal Miners in the United States* (Columbus: J. L. Tauger Printing Co., 1903), 382. Courtesy of West Virginia and Regional History Collection, West Virginia University Libraries.

ground at eleven. Before he was sixteen Tom Lewis was a full-fledged miner. When the family moved to Shawnee in 1879, he attended night school while working in the pits, and finally saved enough money to attend a term at the National University in Lebanon, Ohio. Working days, he read law at night for three years, and he took an active role in labor education through his K of L local assembly, described by Andrew Roy as Lewis's "Workingman's College."[61]

Thomas L., always known as Tom, "imbibed" unionism from his father and older brother W. T., whom he joined in founding the National Progressive Union in 1888, and he later served as a delegate to the founding convention of the UMWA. His union career officially began in 1895 when he was elected president of his eastern Ohio sub-district. From 1897 to 1900 he served as secretary-treasurer of UMWA District 6 (Ohio). He also served as president of the Ohio Federation of Labor from 1896 to 1899, was elected vice president of the UMWA in 1900, and in 1909, the same year W. T. died, was elected president. One of his opponents in the race was another Welshman, John P. Reese, the district president for Iowa. Tom occupied the UMWA presidency until voted out in 1912.[62]

Like so many other successful union men, Tom Lewis became an upright, respectable middle-class member of society. In 1892, he married another Welsh American, Sarah Jenkins; they had two daughters and lived in a handsome house outside Bridgeport, Ohio. Lewis was described as "a man of ambition," but not "the firebrand and radical that so many thought he might be." At forty-two he did not drink alcohol, smoke, chew tobacco, or use profanity; he was regarded as honest and "always conducts himself as a gentleman." Like his brother, with whom he was frequently compared, his biography in the union's paper declared that "in the Lewis blood run the microbes of the true politician."[63]

Serious conflict within the UMWA characterized the presidency of Tom Lewis. The official UMWA historian, Maier Fox, suggests that Lewis's personal qualities were the cause. But Lewis inevitably suffered by comparison with his predecessor, the charismatic John Mitchell, who moved on in 1908 to assume the leadership of the National Civic Federation, a businessman's organization. Fox writes that although Lewis was "undeniably talented," he "apparently had a nasty temper, a dictatorial disposition, and a general inability to get along with associates who disagreed with him." Long before he made so many enemies as president of the national union, an 1896 editorial in the *United Mine Workers Journal* described him as "very rigid in his criticisms, and very steadfast in his leanings." It was noted that he did not resemble his brother W. T. Lewis "either physically or in temperament."[64] Mitchell did not prefer him as vice president, but unlike Tom Lewis, Mitchell was able to work with those who disagreed with him, and so he did not openly oppose Lewis's election.

Nevertheless, it is difficult to blame Lewis for all the turmoil, for he inherited an institutional crisis planted within the UMWA at its founding. Relations between the operators and the union were unraveling because Mitchell had countenanced negotiations by the districts, which in turn undermined the ability of the national headquarters to enforce agreements and also made the markets more unpredictable for the operators. Like his brother, Tom Lewis had always favored a strong, centralized national union. Therefore, in his desire to reestablish interstate bargaining, he met a determined resistance from both operators and district union officials. UMWA politics turned vicious when Lewis riled the district presidents by refusing to support district-approved strikes in Pennsylvania, Arkansas, Kansas, and Indiana, and by sending national organizers into districts without their knowledge. When miners in District 13 (Indiana) went out on strike and the district officers supported them, Lewis ordered the men back to work. When the local refused on constitutional grounds, Lewis revoked their charter and suspended the district officers, who in turn promptly obtained an injunction preventing such action. From then on Lewis found himself in a virtual state of war with district officers and those who supported district autonomy. As the chaos continued, Vice President John P. White refused to run again, and Secretary-Treasurer W. D. Ryan resigned.[65]

The case was an excellent example of why the national officers, like Lewis, favored a strong national union with centralized power over collective bargaining negotiations and strikes, rather than district autonomy. While he made enemies, Lewis also obviously had substantial support among the general membership, for he was reelected handily over Illinois district president John H. Walker, a popular leader with whom Lewis had been locked in a struggle of wills. Lewis's second year in office was filled with as much turmoil as the first. This time it flared up in western Pennsylvania when District 5 president Frank Feehan called the miners out on strike; again Lewis declared the strike unconstitutional and ordered the men back into the mines, and the district president charged Lewis with unconstitutionally meddling in district affairs.[66]

Lewis was again reelected easily in a race against William Green in 1910, but the ease of election did nothing to dampen the internal friction. The operators were intransigently opposed to negotiating district contracts because it opened the way for operators in other districts to undercut them in the market, and Lewis found himself in the hot seat as the ideological struggle broke down into bitter personal wrangling. Just how personal and vindictive was demonstrated when Frank Hayes, who was elected vice president in 1910, immediately opposed Lewis at every turn. In response, Lewis eliminated the vice president's office space. Lewis ran for reelection in 1911 and lost decisively to John P. White. He made another attempt to regain the presidency later that year, but he was soundly defeated again by White, whose moderation helped to calm the fires of internal conflict.[67]

Thomas L. Lewis might well have been temperamentally too inflexible to make the compromises necessary to be a successful president of so large and diverse a union as the UMWA, although his rigid adherence to the idea of one strong miners' union undoubtedly represented the opinion of a majority of the membership. His loss in the struggle over this issue with the district presidents was instrumental in demonstrating that some resolution of this problem was necessary if the union were to exert any real power. Resolution of this issue would have to await the ascent of the most famous Welsh American mine leader of them all, John L. Lewis, who finally won this very uncivil inner war.

Like previous UMWA presidents, most of whom went to work as industry officials when their terms in office were completed, Tom Lewis also switched sides when he left the presidency. His new position as "labor advisor" took him to Charleston, West Virginia, where he worked for the virulently anti-union West Virginia Operators' Association. From his home in Charleston he also edited a coal trade journal, the *Coal Mining Review*, and served as secretary of the Sprint and Gas Coal Association, a marketing agency. He was then selected to serve as secretary of the New River Coal Operators Association in 1918. Subsequently, Lewis helped to found the National Coal Association, an operators' organization, and toured the United States promoting the organization. Thomas L. Lewis died on May 1, 1939, in Charleston after some years of retirement.[68]

Lewis's swift adjustment to working with the operators who fought so vigilantly against recognizing the union certainly raises questions about his integrity, but the same questions might be raised about nearly every UMWA president before John L. Lewis assumed control in 1920. Miners' leaders of this period took their new-found skills and employed them on the side of industry; after all, those skills were of no use down in the pit, and returning to the pick and shovel was a reduction in status. Tom Lewis, like the others, was an ambitious, "get ahead" kind of fellow. When the issue of a pay raise for officers came before the convention in 1900, Lewis was candid: "I am one of the people who if I think my services are worth a certain sum are going to ask for it, and if I don't get it I am going on strike."[69]

Thomas Lewis was not the last of the Lewis brothers to use organized labor as a career springboard. Another brother, Llewellyn, nine years Tom's junior, moved from Shawnee to join his brothers in Martins Ferry, Ohio, across the Ohio River from Wheeling, West Virginia, and went to work in the steel industry. Apparently he was imbued with similar organizational skill for by 1909, at only thirty-four, he was already serving as vice president of the Sheet Division, Amalgamated Association of Iron, Steel, and Tin Workers. Another brother, Isaac, who was three years younger than Llewellyn, also seems to have followed in his brothers' footsteps. Little is known of Isaac, but in 1909 the *Wheeling Majority* reported that "Ike" Lewis had become mayor of the city of Martins Ferry but that after nearly two years in office he resigned to "go back to the mill." During the 1910 steel strike, Ike Lewis and eight other Aetna mill strikers were arrested and indicted for attacking strikebreakers and "shooting with intent to kill." The court reduced the charges and the defendants pleaded guilty to assault and battery and were fined $50 each, plus court costs.[70] Isaac apparently lacked some of that "respectability" his brothers worked so hard to attain.

How conscious the Lewis boys were of their Welshness, and to what degree this shaped their lives, can only be surmised. But there are indications that at least the oldest two were raised within, and conscious of, their Welsh heritage. The *Druid* carried an article in March 1909, announcing a farewell reception for the Reverend William Lewis, sponsored by the Brotherhood of the Welsh Congregational Church of Martins Ferry. The item noted that "several brilliant Welsh Americans" had attended Rev. Lewis's Sabbath school at the Aetnaville church, including T. L. Lewis, president of the UMWA, and William T. Lewis, the Ohio commissioner of labor.[71] Twice in the previous year, Thomas L. Lewis was feted by Welsh societies. The Lackawanna Druid Society, with Colonel R. A. Phillips presiding, and remarks offered by Hon. H. M. Edwards, Hon. George Howell, Hon. John R. Farr, and Hon. T. D. Nicholls, accompanied by a choir of twenty voices, honored Lewis on October 30 while he was in Scranton on business. In Canton, Ohio, the Welsh American Society honored Lewis at a social in December, and the following March Lewis spoke at a Youngstown St. David's Society gathering. His address included comments that lead us to conclude that he retained a Welsh identity: "Every Welshman and Welsh woman ought to be proud to claim they belong to the nationality. . . . and I take pride wherever I go that I am the son of Welsh parents and am proud of that fact."[72] Not only the words, but also the frequency of his appearances before Welsh American organizations, indicate that Welshness was not an abstraction for him. In May 1909, the *Cardiff Weekly Mail* characterized Lewis as the "Mabon" of American miners, referring to the Welsh miners' leader and member of Parliament, and suggested that "Welsh miners' leaders be sent for a short course of instruction in the American miners' leader's school." The *Weekly Mail*, a consistent friend of the South Wales coal owners, approved of Lewis's refusal to become involved in American elections by consistently refusing to instruct the 300,000 UMWA members how to cast their votes.[73]

Both William T. and Thomas L. Lewis were mired in the larger ideological issue of centralization of power in the UMWA, and both believed that the miners would find greater protection and strength in a strong national union rather than in a confederation of semi-autonomous districts. They envisioned one powerful union army led by a general who orchestrated the battle with capitalists, using field commanders followed by disciplined regiments of loyal miners. The operators wielded the power that came from money and government influence; the miners had only numbers and unity. Proponents of district autonomy envisioned the union as a democracy through which the will of the members was expressed, under the control of

United Mine Workers president John L. Lewis (right) with District 17 UMWA official Fred Mooney and his wife in the early 1920s. Courtesy of West Virginia and Regional History Collection, West Virginia University Libraries.

district presidents, of course. For them, concentrating the decision-making powers in a distant headquarters seemed to be serving a vision that was contradictory to the union as a democratic organization of miners. Their union was one through which the miners' will was expressed from the grassroots up through their representatives. While the former thought of the union as improving the living standard of its members by concentrating its power on bread-and-butter issues and following the orders of a national leader, the latter saw this as despotism inimical to a reform movement. Unlike the K of L, with its broader vision of social reform and features resembling a secret order, the UMWA was an open organization that accepted industrial capitalism, sought to organize all those who worked in and about the mines, and was dedicated to improving the material conditions of life and labor for coal miners. The internal UMWA struggle over power relations vexed coal miners and leaders for several decades. Welsh union men were found on both sides of the ideological divide, but the growth in scale and power of industrial capitalism during this period ordained that a strong central union would be the final result if the UMWA was to mount a challenge.

## Business Unionism: John L. Lewis

The UMWA struggled with this issue of power more or less from its founding in 1890 into the 1920s, when a son of Welsh immigrants emerged with the ruthlessness and political skills to seize and hold power for the next forty years. Unlike Tom Lewis, to whom he was unrelated, John L. Lewis was able to crush the district officers who opposed him to become a caricature of the union "general" at the head of a large army of loyal miners. Even though he nearly wrecked the UMWA in consolidating his power over the organization by the end of the twenties, it rebounded to become the most powerful union in the United States at the same time that John L. became the most powerful voice of the labor movement.

So much has been written about John L. Lewis as a labor leader that little more can be offered here that would contribute to this extensive literature or the debate over whether he was a strong visionary leader or a power-hungry despot. Scholars have come to characterize John L. as the prototype career labor leader who emerged in the first half of the twentieth century. If the first generation of union leaders were social reformers who often sacrificed themselves as martyrs for the cause, and the second generation of miners' leaders used the union as a stepping stone to corporate careers, the third generation embraced the union itself as a career. John L. Lewis found the practice in place when he assumed control of the UMWA in 1920, but he expanded on careerism and became the ultimate powerful "labor bureaucrat." His major biographers raise the question as to why, "given Lewis's belief in individualism, the gospel of success, and status striving . . . he was content to act in the role of labor leader." Surely he could have followed a path similar to that of Tom Moses, who climbed the steep ladder from an Illinois coal mine to the highest echelons of U.S. Steel, or at the very least the footsteps of his predecessors as UMWA president, Tom Lewis, John Mitchell, and John White, who became industry executives. The answer, they argue, is that "Lewis's colossal ego . . . required more; it demanded attention, esteem, and most of all, social, economic, and political power."[74]

The scholarship on John L. Lewis the public figure has arrived at a consensus that views his long career as head of the UMWA within this basic personality profile. But Lewis's motives and psychological makeup remain shrouded in myth and mystery because he was so successful in hiding his private life. Biographers Dubofsky and Van Tine's description of his private life should sound familiar to readers who have reached this point: "Victorian respectability characterized the Lewis family. Nary a hint of social deviancy touched any member of the Lewis clan, an extended family that included sons, daughters, brothers, sisters, nephews, nieces, and in-laws. . . . Neither John L.; Myrta; the daughter, Kathryn; nor the son, John Jr., touched alcohol. At the Lewis's Sunday afternoon parties for Washington influentials, presided over by Myrta and Kathryn, tea, not liquor, was the beverage served. Welsh temperance and Iowa Presbyterianism, if not formal church membership, exemplified the Lewis family's value system."[75] These words might have been written about any number of Welsh miners and their families who came to America seeking "respectability." How John L. controlled the union is examined in an extensive literature, but how he came by those staunchly middle-class values associated with temperance, the Protestant ethic, and the Republican Party is traceable directly to the Welsh heritage that surrounded him in the Iowa coalfields of his youth.

Scholars are able to reconstruct only the barest outline of John L.'s early life, but even less has been written about his roots in the Welsh coal community that nurtured him. Ron E. Roberts, a sociologist from Lewis's hometown of Lucas, Iowa, whose grandparents were family friends of the Lewises, has written a revealing account from local sources of Lewis's early life. It sheds additional light on his Welsh upbringing amongst "the wandering Welsh miners of the nineteenth century and their daily lives in their native Wales and American mining camps."[76] Lewis's Welsh roots were distinctive even amongst Welsh immigrants. Few writers do little more than note Lewis's Mormon parents, and John L. certainly never did, but his father and mother both were members of the Reorganized Church of Jesus Christ of Latter Day Saints. This group followed the teachings of Joseph Smith's son, who broke away from the main body because they could not accept polygamy and other controversial ideas emanating from Salt Lake City. His maternal great-grandparents, John Jeremiah and Rachel Lewis, were both born in the South Wales coal mining valleys. One of eleven children, John became an engineer for the Powell Duffryn Coal Company. John's fifth child, Jeremiah Jeremiah, converted to the Reorganized Church and was ordained as a minister sometime prior to 1863. Jeremiah's older sister, Sarah, also was converted by her husband, John Henry Watkins of Glamorganshire. He was a coal miner, musician, and poet, a learned man who became known as "Father Watkins" after he immigrated to America with friends and relatives in 1869. He died at age ninety in the house of his favorite grandson, John L. Lewis.[77]

At the western end of the South Wales coalfield, probably in Pontarddulais, Thomas and Gwenllian Lewis had a child in 1854 they named Thomas H. Unfortunately, both parents died when Thomas H. was quite young, and he was sent into the pits at Mynydd Newydd Colliery near Swansea. In 1869, he departed Wales for the Australian gold fields, probably in company with his uncle Llewellyn. By 1872, the adventurers had crossed the Pacific Ocean to the gold fields of northern California. Not much else is known about the early life of Tom Lewis, but he was in the northern California gold fields at exactly the same time that his future brother-in-law, John J. Watkins, was there on missionary work. It was no mere coincidence, therefore, that 1878 found Tom and his uncle in the town of Lucas, Iowa.[78]

The Welsh were always a relatively small proportion of the foreign-born in Iowa. In 1885 only 3,436 were listed as natives of Wales, and that number declined over the years to 2,048 by 1915. In Lucas County the peak was 282 in 1885, but fell to only 68 in 1915. Most of them lived in and around the town of Lucas. The largest concentration was next door in Mahaska County, which had 406 Welsh in 1885, peaked at 442 in 1895, but declined to 157 in 1915. Most of the Welshmen were engaged in coal mining so naturally they were concentrated in towns near mine sites, such as the Cleveland section of Lucas where the Watkins and Lewis clans lived. According to one contemporary scholar, the Welsh were small in number but "wherever they are, their eisteddfods or annual singing contests and their cymanfa, or church conventions, have survived the transplanting of these folk from their tiny fatherland." He noted that Y Drych had "many readers among the Welshmen of Iowa."[79]

Welsh families moved in clusters of family and friends from one Welsh settlement to another, and the same pattern pertained to Mormons who found islands of kindred spirits in the Reorganized churches; this was common for other Protestant Welsh denominations as well. The church provided contacts, made trustworthy information and decision-making possible, and eased the impact of uprooting families. In Lucas, the Welsh launched a chorale group and two churches, the Reorganized LDS, and the Welsh Congregationalist Chapel. Father Watkins became the presiding elder and Evan B. Morgan of Merthyr was the presiding priest over the two hundred saints who attended the Reorganized church. Hymns were sung in Welsh. To combat the evil of alcohol among the miners, the Welsh established a temperance society, the Knights Templar; to fight for their rights against the operators, they founded a local assembly of the Knights of Labor in 1878. Some Welsh traditions apparently were still practiced into the twentieth century; one elderly resident remembered the miners singing Welsh songs on the front porches in the evenings.[80]

Tom Lewis was a staunch union man, joining the new K of L local and probably the Miner's National Association. He was described as a large extroverted man with red hair who possessed the gift of gab both in Welsh and English. He and Louisa Watkins were married on May 20, 1878, and John Llewelyn Lewis was born on February 12, 1880. That same year Tom Lewis was baptized into the Reorganized Church by his father-in-law, Father Watkins. The couple made their home in the Cleveland section of Lucas with other Welsh families.[81]

In March 1880, when the operators of the Lucas mines put in screens that discarded all but the large lumps of coal, the result was a significant wage cut for miners who were paid by the ton. The operators' action brought work stoppages over the next several years, and a number of miners were black-listed, including Tom Lewis. Tom and Louisa Lewis and their young family moved more or less continuously over the next several years trying to stay ahead of the blacklist. A miner who had worked with Tom Lewis during the "Big Screen Strike" said he could understand why John L. took such a militant stance against the coal corporations "because of the way his father and grandfather were punished by the company" in Lucas. Because of the family's financial straits John L. did not finish high school. By 1897 Tom Lewis and his now large family had moved into the boardinghouse Father Watkins operated in Lucas. The Whitebreast Company was now under new management, and Tom Lewis went back to work in the Lucas mines with his sons John L., Tom Jr., Howard, and Judd.[82]

Several of John L.'s relatives were active in the UMWA. There were two locals serving the Lucas area in the 1890s, and John L.'s uncle George Watkins was president of one of them. Another uncle, John Cochran, was president of the second local, and John J. Watkins was listed in union records as an officeholder between 1899 and 1905. In 1905 John's brother Tom was elected vice president of his local. John L. belonged to the nearby local at Chariton mines in 1901, and became its first secretary that year. Most of the Welsh miners in Lucas began to move to more prosperous coal towns in the area during the 1890s, particularly to Hiteman. The Welsh Presbyterian church relocated to Hiteman, as did the local eisteddfod presided over by John L.'s grandfather Watkins, the chief bard of the *gorsedd*. Although John L. did not speak Welsh, like so many of the second generation, he undoubtedly understood much of what he heard spoken in Welsh.[83]

He could not escape the imprint of Welsh-Mormon culture and values of his early life, however. Through them he absorbed the commitment to self-improvement and respectability. A miner who remembered John L. informed an interviewer that, as a youth, John L. "never drank, nor smoked, nor cussed and raised Cain, or anything like that. Yeah, he was a gentleman. He tried to be a classy sort of fellow." These characteristics became a permanent part of his behavior throughout his life. In Lucas he was elected vice president of the Literary and Gymnasium Society in 1904, and used the forum to develop his oratorical powers. John L. also availed himself of the library and was in fact surrounded by immediate and extended family members who valued and possessed books. His grandfather owned his own library, and although he possessed a limited formal education Father Watkins had achieved a considerable level of cultural attainment himself. Since John L. was his favorite grandson, we can safely assume that Father Watkins shared his vast knowledge of Welsh history and culture, and that John L. availed himself of the many books in his grandfather's library. Given John L.'s receptivity to the power of rhetoric, not surprisingly he was attracted to performing in amateur productions at the Knotts Opera House in Lucas, including challenging plays such as *King Lear*. John L. was sufficiently interested in the theater that he leased the opera house in 1906 and staged performances for a year.[84]

During these years John L. made a number of trips west to work as a miner. In 1902 he was in Wyoming when the mine at Hannah exploded, killing 169 men. He "helped in the rescue work, and went around to the widows' houses to take a look and help out." It was a searing experience that shaped him for life. As a seasoned labor union leader most issues would become negotiable, but throughout his life few issues inflamed his passions more than a disregard for human life by coal operators. In 1904 he moved on to Chihuahua, Mexico, and worked in a gold mine; from there he headed to the Bisbee, Arizona, copper mines of Phelps-Dodge.[85]

Like many young, single, "tramping" miners Lewis worked his way around the country, but he always came back to Lucas. At twenty-three he was seriously thinking about settling down with his own family. In 1907 he married the woman he had courted on and off, Myrta Bell, the daughter of the local physician who worked in her father's office and taught school. Louisa Lewis probably was hurt that her son chose to marry outside the LDS church, and perhaps Myrta's conservative Protestant father had reservations about his daughter marrying outside of her own church, for the couple took the vows in Osceola without the presence of either family.[86] The reluctance of Mormons to discuss their religion or personal lives with "heathens," who in turn shunned Mormon "heretics," and John L.'s desire to avoid family friction, probably accounts for his public silence on all personal or family matters.

When it was time to become serious about a career, the most obvious choice was to become active in union politics. In June 1907 he was elected president of his union local after having lost his first bid for the office. John L. also cast about for other opportunities. He ran a stockyard briefly, and then opened a cooperative dry goods store. Both ventures failed. So did his campaign to become mayor of Lucas in 1907. Although from humble beginnings, many saw in him a man of ambition and intelligence who could realize his full potential only if he left Lucas. It was John L.'s good fortune to come to the attention of another mine official from Lucas, John P. White, an official of UMWA District 13 in Iowa. White knew both the Watkins and Lewis families. He came to town frequently and developed a highly favorable opinion of the young local president. White became international president of the UMWA five years later. Meanwhile, in 1908 John L. and his entire family, including parents and siblings, had moved to Panama, in central Illinois, where he was elected president of the UMWA local in 1909. Illinois was the home district of numerous UMWA politicians, and Lewis hitched his political wagon to several of the most prominent of them. In the election of 1911, John L. threw his support behind White for the union presidency, and when White won he assisted Lewis's elevation in national UMWA politics. John L. would have found another Welshman from Iowa holding a prominent office in the national headquarters during this period, Edwin Perry, who had been elected national secretary-treasurer in 1909. Perry was born in Brymbo, North Wales. He migrated to Pennsylvania in the 1860s where he had been an official in the Workingmen's Benevolent Association, but by the late 1870s he had moved to Oskaloosa, Iowa. There he served as district secretary-treasurer of the Knights of Labor, and was elected UMWA District 13 president in 1900. Even though he had been in the United States for more than forty years, in 1913 he attended the national eisteddfod in Pittsburgh and planned a "pilgrimage to Wales."[87] He obviously had retained some semblance of his Welsh identity, but it is unknown whether he assisted in John L.'s rise to power.

White resigned the presidency in 1917, and when vice president Frank Hayes assumed the office he appointed Lewis to his vacated post. Having been appointed to numerous important positions by the national officers, Lewis became acting president in 1919 and was elected to the post in 1920. Between 1920 and 1960 John L. Lewis controlled the largest and most powerful union in the United States. Peaking at close to 700,000 members in the 1920s, the organization was turned into an efficient national machine.[88] Welsh ethnicity seems to have played no role in Lewis's long tenure as UMWA president. Times had changed, and ethnic chauvinism was destructive to a national organization that depended on organizing all those who worked in and about the mines.

This can be seen in Lewis's long-serving secretary-treasurer, Owen John Owens. Born in Clydach Vale, South Wales, in 1890, he migrated to Ohio with his parents as a child. He entered the pits at age nine and became active in union politics at an early age. In 1935 Owens was elected president of UMWA District 6 (Ohio), and held that post until 1947 when he replaced Thomas Kennedy as international secretary-treasurer, retaining that position until his retirement in 1972. While district president, he also served as the president of the Ohio Industrial Council, as president of the Ohio Congress of Industrial Organizations, and during World War II as a member of the National War Labor Board. As Lewis's trusted right-hand man, Owens became one of the more progressive voices at UMWA headquarters.[89] Owens was a loyal Lewis man, but there is no evidence that they were close personally, and no evidence at all that Owens's Welsh birth meant anything at all to Lewis.

Lewis was American by birth, but he was raised in a decidedly Welsh family and community. John L. was secretive about his personal and family life, and when he occasionally made public reference to his Welsh heritage it was usually for rhetorical effect. In March 1923 John L. and Myrta visited Wales. They stayed in Cardiff and visited the Rhondda before going on to London for a convention of the Miners Federation of Great Britain. The *South Wales News* reporter tried to pry out of him his opinion of labor politics in Great Britain, but Lewis deflected the questions. Nevertheless, the reporter praised Lewis as an excellent example of how the Welsh immigrants had distinguished themselves abroad.[90] Apparently, Lewis compartmentalized his Welshness in a private place along with his personal and family affairs.

Welsh nepotism as practiced during much of the nineteenth century no longer was possible in the new industrial order of the twentieth century, but personal connections remained vital to upward mobility even in the union. Union bureaucracy provided many with that rise to respectability that was so central to success-oriented Welsh miners. They played important roles in shaping not only the union movement, but also labor-capital relations in the twentieth century. Twentieth-century business union leaders, however, often stacked their administrations with sycophants, and success for upper-echelon union leaders was their acceptance by their counterparts in business rather than a stint in jail. In this regime ethnic identity seemed more like a handicap than a goal.

## FROM NANTYMOEL TO
## HOLLYWOOD THE INCREDIBLE
## JOURNEY OF MARY THOMAS

Women played no official role in the United Mine Workers of America because they were barred from working in the mines. Unofficially, however, women did play a significant part in the union's struggle for recognition. Operator policies in coal company towns affected the entire community—men, women, and children—particularly during periods of labor conflict. Everyone was dependent on the coal company, and what affected the miners affected their families and friends. Therefore, women became militant partners in strikes because they had a direct interest in their successful outcome. Workers in early-twentieth-century America came from ethnically diverse backgrounds, but serious conflicts with capital often forged a class unity among coalfield families that led them to expand the definition of "family" to incorporate the entire community. The infamous Ludlow Massacre, which occurred during the Colorado Coalfield War of 1913–14, provides an excellent example of the influence of a single Welsh woman in this process.

The only published eyewitness account of the Ludlow Massacre, *Those Damned Foreigners*, appeared in 1971. The author was Mary T. O'Neal, known to history as Mary Thomas.[1] Mary's story reads like fiction, but the events she described were all too real. Her saga is told from the perspective of a Welsh woman whose first experiences in America were shaped by the vicious class struggle in the Colorado coalfields. Although not representative of immigrant women in the coalfields, she personifies the range of risks and hardships they encountered, as well as the potential rewards, and the psychological, cultural, geographic, and gender borders they crossed on the way to becoming Americans.

Mary Thomas emigrated from Wales at the age of twenty-two in the summer of 1913 with two young daughters. Only twice before had she ventured beyond her valley on brief visits. During the ten months following her departure from Wales, however, her previously uneventful life took a dramatic turn. In less than a year, Mary crossed the Atlantic Ocean and then the United States from New York to Colorado. Within two months of reaching the Colorado coalfields she became embroiled in one of the most violent coal strikes in American history, was jailed several times by the militia as one of the strike's ringleaders, and survived a fierce Colorado winter in a strikers' tent colony as well as the Ludlow Massacre. At the request of the UMWA Mary met with President Woodrow Wilson in the White House to present the miners' side of the affair, testified about the massacre before the United States Commission on Industrial Relations, joined a sit-in at the offices of company owner John D. Rockefeller Jr., and went on a month-long speaking tour of eastern cities relating the Colorado story to large audiences. Along the way, she was befriended by some of the most powerful labor leaders of the day. About 1920 Mary Thomas remarried, adopted her new husband's surname, O'Neal, and moved to Hollywood, where she spent the remainder of her life in material comfort. But it was as Mary Thomas that her life had historical significance, and it was that formative experience during the Colorado mine war that shaped her identity and worldview for the rest of her life. Mary's saga is worth retelling because it suggests the range of individual paths taken by immigrants on their personal journeys from Welsh to American identities.

She was born Mary Hannah Williams in 1887 in the Ogmore Valley. Her father, James Williams, was a coal miner born just north of Port Talbot; her mother, Mary A. Williams, was born near Bridgend. Mary described her hometown as located at "the very end of the dinky line" at the very head of the Ogmore Valley. The only town that fits this description is Nantymoel, a community dependent on the Ocean Colliery. Apparently, the Williamses were talented singers. James loved to sing, and the church offered to train his wife for the National Eisteddfod, but she chose a family instead and operated a small grocery shop out of her front room. Mary was also trained to be a singer and won several local competitions as a child. Her earliest memory was of her father lifting her atop a table at a union meeting to sing for the miners. Mary's Aunt Kathy was an active suffragette and an early feminist who encouraged young Mary to become a performer.[2]

Mary loved to sing, but she wanted to follow in the path of her mother and many Welsh girls of her day by marrying when she was sixteen. The boy Mary had promised to marry when she reached that age died tragically from miners' tuberculosis before the date was set. To lift herself out of the doldrums, Mary went to work in Maesteg for three months in a shop belonging to a friend of her mother. There she met Tom Thomas, a coal miner born in Pennsylvania to parents from Wales who had come back to live with his great aunt. After three months of courtship and against the wishes of her

parents, who disapproved of Tom's hard drinking and incorrigible wom-
anizing, Mary and Tom were married. She had just turned sixteen and he
was twenty-five. After a two-day honeymoon in Cardiff, life settled into a
grim routine in the house of Tom's great aunt, who opposed her nephew's
choice of a bride and refused to speak to Mary during the entire five years
the couple lived under her roof. (During that period Mary gave birth to two
daughters.)[3]

Just when Mary thought she could endure her situation no longer, Tom
announced that a good job was waiting for him in Pennsylvania. He said he
would send for Mary and the children, Olga and Rachael, as soon as he
settled in. She worked in her mother's shop and then opened one of her
own, but about three years elapsed without word or money from him.
Finally, Mary's friend, who kept house for Tom's great aunt, secretly showed
Mary a letter Tom had written to his aunt from Colorado, not Pennsylvania,
which confirmed her deepest suspicion that she and the children had been
deserted. Fortuitously, her mother's eldest brother, Uncle Davy, was visiting
from America, where he had gone when he was fifteen and become "some
kind of mine expert." Mary told him Tom was in a place called Delagua, near
Trinidad, Colorado. As it turned out, Uncle Davy not only knew that mine,
he knew her husband. Instantly, Mary determined to go to Colorado and
force Tom to support his children. Uncle Davy booked passage for her and
the girls on the *Oceanic*, a ship of the White Star Line out of Liverpool, and
arranged for their train fare to Colorado as well. They departed in late June
or early July 1913.[4]

On board ship she immediately became a popular figure by leading the
passengers in nightly song in the lounge. During the Atlantic passage Mary
and fellow passenger Don O'Neal fell in love. He was a ranch foreman who
had been in England buying cattle. He begged Mary to divorce Tom and
marry him, and, even though she recounted how it broke her heart, she did
what she regarded as proper by declining. Reluctantly, he disappeared into
the crowds disembarking from the ship, and Mary thought she would never
see him again.

It was then, upon arrival in New York, that Mary discovered she was
required to have "landing money." She had paid for her passage, but now
she would need money to disembark as well as to provide for the children en
route to Colorado, and the ten dollars in her purse was not enough. At that
point, the first of many strokes of good fortune befell her: the ship's master
of ceremonies arrived with a huge box lunch that would last the entire trip
west, taxi fee to take her to the railroad station, and a collection taken up

from the ship's staff as payment for the onboard entertainment. Mary and the girls were then permitted to leave the ship.[5]

After what seemed like an endless journey by train, she and the children finally arrived in Trinidad, Colorado, in late July 1913 to confront her husband with his responsibility. She found Tom sharing a company house with an Irishman named John in the nearby mining camp of Delagua. After a strained and awkward interlude, Tom and Mary came to a mutual arrangement: she did not want him for a husband but was confronted by the fact that there were no jobs for women in coal camps, and she needed a place to live. On the other hand, he did not want his desertion made public because he would lose his job and then both of them would be out of luck. In a mutual survival pact, Mary presented the public face of a wife, but ran the house as though the two men were boarders.[6]

Mary was bilingual in Welsh and English, but she experienced to some degree what all immigrants felt upon arrival in America. Standing on the platform in Trinidad, she became self-conscious about how she and her children were dressed. "I thought we were very well dressed when we left Wales. I had on my best tucked blouse with leg-o-mutton sleeves, my skirt touching the ground. I wore my sailor hat, so fashionable then, on the back of my head with an elastic band under my chin to keep it from blowing off. I had too much hair to pin up when wearing a hat, so I let it hang down my back. My children came in for a lot of attention too. They wore Welsh pinafores over their dresses, close fitting bonnets tied with ribbon under their chins, and red drawers edged with white lace showing two inches below their dresses. But the stares made me uncomfortable." Like most immigrants, Mary had "brought every pound of baggage the steamship company allowed us on our tickets. We looked the typical immigrants we were, with our pathetic bundles of belongings. I had brought everything I owned, even the traditional wedding gift of a feather bed given every bride by her mother."[7]

In the coal camp Mary experienced the miner's life from a woman's perspective. She quickly learned that the company owned everything, guarded the entrance to the mine, fired union men, and was, in effect, a law unto itself. Her first impression of Delagua was that it was "the most desolate place I'd ever thought could be. Not a tree or anything green in sight. Only a mass of unpainted shacks and bungalows along dust covered streets, if one could call them that." The shock of coal-camp drabness overwhelmed her senses: "My thoughts turned to my green and beautiful Wales, and the neat homes. . . . Had I lost everything by coming here to this desolate place? My heart was heavy, and I was physically and mentally tired. My emotions got the better of me and I began to cry. What if my pride had wrongly told me to come to America to face Tom." But like most survivors, she knew that there was no turning back, and the only alternative was to make the best of it.[8]

The wage labor available for women in the coal camps was limited to washing and scrubbing for managers or boarders. Because of high prices at the company store, Mary noted, as well as deductions from their paychecks for rent, water, lights, coal, and other charges, most of the miners were indebted to the company and hardly ever saw "the color of money." Consequently, men, women, and children coped daily with poverty. While the men labored underground during the day, the women experienced at least the threat of sexual harassment. Managers and gunmen often used their absolute power to harass women for sexual favors or unpaid labor, such as scrubbing the floors in the boss's house. If the woman's husband was disabled or killed, her grief was compounded with an immediate economic catastrophe and no means to support her family.[9]

Mary was astounded by the perplexing range of nationalities among the miners. A 1912 UMWA survey counted twenty-four different nationalities among 14,258 Colorado miners, with more than 70 percent having a first language other than English. The three major groups were Spanish-speaking Mexicans; English-speaking miners, many of whom were of British origin; and European miners from various nations. Like other women in the Colorado coal camps, Mary was young, married, and the mother of young children whose introduction to American life took place in the coalfields.[10] Most of them encountered American xenophobia to some degree and all were homesick for the old country, but they were also determined to make a go of it in America.

In the heterogeneous American coalfields, ethnic differences often took a back seat to a shared class experience. Almost immediately Mary was befriended by Italian Margo Gorci, her next-door neighbor. Mary wrote that the mine guards lumped all the immigrants together as "those Damned foreigners," hence the title of her reminiscence, but shared troubles brought miners and their families to function "as one nationality" when backed against the wall. Women of all nationalities also believed that, whatever their native customs, things were going to be different in America. This applied to the women's sense of their duties to their husbands as well, and they shared their knowledge. When Mary picked up her husband's shoes to clean them, her friend Margo chided her. "We always did in Wales," Mary said, but Margo cut her off: "We did in Italia too," but "American women are not slaves like we were in Europe." Together they vowed that there would be "no more shoe shining" and "no more buttering bread either." The Italian and Welsh tandem shared a laugh. The Welsh girl had been "liberated," Mary noted, by an Italian woman in Colorado.[11]

Mary and Margo were soon sharing their most intimate thoughts and showed each other the contents of their steamer trunks they had brought over from the old country. Margo especially admired a nine-inch carved wooden statuette of Adelina Patti, the famous Italian opera singer who lived in Wales, which Mary had won in a contest. Margo's husband, Tony, was also musical, and they invited Mary to a party of their friends, where many spoke Italian, but others spoke German and French. They were all anxious to hear Mary talk about the old country. Someone observed that, even though they were all from different places, "most of us Europeans are alike in our ways. It's all the mother country, and the longer you are away the more you realize it. Over here, Europeans are like one people." Another responded, "But let us not forget that we are Americans now." Upon request, Mary appropriately chose to sing "O Sole Mio." "I sang the song at least six more times with all of the Italians joining in, some weeping, others grinning from ear to ear. . . . I was accepted by everybody from then on." Mary helped Margo to improve her spoken English so she could be "a real American." Mary was particularly touched by foreigners learning English; she described them as "these wonderful people."[12] Some of the strict Welsh Calvinistic church folk made no secret of their dislike for Catholics, but Mary was not one of them.

Little did Mary know that her life would soon be turned upside down again. On September 23, 1913, thousands of coal miners walked off the job, and, with their wives and children, were evicted from the company houses. About 24,000 people went on union strike relief. Among union demands were the abolition of the hated guard system, the right to trade in any store rather than just the company store, the right of miners to choose their own boarding house and their own doctor, the right to join a union, the right to select their own checkweighman, and a 10 percent raise.

Although coal mining was exclusively the domain of men in Colorado as elsewhere, their families and others in the community who served mining families were directly affected by company policies that precipitated the strike. The women were militant supporters of the strike effort, and they played a strategic role in the long campaign. And while the women fought to improve conditions in the mines, they also fought to improve their own lives. Examining the role of women in the strike, historian Priscilla Long concludes that "class consciousness was the strongest component in the

Mary Thomas (far right) with daughters Rachael and Olga in Welsh pinafores at the Ludlow Tent Colony. *United Mine Workers Journal*, October 16, 1913, 2. Courtesy of Paterno Library, Pennsylvania State University.

world-view of the miner's wife, as it was for her husband. This grew out of the fact that the conditions of life and work for women in America's coal-fields were directly affected by company policies. But their separate work and gender roles gave husband and wife separate experiences. As a result, the class consciousness of the miner's wife had its own qualities."[13]

The UMWA set up tent colonies to house the striking families. The tents at Ludlow had wooden floors, and the walls were partially timbered as well. The union installed heavy stoves inside and arranged for fuel and water, storage pits and sanitation trenches, and a telephone line linking the colony with union headquarters in Trinidad. A wooden stage was erected for meetings and a baseball diamond was marked out. Also, a large tent was erected to serve as a school, meeting place, and recreational center. The local union chief, John Lawson, organized camp police and established committees to deal with community affairs.[14]

The Ludlow tent colony was inhabited by 1,200 residents. As the cold, wet, and tired mining families straggled into camp, they were met by women who had come to feed the new arrivals. Mary Thomas was the first woman there, working in the union's canteen and helping to take care of the miners' children. (She also established herself in a separate tent from Tom and John, thus ending the married couple charade.) Mutual support among residents in the colony unified the diverse population from the start, and linguistic and cultural differences were overcome by the collective effort. Slavs, Germans, Russians, Portuguese, French, Italians, Greeks, Hungarians, and other European nationalities all worked together to survive. Mary wrote: "Looking back now on these bitter days, I can see a wonderful thing in them despite the terror, the disappointments, the deprivations. . . . The mine guards had lumped us together as being 'you Damned foreigners,' but we Damned foreigners became as one nationality. If anyone was sick, all were concerned, and would bring whatever medicines we had on hand, or warm soup. No one thought of anybody as being different in color or national origin. We had become a 'family' of world citizens, petitioning for the right to make an honest living as free human beings, and to realize a portion of the fruits of our labor."[15]

Music was an essential ingredient of camp life, and one could hear songs in Spanish, Slavic, Italian, and Greek on any given day. "Ludlow was blessed with several indefatigable young wives," writes George McGovern in his study of the strike. "An attractive Welsh redhead named Mary Hannah Thomas was appointed the colony's official greeter, and her melodic soprano was to be unfailingly heard when the occasion required the national anthem, Sunday School hymns, concert arias, or the strike song that Frank Hayes had just written, sung to the tune of 'The Battle Cry of Freedom' ":

We will rally from the coal mines
We'll battle to the end,
Shouting the battle cry of union.
The union forever! Hurrah, boys, hurrah!
Down with the Baldwins, up with the law;
For we're coming, Colorado, we're coming all the way,
Shouting the battle cry of union![16]

Because she spoke English and was trusted by the non-English-speaking foreigners, Mary met and worked with numerous union leaders, including local strike leader John Lawson and second-in-command Louis Tikas. Frank Hayes, the union vice president, came to Ludlow to show his support (and write the union strike song), and Mary "Mother Jones" Harris, the octogenarian "Miners' Angel," visited as well. This was the first of several meetings Mary had with Mother Jones, for whom Mary developed a life-long admiration. Indeed, Mother Jones's power to organize miners prompted some to claim that she was "the most dangerous woman in America."[17] In Trinidad, however, it was Mary whom company guards and militia regarded as a firebrand and troublemaker, because she led the women and children in union songs and in heckling the guards when they passed by on the road.

As tensions rose, sporadic gunfire frequently erupted between company guards and the miners, and the governor of Colorado was under pressure from the operators to declare martial law and send in the National Guard. When he came to Trinidad to investigate conditions, Mother Jones led a parade on October 21, 1913, to protest against sending in the guard. The parade was led by a band, followed by hundreds of women and children; taking up the rear were the miners, more than one thousand strong. Nevertheless, on October 28, the Colorado National Guard arrived. Initially, the miners welcomed them, reasoning that they would be better than the company's gun thugs; however, when the National Guard began escorting strikebreakers to and from work, relations turned ugly. The women marched in the forefront of strikers' parades and demonstrations and organized the picketing. And they were aggressive about it. For example, in late November the Ludlow women turned out in force to block a train of strikebreakers heading up the canyon behind the colony. A National Guard officer described the confrontation: "Opposed to ten sentries [guardsmen] was a solid mass of strikers, with their club swinging women in the front rank, giving vent to all manner of profanity, and a sullen bunch of men in the rear urging the women to violence." When the militiamen came to the tent colonies to search for weapons, the women taunted them with profane derision.[18] Mary Thomas was identified by the guardsmen as one of the ringleaders among the Ludlow women.

On January 4, 1914, the militia deported Mother Jones, but, upon arrival at the train depot in Denver, she informed the press that she would return. One week later she did exactly that and was promptly arrested. On January 14 two hundred women marched from the union hall to military headquarters waving flags, chanting, and singing union songs, to demand that General John Chase, the officer in charge of the strike zone, release the miners' matron saint. When Chase refused to release her, the UMWA organized a large women's demonstration on January 22. Initially, the demonstration proceeded peaceably, but, as the throng of one thousand women and children followed by a large contingent of men turned onto Main Street, they confronted one hundred troops on horseback. General Chase ordered the women to stop, but, according to sixteen-year-old demonstrator Sarah Slator, he fell to the ground when his horse was spooked and "everybody screamed and laughed at him and that made him angry." Chase jumped to his feet and ordered the troops to charge, and the women scattered as the horsemen approached with swinging rifles and sabers. The women responded by throwing sticks and bottles.[19]

Mary Thomas had not participated in what the military called the "Mother Jones Riot" because she had missed the train from Ludlow to Trinidad. Three men in an automobile offered her a ride into town, but through their questions it was obvious to Mary that they were company men. Upon reaching Trinidad, the driver stopped on the square near the Columbian Hotel and hurried inside; Mary assumed that he was pointing her out to his superiors. Indeed, she later wrote, after she left the car to enter a hairdressing salon a militiaman "caught me by the collar and pushed me to the floor, and I got up and he knocked me down again, and I got up and he knocked me down again."[20] In another account of the episode, the militiaman ordered her to move on and she taunted him: "You go on and go wash your dirty clothes you have on before you order me off of the sidewalk." When he tried to force her along she fought back, "scratching and clawing at him," while the people crowded around them hissed "shame" upon the soldier.[21]

Militiamen arrested her and marched her at bayonet point before General Chase. One of the militiamen informed him that "this is Mrs. Thomas from Ludlow," to which the general replied, "Oh, that is her, is it. Well, you keep her here until I give you further orders." After holding her there for four hours, they marched Mary to the county jail. Always saucy and hostile toward the troops and "Rockefeller thugs," she described being booked: The officer "took my description and size and weight and the color of my eyes and the color of my hair and they couldn't decide what color my hair was; and they asked me what color would I call that, and I said pale blue." She was put into a jail cell with two other women who had been arrested during the parade; they were released during the night, but Mary stayed behind bars in a filthy cell where "rats were running around like horses." The following day the women of the tent colonies joined in an indignation meeting at Trinidad's Castle Hall to denounce the militia's actions, with Mother Jones's presence keeping the enthusiasm high. Mary probably could not have heard the shouting and cheering from her cell.[22]

Tom Thomas came with the children to speak to her. The jailer said, " 'Mrs. Thomas, I have got to hear your conversation.' 'All right,' I says. So we spoke Welsh and so he couldn't understand it. And he left me stand there for about three to five minutes, then he ordered my husband away; and then after I got my children in with me for about three or four days they were crying something terrible. They would throw the food in to me as if I was a dog and leave it on the floor, and they gave them little children the same kind of food as the worst criminal in America." She repeatedly sent notes to General Chase inquiring of the charges against her, but he was not required to formally charge her because the strike district was under martial law. The general "kept me in there 11 days; and then he released me without any trial whatever, and I don't know even yet what I was confined in there for."[23]

If Mary did not know the reason for her incarceration, the militia certainly did. According to General Chase's official report to the governor, Mary Thomas was "a vociferous, belligerent, and abusive leader of the mob. She forcibly resisted orders to move on, responding only with highly abusive and, to say the least, unwomanly language. She attacked the troops with fists, feet, and umbrella." Mary had been under surveillance by the militia for a long time. When her husband was arrested for "knocking down a woman," she "strenuously defended her spouse," the report stated. "The next day she appeared at the office of the *Trinidad Advertiser* and professed her intention to kill the editor for having printed as a news item the incident concerning her husband, and returned a little later with a pistol to carry out her purpose; but, being excluded from the office, she remained for some time upon the sidewalk, attracting a crowd by her loud, vile, and boisterous denunciations. She is altogether a violent and, upon occasions like the Mother Jones riot, a dangerous woman."[24]

There is little doubt that Mary Thomas was targeted by the militia for reprisal for being one of the ringleaders of the Ludlow opposition, although the general's report certainly was exaggerated. Mary was no shrinking violet, but it was a common tactic for strikebreakers to fabricate stories to discredit strikers before the judge and in the court of public opinion. It is unlikely that Mary would have gone to such lengths to avenge her estranged husband's honor, for she clearly thought he had none to avenge. Moreover, guns had no place in her life. She testified that the company guards menaced the evicted families: "These gunmen just would stand a few yards from us and would point their revolvers at us . . . and that was the very first time I ever had seen a gun."[25] It would not be the last.

The Sunday before the Ludlow Massacre was the Greek Easter, and the entire colony turned out on a beautiful day to celebrate their survival of the harsh Colorado winter. Everyone was dressed in their best clothing and joined in singing hymns. This was Mary's first Easter away from home, "where Easter meant so much, with the family singing hymns together. Suddenly I became homesick and despondent," she recollected. Back at their tents, Mary broke into a Welsh hymn. Her closest friends, Margo Gorci and Cedi Costa, stopped to listen. " 'What is that you are singing, Maria?' I explained it was my mother's favorite hymn, 'Aberystwyth.' Margo and Cedi were spellbound by it, and singing it helped soothe some of the feeling of loneliness for my homeland this Easter morning." In the afternoon everybody gathered at the ball field for a baseball game, but the day was ruined when the company guards, now sworn in as state militia and wearing cavalry uniforms, rode onto the field "shouting vile remarks. The men dared not to answer back for fear some of the women and children might be hurt. But this didn't stop the women from yelling at them, telling them what they were, and in no uncertain terms." The guards retorted: "Go ahead and have your fun today. Tomorrow we'll have ours," and rode off.[26]

Around 9:00 A.M. on Monday, April 20, 1914, Mary's girls had just finished their oatmeal breakfast when a "terrific explosion" was heard outside. Using a megaphone Louis Tikas informed the colony that the explosion was a warning bomb from the company militia, and that two more would follow, after which the colony would come under attack. All the women and children were advised to run for their lives to the arroyo. Mary recollected that "suddenly the prairie was covered with human beings running in all directions like ants. No one had time to get anything, save to pick up whatever food was on the table. We all ran as we were, some with babies on their backs, in whatever clothes we were wearing, leaving our tent homes behind us."[27] In a panic Mary and the girls broke into a run for the arroyo a half mile away. In the rush they forgot their coats. Halfway there, they heard the third bomb explode and the shooting at the tent colony begin; its inhabitants fled. "My shoe came off. I stooped to put it back on, and a bullet hit me in the wrist, a mark I have to this day," Mary wrote. Margo used a piece of her petticoat to bind Mary's bleeding wrist.[28]

The women and children huddled in the arroyo most of the day, while the men took their guns to strategic locations where they could shoot from above any guards who attempted to enter the tent colony. By 5:00 P.M. a chill was already settling in, and the women had to decide how to keep the children warm during the night. Mary suggested that they head for an abandoned dry well once used by the railroad. She had learned about the well from one Mrs. Lowe, whose husband worked for the railroad; both were sympathetic to the miners. The dry well was warm, so it provided the perfect solution. They carefully picked their way toward the well and reached the haven about dusk. Armed miners were watching over the tent colony and informed the women that the guards were right in front of them and would shoot anything that moved. So the women and children hunkered down to wait until the next train passed through. Then, as the mile-long freight train blocked the guards' view, the women and children dashed for the safety of the dry well.[29]

While the women secured the children in the well, Mary took some food to the miners watching the tent colony. It was now dark, but she could see three lifeless forms lying on the ground. One of them was Charley Costa, Cedi's husband and a good friend to Mary. Six miners had been there earlier; now there were three. The miners were low on ammunition, and Tikas had not sent the supply he had promised. Little did they know that Tikas himself had been dead for several hours, killed by a crashing blow from the butt of a rifle. His body lay out on the road until the next day.[30]

As Mary stood with the miners, a sentinel exclaimed that the tents were on fire. Mary scrambled up the knoll to see a blazing inferno. The leader of the miners informed her that the women and children in the well must leave quickly, for just as soon as the mine guards were finished looting the tents, they would look for the miners and their families. The guards were now drunk and wild with excitement, and it would not be safe for anyone to stay there. Another freight train was due shortly; when it arrived, the women and children would be directed to a ranch about two miles away on the open prairie. The ranch's owners were also sympathetic to the miners. About 11:00 p.m. a miner lifted the well door and sent the women ahead to a safe place. After wandering in the desert like the Children of Israel, they finally reached the safety of the ranch, where they were fed and warmed and then left to sleep in the stable, covered with hay. Exhausted as she was, Mary could not sleep for worrying about "what work I could do to support my children, knowing no trade, everything gone. I had held my nerve until now without a tear, but felt on the verge of hysteria. Suddenly I imagined I felt my mother's hand tap me on the shoulder . . . 'Pray,' she seemed to say. 'Pray. God will find a way.' How often I had heard my saintly mother speak those very same words to anyone in trouble." Mary lost track of how long she was on her knees, but she "saw the sun rising on another day." When she arose, she wrote that "there was Margo on her knees along with the other women. We were all of different nationalities and faiths, but our prayers were universal." A union truck arrived in the afternoon and transported the women and children to Trinidad. Sadly, that day the "bullet riddled bodies of those three heroic men who helped us escape were found."[31]

The women of Trinidad turned out to help the truckloads of women and children taking refuge in temporary quarters at town hall. One of them who helped Mary and her girls was Harriet Eden, a waitress from Salt Lake City.

Harriet allowed them to use her apartment to take a bath and change into clean clothes, and then promised to help Mary find a job in Salt Lake City. The two women were to become fast friends. Just after the girls were put to bed, Mary learned the tragic news about what would become known as the Ludlow Massacre, one of the most infamous episodes in America's bloody labor history. The tent homes were burned to the ground and family possessions looted. "Everything we had was in those tents," Mary observed. "Most of us had brought beautiful, highly valued things from our own countries. Now all that any of us had was the tattered cotton dress on our back." The real tragedy of Ludlow, however, was that two women and eleven children who had sought shelter in the basement that was dug out under their tent had been trapped and burned alive. Her friend Cedi Costa and her three children were among them. With Charley Costa killed as well, the entire Costa family died at the hands of mine guards now deputized and wearing uniforms of the National Guard.[32]

The bodies of the dead were brought to Trinidad, and miners stood a twenty-four hour watch at each casket until it was buried. With a cessation of the shooting, the miners came down out of the hills. "Strangers wearing union buttons began flocking in from other states. The mine guards were now conspicuous in their absence," she remembered, and the miners "became moody and quiet. You could see and feel their hatred as they silently watched every move of the military."[33]

Mother Jones had been in New York trying to get an audience with John D. Rockefeller Jr., and then in Washington in an effort to get hearings instituted on conditions in Colorado, when she learned about the Ludlow Massacre. She returned to Colorado immediately; again the governor warned her to stay out of the strike zone; again Mother Jones ignored him. Mary was helping to prepare a meal for the refugees when Mother Jones sent for her. "Mother Jones was known for her coldness toward women unless, in her opinion, they were doing something constructive," Mary recollected, and indeed that was true. She must have respected Mary, however, for it was Mary whom she asked for a firsthand account, and it was Mary whom Mother Jones charged with carrying on the fight. Ludlow was a terrible tragedy, and the operators had made a few concessions, but Mother Jones was not impressed: "You ain't won a Damned thing until they allow the men the right to organize," she snorted. "You have to keep fighting, Girl." Mary promised she would try to get the women to go back to Ludlow after the funerals. "Good for you, Girl," she exhorted Mary with a smile and a slap on the back.[34]

On the day of the funerals a quiet pall fell over Trinidad. Mother Jones led the procession with her head bowed, and women, children, family, and friends followed behind. The next day Mary and a few others moved back to Ludlow. She looked through the ruins of her old tent for the trunk that contained all her personal treasures brought over from Wales, but it was gone. Returning to Trinidad on the union truck the next day, she went to say goodbye to Mother Jones, who was leaving that night, and was pleased to hear that "the trek back to Ludlow had started." On her way back to the truck a soldier detained Mary while another brought the commanding officer. " 'So this is Mrs. Thomas,' he said. 'Just what is this all about?' I questioned. 'You'll know soon enough,' he answered. He marched me between ten soldiers to jail, took me upstairs to the women's quarters and locked the door." Two other women unknown to her were also there. When she asked the jailer why she was there, he responded: "I don't know lady. Maybe it's so the flame in that red hair of yours won't ignite a war."[35]

Mary worried about her two children, who were in the care of Mrs. Lowe, but they were delivered to her within a few hours. Again Mary Thomas and her two daughters were in jail, and again she did not know the charge against her. This time, at least, the food was better than what they had been eating. A small window with a broken pane faced out onto the street. According to Mary, "I was becoming tense, and when I was tense I'd either scream or sing." She decided to sing, and went to the window and began singing arias. Soon a crowd gathered beneath the window and applauded. They could not see her because the window was too high, but she was able to put her hand out the window and led them in singing the union's fight song. Soon hundreds of men incarcerated in the jail began singing along with Mary's lead of "Union Forever," while sympathizers in the streets joined in. This became a daily event, with crowds growing increasingly larger until the police dispersed them. Mary and her girls had been in jail three weeks when, one night, Mary sent the children to the bathroom to wash before going to bed. They must have forgotten to turn off the faucet for the cell flooded, prompting the angry jailer to unlock the cell door and order Mary to "get out, and take that wrecking crew with you!" Once on the street Mary went immediately to union headquarters.[36]

William Diamond, the UMWA's international organizer in the southern Colorado strike zone, was sitting behind the desk at headquarters when Mary entered. He was surprised to see her. "Did you know," he said, "that you and your children being jailed is coming up before the House in Washington?" In jail Mary received no news at all, so she was unaware of the hearings being initiated by the House Commission on Industrial Relations. Mary inquired about getting back to Ludlow to join her women friends, but Diamond informed her that there were "no women left in Ludlow, and it wouldn't be safe for you to go back right now" because all the families had moved away. Many of the single men were up in the hills still fighting. "There's been a regular war," he continued. "It started after we buried our dead . . . it must have been the day you were arrested. The miners went completely mad," burning company buildings and shooting company men and scabs who did not flee. He handed her a file of newspaper clippings, one of which reported the arrest of a Welsh girl and her two children in Trinidad. " 'Oh dear,' I said . . . 'this is an international news service. I hope my mother in Wales doesn't see this.' 'That reminds me,' he said, 'a letter came in for you from Wales.' " The letter, from Mary's sister, informed her that her mother had in fact seen the article and was convinced that Mary had become a "criminal." Mary used some of her three weeks of union dole money to cable her mother that she was out of jail now and that she and the girls were fine.[37]

Both sides in the conflict used Mary's experience for its full propaganda value. While the militia portrayed her as "a belligerent and abusive leader of the mob," union propagandists represented her as an unoffending, "frail little Welsh woman." Neither were accurate descriptions, of course. It was her notoriety that prompted UMWA's Frank Hayes to seek Mary's assistance in a public relations project on the union's behalf. She hardly had time to recuperate from her ordeal in jail when Hayes asked her to join a delegation headed to Washington to meet with President Woodrow Wilson in hopes of convincing him to force the operators to intervene and settle the strike. Mary and her daughters, ages four and six, were to join two other female survivors of the Ludlow Massacre, Pearl Jolly, a Red Cross nurse in the camp, and Mary Petrucci, still too traumatized to speak following the death of her three children when the tent was set ablaze during the massacre. Leading the party was Judge Ben B. Lindsey of Denver and his wife, and Mrs. Lee Champion, wife of the Colorado district judge active in relief work for the strike district. They were joined by James Lord, head of the mining department of the American Federation of Labor. The women's expenses were paid by the Denver Labor League. The trip to Washington became a major speaking tour involving stops in many industrial cities. Their first stop was Hull House in Chicago, where they were guests of Jane Addams, and the miners' wives spoke to a large gathering.[38]

The party disembarked from the train outside Washington on May 20,

1914, to be briefed by labor leaders. Hayes introduced Mary to William Green, secretary-treasurer of the UMWA and future AFL president. The delegation arrived at the White House the following day and met with President Wilson for twenty minutes. Mary thought that Wilson seemed more interested in the women's experience than in the cause, which he had determined was a conflict that must come to an end because the Italian and Austro-Hungarian ambassadors were demanding protection for their nationals. On the other hand, the British vice consul in Denver had rejected Mary's complaint that she had been arrested illegally, and informed State Attorney General Fred Farrar that he would not intercede on behalf of British subjects who flaunted the law.[39]

Wilson bounced Olga on his knee and held Rachael's hand, but he remained noncommittal. "Mrs. Thomas, you tell me the whole story in your own way," and so she did. Although Mary had fretted that meeting the president was the equivalent of meeting a queen, once she began to talk she decided it was "more like I was talking to my father," she wrote. After the interview the women were met by dozens of reporters and then were taken to meet John P. White, president of the UMWA, and other union officials, including William Green. They also met with influential members of Congress, including Representatives Edward Keating of Colorado and William Kent of California, and a Welshman from the British consulate. That night they spoke at the packed armory hall with a number of prominent men and women in attendance, including the president's daughter Margaret.[40] The delegation spent four days making the rounds in Washington. Mary told her story to AFL president Samuel Gompers, and on May 27 she and Pearl Jolly testified on the Ludlow Massacre before the Commission on Industrial Relations at the urging of Melinda Scott, president of the Women's Trade Union League, Jane Addams, and J. Borden Harriman, a commission member. During that time, she wrote, "I met many influential people of Welsh parentage, and at that time Wales meant a lot to me." If she had had the money she would have gone home "in a flash."[41] Then it was off to New York.

From Washington the party traveled to New York, where they hoped to meet with John D. Rockefeller Jr. Mary joined Upton Sinclair and other reformers in picketing in front of Rockefeller's offices at 26 Broadway. The famous tycoon refused to grant them an audience, but Upton Sinclair's wife, Craig, led the miners' wives to Rockefeller's offices by way of a private elevator. When the women stepped off the elevator, the secretaries in the office were startled. Informed that the industrial titan was out, the women

sat down to wait and eat their lunches. Mary's children entertained themselves on the floor. Mary recalled that "a sad looking man came out of the
Rockefeller office and smiled as he watched my children play. I smiled back
and he took a step toward us. Just then newsboys in the street below yelled,
'Extra, Extra, Three Miners' Wives Here to Kill Rockefeller,'" and the man
was rushed behind closed doors. Mary believed the man was Rockefeller
and that he would have talked to them had the newsboys not cried out the
headline. Shortly after, a policeman asked them to vacate the premises and
they complied.[42]

Mother Jones was convinced that Rockefeller would take action only if he
were to go to Colorado and see conditions in the coalfield with his own eyes.
When he agreed to do so, Mother Jones told union miners to call off the
strike, but the miners thought she had turned against them. Mary rejected
that charge and expressed irritation with the radicals and anarchists she
encountered in New York.[43] In New York the Ludlow women spoke to large
crowds. The same theme and format was repeated everywhere they went.
Jolly told the crowds that her Red Cross badge was a target for the militia,
while Mary recounted how she led the women and children to safety through
a rain of bullets and how she watched as the militia looted and burned the
Ludlow tent colony to the ground. The complete itinerary of the speaking
tour is unknown, but large sympathetic crowds reportedly greeted them in
"all the great industrial cities." The *United Mine Workers Journal* reported that
preparations for a "monster demonstration" were underway in Indianapolis
for June 5, and that large crowds assembled in other cities demonstrated the
"great interest in the message these women have to deliver."[44] The Central
Labor Union organized a large turnout at Tomlinson Hall, the largest audi-
torium in Indianapolis. On stage were representatives of the many international unions headquartered in the city. Mary held the audience spellbound
with her recounting of the injustices perpetrated on miners in the Colorado
coal camps. "Her story of the horrors of the destruction of the peaceful tent
colony brought tears to the eyes of men inured to hardships, accustomed to
wrongs and abuses," the *UMWJ* reported, and "the vast audience departed in
silence" after hearing firsthand about the Ludlow tragedy.[45]

Even though all their expenses were paid, the women received no money
for their efforts and returned to Colorado penniless. In Trinidad, Mary
found that the strikers had mostly dispersed to other coalfields. Worse, in
order to join the UMWA speaking tour, Mary had left her daughters with a
caretaker in Washington, and so now was separated from them by nearly
2,000 miles. But in the union hall she was given a letter sent to her from

Harriet Eden, informing her that work as a waitress was available if she joined her in Salt Lake City. Just as Mary was about to leave the hall, Upton Sinclair entered to speak to her. "He said he was waiting for me to get back to ask questions for a new book called *King Coal* . . . 'and you, Mary, are its heroine.'" Mary was "stunned" and obviously flattered to be the heroine of a Sinclair novel. She recounted as much of the strike as she could for him, but in her reminiscence she provides no additional information about the interview with the famous author.

That the protagonist of *King Coal* and its sequel, *Coal War*, was based on Mary Thomas might be confirmed by the character's name, Mary Burke, possibly a conflation of Mary's name with that of the actress and singer Billie Burke. Newspapers at the time reported that Mary closely resembled Burke, who was then at the height of her musical comedy career on the New York stage. Indeed, when she first arrived in the mine camp of Delagua, her husband's friend John had remarked that Tom was right: "Your wife sure does look like that color picture of Billie Burke my brother sent me from London when she was playing there. Even the same size and same color of hair." Tom replied that back in Wales "she was written up as her double when Mary won a contest for the best potential opera singer under twenty."[46] And in his novels, Sinclair describes Mary Burke as a small, feisty redhead who unambiguously identified with the working class and proved to be one of the true leaders in the war. Although the character was Irish rather than Welsh, she was described as having deep red hair and being tough but highly principled, all true of Mary Thomas as well.[47]

There is a curious six-month lapse in *Those Damned Foreigners* between the summer of 1914, when Mary returned to Colorado, and the following spring of 1915 when she left the state for good. A letter to UMWA president John P. White, dated January 4, 1915, from Pittsburgh, reveals personal difficulties she omitted in the book. Mary informed White that when she returned to Trinidad Frank Hayes provided her with the financial assistance to pay for her return to Washington in August 1914 and for the children's board. While in Washington, Mary wrote, she received a letter from her husband back in Colorado informing her that the police had a warrant for her arrest. Therefore, a union official advised her to leave her children with the caretaker and try to find employment in Pittsburgh; her children could rejoin her once she was established. Why he suggested Pittsburgh is unclear, but Mary "tramped the streets" of that city looking for work without success. She pleaded with White to help her for she could not retrieve her children until the five-month board bill, which amounted to at least $80, was paid. "I am nearly going crazy," Mary pleaded, and "if I could only have my babies out from there I would beg for food for them." She was completely destitute and was coping only with assistance from her church and Van A. Bittner, a UMWA official in the Pittsburgh region. White promised to present her case at the next meeting of the International Executive Board, which responded favorably by authorizing Philip Murray, a board member from Pittsburgh, to provide her with financial assistance. Apparently he followed through, for Mary's memoir resumes her saga in Colorado with her children back from Washington.[48]

It was then that Mary joined Harriet in Salt Lake City. No sooner had she gone to work, however, than the restaurant closed. The employment agency found waitressing jobs for Mary and Harriet in Lockwood, Nevada, a true Wild West town. An opportunity presented itself for the women to own their own dance hall and restaurant. Harriet married a local rancher instead, so Mary went into business for herself. The dance hall and restaurant enabled Mary to make a good living. She did not like the business, but it was a way to establish a life for herself and the girls until she could save enough money to leave Lockwood. Soon, World War I came and so did Prohibition; ever adaptable, Mary bought bootleg whiskey to stay in business and protect her investment.[49]

By this time Mary knew where she wanted to live after Lockwood. Several years earlier her sister Gwen and her husband had moved to Hollywood, and on a visit there Mary found she loved "the pretty little village" so well that she rented a cottage behind Gwen's house. She then placed Olga and Rachael in a Hollywood boarding school and commuted from Nevada on the weekends. Her reminiscence does not indicate the year, but it was probably in the early 1920s that she finally had saved enough money to sell her business and move to Hollywood for good.

Then, on the very day she was to leave Lockwood, something happened that might have seemed to come straight out of a Hollywood movie. Three men entered the restaurant and sat down at a table. One of them was Don O'Neal, the man who had fallen in love with Mary on their transatlantic passage on the *Oceanic* in 1913. He had gone into the mining and land business after the war, and the three men sitting at the table were engaged in a discussion about mining. Don's back was to Mary, but she instantly recognized his voice. She stood there transfixed. Seeing Mary he leaped to his feet, took her in his arms, and declared that she must marry him before he lost her again; Mary agreed on the spot. Following a brief ceremony the next day, the couple departed for Hollywood and moved into the house next to Gwen.[50]

We do not know if they lived happily ever after because Mary Thomas's reminiscence gives short brush strokes to the remainder of her life, as though the significant portions were over. Don was out of town for extended periods on business, her daughters married, and to pass the time she opened a ladies' sportswear shop on Hollywood Boulevard. In late 1949 or early 1950 Mary and Don arranged a trip to Europe, with a side visit to Wales, on the same White Star liner where they first met. At the last moment business prevented Don from going, but he insisted that Mary go without him. For the first time in the thirty-six years since she had left the Ogmore Valley in 1913, Mary Williams Thomas O'Neal returned to her homeland. At the station in Bridgend a busload of relatives and friends met her with a big banner proclaiming, "Welcome Home Mary." While many changes had taken place, much remained as she remembered. Mary spent "many wonderful days" with family and friends, and then she left to continue her European vacation. On her way back to Hollywood, the former labor rebel, now Hollywood shopkeeper, stopped at Ludlow to see the monument that had been erected by the UMWA in 1915 to commemorate that dark episode in the nation's history. It seems telling that an equal amount of space in her memoir is devoted to her visit to the Ludlow monument as to her family reunion in Wales.[51]

In March 1950, two weeks after returning from Europe, Mary read in the newspaper that the AFL-CIO would soon be celebrating fifty years of unionism at the Hollywood Palladium. At Don's urging she decided to attend. William Green, now president of the AFL-CIO, was the main speaker. Decades had elapsed since she had last seen him, but when she approached he recognized her. "Well, well, well! Mary Thomas!" he said. "The years have been kind to you, Mary. You don't look much different from the pretty little redheaded girl from Wales I knew then when you sang so beautifully for us." Looking around the large room at the women in furs and jewels, and the well-fed and well-dressed men, Mary concluded that organized labor had finally entered the mainstream of American life, for "one couldn't tell the employers from the employees." Watching the audience, she wrote, she felt like screaming: "If you only knew the price which was paid for this splendor."[52]

Sixty years after the Great Colorado Coalfield War of 1913–14, a writer met with Mary Thomas O'Neal in a Hollywood restaurant to hear her recollections of the strike: "I imagined her a girl of twenty-two standing at the Trinidad depot with her two small daughters beside her and that deep red hair she had been so proud of falling down her back, still wearing her Old Country leg-o-mutton blouse and a sailor hat stuck on the back of her head." Listening to her recollections, the interviewer noted that she barely topped five feet tall; "with her picture hat and her animated hands and her intemperate Welsh twang and her memories of Colorado she must have been something then."[53] And indeed she was.

Wales influenced the girl, but Ludlow molded her into the woman she became. During her first twenty-two years she lived as a miner's daughter; the mines injured her father and killed her fiancé. She grew up in the shadow of the Ocean colliery in a mining culture shaped by the rhythms of the industry. She was brought up a Baptist but resented the religious bigotry against the Irish Catholics and blamed it on Protestant zealots. Perhaps her Irish-Catholic paternal grandmother felt the sting of those zealots back in Wales. Mary's father apparently was not religious, but he was a devout union man who had shown her its importance to the miners.[54] In the Colorado coalfields there was no middle ground; one took sides and Mary identified with the miners completely. She opted for class consciousness over religious or ethnic bigotry, and her first and closest friends were Italian Catholics. Eventually, Mary became an independent businesswoman, married a wealthy businessman, and lived an affluent life in Hollywood. In the final analysis, however, Mary Thomas was and remained a class-conscious labor rebel; it was culturally engrained in her, and fighting for the miners validated her identity. She experienced firsthand capitalist oppression in its rawest form, and believed the union's crusade was a moral struggle for justice and democratic values. Given her background, there was little else she could do and still maintain her sense of honor.

In the early years when the industry was founded in eastern Pennsylvania, coal companies hired British miners to operate the mines. In time they claimed a customary right to their employment and resisted when non-British workers threatened their grip on the craft. It was, therefore, difficult for many of them to achieve working-class unity beyond their own ethnic group. Later in the nineteenth century, as the industry expanded, operators frequently followed a policy of "judicious mixture," recruiting a workforce fragmented by nationality, culture, and language in order to create divisions that would inhibit unionization. In these fields where no established ethnic group could claim ownership of the craft, the only way forward was class solidarity. Twenty-four different nationalities were represented in the Colorado coalfields, but Mary intuitively understood that their interdependency and class interests gave them common purpose. Women like Mary Thomas played an important role as strike leaders because of their facility with English, and because they were accustomed to direct participation in conflicts that affected the mining community. Class consciousness was an important element of the miners' wives, and when judicial injunctions barred men from picketing or demonstrating, women often became the shock troops of the movement, confronting the company's gendarmes and occasionally filling the jails for outraging the powers of property. Separate spheres were the working norm in the British and American coalfields, but when the entire community was threatened, as during strikes, the role of British and American coalfield women extended to collective action. This stood in contrast to many of the southern and eastern European women from non-mining cultures, who found themselves for the first time in tent colonies like Ludlow sitting next to their husbands in meetings and discussing affairs outside their own homes.[55]

Like most other immigrants, Mary embraced reform but rejected radicalism. Fighting for your rights as Americans was a worthy cause, but overthrowing the system itself was not what they came to America to achieve. They were believers in American exceptionalism who had emigrated to improve their chances in life. Mary's complaint was not with capitalists so much as with what she saw as their calculated abuses of power against her people, actions that were inconsistent with her sense of justice and the American creed. Like so many Welsh miners, Mary was upwardly mobile. She thought of America as a land of opportunity with a fluid class structure, a country where one could get ahead and gain respectability by hard work. Indeed, the British encountered little that would tell them otherwise. Mary Thomas embodied these cultural values, but she was also unique among the Welsh women of the coalfields because she was a single mother with two daughters to be raised. The coalfields operated as a closed system that trapped mining families in permanent debt and lower-class status. In rebelling against the "un-American" power structure found in the Colorado coalfield, Mary Thomas was validating her identity as a daughter of Welsh mining culture.

More than distance was navigated during the incredible journey of Mary Williams Thomas O'Neal from Nantymoel to Hollywood. She also traversed the psychological wilderness of dramatic cultural change and the construction of a new identity. Her remarkable success in this project after encountering so many obstacles symbolizes the high personal cost of Americanization, but also the reward for those who succeeded. Along the way, Mary became less and less Welsh and more and more American. She returned to Wales thirty-six years after her departure and then only on a European vacation, even though her financial independence would have allowed her to return at any time. Sixty years after Ludlow, an interviewer reported that tears came to Mary's eyes as she "told me she often dreamed about Ludlow. Dreamed about it yet."[56] There is no account by her hand or any other, however, that memories of her Welsh homeland still brought tears to her eyes. Sometime during the years following Ludlow, Mary Thomas's incredible journey carried her across that intangible boundary of identity when she came to regard herself as American rather than Welsh.

Welsh cultural distinctiveness began to decline with the first generation. Welsh *hiraeth*, "the deep affection-ate remembrance of absent loved ones and localities," as the Reverend Dr. Erasmus W. Jones defined the word, was present among all first-generation Welsh Americans to some degree, particularly at times like Christmas that elicited powerful nostalgic emotions. After seventy years in America, living as a citizen for sixty-four of them, Rev. Jones still felt the *hiraeth*. "Ah, my dear native American friend, by experience you know nothing of those heart-throbbings felt by thousands among us. . . . The emigrant parts not only with friends and kindred dear, but also with scenes and objects with which he has been familiar from his earliest remembrance."[1]

Most Welsh emigrants did not go to America with the intention of pre-serving their Welsh identity, but they did transplant much of their culture with them. As time passed, however, the old ways were bound to experience the flux of memory. "There is strange how things come back if you start to think of one thing and become tangled up in memory," mused Huw Mor-gan, the narrator in Richard Llewellyn's ever-popular novel *How Green Was My Valley*. "Sometimes you think of a thing, and it reminds you of some-thing else, but nearly always you forget why it should remind you, and you find you have forgotten the link between them."[2] Huw longed to return to that "home" before coal had turned his valley black, a time and place that no longer existed except in his memory. Like other immigrants, first-gener-ation Welsh Americans became painfully aware that they could not go "home" again. Without memories of the old country, however, second-generation Welsh Americans felt little sense of loss with the demise or Americanization of Welsh cultural institutions that had helped to ease the transition for their parents to a new home. Welsh heritage did not present an obstacle to assimilation into American society, so there was no second "ill-adjusted" generation; they simply and quickly became Americans.[3] Americanization was the result of a two-way process whereby the Welsh increasingly participated in the dominant culture and mainstream Americans accepted them. It was a function of life experience as well. Cultural identity might be likened to a scale balancing Welsh and American experience. As years passed into decades, the scale of experience tipped toward America, and barring mitigating restraints the immigrant gradually became more American than Welsh. The process was slower in the rural areas, where religious groups in particular chose to preserve what they regarded as a traditional Welsh identity. Over time, however, all Welsh communities were affected by the dramatic generational shift from Welsh to Welsh American and then to American of Welsh descent. Like all immigrants, the Welsh confronted an assault on their ethnic identity and their cultural institutions immediately upon arrival in America. Unlike the millions of immigrants from southern and eastern Europe who encountered formidable language and religious barriers, the Welsh met with few obstacles to assimilation.

A number of factors smoothed their way. Most obvious was race and nationality. In an era of overt racism and xenophobia, the Welsh were indistinguishable from mainstream white Americans. Moreover, the timing of the Welsh migration preceded the influx of eastern and southern Europeans that began in the late nineteenth century. By then Welsh migrants were "old stock" Britons whose status, occupation, and standard of living placed them among the "established," native population. Also, their strict brand of Protestantism nested them neatly with the vast majority of Americans prior to the great European migrations, and aligned them with the nativists who feared what the influx of Catholics would do to the American Protestant identity. "Among the Welsh, prejudice against Roman Catholicism can hardly be over-estimated," Emrys Jones writes, and when nativists made Protestantism synonymous with Americanism, they saw the Welsh as supporters of the Protestant American nation.[4]

The socioeconomic status of the Welsh also facilitated their acceptance by Americans. Unlike the Irish, Slavs, and Italians, most of whom arrived without industrial experience, and whose economic circumstances bordered on desperation, the Welsh were disproportionately skilled workers in great demand who fetched handsome wages in labor-scarce America. Since they began at a higher rung on the socioeconomic ladder, upward mobility was correspondingly easier for even the first generation. The Welsh, therefore, enjoyed a higher standard of living than newcomers from Europe and were disproportionately middle rather than lower class. Even lower-class Welshmen were less visible than "respectable" Welshmen, so they escaped scrutiny. These social characteristics facilitated the integration of the Welsh into American society and accelerated the cultural identity shift. The British generally escaped American ridicule, and while the Welsh might object to being called "taffy" or "goat," few Americans understood their cultural context or used them. Some regarded the Welsh immigrants as "clannish" because they were slightly less inclined to intermarry with native-born Americans than their British counterparts, and there was a stronger tendency to band together around Welsh language churches in their own communities. On the other hand, the Welsh seldom lived apart from Americans and they were never segregated either by law or custom.[5]

Although one might expect that the Welsh language would serve as a disincentive to acquiring American citizenship, the great majority of Welsh immigrants were bilingual, and a higher proportion of them were fully naturalized citizens than the English or Scots. Well over 90 percent of Welsh immigrants had either become naturalized or had applied for citizenship in 1900, one of the highest rates among all foreign immigrant groups, including the English and the Scots. As one historian of British immigration observed, most British immigrants passed almost unnoticed into American life; the "immigrant problem" had nothing to do with the English, Scots, "or even the more clannish and foreign-speaking Welsh." The Welsh in America were no less attached to their homeland, but in an era when Welsh nationalism had stirred their consciousness of longstanding grievances against the English, they were not equally loyal to the queen of England. They had no difficulty, therefore, in renouncing their allegiance to the crown as required for American citizenship. In short, the Americans embraced them because they were skilled workers of British stock, English speakers, Protestants, Republicans in politics, and exemplars of middle-class values.[6]

As the Welsh immigrants became Americanized they and especially their children abandoned the coal industry. The dramatic recomposition of the mining workforce in the American coalfields, particularly in anthracite country, resulted from mine mechanization, the corporate centralization of control over the production process, and a flood of unskilled Europeans. Already by 1880 corporate and technological changes in the industry had shifted employers' preferences away from skilled British miners to the new unskilled agricultural immigrants who employers believed would work for less and be more pliable. The changing workforce enabled those Welsh who remained to gain an even greater proportion of the supervisory positions. The Scranton city directory for 1900 listed as many mine bosses as miners. In 1910, an anthracite mine once worked exclusively by Welshmen now employed Welshmen only as managers and superintendents, while the Irish worked as foremen, the Poles and Lithuanians as contract miners, and the Slovaks, Ruthenians, and Italians at the bottom of the hierarchy as outside laborers.[7] Welsh anthracite miners who could not achieve upward mobility within the industry were forced to choose other occupations or leave the anthracite fields for the developing bituminous fields further west. A significant number returned to Wales. A reputation for strident unionism provided added inducement for mine owners to replace Welshmen with more pliable workers. The miners themselves understood this well, and frequently complained about the changing preference among mine owners.[8]

Finally, there was the influence of geographic scale in the transition from Welsh to a Welsh American identity. Rev. R. D. Thomas recognized the importance of space in his 1872 book on the Welsh settlements in the United States. He counted over two hundred of them scattered over twenty-three states, "and the majority of the states are ten times the size of the whole Principality of Wales." Sprinkled across this vast expanse was a comparatively small Welsh population representing only one 332nd part of the total American population. In such a large kettle, the Welsh were simply blended into the American ethnic stew with scarcely a trace.[9]

The Americanization of the Welsh, and their upward mobility within the coal industry as well as the broader economy, is generally regarded by scholars as a mark of progress. And so it is, but clearly at the price of their Welsh identity. Measuring how this affected individuals at the personal, emotional level is impossible. Nevertheless, by the turn of the twentieth century, the dominant position of the Welsh in the American coal industry was well on its way to becoming a thing of the past, as was the work culture that shaped their communities. With the decline of community went the institutional means for preserving Welsh cultural memory.[10]

The agricultural migrants of the early nineteenth century fully intended to preserve Welsh culture and values from Anglicization and industrialization. Led by Nonconformist preachers, they settled in rural agricultural communities held together by chapels. The industrial Welsh migration, however, began in the mid-nineteenth century and consisted of emigrants who left the homeland one by one, generally to elevate their economic status. Their interest in preserving Welsh culture and institutions took a back seat to practicality and usefulness. The first Welsh immigrants to the United States arrived before the Civil War, fully intent on preserving Welsh culture and values. Naturally, the industrial immigrants were much more amenable to change, and their children, who were born and raised in the United States, were products of a very different set of values derived from the mainstream majority. Rapid change among them would seem to have been inevitable.[11]

Americanization proceeded swiftly in Welsh coal-mining communities. South Wales was in the vanguard of Anglicization and modernity in Wales, so migrants from this region did not generally share the same commitment to preserving Welshness as the rural agricultural migrants. If culture is defined as a fixed set of immutable traits, then Americanization was a tragic, irreversible loss—like the extinction of a species or death of a loved one. On the other hand, if culture is understood as a dynamic process of human adaptation to new circumstances and the abandonment of traditional ways that are no longer useful, then cultural change is a healthy sign of vitality. However "Welshness" is defined, the memory of Wales among the first generation began to fade almost immediately, and subsequent generations with no memory of Wales were proud of their Welsh ancestry, but prouder still of being Americans.[12]

Economic success spurred the disintegration of Welsh community co-hesiveness, and a distinctive ethnic culture, as prosperity reduced the need for mutual support and cooperation. Settlement patterns that made the Welsh appear clannish—speaking the Welsh language, occupational net-working and nepotism, separate churches—all were displaced by American-ization. The signs had been present for decades but Welsh community leaders disagreed on what, if anything, should be done about it. For many there could be no distinctive Welsh identity without the Welsh language, which was threatened almost from the beginning. During the 1860s and 1870s most Welsh immigrants spoke Welsh, although undoubtedly the great majority were bilingual to some degree. The old language was indeed a principal link in the transnational Welsh culture. Welsh writer Gwyn Thomas experienced the language shift firsthand. "My father and mother were Welsh-speaking," he observed in 1979, and yet "I did not exchange a word in that language with them. The death of Welsh ran through our family of twelve like a geological fault. Places like the Rhondda were parts of America that never managed to get to the boat." South Wales, the "Ameri-can Wales," which sent so many Welsh to the United States, was trans-formed during the late nineteenth and early twentieth centuries by indus-trialization, urbanization, a large influx of English immigrants, and a materialist interpretation of progress. The new understanding of progress magnified the importance of the English language in getting ahead in South Wales, just as it did for Welsh immigrants in America.[13]

Historical change is marked in institutional shifts, but individual human behavior is the immediate agent of cultural change. Welsh immigrants came to the United States with values nurtured in Wales and embedded in the language and the Nonconformist chapel. Children in the rural agricultural communities might retain the language and values of their parents longer, but those raised in urban industrial places were soon overwhelmed by the multitudes. Welsh children may have heard Welsh spoken in the home, but as soon as they stepped out the door the dominant culture crowded in from all corners. School, play, work, and popular culture all were conducted in English. Consequently, a struggle for cultural hegemony often was waged day by day, household by household, and the outcome was achieving results.[14]

The Welsh scholar Emrys Jones experienced two episodes during a Welsh prayer meeting that captured the point of change: "A prayer was being offered by an old Welshman who had lived in Utica for some forty years. He thanked God that he was a Welshman, and for the religious heritage that was his by virtue of this fact. Then he began referring to heaven as . . . another name for Wales! His identification of the two 'realms' became complete, and his reference to those who were on 'the other side' became so ambiguous that they could have referred to the dead or to those on holiday in Wales! Spiritually that man's home was still Wales—he was a spiritual exile. It would not be too much to claim that he represented many of his own generation." Immediately following that meeting, Jones was approached by a second-generation Welshman whose "indignation knew no bounds after reading in a passage in a newspaper from Wales a reference to 'Welsh exiles in the United States.' 'We are not exiles,' was his emphatic answer, 'We are Americans.' The last phrase was uncompromising. Those two incidents on the same evening demonstrated the schism and the sudden change all too clearly."[15]

The identity of second-generation Welshmen was a bifurcation of Welsh and American. "Welsh" offered an identity based on group continuity and solidarity, reinforced through family, church, and ethnic societies; the "American" identity offered new and exciting possibilities for material advancement and acceptance, its influence exerted through education, work, recreation, and the media. So long as a steady flow of immigrants arrived from Wales to provide a transfusion of traditional values from the homeland, their institutions remained Welsh-language institutions; however, the tide shifted when emigration from Wales came to a halt. Within two or three decades the second and third generations became the majority, and Welsh institutions faced a life-changing choice: adapt or die.[16]

The Welsh language in America found its widest public expression in those cultural institutions that preserved the memory of what it meant to be Welsh in the native tongue. Conversely, decline of the "ancient tongue" also may be tracked in the shift to English in these institutions. No other cultural institution even came close to rivaling the importance of the Welsh churches in this mission. Wherever the Welsh congregated, chapels grand and small immediately followed. Welsh Nonconformity presented a unifying element that bound all the Welsh together, not unlike Catholicism unified the Irish. The churches were tight little communities unto themselves. They held Sunday and Weekly Schools where the language and a wide range of topics were taught to young and old of both sexes. Each one had auxiliary societies through which members learned leadership skills and organized popular preaching and singing sessions. In their activities and demeanor the chapels emphasized to Americans and to the Welsh themselves "the similarities between the respectable, utilitarian and even 'middle-class' character of Welsh culture and the dominant White Anglo-Saxon Protestant (Anglo-American) ideology of the host country."[17]

The vitality of the Welsh churches served as a weathervane of Americanization. The once-thriving Welsh-language culture it had incubated began a precipitous decline after the 1870s until it had all but disappeared by the early twentieth century. Coming from the most Anglicized parts of South Wales, most Welsh coal miners and mill workers were able to make the shift to English within one generation. Most Welsh churches converted to English out of fear that young people would abandon religion entirely. The inability to recruit new blood, either among the American-born or new immigrants from Wales, ensured the decline of not only the Welsh church but also the language it perpetuated.[18]

The Reverend R. D. Thomas read the signs as early as 1872. In his book published that year, he observed that "in the old Welsh settlements, the children of the old settlers are scarcely without exception totally indifferent about speaking, reading and writing the Welsh language; many of them are unable to do it." In the newer settlements, which included the numerous coal mining communities, the language was still spoken, and he anticipated that it would continue to be spoken for another twenty to forty years. But in all the Welsh settlements, he wrote, the children spoke English at home. "ENGLISH is *the language of the country*, and it is necessary for us and for our children to learn to understand it, to speak it, to read it, and to write it before we are able to feel happy and successful and gain influence and respect here." This was a "painful" disappointment to those committed to the

Welsh language, such as Rev. Thomas, but he saw its loss as both inevitable and irreversible.[19]

Scholars have documented the language shift in church records and publications. Late-nineteenth-century trustee and committee reports, pastoral addresses, and sermons generally were still being written in Welsh, but the shift to English began in earnest during the first decade of the twentieth century. By the 1930s church business ceased to be conducted in Welsh. Interestingly, women's society activities experienced the shift earliest, in the 1920s, at the same time the trend was noticed in Wales. A study at a Welsh grammar school during the same period showed that boys preferred to be taught in Welsh, but girls increasingly preferred instruction in English as they grew older and adopted English on the playground. The "last stand" occurred in the Sunday services. Initially, Sunday morning and evening services were conducted in Welsh, then the evening service became English, then the order was reversed. Finally, in the twentieth century, Welsh was preserved only in a few large urban churches.[20]

All Welsh churches confronted the choice of either shifting to English in order to serve the spiritual needs of the younger generation of Welsh Americans or continuing as Welsh churches and dying on the vine for lack of new members. Emrys Jones called this the "inner nexus of the culture complex," the intersection of religion and language where the most cherished values of Welsh culture resided for the first generation. Throughout the nineteenth century, but particularly in the 1880s and 1890s, the debate over the fate of the language and the institutions in which it was embedded raged in the columns of both Welsh- and English-language publications. They reflected a deep ambivalence. A minister who dreaded the merging of Welsh and American churches exclaimed: "One organization—one language—God help us!"[21] But an 1882 editorial in the *Cambrian* declared that to deny young people the benefit of a sermon because it was delivered in a language they did not understand was a "folly" and probably "sinful." Even the strongest Welsh churches would have to calculate "how long will the old people live" and "how long will the churches live." Another *Cambrian* editorial of 1893 thought it possible that Welsh churches might stem the tide for a time, "but then they should yield gracefully to the shift to English."[22] And this is precisely what happened.

A similar quandary confronted the eisteddfod with the same outcome. The shift was gradual but inexorable, a struggle between continuity and change at both the individual and institutional levels. A distinctively Welsh institution that migrants transplanted nearly everywhere they settled, the eisteddfod celebrated creative work in the Welsh language. Language shift in the eisteddfod, therefore, was a significant measure of Americanization that occurred during approximately the same period as it did in the church. English was nearly absent before the First World War, and as late as 1910 only 12 percent of the program was performed in English. By 1930 English accounted for nearly 45 percent of the competition, and by 1948 Welsh had disappeared entirely. In form the eisteddfod remained a musical and writing competition for the Welsh, but it gradually became a festival for the entire community with Poles, Germans, Americans, and Italians competing and taking prizes, all in English. The Welsh-language press followed a similar pattern in the shift to English. *Y Drych*, the leading Welsh American publication, was the staunchest holdout; between 1851 and the 1920s very little beyond the occasional advertisement was in English. By the late 1940s, however, even *Y Drych* had shifted to English.[23]

There is no precise way to measure language use before World War I, but the loss of native language ability among the Welsh in America was significant throughout the nineteenth century. Only continued emigration from the homeland in the late nineteenth century forestalled its demise. The language question was cause for agitation in many quarters. The dwindling few who lamented the demise of their native tongue charged their countrymen with abandoning their Welsh identity. Complaints that parents were not teaching their children Welsh, particularly in the industrial regions, were a regular feature in Welsh American publications. The *Cambrian* printed a letter from one critic who declared: "While every Welshman is in the habit of saying '*Oes y Byd I'r Iaith Gymraeg,*' very few have a hearty desire to see it live on. . . . We cannot see how it [Welsh language] is going to continue much longer when Welsh folks persist in nursing their little ones in utter ignorance of their mother tongue. . . . Cases are met with where parents with but a slight knowledge of English teach their children in that tongue." Another critic complained in *Y Drych* that one-half of those espousing Welsh at eisteddfodau were raising their children to speak English. A correspondent praised *Y Drych* for refusing to shift and thereby "prostitute itself for Americanism."[24]

Those unconcerned about the fate of the language responded that they had immigrated to America to improve their position in the world and not to preserve the Welsh language and culture. Many thought efforts to preserve the Welsh language were misplaced. As one proponent of Americanization declared in 1909, "to perpetuate the many languages in this country would be folly beyond imagination." More specifically, he continued, "the effort to perpetuate the Welsh language in this country is as useless as trying to stem the tide with a broom. It would be far better for those who wish to keep it to go back to Wales."[25] By the turn of the twentieth century, Welsh was seldom heard in the streets of Welsh American communities, including even leading centers like Scranton. There seemed little regret, and the inability to speak Welsh was not, in William Jones's phrase, regarded as a "negation of Welsh identity."[26]

Judge Henry M. Edwards articulated the perspective of the elite Welsh American community leaders on preserving the language. Born in Ebbw Vale, Monmouthshire, he emigrated in 1864 at the age of twenty, and settled in Hyde Park, Pennsylvania, where he lived until his death in 1925. There he became a lawyer and Lackawanna County judge who was elected to that post continuously from 1893 through 1923. Even though he rose in society, he abandoned neither the language nor his ethnic identity. He managed the Welsh language newspaper *Baner America*, served as president of the local Cymmrodorion Society, and was a trustee of the Welsh Philosophical Society and the Welsh Congregational Church. Edwards also was one of the most accomplished Welsh American poets and orators (in Welsh and English), a member of the Gorsedd in Wales, Deputy Archdruid of the American Gorsedd of Bards in 1913, and an active supporter and adjudicator at eisteddfodau.[27] Consideration was certainly given to a man of his status and commitment to Welsh culture when he spoke about the issue of language preservation.

As early as 1871, Judge Edwards took first prize in the essay competition at the Youngstown Eisteddfod in which he chastised Welsh Americans for their cultural shortcomings. He complained that Welsh Americans were ashamed to speak in their mother tongue. "The Welsh spend most of their time convincing their neighbors that there is no virtue in being a Welshman, and they would be overjoyed if they and their children were something else," he lamented.[28] However, in a reminiscence published in the *Druid* in 1909, the judge obviously had changed his mind. He noted the dramatic changes in his own Hyde Park, perhaps the most prominent of the Welsh American communities, and one where coal miners made up a major segment of the population. "In the last fifteen or twenty years," he observed, use of the Welsh language had declined and "it is safe to say that fifteen years hence there will be very little Welsh spoken. The Welsh churches will be altogether English, instead of half English, as they are now." Did the noted Welshman regard this as a problem? Not at all, for this was as it should be, and yet "the glory of a language and a people that have existed for so many centuries will continue to live in poetry and song for centuries to come, although sung in another tongue."[29]

H. M. Edwards's views on the significance of the Welsh language in the United States had changed between 1871 and 1909, no doubt reflecting his own assimilation. By 1909, Judge Edwards had come to believe that a Welsh identity could be maintained in English, and that Welsh and American cultures were complementary rather than mutually exclusive identities. In a speech at Welsh Day in Pittston, Pennsylvania, in 1909, H. M. Edwards confirmed this opinion by declaring, "No race ever comes to America that gets into the American spirit more quickly than a Welshman. . . . There is no essential element or principle loved by the American people [which has not been] part of the blood and principle of the Welsh people for the past 1000 years. . . . I was an American citizen 1000 years before I was born."[30]

The notion that Welshmen possessed a cultural affinity with America was, as discussed elsewhere, a recurring theme throughout a century of Welsh migration to the United States. Characteristics that leaders defined as essentially Welsh, including loyalty, love of truth, liberty, and an innate proclivity for democracy, were the very foundation of the American republic. Here the two identities constructed by intellectual leaders like Edwards merged; the essential ingredients of "Americanness" were possessed in spades by Welshmen at birth, whether they communicated in Welsh or English. In this construction of Welsh/American identity, language was not the central, defining feature. Preservation was desirable but not essential to the Welsh American identity.[31] In this view, Judge Edwards was only one of the most recognizable Welsh American spokesmen. Anthony Howells, a prominent mine owner, businessman, Ohio politician, U.S. consul to Cardiff, and ardent supporter of Welsh American cultural organizations, articulated the same idea. At the St. David's Day banquet in Youngstown, Ohio, in 1893, Howells declared that he disagreed with those who believed that Welsh American institutions should conduct their affairs only in the Welsh language "because that would lose us the presence of our sons and daughters . . . and as true American citizens we want men of all nationalities to meet with us, and forget themselves for the time being and think of themselves as Welshmen."[32]

Welsh American identity could became extremely ambiguous as constructed by the upwardly mobile elite who found it advantageous to shift the definition of Welshness away from restrictive criteria, such as language, to general concepts that reconciled their Welsh identity and their success as Americans. Elites like Edwards and Howells were not men who merely reflected on the meaning of Welsh American identity; rather, they were national leaders in the Welsh cultural institutions who played a pivotal role in Americanizing those institutions. Those who expressed their opinions in the Welsh American publications and were leaders in Welsh cultural organizations and communities, however, were but a small if articulate segment of Welsh America. They loom large in historical accounts because they left a record, and they were influential in setting an agenda. Maldwyn Jones has cautioned historians that focusing on institutions and their leaders may give "undue prominence to a particular type of newcomer," namely those immigrants most concerned with preserving "traditional ways and who, for that reason, have tended to leave more tangible evidence of their lives and attitudes than did those whose aim was rather to become Americanized with all possible speed."[33]

The frequent complaints from "respectable" Welshmen about drunkenness, course and violent behavior, questionable entertainments such as prizefighting and cockfighting, and breaking the Sabbath suggest that there was a substantial number of Welsh Americans who either did not think about their culture at all or were assimilated through participation in American popular culture rather than thoughtful discourse in ethnic publications. For the vast majority, the Welsh language was simply a matter of functionality that was of little value in the struggle to get ahead in America. Except for the occasional pang of nostalgia, the language fell into disuse and eventually was forgotten. In 1920, a correspondent to the *Druid* opined that the Americanization of the Welsh came so swiftly because "the general tendency of the Welsh people has been to join and affiliate with other social and fraternal organizations, thus losing their national distinction," and abandoned their own cohesive national institutions. More analytical than lamentacious in tone, he observed that the Welsh lacked the interest or will essential to maintain national ethnic organizations, "but mix us up in other societies and our caliber comes rapidly to the surface." In addition to suggesting that the Welsh were a leavening minority, the author was stating what seemed obvious to him, that the Welsh contribution to America was to become American.[34] If this observation is correct, it is contribution enough.

In her fine study of the Welsh in Gallia and Jackson Counties, Ohio, Anne Knowles argues that the "worship of respectability" that characterized the first- and second-generation Welsh was rooted in the Calvinistic religion of the chapel and in American Puritanism. In this religious tradition, the strict moral code, emphasis on hard work, deferred gratification, and spiritual asceticism predisposed the Welsh for success in the capitalist system of the United States. But success and prosperity altered the meaning of these markers over time. Like Huw Morgan, the main character in Richard Llewellyn's *How Green Was My Valley*, many Welsh Americans longed for the South Wales valleys of memory. Their memory, like Huw's, was mysteriously triggered by an association, but what linked the two had been forgotten. The same was true with their construction of culture. Welsh Americans reconstructed a Wales of symbolic remembrance conveniently devoid of change. Better they had constructed a memory of Wales portrayed by Matthew Price, another novelistic native cast out of his own land in Raymond Williams's *Border Country*, who encountered that eternal bit of wisdom, "You can't go home again." Why not? Identities are constantly being constructed and reconstructed, and there can be no going back to the remembrance, for the place and the people all will have changed with the passage of time. Like Matthew Price, Welsh immigrants undoubtedly longed for what seemed like a simpler and emotionally vital time and place at "home" in Wales. Unfortunately, both existed only in memory.[35]

The Welsh scholar Hazel Davies has astutely observed that nineteenth-century America was a nation of the uprooted with few restraining traditions. The American ethic was, therefore, to push forward; the "American Dream" was neither about preserving nor opposing ethnic identities but rather about "endlessly becoming." There was little or no value in looking back. Most American immigrants navigated these turbulent cultural waters, and descendants measure their history by the ease with which their forbears were able to lay claim to their part of the dream. Like most immigrants, the Welsh looked ahead toward success in America, and only later took stock of what they had left behind in Wales.[36]

# NOTES

### INTRODUCTION

1 R. Merfyn Jones, "Beyond Identity?," 331–32.

2 Ibid., 345; Church, *History of the British Coal Industry*, 304–5.

3 R. Merfyn Jones, "Beyond Identity?," 331.

4 Ibid., 346; Borrow, *Wild Wales: Its People, Language, and Scenery*, documents an 1854 tour by Borrow primarily through North Wales (only 9 of the 109 chapters describe industrial South Wales).

5 Wittke, *We Who Built America*.

6 Hansen, *Atlantic Migration*; Easterlin, *Population, Labor Force*; Vecoli, "Contadini in Chicago"; Smith, "Religion and Ethnicity in America."

7 Bodnar, *The Transplanted*; John Higham, "Current Trends in the Study of Ethnicity."

8 Bukowczyk, "*The Transplanted*: Immigrants and Ethnics," 238–39.

9 *La Pietra Report*; Bender, *Rethinking American History*.

10 Kenny, "Diaspora and Comparison," 134–35, 137.

11 Bryce, *American Commonwealth*, 2:360–61; Murdoch, *British Emigration*, 113.

12 Carnegie, *Triumphant Democracy*, 82–83; Murdoch, *British Emigration*, 114.

13 Erickson, *Invisible Immigrants*; Murdoch, *British Emigration*, 115–17, 125.

14 Hoerder, *Cultures in Contact*, 344–45; Fones-Wolf, "Transatlantic Craft Migrations," 299.

15 William D. Jones, "Wales in America," xvii–iii.

16 *Pottsville Miners' Journal*, June 16, 1827, July 11, 1829; Berthoff, *British Immigrants in Industrial America*, 48–49.

17 William D. Jones, "Wales in America," 25.

18 Hartmann, *Americans from Wales*, 79–81; William D. Jones, "Wales in America," 20, citing *Tarian y Gweithwr*, August 22, 1879.

19 William D. Jones, "Wales in America," 21, citing the *Llanelly and County Guardian*, June 5, 1890.

20 Hartmann, *Americans from Wales*, 80–81, 85–86.

21 Berthoff, *British Immigrants in Industrial America*, 48–51; Hartmann, *Americans from Wales*, 76–85.

22 William D. Jones, "Wales in America," 19–20; Hartmann, *Americans from Wales*, 79; Ashton, *Welsh in the United States*, 90–91.

23 Hartmann, *Americans from Wales*, 90–95; Vugt, *British Buckeyes*, 143–58; William D. Jones, "Wales in America," 19–23.

**CHAPTER 1**

1 Conway, "Welsh Emigration to the United States," 183–84.

2 Ibid., 185–88; William D. Jones, "Wales in America," 2; David Williams, *Cymru ac America*, 23; Dodd, *Character of Early Welsh Emigration*, 6–11, 31. For the Pennsylvania settlement, see also Rees, *Quakers in Wales and Their Emigration to North America*; Browning, *Welsh Settlement of Pennsylvania*; and Glenn, *Welsh Founders of Pennsylvania*.

3 Geraint Jenkins, *Foundation of Modern Wales*, 312, 317–18; William D. Jones, "Wales in America," 2–3; Gwyn A. Williams, *When Was Wales?*, 167–69.

4 G.B. Parliament, Parliamentary Papers, *Reports from the Commissioners on the State of Education in Wales*, Part III, 3; Conway, "Welsh Emigration," 193.

5 Conway, "Welsh Emigration," 194 (quotation). See also David Williams, *Rebecca Riots*, particularly chapters 3 and 4 on economic and social conditions in the countryside.

6 Conway, "Welsh Emigration," 194–95. For similar circumstances in pre-famine Ireland, see Miller, *Emigrants and Exiles*, 26–101.

7 Conway, "Welsh Emigration," 199–204; David Williams, *Rebecca Riots*, 251–52, 286–89.

8 Parliamentary Papers, *Reports from the Commissioners on the State of Education in Wales* (1847). The *Reports* were issued in blue bindings. The title was based on *Brad y Cyllyll Hirion* (Treachery of the Long Knives), an incident in the wars between the Welsh and Saxons. For a scholarly study see Gwyneth Tyson Roberts, *Language of the Blue Books*, particularly 140–67 on female sexual morality.

9 Morgan, *Wales in British Politics*.

10 Gwyn Williams, *Search for Beulah Land*; *The American, Which Contains Notes on a Journey from the Ohio Valley to Wales*, 1–41.

11 Stephen Williams, *The Saga of Paddy's Run*, 18–28, 167–85; Hartmann, *Americans from Wales*, 67, 208; Knowles, *Calvinists Incorporated*, 18–22; Shepperson, *Samuel Roberts*; Conway, "Welsh Emigration," 216–17. For Michael D. Jones and the Patagonian settlement see Glyn Williams, *Desert and the Dream* and *Welsh in Patagonia*.

12 William D. Jones, "Wales in America," 5; Hartmann, *Wales in America*, 68–70; Conway, "Welsh Emigration," 226; Glanmor Williams, *Religion, Language, and Nationality in Wales*, 225–26.

13 Douglas Davies, *Mormon Spirituality*, 7–9; Shepperson, *Samuel Roberts*, 17–18.

14 Douglas Davies, *Mormon Spirituality*, 48; Conway, "Welsh Emigration," 240; Hartmann, *Wales in America*, 73–75.

15 Dodd, *Industrial Revolution in North Wales*; A. H. John, *Industrial Development of*

South Wales; Brinley Thomas, "Migration of Labour into the Glamorgan Coal-field," 275–94.

16  Morris, "Coal and Steel," 177–84; Dai Smith, Wales! Wales?, 16, 18 (quotation).

17  Peter Williams, David Thomas: Iron Man from Wales, 4–5, 16, 22.

18  Morris, "Coal and Steel," 177–84; John, Industrial Development of South Wales, 23–57; Walters, Economic and Business History of the South Wales Steam Coal Industry, chapters 1–3; Phillips, History of the Pioneers of the Welsh Coalfield. Two essays provide evocative portrayals of the social changes that accompanied the industrial transition in South Wales: Neil Evans, " 'As Rich as California . . . ,' " 111–44, and Bill Jones, "Banqueting at a Moveable Feast," 145–78.

19  Conway, "Welsh Emigration," 229–31; Williams, When Was Wales?, 178; Wal-ters, "Capital Formation in the South Wales Coal Industry," 69–92.

20  Dai Smith, Wales! Wales?, 20.

21  Ibid., 14–15, 21; Holmes, "South Wales Coal Industry," 162–207, esp. 163; Gwyn Williams, When Was Wales?, 222; Brinley Thomas, "Growth of Industrial Towns," 186; D. Gareth Evans, History of Wales, 186–89.

22  Morris and Williams, South Wales Coal Industry, 209–10; Parliamentary Pa-pers, Report of the Commissioner Appointed to Inquire into the State of the Popula-tion in the Mining Districts (1849), Part II, xxiv, 31–32; Parliamentary Papers, Reports from the Commissioners on the State of Education in Wales (1847), Part II, xxvii (quotation from 293).

23  Parliamentary Papers, Report of the Commissioner Appointed to Inquire into the State of the Population in the Mining Districts (1847), 3–4; Morris and Williams, South Wales Coal Industry, 211–14.

24  Morris and Williams, South Wales Coal Industry, 215–16; Parliamentary Papers, Report of the Commissioner Appointed to Inquire into the State of the Population in the Mining Districts (1847), 34, (1850) 59–64, and (1851) 20.

25  Conway, "Welsh Emigration," 235; Morris and Williams, South Wales Coal In-dustry, 239–42. Because coalfields last only as long as the coal, some scholars have questioned whether Wales was in fact industrialized. See John Williams, Was Wales Industrialized?, 14–36.

26  E. W. Evans, Miners of South Wales, 10; Morris and Williams, South Wales Coal Industry, 242–44.

27  E. W. Evans, Miners of South Wales, 9–14; John, Industrial Development of South Wales, 87; Morris and Williams, South Wales Coal Industry, 224–26.

28  Parliamentary Papers, Report of the Commissioners Appointed to Inquire into the Truck System (1871), XXXVI, Part I, v–xiv, xxi–xlvii, Part II, xlix–lxx, 31–60, 496–509; Parliamentary Papers, Report of the Commissioner Appointed to Inquire into the State of the Population in the Mining Districts (1846), Part I, 30–51; Morris and Williams, South Wales Coal Industry, 226–29; John, Industrial Development of South Wales, 79.

29  John Williams, *Was Wales Industrialized?*, 150–91; Conway, "Welsh Emigration," 238.

30  D. Gareth Evans, *History of Wales*, 188.

31  Philip Jenkins, *History of Modern Wales*, 211–15; Gwyn Williams, "Emergence of a Working-Class Movement," 142–43; Gwyn Williams, *When Was Wales?*, 192.

32  Gwyn Williams, "Emergence of Working-Class," 143–44. For a full account see Gwyn Williams, *Merthyr Rising.*

33  David Williams, *John Frost*; Wilks, *South Wales and the Rising of 1839*; David J. V. Jones, *Last Rising*; Humphries, *Man from the Alamo.*

34  E. W. Evans, *Miners of South Wales*, 213–15.

35  Ibid., 216–21.

36  Morris and Williams, *South Wales Coal Industry*, 269–73, 282–84.

37  D. Gareth Evans, *History of Wales*, 76–77, 219.

38  Ibid., 79–80.

39  Ibid., 86–88, 94 (quotation), 133–36, 139–44. For the Scotch Cattle see David J. V. Jones, *Before Rebecca*, especially chapter 4. For the Merthyr Uprising see Gwyn Williams, *Merthyr Rising*. For the rural rebellions see David Williams, *Rebecca Riots*. Standard works on the Chartist movement in South Wales are Wilks, *South Wales and the Rising of 1839*, and David J. V. Jones, *Last Rising.*

40  E. T. Davies, *Religion in the Industrial Revolution in South Wales*, 76–82; D. Gareth Evans, *History of Wales*, 144–45, 166–67.

41  D. Gareth Evans, *History of Wales*, 220; Weber, *Protestant Ethic and the Spirit of Capitalism*; Berthoff, "Peasants and Artisans," 581; Gwyneth Roberts, *Language of the Blue Books.*

42  D. Gareth Evans, *History of Wales*, 228–29.

43  Gwyther, "Sidelights on Religion and Politics in the Rhondda Valley," 32–35.

44  D. Gareth Evans, *History of Wales*, 240–43; E. T. Davies, *Religion in the Industrial Revolution*, 82–89.

45  E. T. Davies, *Religion in the Industrial Revolution*, 91, quoted in Gwyther, "Sidelights on Religion," 22.

46  Quoted in Gwyther, "Sidelights on Religion," 34.

47  *National Labor Tribune*, May 28, 1914.

48  *Druid*, December 19, 1912; *Cambrian* 29 (September 1, 1909), 11 (quotations); Hartmann, *Americans from Wales*, 135.

49  *Cambrian* 32 (August 1, 1912): 6–7.

50  For a history of the Fed see Francis and Smith, *The Fed.*

51  March 9, 1859, quoted in Conway, "Welsh Emigration," 246.

52  *Baner Cymru*, August 10, 1859, quoted in Conway, "Welsh Emigration," 246.

53  Conway, "Welshmen in the Union Armies," 143–74; Griffiths, "Welsh and the American Civil War," 231–74.

54  *Merthyr Telegraph*, August 29, 1863, cited in Conway, "Welsh Emigration," 250.

55  Bill Jones, " 'Raising the Wind,' " 5; Baines, *Emigration from Europe*, 9.

56 Hywel Davies, "'Very Different Springs of Uneasiness,'" 368–98; Knowles, *Calvinists Incorporated*, 43–130.

57 Bill Jones, "'Raising the Wind,'" 8, citing Walter Davies, *The Right Place, The Right Time*, 46–47.

58 *Baner ac Amserau Cymru*, May 19, 1869, and *Seren Cymru*, August 7, 1863, cited by Bill Jones, "'Raising the Wind,'" 24.

59 *Cardiff and Merthyr Guardian*, March 27, 1869; *Aberdare Times*, June 7, 1862; *Merthyr Telegraph*, July 17, 1869; *Seren Cymru*, April 17, August 7, 1863, cited in Bill Jones, "'Raising the Wind,'" 23–24.

60 *Tarian y Gweithwr*, August 18, 1881, cited in Bill Jones, "'Raising the Wind,'" 9.

61 Bill Jones, "Inspecting the 'Extraordinary Drain,'" 109.

62 *Merthyr* (Wales) *Telegraph*, April 24, 1869, quoted in ibid.

63 May 16, 1868, quoted in Bill Jones, "'We Will Give You Wings to Fly,'" 27.

64 January 19, 1861, quoted in Bill Jones, "Inspecting the 'Extraordinary Drain,'" 112.

65 Ibid., 110–11. The press complained of this throughout the first half of the nineteenth century. See Chris Evans, "*The Labyrinth of Flames*," 145–77.

66 Bill Jones, "Inspecting the 'Extraordinary Drain,'" 112; *Merthyr Express*, March 31, 1866; *Merthyr* (Wales) *Telegraph*, March 2, 1861, May 2, 1863, April 30, 1869; *Merthyr Star*, August 15, 1863, February 4, 1864.

67 Gottlieb, "Immigration of British Coal Miners," 362; Maldwyn Jones, "Background to Emigration," 50–51; Erickson, "Encouragement of Emigration by British Trade Unions," 248–73.

68 *Miner and Workman's Advocate*, February 4, 1865; Gottlieb, "Immigration of British Coal Miners," 366.

69 *Miner and Workman's Advocate*, July 11, 1865; Gottlieb, "Immigration of British Coal Miners," 366.

70 *Merthyr Star*, March 17, 1868, in Bill Jones, "'We Will Give You Wings to Fly,'" 29.

71 Bill Jones, "'We Will Give You Wings to Fly,'" 30–34.

72 Ibid., 36–41.

73 *Times* (London), November 25, 1969, 7; Gottlieb, "Immigration of British Miners," 369.

74 *Tarian y Gweithwr*, December 19, 1879, cited in Bill Jones, "'Raising the Wind,'" 18–19.

75 Bill Jones, "'Raising the Wind,'" 17; Johnston, "Welsh Diaspora," 68; Glanmor Williams, *Religion, Language, and Nationality in Wales*, 224.

76 Maldwyn Jones, "Background to Emigration from Great Britain," 54–55; Vugt, *Britain to America*, 13; Johnston, "Welsh Diaspora," 56–57.

77 Vugt, *Britain to America*, 13; Baines, *Emigration from Europe*, 41.

78 Vugt, *Britain to America*, 14–16; *Merthyr Express*, May 23, 1868; Bill Jones, "Raising the Wind," 1.

79 *Baner ac Amserau Cymru*, October 20, 1869, cited in Bill Jones, " 'Raising the Wind,' " 20.

80 Vugt, *British to America*, 122.

81 *Carmarthen Journal*, September 19, 1879, quoted in Bill Jones, "Raising the Wind," 20.

82 *Baner ac Amserau Cymru*, October 1, 1879, in ibid., 46.

83 *Tarian y Gweithwr*, November 12, 1880, cited in ibid., 20.

84 O'Neal, *Those Damned Foreigners*, 27–33.

85 *Merthyr Telegraph*, April 29, 1865; *Cardiff and Merthyr Guardian*, June 6, 1868; Bill Jones, " 'Raising the Wind,' " 22.

86 *Cardiff and Merthyr Guardian*, March 20, 1869; *Baner ac Amserau Cymru*, March 31, 1869, cited in Bill Jones, " 'Raising the Wind,' " 28–29.

87 William Jones, "Wales in America," 6; Berthoff, *British Immigrants in Industrial America*, 5–10; Gwyn Williams, *When Was Wales?*, 179.

88 Brinley Thomas, "Wales and the Atlantic Economy," 1–29. See also, by the same author, *Migration and Economic Growth*, particularly chapters 7 and 14, and *Industrial Revolution and the Atlantic Economy*.

89 Brinley Thomas, "Wales and the Atlantic Economy," 1–29. Thomas argues that the Welsh language was saved by the redistribution resulting from industrialization because the absorptive power of the coal valleys allowed Wales to retain its native Welsh speakers. William Jones, "Wales in America," 9; Knowles, *Calvinists Incorporated*, 6–10; Baines, *Migration in a Mature Economy*, 220–49, 266–82; Conway, "Welsh Emigration," 265.

90 Berthoff, *British Immigrants in Industrial America*, 23, 28–29, citing *Eleventh Census of the United States* (1890), II, 484–89; "Reports of the Immigration Commission," Senate Document, 61 Cong., 2nd sess., no. 633 (June 15, 1910), VI, 44, 50; VIII, 41, 48; X, 73, 83, 665; XI, 34, 37; XVI, 24, 27–28, 227, 230; XIX, 95, 104, 111.

91 Berthoff, *British Immigrants in Industrial America*, 28–29.

92 Harvey, *Best-Dressed Miners*, 20; R. D. Thomas, *Hanes Cymry America*, 336–37; Glanmor Williams, *Religion, Language, and Nationality in Wales*, 225–26.

93 Gwyn Williams, *When Was Wales?*, 180.

**CHAPTER 2**

1 Daniel Williams, *One Hundred Years of Welsh Calvinistic Methodism*, 113–14.

2 Ibid., 102–4.

3 Ibid., 106–7.

4 Ibid., 111, 113.

5 R. D. Thomas, *Hanes Cymry America*, 26–28; Daniel J. Williams, *One Hundred Years of Calvinistic Methodism*, 116–17, 121; R. D. Thomas, *Hanes Cymry America*, 32.

6 R. D. Thomas, *Hanes Cymry America*, 30.

7 Wallace, *St. Clair*, 103.

8 R. D. Thomas, *Hanes Cymry America*, 21–22 (emphasis in original).

9 Wallace, *St. Clair*, 85.

10 Samuel Thomas, "Reminiscences," 901–7; Peter Williams, *David Thomas*, 1–10; Wallace, *St. Clair*, 88.

11 Samuel Thomas, "Reminiscences," 908–28; Peter Williams, *David Thomas*, 11–18; Wallace, *St. Clair*, 88–89. See also Adams, *Old Dominion, Industrial Commonwealth*; Chandler, "Anthracite Coal," 141–81; Yates, "Discovery of the Process for Making Anthracite Iron," 206–23; Stapleton, *Transfer of Early Industrial Technology to America*, 169–207.

12 Wallace, *St. Clair*, 89–90.

13 Sheppard, *Cloud by Day*, 29–31; Eavenson, *The First Century and a Quarter*, 225–27.

14 Sheppard, *Cloud by Day*, 32–36, 43; Eavenson, *First Century and a Quarter*, 178; Long, *Where the Sun Never Shines*, 116–25. For a description of the coke region, see MacFarlane, *Coal-Regions of America*, 216–25. For a brief description of the Bessemer process and its revolutionary results, see Krause, *Battle for Homestead*, 52–56.

15 U.S. Department of Interior, *Ninth Census of the United States, 1870: Population*, Vol. I, Table VIII, 388–89; *Tenth Census of the United States, 1880: Population*, Vol. I, Table XIV, 525–26; *Compendium of the Tenth Census, 1880*, Part I, Table XXXI, 527–28; *Twelfth Census of the United States, 1900, Population*, Part I, Table XXXIV, 780. The eight major bituminous coal-producing counties of western Pennsylvania referred to in the text are Allegheny, Cambria, Clearfield, Fayette, Mercer, Tioga, Washington, and Westmoreland.

16 R. D. Thomas, *Hanes Cymry America*, 22–25, 55, quotation from 24. For a description of the several mines in Tioga County, see MacFarlane, *Coal-Regions of America*, 124–50.

17 Daddow and Bannan, *Coal, Iron, and Oil*, 414–15, 450–53; Wallace, *St. Clair*, 8–9; Dix, *What's a Coal Miner to Do?*, 1–2; Schwieder, *Black Diamonds*, 27–28.

18 Daddow and Bannan, *Coal, Iron, and Oil*, 415–28; Dix, *What's a Coal Miner to Do?*, 2–3; Schwieder, *Black Diamonds*, 29.

19 Daddow and Bannan, *Coal, Iron, and Oil*, 418–19; Wallace, *St. Clair*, 10–14.

20 Dix, *What's a Coal Miner to Do?*, 5–6; Goodrich, *The Miner's Freedom*, 37.

21 Aley, *Heritage to Share*, 45.

22 Ohio Inspector of Mines, *Sixth Annual Report*, 59–60.

23 U.S. Department of Interior, *Tenth Census of the United States, 1880: Population*, Table III, 292, 296, Table XIII, 494, and Table XIV, 523–24; Ulam and Ulam, *1880 Census Index of Trumbull County, Ohio*; Ohio Inspector of Mines, *Sixth Annual Report for the Year 1880*, 24.

24 Ohio Inspector of Mines, *Second Annual Report for the Year 1875*, 71–75. The names of managers were taken from the inspector's report, and their ethnicity

confirmed when possible from a variety of sources, such as the censuses, newspapers, or local histories and directories.

25  *Druid*, June 26, 1913; *Cambrian* 17 (July 1897): 337–38.

26  *Stark County Bicentennial Story*, 70; U.S. Department of Interior, Statistics of the Population, Tenth Census, 1880; Lane, *Fifty Years and Over*, 1049–50.

27  Kenfield, *Akron and Summit County, Ohio*, 1:150; Grismer, *Akron and Summit County*, 575.

28  Lane, *Fifty Years and Over*, 986.

29  *Manuscript Census Schedules, 1880*, Ohio, Summit County, Springfield and Coventry Township, Thomastown Village. Manually tabulated.

30  *Meigs County, Ohio, from Hardesty's Historical and Geographical Encyclopedia, 1883*, 279.

31  *Cambrian* 2 (November–December 1882): 279–81. Ebenezer Williams (1816–1886) was opening another mine at Energetic, Putnam County, West Virginia, during the summer and overworked himself. *Cambrian* 6 (September 1886): 253.

32  This story is brilliantly told by Anne Knowles in *Calvinists Incorporated*.

33  Tribe, "Empire of Industry," 60–165; *Cambrian* 5 (January 1885): 36.

34  *Manuscript Census Schedules, 1880*, Ohio, Perry County, Village of Shawnee. Manually tabulated.

35  Gibson, *History of Shawnee*, 1–47.

36  Vugt, *British Buckeyes*, 174. He cites W. G. Wolfe, *History of Guernsey County*, Vol. 2 (St. Peter Port, Guernsey: privately published, 1943), 688–89.

37  *Druid*, April 18, 25, May 16, 30, 1912. Rev. Thomas himself had lived in the Mahoning Valley and remembered some of them.

38  Powell, *Next Time We Strike*, 14–16.

39  Ibid., 19–21, 229; Milan, "Winter Quarters Explosion," 15.

40  Milan, "Winter Quarters Explosion," 19; Taniguchi, *Necessary Fraud: Progressive Reform and Utah Coal*, 59.

41  Olson, *Black Diamond*, 13–14.

42  Sullivan, "Coal Men and Coal Towns," 1–5. For an overview of the development of the Appalachian coalfields see Eller, *Miners, Millhands, and Mountaineers*.

43  Sullivan, "Coal Men and Coal Towns," 113, 135–36, 280; Sullivan, "Coal Men of the Smokeless Coalfields," 146–47. Note that in the latter reference Sullivan states that forty-four operators were studied, eleven of whom were Pennsylvanians.

44  Sullivan, "Coal Men of the Smokeless Coalfields," 148–49, 152–54, 156.

45  *Men of West Virginia*, 2:743–44; Miller and Maxwell, *West Virginia and Its People*, 2:230.

46  "Kanawah Valley, West Virginia," *Cambrian* 3 (March–April, 1883): 73; Marsh, *1880 Census*, Vol. 4.

47  *Men of West Virginia*, 2:745; *Montgomery News*, September 22, 1916, 1; Miller and

Maxwell, *West Virginia and Its People*, 2:230–31; *History of Fayette County, West Virginia*, 26; Alexander, *West Virginia Tech*; Cox, *Pictorial History of the New River Gorge*, 56–57.

48 *Men of West Virginia*, 2:745; *Montgomery News*, September 22, 1916, 1; Miller and Maxwell, *West Virginia and Its People*, 2:230–31.

49 Vuranch, "Influence of the Welsh Immigrants," 72–73; *Charleston Daily Mail*, July 3, 1940, 4, 7; Athey, "William Nelson Page," 1–2.

50 E. L. Kirk, interview by Fred Barkey, October 28, 1972, quoted in Vuranch, "Influence of Welsh Immigrants," 74.

51 Barkey, "Working Class Political Activity"; Vuranch, "Influence of Welsh Immigrants," 75.

52 Corbin, *Life, Work, and Rebellion*, 28.

53 *West Virginia Department of Mines Reports, 1908, 1910*; Lewis, *Black Coal Miners*, appendix, 191, based on U.S. census.

54 Hager, "Millionaires' Town," 43–54; Becker, *Bramwell*.

55 *Bluefield Daily Telegraph*, November 1, 1896, Industrial Edition; Smith, *Fire Creek*; West Virginia Inspector of Mines, *First Annual Report*, Table 1. The Erskine Company Records, 1815–70, contain voluminous records of the coal mines in which the company invested, including the New River (see bibliography, West Virginia and Regional History Collection, West Virginia University). Tams, *Smokeless Coal Fields*, 37; McGehee, "Jenkinjones Fights Back," 13–15.

56 "Pocahontas Fuel," 416–17 (quotation); "W. G. Freeman," *Men of West Virginia*, 2:745; Becker, *Bramwell*, 84–86.

57 *Druid*, June 6, 1907.

58 *Druid*, March 26, 1908, March 13, 1913 (quotation).

59 *Druid*, May 28, 1908.

60 *Druid*, September 24, 1908.

61 *Druid*, November 19, 1908.

62 *Druid*, May 28, 1908.

63 *National Labor Tribune*, February, 9, 23, March 23, 1889.

64 *Druid*, November 16, 1911, July 18, 1912, and October 30, 1913 to February 5, 1914. For the disaster see Lieven, *Senghennydd: Universal Pit Village*, 215–68.

65 *Bluefield Daily Telegraph*, December 20, 1916, 1; Becker, *Bramwell*, 85; Battlo, "Jones Mansion," 53.

66 *Bluefield Daily Telegraph*, December 7, 8, 10, 1899, July 12, 1918, and November 1, 1896, Industrial Edition; "Mill Creek Mine First in West Virginia in Pocahontas Field," *West Virginia Review*, 144–45; McGehee, "Cooper Family," 16–17; Becker, *Bramwell*, 17–18, 76–78, 92; Hager, "Millionaires' Town," 49–50.

67 Becker, *Bramwell*, 92–93; *Bluefield Daily Telegraph*, January 12, 1918.

68 John A. Williams to Mr. and Mrs. [William] Thomas of Brynawel, Aberdare, November 10, 1895, Ms. 3293E, National Library of Wales, Aberystwyth, Wales. This document is partially reprinted in Conway, *Welsh in America*, 204–10.

69  Walters, *Economic and Business History*, 60, 186–89; Obituary, *Colliery Guardian* 86 (March 13, 1903): 583.

70  Becker, *Bramwell*, 94–95.

71  John A. Williams to Mr. and Mrs. [William] Thomas of Brynawel, Aberdare, November 10, 1895, National Library of Wales. For mine managers, see West Virginia, *Reports of Mine Inspectors for the First, Second and Third Districts*, 15–16.

72  John A. Williams to Mr. and Mrs. [William] Thomas of Brynawel, Aberdare, November 10, 1895, National Library of Wales.

73  *Bluefield Daily Telegraph*, November 1, 1896, Industrial Edition; *Men of West Virginia*, 2:580–82; "Booth-Bowen Mine, Fourth One in Pocahontas-Flat Top Field," 458–59; Becker, *Bramwell*, 81–82.

74  Becker, *Bramwell*, 106.

75  DuBose, *Jefferson County and Birmingham, Alabama*, 561; *Birmingham Age-Herald*, February 5, 1911; U.S. Senate, *Report . . . upon the Relations between Labor and Capital*, 444; 1851 Manuscript Census, Great Britain, Pontypridd, piece 2456, folio 465, schedule 099. Llewellyn apparently changed the family name of John to Johns after he reached America.

76  Fuller, "History of the Tennessee Coal, Iron, and Railroad," 279–82; DuBose, *Jefferson County and Birmingham*, 562–65; Armes, *Story of Coal and Iron in Alabama*, 292.

77  *Druid*, March 19, 1908.

78  *Birmingham Age-Herald*, February 5, 6, 1912, and June 6, 1943 (quotation); *Druid*, October 19, 1911.

79  *Birmingham Age-Herald*, February 6, 1912. The quartet was composed of Arthur Thomas, Idris Thomas, Steven Allsop, and Robert Morgan.

80  *Druid*, January 11, 1912.

81  *Cambrian* 26 (April 1906): 180–81, and 29 (May 1, 1909): 13.

82  DuBose, *Jefferson County and Birmingham*, 561.

83  *Druid*, April 22, 1909, and April 18, 1912.

84  *Druid*, January 1, 1920.

85  Armes, *Story of Coal and Iron*, 330–32.

86  Ibid., 330–36, 425; Fuller, "Tennessee Coal and Iron Railroad," 92–93, 121–67.

87  DuBose, *Jefferson County and Birmingham*, 564; *Birmingham Age*, February 5, 1886.

88  *Birmingham Age*, February 5, 1886; *Birmingham Chronicle*, September 27, 1886.

89  U.S. Commission on Immigration, *Reports on Immigrants in Industries*, 2:218; *Report on Relations between Labor and Capital* (1885), 4:434 (quotation).

90  For other British coal and iron managers in Birmingham district, see Armes, *Story of Coal and Iron*, 68–69, 355–57, 450–51; *Report on Relations between Labor and Capital*, 4:443; Council, Honerkamp, and Will, *Industrial Technology*, 74–75.

91  Armes, *Story of Coal and Iron*, 174–75; Council, Honerkamp, and Will, *Industrial Technology*, 69, 74.

92 Council, Honerkamp, and Will, *Industrial Technology*, 88; *Report on Relations between Capital and Labor*, 4:383.

93 Armes, *Story of Coal and Iron*, 356.

94 Ibid., 230–31 (quotations); Council, Honerkamp, and Will, *Industrial Technology*, 88.

95 *Report on Relations between Labor and Capital*, 4:384–85 (Edwards testimony), 445–46 (Johns testimony). For labor costs at Johns's Pratt Mines, and the racial wage scale in Alabama coal, see Lewis, *Black Coal Miners*, 32–33, 47–48.

96 *Report on Relations between Capital and Labor*, 4:386–87.

97 U.S. Census of Population, 1900.

98 *Report on Relations between Labor and Capital*, 4:446.

**CHAPTER 3**

1 Glanmor Williams, *Religion, Language, and Nationality in Wales*, 235.

2 Quoted in ibid., 221–22.

3 Conway, *Welsh in America*, 178–79. See also Glanmor Williams, *Religion, Language, and Nationality in Wales*, 222.

4 Glanmor Williams, *Religion, Language, and Nationality in Wales*, 233 (quotation), 234–35.

5 Ibid., 226–27; Dai Smith, *Wales! Wales?*, 42; Maldwyn Jones, "From the Old Country to the New," 89–90.

6 Berthoff, *British Immigrants*, 125 (quotation), 134; *Pottsville Miners Journal*, May 26, June 30, August 18, 1855.

7 Berthoff, *British Immigrants*, 140; Wyman, *Round-Trip to America*, 11.

8 See Harrison, *Independent Collier*, and Dick Geary, "Myth of the Radical Miner," 43–64.

9 R. D. Thomas, *Hanes Cymry America*, 332.

10 The difficulties of conducting a scientific sample across the censuses would far outstrip the value of the results. The Welsh Coal Miners in Ohio database (hereafter cited as Ohio database) was constructed from the U.S. Census, Manuscript Schedules (Schedule 1) of Population, microfilm edition, for Meigs County, which includes the towns of Syracuse, Minersville, and Pomeroy (1860, 1870, 1880); Perry County: Shawnee Village (1880); Stark County: Lawrence Township (1880); Mahoning County: Youngstown Township and Austintown Township (1860, 1870, 1880); Trumbull County: Weathersfield Township and Brookfield Township, which includes the towns of Niles, Girard, and Mineral Ridge (1860, 1870, 1880); Hubbard Township: which includes the town of Hubbard (1880); and Liberty Township, which includes the town of Church Hill (1860, 1870, 1880). A total of 9,209 individuals are in the database, including first- and second-generation Welsh coal miners and their families. Also included are Welsh women married to miners who may not be Welsh, a fact that is not always discernible from the census. Boarders were included in the house-

hold if present. Their numbers were relatively few (a total of 198), and their nativity was not always noted, but two-thirds of them were single males, the great majority of whom were probably kith or kin.

11  Ohio database.

12  Census database.

13  Ohio database.

14  Ohio database. See also *Census of Population*, 1900, Part I, Table LXXXVIII, pp. cxc, cxci, cxcii. Note that seventy-one "colored persons" were listed as having Welsh parentage, twenty had two parents who were born there, and fifty-one had one Welsh-born parent and one native American parent.

15  Berthoff, "Peasants and Artisans," 579.

16  Foner, *Free Soil*, 11–13; Weber, *Protestant Ethic*.

17  Foner, *Free Soil*, 12–13, 15.

18  Ibid., 17–20, 26. For an analysis of the extensive literature on "republicanism," see Rodgers, "Republicanism," 11–38.

19  Foner, *Free Soil*, 22–23, 32; Montgomery, *Beyond Equality*, 26–27.

20  Foner, *Free Soil*, 33, 38–39; Cawelti, *Apostles of the Self-Made Man*, especially chapter 5.

21  The literature on the modern industrial economy is extensive. See, for example, these standards: Cochran and Miller, *Age of Enterprise*; Kirkland, *Industry Comes of Age*; Chandler, *Visible Hand*; and Bensel, *Political Economy of American Industrialization*.

22  Gutman, *Work, Culture and Society*, 50–51.

23  *National Labor Tribune*, October 2, 1880.

24  *United Mine Workers Journal*, June 28, 1894; Gutman, *Work, Culture and Society*, 112.

25  Gwyther, "Sidelights on Religion," 35–39.

26  Rev. W. R. Evans, "Trusts and Trade Union," 133–36, quotations from 134–35. There are numerous examples of Welsh coal miners who became ministers and articulated an ideology linking republicanism and evangelical religion in support of upward mobility as a reward for a virtuous life. See, for example, *Cambrian* 24 (April 1904): 177–79.

27  *National Labor Tribune*, December 12, 1874; Gutman, *Work, Culture and Society*, 51–52.

28  A number of these studies appeared in an influential collection of essays edited by Miller, *Men in Business*. Other scholars generally supported this thesis. See Mills, "The American Business Elite," in *Power, Politics and People*, ed. Irving Horowitz, 110–39; Bendix and Howton, "Social Mobility and the American Business Elite," in *Social Mobility in Industrial Society*, ed. Bendix and Lipset, 114–43; Miller, *Men in Business: Essays in the History of Entrepreneurship*.

29  Thernstrom, *Poverty and Progress*; Tine, *Making of a Labor Bureaucrat*.

30  Gutman, *Work, Culture and Society*, 221, 225, 233.

31  Edward Davies, *Anthracite Aristocracy*; Ginger, "Managerial Employees in An-
    thracite," 147–48, 156.

32  Ginger, "Managerial Employees in Anthracite," 156–57.

33  Bodnar, "Socialization and Adaptation," 147–62.

34  Ibid., 149–50.

35  Ibid., 151–54.

36  Ibid., 155–57.

37  Ibid., 157–60.

38  Ibid., 162.

39  Gottlieb, "Immigration of British Coal Miners," 374–75; Harvey, *Best-Dressed
    Miners*, 85–86.

40  Knowles, *Calvinists Incorporated*.

41  Bradsby, *History of Luzerne County*.

42  Ibid.

43  *Cambrian* 14 (August 1894): 225–26.

44  *Druid*, June 6, 1907, April 18, 1912, and January 1, 1924.

45  Montgomery, *Beyond Equality*, 215; Dawley, *Class and Community*, 216.

46  Montgomery, *Beyond Equality*, 211; Bradsby, *History of Luzerne County*, 1466;
    *Cambrian* 8 (June 1888): 162–63.

47  *Cambrian* 15 (January 1895): 1–5, and 20 (May 1900): 232–34.

48  Pugh, *Shaftdiggers*, 12–13. The book does not provide an emigration date.

49  U.S. Anthracite Coal Strike Commission, *Report on the Anthracite Coal Strike
    1902*, 58th Cong., special sess., serial doc. 16, 79; Peter Roberts, *Anthracite Coal
    Communities*, 203, 238 (quotations); U.S. Immigration Commission, *Report on
    Immigrants in Industry*, 61st Cong., 2nd sess., serial doc. 633, 672.

50  Vugt, *British Buckeyes*, 143–46; U.S. Department of Interior, Census Office,
    *Statistics of the Population at the Tenth Census*, Vol. 1, Table 31, 735.

51  Vugt, *British Buckeyes*, 155–56, 174.

52  Summers, *Genealogical and Family History*, 144. See also Butler, *History of
    Youngstown*; Upton, *Twentieth Century History*.

53  Hereafter this collection is referred to as Ohio biographies.

54  Ohio biographies.

55  Thomas Bruce Carpenter, Thomas-Redman-Hughes Families, MS 91–19, West
    Virginia State Archives, Charleston, W.Va.

56  Death Certificate Stark Co., Ohio Bureau of Vital Statistics; Marriage Cert.,
    Pontypool, Monmouthshire; Record of Deaths, Probate Court, Stark County,
    2:73; Obituary, *Canton Daily News*, May 26, 1919.

57  Roy, *History of the Coal Miners*, 130, 158, 348–49, 366; Danner, *Old Landmarks*,
    1445–47.

58  Chris Evans, *History of the United Mine Workers*, 2:4, 9, 34–39; *National Labor
    Tribune*, May 25, 1889.

59  Biographical information gleaned from Danner, *Old Landmarks*, 1445–46; *Can-*

ton Repository, May 31, 1894; *Canton Daily News*, May 26, 1919, 11; Roy, *History of the Coal Miners*, 170–73; Ohio Mine Inspector, *Thirtieth Annual Report, 1904*, 393–95.

60 Ohio database.

61 Ohio database.

62 Laslett, *Colliers across the Sea*, 93–94.

63 Ibid., 24. For an exploration of the concept, see Harrison, *Independent Collier*.

64 John E. Williams, "Christmas Day in Old Dowlais," *Druid*, December 26, 1912; Clark, "John Elias Williams," 12.

65 *Rotary Spokesman*, June 15, 1923, quoted in Clark, "John Elias Williams," 13–15. On the split between John James and Daniel McLaughlin see Laslett, *Colliers across the Sea*, 120–23.

66 Clark, "John Elias Williams," 16–17.

67 Quoted in ibid., 18; Petofsky, *John E. Williams*, 10.

68 Clark, "John Elias Williams," 21–29; Petofsky, *John E. Williams*, 10. For a general discussion of the disaster that incorporates Williams's negotiation of the claims settlement, see Tintori, *Trapped*.

69 John E. Williams, "The English Law as a Basis for settling the Cherry Case," *Streator Daily Independent Times*, January 22, 1910; Clark, "John Elias Williams," 30–31, 33–36.

70 Petofsky, *John E. Williams*, 18–19, 37–38, quoting Williams.

71 Williams's testimony before the U.S. Commission on Industrial Relations, 2:28, 35, cited in Clark, "John Elias Williams," 77–78.

72 Clark, "John Elias Williams," 87.

73 Angela John, *By the Sweat of Their Brow*, 49.

74 Humphries, "Working-Class Family," 1–33, 28 (quotation).

75 For where they worked, see Ashton and Sykes, *Coal Industry of the Eighteenth Century*, and Nef, *Rise of the British Coal Industry*, 166–67.

76 Humphries, "Protective Legislation," 8–11; Angela John, *Sweat of Their Brow*, 21–23.

77 Angela John, *Sweat of Their Brow*, 38.

78 Ibid., 24–25, 39–42; *Parliamentary Papers* (1842) XVI, 243, 254, 201–4, 244, 458, 501; XVII, 11, 647, 513, 552, 577, 580.

79 Humphries, "Protective Legislation," 13–14; *Parliamentary Papers* (1842) XVI, 237, 291, 124, 447, 456, 458.

80 Humphries, "Protective Legislation," 15–16; *Parliamentary Papers* (1848) XVI, 291, 452.

81 Humphries, "Protective Legislation," 21.

82 Ibid., 22–23, 26; *Parliamentary Papers* (1842) XVI, 441–42, 468, 286–87, 248, 263. See also Humphries, " 'Most Free from Objection,' " 929–49.

83 Angela John, *Sweat of Their Brow*, 43–44, quoting *Parliamentary Papers* (1842), XVII, 75.

84 Angela John, *Sweat of Their Brow*, 49–55.

85 Seccombe, "Patriarchy Stabilized," 64.

86 Ibid., 54, 57, quotation from 57.

87 Ibid., 65.

88 Ibid., 65–69; McClelland, "Some Thoughts on Masculinity," 171–73; Humphries, "'Most Free Obligation,'" 931, 947.

89 Milkman, *Women, Work and Protest*, 1; May, "Bread Before Roses"; Kessler-Harris, *Out to Work*, 75–107; Levine, *Labor's True Woman*; Berthoff, *British Immigrants*, 28; Blewett, *Constant Turmoil*; and Blewett, *Men, Women, and Work*.

90 Peter Roberts, *Anthracite Coal Communities*, 14–15. Early marriage and fertility among females in mining populations, particularly Pennsylvania, is examined in Haines, "Fertility, Marriage, and Occupation," 28–55.

91 Bodnar, "Socialization and Adaptation," 161. On the hard lot of a miner's wife, see Peter Roberts, *Anthracite Coal Communities*, 136–40, and MacLean, "Life in the Pennsylvania Coal Fields," 329–51.

92 May, "Bread Before Roses," 6, 8. Samuel Gompers is quoted in Boyle, *Minimum Wage and Syndicalism*.

93 May, "Bread Before Roses," 9 (original emphasis).

94 Greenwald's introduction to Elizabeth Beardsley Butler, *Women and the Trades*, xxii; May, "Bread Before Roses," 9; Milkman, "Organizing the Sexual Division of Labor," 95–144; Gabaccia, *From the Other Side*, 86. For a study devoted to gender relations constructed by craft unions, see DeVault, *United Apart*, particularly 75–104 on the AFL.

95 Casson, "Welsh in America," 749.

96 Gibbons, "Miners of Scranton," 920–21. Others have commented on the neatness of British miners. See, for example, Harvey, *Best-Dressed Miners*.

97 Gibbons, "Miners of Scranton," 923.

98 For contemporary references to home life in anthracite communities, see MacLean, "Life in the Pennsylvania Coal Fields," 329–51, and Peter Roberts, *Anthracite Coal Communities*, 14–16, 136–45.

### CHAPTER 4

1 Dai Smith, *Wales! Wales?*, 29.

2 Ibid., 30–31.

3 Berthoff, *British Immigrants*, 174; Dai Smith, *Wales! Wales?*, 32.

4 Casson, "Welsh in America," 749–54.

5 Berthoff, *British Immigrants*, 127; Parliamentary Papers, *Reports from the Commission on the State of Education in Wales* (1847), XXVII, Part I, 870, 3–10; Part II, 871, 48–55; Part III, 872, 55–59.

6 U.S. Department of Commerce, Bureau of the Census, *Historical Statistics of the United States*, Part 1, 364–65, quotation from 364; Ohio database.

7 Bureau of the Census, *Historical Statistics of the United States*, Part 1, 382.

8 Ohio database.

9 Ibid.

10 William Jones, *Wales in America*, 90, and "Welsh Language and Welsh Identity," 261–63, 266; R. D. Thomas, *Hanes Cymry America*, 38–51.

11 Hartmann, *Americans from Wales*, 176–81; R. D. Thomas, *Hanes Cymry America*, 117–27, 232–33, 254–60; Knowles, *Calvinists Incorporated*, especially 225–58; Daniel Williams, *One Hundred Years of Welsh Calvinistic Methodism*, 126–29, 144–58, 232–36.

12 Hartmann, *Americans from Wales*, 127–30; Aled Jones and Bill Jones, "*Y Drych* and American Welsh Identities," 50, 54; Bill Jones, "Ethnic Journalism."

13 Hartmann, *Americans from Wales*, 130–35.

14 E. C. Evans, "Census Reports of the Welsh Population in the United States," 135.

15 *Druid*, April 24, 1913.

16 E. C. Evans, "Census Reports of the Welsh Population in the United States," 136–37.

17 See, for example, "Hustlers for the *Druid*," *Druid*, February 15, 1912.

18 *Druid*, August 3, 1911.

19 *Druid*, May 15, 1913.

20 *Druid*, July 20, 1911, and April 15, 1909.

21 *Y Drych*, January 9, 1868, and May 26, 1881, cited in Aled Jones and Bill Jones, *Welsh Reflections*, 59.

22 *Druid*, February 15, 1912.

23 The three major Welsh American periodicals were replete with articles on the "Welsh character." See, for example, the following articles in *Cambrian*: Howell Davies, "Individuality of the Welshman" 21 (April 1901): 145–47; Glen.[sic] Edwards, "Welsh Americans" 21 (June 1901): 254–57; Daniel Phillips, "Welsh Life" 24 (December 1904): 530–32; F. M. Davenport, "Spirit of the Welsh Race" 31 (January 15, 1911): 4–5; and E. C. Evans, "Welsh People in America" 31 (March 15, 1911): 4–7.

24 Aled Jones and Bill Jones, "*Y Drych* and American Welsh Identities," 54.

25 *Y Drych*, March 29, 1888, April 28, 1982, March 16, 1893, and October 5, 1893, cited in Aled Jones and Bill Jones, "*Y Drych* and American Welsh Identies," 53.

26 *Y Drych*, August 10, 1893, translation cited in Aled Jones and Bill Jones, "*Y Drych* and American Welsh Identities," 55.

27 Aled Jones and Bill Jones, "*Y Drych* and American Welsh Identities," 55.

28 *Y Drych*, July 4, 1895, cited in Bill Jones, "Ethnic Journalism."

29 Bill Jones, "Ethnic Journalism,"7.

30 Aled Jones and Bill Jones, "*Y Drych* and American Welsh Identities," 57. For journalism and the press in Wales during this period, see Aled Jones, *Press, Politics and Society*.

31 Vecoli, "Italian Immigrant Press," 28.

32  *Y Wasg*, July 5, 1884 (courtesy Bill Jones).

33  Bill Jones, "Ethnic Journalism."

34  Vugt, *Britain to America*, 132–33.

35  Knowles, *Calvinists Incorporated*, 225–55; Vugt, *Britain to America*, 133–34.

36  Hartmann, *Americans from Wales*, 101–2; Berthoff, "Welsh," 1014; R. D. Thomas, *Hanes Cymry America*, 345.

37  R. D. Thomas, *Hanes Cymry America*, 340–43, 345; Hartmann, *Americans from Wales*, 170–91.

38  Daniel Williams, *One Hundred Years of Welsh Calvinistic Methodism*, 39–40; Maldwyn Jones, "From the Old Country to the New," 93–94; Hartmann, *Americans from Wales*, 103–4.

39  Hartmann, *Americans from Wales*, 104, 107.

40  Erasmus Jones, "Welsh in America," 305–13.

41  Berthoff, *British Immigrants*, 127; Hartmann, *Americans from Wales*, 106–7.

42  Hartmann, *Americans from Wales*, 110; Rev. Roberts, "Welsh People and the Christian Religion," *Druid*, October 19, 1911; Llewelyn J. Evans, "The Welsh Pulpit," *Cambrian* 3 (November–December 1883): 299–301.

43  Rev. William A. Powell, "Rev. Howell Powell," *Cambrian* 1 (July–Aug, 1881): 135–38.

44  William Roberts, "The Welsh People and the Christian Religion," *Druid*, October 19, 1911.

45  Hartmann, *Americans from Wales*, 107–9.

46  E. C. Evans, "Census Reports on the Welsh People in the United States," 138.

47  Morgan, *Wales in British Politics*, 12.

48  Maldwyn Jones, "From the Old Country to the New," 94; Berthoff, "The Welsh," 1015.

49  Vugt, *Britain to America*, 137–38.

50  Parliamentary Papers, *Report of the Commissioner Appointed to Inquire into the State of the Population in the Mining Districts* (1852), Part II, 50–61 (quotations from 53).

51  *Y Drych*, July 28, 1870, cited in William Jones, *Wales in America*, 204.

52  William Jones, *Wales in America*, 204–12. See, for example, four articles in one issue of *Druid*, January 11, 1914: "Town without Saloons"; "Drink Evil Again Discussed"; "Temperance Wage High in Scranton"; and "Scranton Churches Vote for Prohibition." David Jones, *Memorial Volume of the Welsh Congregationalists of Pennsylvania, U.S.A.*, 353.

53  David Jones, *Memorial Volume of the Welsh Congregationalists of Pennsylvania*, 346–47.

54  Daniel Williams, *One Hundred Years of Welsh Calvinistic Methodism*, 113–14.

55  Gibbons, "Miners of Scranton," 923.

56  *Druid*, February 13, 1908; Hartmann, *Americans from Wales*, 156–57.

57  *Druid*, January 22, 1914, and February 5, 1914; *United Mine Workers Journal*, January 22, 1914.

58 *Hazleton Daily Standard*, October 5, 1897; *Morris Herald*, March 2, 1888; *Druid*, December 9, 1909, November 23, 1911, and January 8, 1914, respectively.

59 *Merthyr Express*, quoted in *Cambrian* 33 (January 1, 1913): 4. See also *Druid*, October 10, 1907, September 24, October 8, 1908, and September 23, December 23, 1909, for other examples.

60 Hartmann, *Americans from Wales*, 158–60; William Jones, *Wales in America*, 95; Buskirk, "History of the Philanthropic Order of True Ivorites in Wales and in North America," *NINNAU*, July 1, 2006.

61 William Jones, *Wales in America*, 96.

62 Hartmann, *Americans from Wales*, 139–51; Berthoff, *British Immigrants*, 173–75.

63 Hartmann, *Americans from Wales*, 146–47.

64 William Jones, *Wales in America*, 99–100; *Scranton Republican*, March 11, 1871.

65 Gibbons, "Miners of Scranton," 919. See also Casson, "Welsh in America," 751–52, and Erasmus Jones, "Welsh in America," 310–11. The Welsh American press is filled with notices for, and descriptions of, eisteddfodau.

66 *Scranton Republican*, May 11, 1875, June 10, 1875.

67 William Jones, *Wales in America*, 101, 105.

68 Hartmann, *Americans from Wales*, 151–52. See also Wendell Jones, "Gymanfa Ganu," 7–22, 28, 33.

69 Berthoff, *British Immigrants*, 172; *Druid*, July 24, 1907.

70 Wendell Jones, "Gymanfa Ganu," 17.

### CHAPTER 5

1 Wallace, *St. Clair*, 249–51.

2 *Pottsville Miners Journal*, December 18, 1858; Wallace, *St. Clair*, 253.

3 Korson, *Minstrels of the Mine Patch*, 278. According to Archie Green, "Down in a Coal Mine" was already a traditional ballad in 1908 when it became the first coal folk song ever recorded in the United States. Green, *Only A Miner*, 48.

4 Trachtenberg, *History of Legislation*, 3–8; Parliamentary Papers, *First Report from the Commission of Inquiry into the Condition of Children in Mines and Manufactories* (1842), XV, XVI, and XVII; Parliamentary Papers, *Second Report from the Commission of Inquiry into the Condition of Children in Mines and Manufactories* (1843), XII.

5 Trachtenberg, *History of Legislation*, 8–9.

6 MacDonagh, "Coal Mines Regulation," 68, 84; Benson, *British Coal Miners*, 41–43.

7 Trachtenberg, *History of Legislation*, 10.

8 Ibid., 10–11; Roy, *History of the Coal Miners*, 35–40; Curran, *Dead Laws for Dead Men*, 52–56. For the Hartley and Oak Colliery disasters see Helen and Baron Duckham, *Great Pit Disasters*, 95–140.

9 Trachtenberg, *History of Legislation*, 25–27; *Pottsville Miners Journal*, May 6, 1854.

10  *Pottsville Miners Journal*, August 28, 1858, January 26, 1861; Trachtenberg, *History of Legislation*, 30.

11  Pinkowski, *John Siney, the Miners' Martyr*, 52; Wallace, *St. Clair*, 294–95; Trachtenberg, *History of Legislation*, 32–34.

12  Wallace, *St. Clair*, 296–97; Ellis Roberts, *Breaker Whistle Blows*, 7; O'Malley, *Adventures in the Mines*, 139.

13  O'Malley, *Adventures in the Mines*, 140–41; Wallace, *St. Clair*, 297; Ellis Roberts, *Breaker Whistle Blows*, 7; Campbell, "For 110," 17.

14  Wallace, *St. Clair*, 298; O'Malley, *Adventures in the Mines*, 140–41; Roberts, *Breaker Whistle Blows*, 8; Campbell, "For 110," 17.

15  Chase, *Account of the Unparalleled Disaster*, 7. There is a report filed by the West Virginia Chief of Coal Mining Investigation, John W. Paul, dated September 25, 1922, which draws on Chase, in the National Mine Health and Safety Academy, Beckley, West Virginia.

16  Chase, *Account of the Unparalleled Disaster*, 8.

17  Ibid., 8.

18  Ibid., 10.

19  Chase, *Account of the Unparalleled Disaster*, 12.

20  Ibid., 13–17.

21  Ibid., 18.

22  *New York Times*, September 10, 1869; Chase, *Account of the Unparalleled Disaster*, 20.

23  Chase, *Account of the Unparalleled Disaster*, 22–23, 33–38; *Frank Leslie's Illustrated Newspaper*, September 25, 1869, 16–25, and "Coal Mine Calamity Supplement to *Frank Leslie's Illustrated Newspaper*," September 25, 1869; *New York Times*, September 13, 1869 (quotation).

24  *New York Times*, September 11, 12, and 13, 1869; Wallace, *St. Clair*, 301 quoting *Philadelphia Press*, September 21 and 17, 1869; Chase, *Account of the Unparalleled Disaster*, 23, 30–31.

25  Pinkowski, *John Siney*, 51; Powderly, *Path I Trod*, 24; *United Mine Workers Journal*, May 18, 1916.

26  Wallace, *St. Clair*, 303–4; Campbell, "For 110," 21.

27  Wallace, *St. Clair*, 303–4; Trachtenberg, *History of Legislation*, 42–43.

28  Trachtenberg, *History of Legislation*, 44–45.

29  Pennsylvania Department of Internal Affairs, *Reports of the Inspectors of Mines of the Anthracite Coal Regions of Pennsylvania* (hereafter cited as *Reports of the Pennsylvania Mine Inspectors*). The reports were issued annually and in 1888 included "Anthracite and Bituminous Coal Regions." By 1900 they were called *Report of the Bureau of Mines of the Department of Internal Affairs of Pennsylvania*.

30  *Reports of the Pennsylvania Mine Inspectors, 1888*, 9–11; 1900, 1910, and 1920, as listed in the index of inspectors.

31  *Scranton Morning Republican*, Evening edition-extra, May 27, 1871.

32  Ibid., May 29, 1871.

33  Ibid., May 29, 30, 1871.

34  Ibid., May 31, 1871.

35  Ibid., June 6, 1871.

36  Ibid., May 29, 1871.

37  Ibid., May 30, 31, 1871 (quotation).

38  Ibid., June 1, 1871; June 9, 1871; and June 15, 1871.

39  Ibid., June 24, 1871. See chapter 6 for the 1871 political struggle.

40  See, for example, *Reports of the Pennsylvania Mine Inspectors, 1879*, 171–253, where William S. Jones, another Welshman, reports on the explosion at the Dinas colliery in January 1879, Rhondda Valley, South Wales, and other British reports on such issues as ventilation.

41  *Reports of the Pennsylvania Mine Inspectors, 1877*, 57–58.

42  Ibid., 57, 59.

43  Ibid., 59–61.

44  Ibid., 62 63 (quotations); Pinkowski, *John Siney*, 278.

45  *Reports of the Pennsylvania Mine Inspectors, 1877*, 100.

46  *National Labor Tribune*, May 18, 1889.

47  *Cambrian* 17 (November 1897): 520–22 (quotation from 522); Bradsby, *History of Luzerne County*, 1040.

48  *Colliery Engineer and Metal Miner* 15 (March 1895): 175–76, and 15 (April 1895): 204 (quotations).

49  Brenckman, *History of Carbon County*, 428–30.

50  Bradsby, *History of Luzerne County*, 1463; *Cambrian* 24 (October 1904): 454–55.

51  Roy, *History of the Coal Miners*, 135; Robertson, "Andrew Roy," 23–25.

52  Roy, *History of the Coal Miners*, 116; Kerr, "Movement for Coal Mine Safety," 7–8.

53  Roy, *History of the Coal Miners*, 120–26; *Warren Western Reserve Chronicle*, September 28, 1870.

54  *National Labor Tribune*, November 3, 1883, 3; Robertson, "Andrew Roy," 29–33.

55  *Report of the Ohio Mining Commission, 1871*, 27–51, 55–96, 189.

56  Kerr, "Movement for Coal Mine Safety," 13–14; Roy, *History of the Coal Miners*, 130–31; O'Malley, *Adventures in the Mines*, 148–49; Robertson, "Andrew Roy," 38–40.

57  *Workingman's Advocate*, March 14, 1874; Kerr, "Movement for Coal Mine Safety," 14.

58  Robertson, "Andrew Roy," 44–45; Kerr, "Movement for Coal Mine Safety," 15; *National Labor Tribune*, April 6, 13, and May 4, 1878. Roy campaigned for secretary of state on the Greenback ticket in 1878.

59  Kerr, "Movement for Coal Mine Safety," 16; *National Labor Tribune*, April 20, May 11, June 1, 15, July 20, 1878; Ohio Inspector of Mines, *Eighth Annual Report 1882*, 8 (hereafter cited as *Ohio Inspector of Mines Report*); *Ohio Inspector of Mines Report, 1884*, 129.

60  *Ohio Inspector of Mines Report, 1875*, 15, 31; *1876*, 79.

61  Names of the Ohio mine inspectors were taken from the annual reports of the chief inspector, and nativity determined from references generated from other research sources, from the census index, and from biographical sketches in county and local histories.

62  Gottlieb, "Regulation of the Coal Mining Industry," 288.

63  Ibid., 288, 119; Boston, *Chartists in America*, 84.

64  Gottlieb, "Regulation of the Coal Mining Industry," 119–25.

65  Ibid., 127–33; *Workingman's Advocate*, January 11 and March 18, 1871; Chris Evans, *History of United Mine Workers*, 1:29; Roy, *History of the Coal Miners*, 141.

66  Roy, *History of the Coal Miners*, 142; Gottlieb, "Regulation of the Coal Mining Industry," 288, 148–49, 195.

67  U.S. Department of Labor, Mine Safety and Health Administration, *Historical Summary of Coal-Mine Explosions*, 6–17.

68  Illinois, Bureau of Labor Statistics, *Annual Coal Report, 1883*, 97–108; Gottlieb, "Regulation of the Coal Mining Industry," 192 n. 3; Roy, *History of the Coal Miners*, 202–7.

69  Gottlieb, "Regulation of the Coal Mining Industry," 205. For examples of inspectors in the crossfire, see *National Labor Tribune*, June 21, 1884; December 27, 1884; July 11, 1885; August 7, 1886.

70  Gottlieb, "Regulation of the Coal Mining Industry," 91, 289, 231, 82.

71  Ibid., 312–13.

72  Ibid.

73  Ibid., 332–33; Roy, *History of the Coal Miners*, 134–36; *National Labor Tribune*, January 16, 1902; March 25, 1897; June 3, 1897; January 16, 1902.

74  Gottlieb, "Regulation of the Coal Mining Industry," 337–38.

75  Taniguchi, "Explosive Lesson," 141. The first inspector, Robert Forrester, became geologist for the Pleasant Valley Coal Co. and agent for the Clear Creek mine. See Utah Coal Mine Inspector, *Report of the Coal Mine Inspector*, 5 (hereafter *Utah Mine Inspector's Report*), and Taniguchi, "Explosive Lesson," 147.

76  Milan, "Winter Quarters Explosion," 16–17; Powell, *Next Time We Strike*, 27.

77  Dilley, *History of the Scofield Mine Disaster*, 110, 113; Powell, *Next Time We Strike*, 29.

78  Dilley, *History of the Scofield Mine Disaster*, 86, 99–100, 103.

79  Ibid., 77–78, 104. There is an internal conflict here; he says 19 and 20 on p. 77 but 19 and 21 on p. 104.

80  *Utah Mine Inspector's Report, 1899–1901*, 92–94; Dilley, *History of the Scofield Mine Disaster*, 28, 69–70, 116, 139.

81  Dilley, *History of the Scofield Mine Disaster*, 196–97, 241, 247, 252–53, 280–81.

82  Taniguchi, "Explosive Lesson," 141–42.

83  *Utah Coal Mine Inspector's Report, 1899–1901*, 5, 17, 19, 22–23.

84  Taniguchi, "Explosive Lesson," 147–49, 151–52; *Utah Mine Inspector's Report, 1900*, 65–80 ; Powell, *Next Time We Strike*, 33–34.

85  *Utah Mine Inspector's Report, 1900,* 63, 67 (quote), 95; Taniguchi, "Explosive Lesson," 153; Milan, "Winter Quarters Explosion," 18–19.

86  Whiteside, *Regulating Danger,* 70–72, 151–52; Taniguchi, "Explosive Lesson," 155; *Utah Mine Inspector's Report, 1901,* 17, 19; *1902,* 78; and *1906,* 46.

87  Price, *Eastern Utah Advocate,* April 26, 1906, quoted in Taniguchi, "Explosive Lesson," 156.

88  *Eastern Utah Advocate,* September 5, 1912, quoted in Taniguchi, "Explosive Lesson," 140, 157 (quotation).

### CHAPTER 6

1  Coleman, "Labor Disturbances in Pennsylvania," 19–20. For the Irish immigration to America see Miller, *Emigrants and Exiles.* For the politics of Irish inequality in the anthracite fields during this period, see Palladino, *Another Civil War,* especially chapter 4.

2  Wallace, *St. Clair,* 171–72; Aurand, *Coalcracker Culture,* 24, 34–36, 70–71.

3  Wallace, *St. Clair,* 172.

4  Conway, *Welsh in America,* 194.

5  For this aspect of discrimination against the Irish during this period, see Ignatiev, *How the Irish Became White,* and Roediger, *Wages of Whiteness,* especially chapter 7.

6  O'Leary, *Immigration and Integration,* 20–21; John Davies, *History of Wales,* esp. chapters 7 and 8 on industrialization and population growth.

7  O'Leary, *Immigration and Integration,* 22–23. See also A. H. John, *Industrial Development of South Wales,* 95–96, 102, and E. D. Lewis, *Rhondda Valleys,* 45–47.

8  O'Leary, *Immigration and Integration,* 32, 36; A. H. John, *Industrial Development of South Wales,* 68.

9  O'Leary, *Immigration and Integration,* 36–38; Hobsbawm, *Labouring Men,* 7; Gwyn Williams, "Locating a Welsh Working Class," 28–29, 36–37.

10  O'Leary, *Immigration and Integration,* 81–89, 100–102, 114, 122–27, 173–74.

11  Ibid., 94, 137.

12  Ibid., 148 nn. 40–41; Lewis, *Rhondda Valleys,* 67, 234; I. G. Jones, *Explorations and Explanations,* 148.

13  O'Leary, *Immigration and Integration,* 150, and "Anti-Irish Riots in Wales, 1826–1882," 33; *London Times,* July 15, 1882, quoted in Parry, "Tredegar Anti-Irish Riots," 21.

14  Parry, "Tredegar Anti-Irish Riots," 21–22, quoting Williams's letter to the Home Office, July 15, 1882.

15  O'Leary, "Anti-Irish Riots in Wales," 34–35.

16  O'Leary, *Immigration and Integration,* 165, 202, 209, 213.

17  Conway, *Welsh in America,* 16.

18  William Jones, *Wales in America,* 31–32; Aurand, *From the Molly Maguires,* 55–58.

19  William Jones, *Wales in America*, 32–33. For biographies of Col. Reese Phillips (1863–1922), see the *Druid*, June 6, 1907, and August 22, 1922.

20  William Jones, *Wales in America*, 33–34.

21  Pinkerton, *Molly Maguires and the Detectives*, 151.

22  William Jones, *Wales in America*, 37–38.

23  *Y Drych*, March 12, 1885, quoted in William Jones, *Wales in America*, 39.

24  *Y Drych*, March 12, 1885, quoted in William Jones, *Wales in America*, 41.

25  William Jones, *Wales in America*, 42; Phelan, *Divided Loyalties*, 50–51, 119–22, 126, 189, 201, 203–5, 297–98.

26  Wallace, *St. Clair*, 134–35, 374.

27  Aurand, *Coalcracker Culture*, 74–75; United States, Coal Strike Commission, *Proceedings of the Anthracite Coal Strike Commission*, 1902, 1514, 5652, 8635.

28  Rees and Sarah Phillips in Hyde Park, Scranton, to a Friend, November 20, 1869, reproduced in Conway, *Welsh in America*, 185.

29  Quoted in Wallace, *St. Clair*, 136.

30  T. Thomas, of Taylorville, Scranton, late of Aberdare, to the editor, *Y Gwladgarwr*, April 25, 1868, trans. and reproduced in Conway, *Welsh in America*, 194.

31  Trachtenberg, *History of Legislation*, 135–36.

32  *Scranton Morning Republican*, May 11, 1871.

33  Coleman, "Labor Disturbances in Pennsylvania," 26.

34  Gibbons, "Miners of Scranton," 925–26.

35  William Jones, *Wales in America*, 53–54; *Scranton Morning Republican*, 10, March 10, 31 (quotation), 1871.

36  *Scranton Morning Republican*, April 21, 1871.

37  W. R. Storrs to Sam Sloan, June 12, 1913, Delaware, Lackawanna and Western Railroad (Coal Department) Papers, Lackawanna Historical Society, Scranton, quoted in William Jones, *Wales in America*, 55, and see also 34, 56.

38  *Scranton Morning Republican*, April 7–10, 1871; *New York Times*, April 8, 9, 10, 1871; William Jones, *Wales in America*, 57–58.

39  *Scranton Morning Republican*, May 3, 4, 1871.

40  *Scranton Morning Republican*, May 9, 1871.

41  Ibid., May 8, 10 (quotation), 11, 1871; *New York Times*, May 11, 1871; William Jones, *Wales in America*, 57. For similar actions in Wales, see Rosemary Jones, "Women, Community and Collective Action," 17–41.

42  *New York Times*, May 11, 1871; *Scranton Morning Republican*, May 10, 1871.

43  William Jones, *Wales in America*, 66; *New York Times*, May 11, 1871; *Scranton Morning Republican*, May 11, 12 (quotation), 1871. For the press coverage, see the *Scranton Morning Republican* and *New York Times*, March through May 1871.

44  William Jones, *Wales in America*, 67; *Scranton Morning Republican*, May 18, 1871 (quotation).

45  *Scranton Morning Republican*, May 22, 25, 1871; William Jones, *Wales in America*, 68.

46  *New York Times*, January 10, 1872.

47 William Jones, *Wales in America*, 72–73.

48 Aurand, *From the Molly Maguires*, 86; *New York Times*, January 10, 1872; Coleman, "Labor Disturbances," 27; W. R. Storrs to Sam Sloan, May 23, 1871, DL&W Papers, quoted in William Jones, *Wales in America*, 71.

49 *Scranton Morning Republican*, June 3, 1871.

50 Ibid., April 15, 17, May 20, and June 8, 19, 27, 1871.

51 William Jones, *Wales in America*, 73. For ethnic considerations in late-nineteenth-century Scranton politics, see Walker, "Terence V. Powderly, Labor Mayor," 8, 36–107.

52 *Scranton Morning Republican*, February 28 (quotation), June 8, and July 24, 31, 1871; William Jones, *Wales in America*, 74; Walker, "Terence V. Powderly, 'Labor Mayor,'" 376.

53 William Jones, *Wales in America*, 75–76; Walker, "Terence V. Powderly, 'Labor Mayor,'" 376; *Scranton Morning Republican*, October 19, 1871, May 8, 1872.

54 William Jones, *Wales in America*, 76–77; Walker, "Terence V. Powderly, 'Labor Mayor,'" 389; Falzone, "Terence V. Powderly: Politician and Progressive Mayor," 291–92; Aurand, *From the Molly Maguires*, 110–13.

55 William Jones, *Wales in America*, 78; Falzone, "Terence V. Powderly: Politician," 191–92; Walker, "Terence V. Powderly, 'Labor Mayor,'" 86–87, 97; *Scranton Morning Republican*, October 3 and November 14, 1877.

56 William Jones, *Wales in America*, 78–79; *Scranton Morning Republican*, January 28, and February 25, 1878.

57 *Y Drych*, February 14, 1878, cited in William Jones, *Wales in America*, 79; Walker, "Terence V. Powderly, 'Labor Mayor,'" 105–7.

58 Aurand, *From the Molly Maguires*, 118–20; W. R. Storrs to Sam Sloan, January 20, 1887, DL&W Papers, quoted in William Jones, *Wales in America*, 79–80.

59 William Jones, *Wales in America*, 80 (quotation); Berthoff, "Welsh," 1011–17.

60 Long, *Where the Sun Never Shines*, 106–8; Schlegel, *Ruler of the Reading*, 10–11, 18; Yearly, *Enterprise and Anthracite*, 16, 57–59, 134. For ethnicity, particularly Irish, as an issue in the politics of the anthracite region, see Gudelunas and Shade, *Before the Molly Maguires*.

61 Long, *Where the Sun Never Shines*, 106–9; Schlegel, "Workingman's Benevolent Association," 250, 253; Yearly, *Enterprise and Anthracite*, 208; Aurand, *From the Molly Maguires*, 88–95; Roy, *History of the Coal Miners*, 99; Schlegel, *Ruler of the Reading*, 62–76.

62 *Pottsville Miners' Journal*, October 10, 1857; Kenny, "Nativism, Labor, and Slavery," 325–61. See also Daddow and Bannan, *Coal, Iron, and Oil*.

63 There are numerous accounts of the Molly Maguire episode. For more modern treatments, see Aurand, *From the Molly Maguires to United Mine Workers*, and Broehl, *Molly Maguires*, which accept the reports of McParlan as eyewitness accounts. Wallace, *St. Clair*, 314–61, suggests there might have actually been a secret society. Kenny, *Making Sense of the Molly Maguires*, accepts the inner circle

theory, but shows that the trials were a farce, and how retributive violence was brought with certain Irishmen from Donegal. McParlan's reports are in the Molly Maguire Papers, Historical Society of Pennsylvania.

64  Kenny, *Making Sense of the Molly Maguires*, 161, 164, 70; Broehl, *Molly Maguires*, 161, 165. McParlan's reports make frequent mention of conflict between the Modocs, Molly Maguires, and the Sheet Iron Gang in 1874. See especially Molly Maguire Papers, Historical Society of Pennsylvania, and Pinkerton National Detective Agency, Library of Congress (Kenny, *Making Sense of the Molly Maguires*, 164 n. 21). For gang violence in Mahanoy City involving Molly Maguires, Modocs, and Sheet Iron Boys, see also Munsell and Company, *History of Schuylkill County*, 240–41.

65  Munsell and Company, *History of Schuylkill County*, 241. See also Broehl, *Molly Maguires*, 181.

66  Kenny, *Making Sense of the Molly Maguires*, 165–66; Broehl, *Molly Maguires*, 181–83, 195–98; Munsell and Company, *History of Schuylkill County*, 241; Wallace, *St. Clair*, 358–59.

67  Kenny, *Making Sense of the Molly Maguires*, 185–86.

68  Pinkerton, *Molly Maguires*, 150–51.

69  Broehl, *Molly Maguires*, 181–83, 195–98, 212–18, 256; Kenny, *Making Sense of the Molly Maguires*, 190–91; *Pottsville Miners Journal*, May 28, June 11, 1875, and March 29, 1878; Wallace, *St. Clair*, 353.

70  *Pottsville Miners' Journal*, August 15, 22, 1873, March 20, 1874, and August 20, 1875; Wallace, *St. Clair*, 346–50; Kenny, *Making Sense of the Molly Maguires*, 191–92; Broehl, *Molly Maguires*, 228–30, 328.

71  *Pottsville Miners Journal*, August 20, 1875; Kenny, *Making Sense of the Molly Maguires*, 192–93; Broehl, *Molly Maguires*, 256.

72  Kenny, *Making Sense of the Molly Maguires*, 193, 198–99; Broehl, *Molly Maguires*, 224–36. See also Dewees, *Molly Maguires*, 235–37.

### CHAPTER 7

1  Warne, *Slav Invasion*, 39–40; Census of Population, Part I, 1900. "English-speaking" includes Ireland, England, Wales, Scotland, Canada, and the United States.

2  Rood, "Mine Laborers of Pennsylvania," 110; Daniels, *Coming to America*, 188.

3  *Annual Report of the Secretary of Internal Affairs of the Commonwealth of Pennsylvania*, Part III, Industrial Statistics, 1904 (Harrisburg, 1905), XXXII, 391–92.

4  Warne, *Slav Invasion*, 51, 58–59; Warne, "Effect of Unionism upon the Mine Workers," 29n. See also Warne, "Slav Invasion of the Anthracite Region," Part 1, *Philadelphia Public Ledger*, September 21, 1903.

5  *Annual Report of the Secretary of Internal Affairs of the Commonwealth of Pennsylvania*, Part III, 1903, XXXI, 431–32; Warne, *Slav Invasion*, 63; "Contract Labor in the Mines," *Collier Engineer and Metal Miner* 12 (February 1892): 156.

6  Warne, *Slav Invasion*, 60–63; *Report of the Department of Mines of Pennsylvania*, Part I, Anthracite, 1915, 35–36.

7  Greene, *Slavic Community on Strike*, 14–15, 21, 23, 26– 27, 30; *Reports of the Immigration Commission: Emigration Conditions in Europe*, 1911, 30.

8  Greene, *Slavic Community on Strike*, 36–38.

9  Ibid., 39, 42–43.

10  Warne, *Slav Invasion*, 70; Greene, *Slavic Community on Strike*, 44–45; Haines, "Fertility, Marriage, and Occupation," 28–55; Peter Roberts, *Anthracite Communities*, 69, 72–74.

11  Peter Roberts, *Anthracite Coal Communities*, 52–53 (quotation), 222–43. See also Peter Roberts, "Slavs in Anthracite Communities," 219 (quotation).

12  Greene, *Slav Community on Strike*, 113–14; *New York Herald*, September 30, 1889 (quotation); MacLean, "Life in the Pennsylvania Coal Fields," 336–38. Peter Roberts, *Anthracite Coal Communities*, 41–44. Roberts devotes pages 87– 150 to the different standards of living for Americans, British, and Slavs.

13  MacLean, "Life in the Pennsylvania Coal Fields," 347.

14  Greene, *Slav Community on Strike*, 49–58; MacLean, "Life in the Pennsylvania Coal Fields," 338; Peter Roberts, *Anthracite Coal Communities*, 41–44. See also "Slav Invasion of the Anthracite Region," Part 3, *Philadelphia Public Ledger*, September 23, 1903.

15  Warne, *Slav Invasion*, 87–88.

16  Peter Roberts, "Slav Invasion of the Anthracite Region," Part 2, September 22, 1903; Part 3, September 23, 1903; Part 4, September 24, 1903; and Part 5, September 25, 1903, all in the *Philadelphia Public Ledger*; Novak, *Guns of Lattimer*, 55–56 (quotation).

17  *Wilkes-Barre Union Leader*, January 25, 1884, and *Wilkes-Barre Public Ledger*, April 9, 1890 (quotations, respectively). See also Greene, *Slav Communities on Strike*, 116; U.S. Department of Labor, Mine Safety and Health Administration, *Anthracite Mine Laborers*, 752–53.

18  *Philadelphia Public Ledger*, April 9, 1890.

19  Warne, "Real Cause of the Miners' Strike," 1053–57; House Select Committee, *Labor Troubles in the Anthracite Regions*, 371, 374, 390 (quotations).

20  House Select Committee, *Labor Troubles in the Anthracite Regions*, 582–83; Greene, *Slavic Community on Strike*, 80–83.

21  For Davis's biography see *Cambrian* 3 (July–August 1883): 158; House Select Committee, *Labor Troubles in the Anthracite Regions*, 52–58, 136–37.

22  House Select Committee, *Labor Troubles in the Anthracite Regions*, 544–49, 548–49 (quotations).

23  Greene, *Slav Community on Strike*, 86–87, 90–92. For an overview of the 1887–1888 conflict, see John Davies, "Authority, Community, and Conflict," 339–63.

24 Novak, *Guns of Lattimer*, 16–17; Bradsby, *History of Luzerne County*, 1034; Aurand, "Lattimer Massacre," 7.

25 *Wilkes-Barre Record*, September 14, 1897.

26 *Cambrian* 16 (July 1896): 223–24; *Colliery Engineer and Metal Miner* 16 (July 1896): 281.

27 *Cambrian* 14 (August 1894): 226.

28 *Cambrian* 14 (August 1894): 225–26, 226 (quotation); Bradsby, *History of Luzerne County*, 1196.

29 *Hazleton Daily Standard*, August 16, 1897 (hereafter cited as *HDS*); W. R. Storrs to Samuel Sloan, August 28, 1897, Delaware, Lackawanna, and Western Papers, cited in Aurand, *From the Molly Maguires*, 137; Aurand, "Lattimer Massacre," 7; Blatz, "Reflections on Lattimer," 43.

30 Quoted in Novak, *Guns of Lattimer*, 17.

31 *HDS*, August 19, 1897.

32 Aurand, *From the Molly Maguires*, 137; Novak, *Guns of Lattimer*, 18–19.

33 *HDS*, August 16, 17, 18, 1897; Novak, *Guns of Lattimer*, 24 (quotation).

34 *HDS*, August 17, 1897; Novak, *Guns of Lattimer*, 27.

35 *HDS*, August 19, 20, 21, 1897; Novak, *Guns of Lattimer*, 43–44, 56.

36 *HDS*, August 27 (quotation), August 28, 1897; Novak, *Guns of Lattimer*, 62–64.

37 Bradsby, *History of Luzerne County*, 1298; *Colliery Engineer and Metal Miner* 16 (July 1896): 275.

38 *Colliery Engineer and Metal Miner* 16 (July 1896): 275.

39 Bradsby, *History of Luzerne County*, 1298.

40 Roderick, in *Reports of the Pennsylvania Mine Inspector, 1882*, 261 (quotation); Aurand, *From the Molly Maguires*, 156–58.

41 *Druid*, June 26, 1913.

42 *HDS*, August 30, 1897.

43 *HDS*, September 4, 5, 1897; Novak, *Guns of Lattimer*, 74–76.

44 *HDS*, September 6, 1897.

45 *HDS*, September 7, 1897.

46 *HDS*, September 7, 8, 9, 10, 1897; Novak, *Guns of Lattimer*, 87–102. For the role of John Fahy and the UMWA in the events surrounding the Lattimer Massacre, see the entire issue of *Pennsylvania History* 68 (Winter 2002), which is devoted to the topic. See also Blatz, *Democratic Miners*, 282.

47 *HDS*, September 11, 1897; Novak, *Guns of Lattimer*, 109–32; Turner, "Lattimer Massacre," 11–12.

48 *HDS*, September 13, 1897; *Wilkes-Barre Leader*, September 14, 1897; Novak, *Guns of Lattimer*, 150–51.

49 *HDS*, September 12, 1897; Novak, *Guns of Lattimer*, 159, 178–79.

50 *HDS*, September 18, 20, 21, 22, 1897; *United Mine Workers Journal*, November 25, 1897.

51  Turner, "Lattimer Massacre," 11–30, and Stolarik, "Slovak Perspective on the Lattimer Massacre," 31–40; Novak, *Guns of Lattimer*, 245 (quotation). For coverage of the funerals, coroner's inquest, and grand jury hearings, see the *Hazleton Daily Standard* and the *Wilkes-Barre Leader* throughout September 1897, and for the trial beginning in February 1898.

52  Aurand, *From the Molly Maguires*, 142.

53  Letter from Richard Edwards, Pottsville, Pa., May 4, 1888, reproduced in Conway, *Welsh in America*, 200–201.

54  John R. Williams at Algoma, McDowell County, W.Va., to William Thomas of Brynawel, Aberdare, Wales, November 10, 1895, Ms. 9393E, National Library of Wales, Aberystwyth. See also Conway, *Welsh in America*, 205, for a partial reproduction.

55  Conway, *Welsh in America*, 166.

56  House Select Committee, *Labor Troubles in the Anthracite Regions*, 306.

57  Warne, *Slav Invasion*, 72, 73, 74, 76, 77 (quotation). See also Warne, "The Real Cause of the Miners Strike," 1054.

58  Warne, *Slav Invasion*, 78, 79, 80.

59  Ibid., 80–82.

60  Ibid., 95–97, 100 (quotation); Peter Roberts, *Anthracite Coal Communities*, 17–18. For a summary of the standard of living argument, and why the English speakers left the coal industry, see Warne, "Real Cause of the Miners' Strike," 1053–57.

61  For an excellent example of recent scholarship that demonstrates that the Slavs were in the vanguard of union organization, see Beik, *Miners of Windber*.

62  William Jones, *Wales in America*, 80, 82, 85 (quotation).

63  *Senate Report of the Immigration Commission*, 1:251.

64  Ibid., 254–55.

65  Ibid., 255–57, 260.

66  Ibid., 261–66, 290. The 515 Scots in the sample had the highest average daily earnings at $2.35, the 209 Swedes were second at $2.33, the English were third at $2.32, and the Welsh were fourth at $2.27 (p. 290). Note that the data collected was for Welsh-born fathers rather than parents. It would be misleading to claim "parentage" for figures collected on the father's nativity because Welsh men increasingly married women of other nationalities.

67  Ibid., 415 (quotation), 416–19.

68  Ibid., 424.

69  Ibid., 290–92.

70  MacLean, "Life in the Pennsylvania Coal Fields," 347.

71  Peter Roberts, *Anthracite Coal Communities*, 25.

72  *Senate Report of the Immigration Commission*, 1:427. See also Long, *Where the Sun Never Shines*, 128; Berthoff, *British Immigrants*, 28.

73  Hirsh, "Coal Miners and the American Republic," 198. Herbert Gutman pi-

oneered the idea of class formation and reconstitution in *Work, Culture and Society*.

74   U.S. Congress, *Testimony Taken by the Select Committee, 1888*, 213.

75   *Annual Report of the Pennsylvania Department of Mines, 1906*, Part I, 36.

76   Quoted in Hirsh, "Coal Miners and the American Republic," 207.

### CHAPTER 8

1   Tine, *Making of the Labor Bureaucrat*, 1, 4–5. Among the classics are Perlman, *Theory of the Labor Movement*, 192–200; Perlman and Taft, *History of Labor in the United States, 1896–1932*, 3–12; Commons et al., *History of Labour in the United States*, 2:308–10; Grob, *Workers and Utopia*; Ware, *Labor Movement*.

2   Tine, *Making of the Labor Bureaucrat*, 10–11, 19–22; Brophy, *A Miner's Life*, 12, 73.

3   Tine, *Making of the Labor Bureaucrat*, 17–18, 24–25, 28–30, 58, 61 (quotations on 25 and 30, respectively).

4   Ibid., 84, 158–59; *United Mine Workers Journal*, July 16, 1917 (hereafter cited as *UMWJ*).

5   Tine, *Making of the Labor Bureaucrat*, 176–77; *UMWJ*, July 6, 1905 (quotation).

6   Tine, *Making of the Labor Bureaucrat*, 180–81.

7   Krause, *Battle for Homestead*, 87–88, 149; Roy, *History of the Coal Miners*, 184–85; Chris Evans, *History of the United Mine Workers*, 1:89–90.

8   Krause, *Battle for Homestead*, 149–50; McBride, "Coal Miners," 242–53; Roy, *History of the Coal Miners*, 179, 184–85; Chris Evans, *History of the United Mine Workers*, 89–90.

9   Roy, *History of the Coal Miners*, 180.

10   *National Labor Tribune*, October 28, 1882 (hereafter cited as *NLT*).

11   Roy, *History of the Coal Miners*, 180; Krause, *Battle for Homestead*, 88; Armstrong to Powderly, January 1, 1880, reel no. 2, D. R. Jones to Uriah Stephens, October 13, 1879, and D. R. Jones to Powderly, October 16, 1879, reel no. 1, microfilm edition, Terence V. Powderly Papers; *NLT*, November 20, 1880.

12   *NLT*, November 15, 1879.

13   Ibid., October 28, 1882.

14   Ibid., October 8 and November 29, 1879.

15   Ibid., August 16, 1879; Krause, *Battle for Homestead*, 150–51.

16   Krause, *Battle for Homestead*, 157–59; *NLT*, November 27, 1880 (quotation), October 29, 1881, and February 26, 1881.

17   Krause, *Battle for Homestead*, 194, 200. The *National Labor Tribune* claimed that there were three hundred thousand onlookers, which is an exaggeration, but the most conservative estimate was thirty thousand (*NLT*, October 28, 1882).

18   *NLT*, January 6, 1883 (quotation). For the series see *NLT*, October 6, 1883, to February 9, 1884.

19   Ibid., October 20, 1883.

20 Ibid., October 27, October 1883, November 3, 10, 1883, and February 9, 1884 (quotation).

21 Ibid., February 20, 1886 (quotation), October 6, 1883, February 9, 1884, February 19, 1887, May 18, 1889; Krause, *Battle for Homestead*, 88.

22 Burgoyne, *Homestead*, 219–20.

23 Krause, *Battle for Homestead*, 88.

24 Manuscript Census of Population, 1880, Perry County, Ohio; *Charleston Gazette*, May 2, 1939; Tine, *Making of the Labor Bureaucrat*, 171; *UMWJ*, February 6, 1908.

25 "W. T. Lewis," obituary, *Cambrian* 29 (May 15, 1909): 10; *Logan Republican Gazette*, September 11, 1890; Tribe, "Empire of Industry," 275; Roy, *History of the Coal Miners*, 248; Ware, *Labor Movement in the United States*, 329–32.

26 *Logan Republican Gazette*, September 11, 1890 (quotation); *Cambrian* 29 (May 15, 1909): 10; Tribe, "Empire of Industry," 275; Roy, *History of the Coal Miners*, 248.

27 *Logan Republican Gazette*, September 11, 1890.

28 Roy, *History of the Coal Miners*, 247–48; Evans, *History of the United Mine Workers*, 237.

29 Grob, *Workers and Utopia*, 99–100.

30 Ibid., 100.

31 Ibid., 60–61, 101–2, 105.

32 Ibid., 105–6, 119.

33 Weick, *American Miners' Association*; Grob, *Workers and Utopia*, 124; Roy, *History of the Coal Miners*, 215–26; Fox, *United We Stand*, 14–16.

34 Grob, *Workers and Utopia*, 125; Chris Evans, *History of the United Mine Workers*, 1:385–86; Roy, *History of the Coal Miners*, 248–50; National Federation of Miners and Mine Laborers, *Proceedings*, 1886 (quotation).

35 Chris Evans, *History of the United Mine Workers*, 1:252–54, 273–75.

36 Roy, *History of the Coal Miners*, 249, 268.

37 *NLT*, May 28, 1887.

38 Ibid., August 27, 1887.

39 Greene, *Slavic Community on Strike*, 82–87, 90–91.

40 Ibid., 92–94; *NLT*, January 5, 1889.

41 Powderly's letter, dated December 21, 1888, was sent to NTA 135 members and reprinted in the *New Lexington Herald*, October 23, 1890, a Democratic paper hostile to Lewis.

42 Chris Evans, *History of the United Mine Workers*, 1:385–86.

43 The story was reprinted in the *NLT*, December 8, 1888, from an undisclosed source, probably the *Ohio State Journal*.

44 Ibid., December 8, 1888.

45 Ibid., December 15, 1888; Fox, *United We Stand*, 17–18; Greene, *Slavic Community on Strike*, 87.

46 Roy, *History of the Coal Miners*, 249–50. See also Ware, *Labor Movement in the*

United States, 216–17; Fox, *United We Stand*, 18; Grob, *Workers and Utopia*, 125; *NLT*, January 26, 1889 (quotation). For the constitution of the NPU, see the *NLT*, December 15, 1888.

47  Chris Evans, *History of the United Mine Workers*, 1:394–402; Roy, *History of the Coal Miners*, 250–51; Fox, *United We Stand*, 18–19. For examples of competing locals at the same mines, see *NLT*, July 27 and August 3, 10, 1889.

48  *NLT*, February 16, 1889.

49  Ibid., January 12, 1889.

50  Ibid., March 2, 1888 (quotations). The corruption investigation committee, composed of Nelson A. Sims, John McBride, and Richard J. Fanning, conducted its work in March 1889.

51  Ibid., March 30, 1889.

52  Ibid., April 6, 1889. See for example, several others in the same issue, and April 13, 1889.

53  Ibid., September 28, 1889 (emphasis in original).

54  Chris Evans, *History of the United Mine Workers*, 1:470–71. Quotations are from the full letter of resignation which was published in the *NLT*, July 20, 1889. For testimonials to Lewis on his resignation see, for example, *NLT*, July 27, 1889.

55  Chris Evans, *History of the United Mine Workers*, 470–71; *Logan Republican Gazette*, September 11, 1890; *NLT*, September 28, December 21, 1889 (quotation); Tribe, "Empire of Industry," 275.

56  *Logan Republican Gazette*, September 4, 18 (quotations, respectively), October 2, 9, 16, 23, and November 6, 1890; Tribe, "Empire of Industry," 275–76.

57  *New Lexington Herald*, October 9, 1890; *Logan Republican Gazette*, October 30, 1890 (quotations).

58  Watchorn, *Autobiography*, 81.

59  *Logan Republican Gazette*, November 13, 1890; Tribe, "Empire of Industry," 277; Tine, *Making of the Labor Bureaucrat*, 171; *UMWJ*, February 6, 1906.

60  Roy, *History of the Coal Miners*, 247–49; Ellis Roberts, *Breaker Whistle Blows*, 24. The *Cambrian* obituary left without elaboration a tantalizing reference to the fact that he was "an inventor of many useful articles" (*Cambrian* 29 [May 15, 1909]: 10).

61  T. L. Lewis biography in *UMWJ*, February 6, 1908; Roy, *History of the Coal Miners*, 353.

62  *UMWJ*, February 6, 1908.

63  Ibid.

64  Fox, *United We Stand*, 126–27; *UMWJ*, April 16, 1896.

65  Fox, *United We Stand*, 126–29.

66  Ibid., 130.

67  Ibid., 132–35.

68  Roy, *History of the Coal Miners*, 351–53; Fink, *Biographical Directory of American Labor*, 355–56; Obituary, *Charleston Gazette*, May 2, 1939.

69 Quoted in Tine, *Making of a Labor Bureaucrat*, 148.

70 *Amalgamated Journal*, 10 (May 6, 1909): frontispiece; *Wheeling Majority*, December 23, 1909 (quotation); *Wheeling Intelligencer*, May 18, 1910.

71 The others included John H. Morgan, chief inspector of factories and workshops of the state of Ohio, Columbus; Ben I. Davis, editor *Amalgamated Journal*, Pittsburgh; Thomas R. Lloyd, guide mill superintendent, Cambridge, Ohio (*Druid*, March 25, 1909).

72 *Druid*, October 8, December 10, 1908, and March 4, 1909 (quotation).

73 Reprinted in *Druid*, May 20, 1909.

74 Dubofsky and Tine, *John L. Lewis*, 292.

75 Ibid., 293.

76 Ron Roberts, *John L. Lewis*, 9. See also Ron Roberts, *Ordinary Ghosts and Everyday People*, for historical sketches from local sources in Lucas, Iowa.

77 Ron Roberts, *John L. Lewis*, 18–19; Dubofsky and Tine, *John L. Lewis*, 4–5.

78 Ron Roberts, *John L. Lewis*, 19–20, 23; Dubofsky and Tine, *John L. Lewis*, 4–5.

79 Zee, *British in Iowa*, 44–45. For background on Welsh settlement of Lucas, Iowa, see Ron Roberts, *Ordinary Ghosts and Everyday People*, 21–29. For coal mining settlements in Iowa generally, see Schwieder, *Black Diamonds*.

80 Ron Roberts, *John L. Lewis*, 26–27. On singing their way home, Roberts cites his interview with Irene Evans Baker, Lucas, Iowa, October 10, 1983. She was eighty-seven at the time.

81 Ibid., 28–29.

82 Ibid., 29–31, 37, 40, 43; *NLT*, June 4, 1881, and July 25, 1883; Dubofsky and Tine, *John L. Lewis*, 8–14; Hutchinson, "John L. Lewis," 187.

83 Dubofsky and Tine, *John L. Lewis*, 8; Ron Roberts, *John L. Lewis*, 42–44, 59.

84 Hutchinson, "John L. Lewis," 192–93 (quotation); Ron Roberts, *John L. Lewis*, 51–52.

85 Hutchinson, "John L. Lewis," 193. See also Alinsky, *John L. Lewis*, 17; Ron Roberts, *John L. Lewis*, 53; Dubofsky and Tine, *John L. Lewis*, 15–16.

86 Ron Roberts, *John L. Lewis*, 54–55; Dubofsky and Tine, *John L. Lewis*, 17–18.

87 *Druid*, February 20, 1913. Perry retired in August 1913. (John P. White to Edwin Perry, May 8, 1913, President's Office Files, International Executive Board 1911–1943, Box 3, F-18, United Mine Workers of America Archive, Pennsylvania State University.)

88 President's Office Files, International Executive Board 1911–1943, Minutes, Box 3, F-18, UMWA Archive, Pennsylvania State; Dubofsky and Tine, *John L. Lewis*, 18–19, 21–42; Ron Roberts, *John L. Lewis*, 55.

89 Biographical description and clippings in the John Owens Collection, Mss. 41, Archives and Special Collections, Ohio University; "John Owens," *Fortune* 34 (November 1946): 146.

90 *Cardiff South Wales News*, March 24, 1923, unbound clippings, John L. Lewis Papers, Microfilm Edition, reel 2, State Historical Society of Wisconsin.

**CHAPTER 9**

1 O'Neal, *Those Damned Foreigners.*

2 Ibid., 12–14, 17; 1891 British Population Census. For Nantymoel, see the *Ogmore Valley Local History and Heritage Society Journal* 3 (December 2002), and Keen, *Llynfi, Garw and Ogmore Valleys in Old Photographs.*

3 O'Neal, *Damned Foreigners*, 16, 23–26.

4 Ibid., 27–31, 42, 57.

5 Ibid., 35, 44–46.

6 Ibid., 46–49, 58.

7 Ibid., 51–54.

8 O'Neal, *Damned Foreigners*, 67.

9 Senate Commission on Industrial Relations, *Final Report and Testimony*, 1916, Vol. 7, "Testimony of Mrs. Mary Hannah Thomas," 6359; Long, "Women of Colorado Fuel," 66–67; Long, *Where the Sun Never Shines*, 247, 262, 264.

10 "Nationalities Employed in Mines of Colorado During the Year 1912, and Percentages," President-District Correspondence, 1911–1932, District 15, Box 71, F-3, United Mine Workers of America Archive, Pennsylvania State University (30 percent were "English" and 29 percent were Italian); Long, *Where the Sun Never Shines*, 262; Long, "Women of Colorado Fuel," 69. Pearl Jolly, the Ludlow camp nurse, testified that there were 21 different nationalities at Ludlow (*Commission on Industrial Relations Report*, 7:6354).

11 O'Neal, *Damned Foreigners*, 124, 68–69 (quotations).

12 Ibid., 70–73, 76, 80, 66.

13 "Nationalities Employed in Mines of Colorado During the Year 1912, and Percentages," President-District Correspondence, 1911–1932, District 15, Box 71, F-3, United Mine Workers of America (hereafter UMWA) Archive, Pennsylvania State University; Long, "Women of the Colorado Fuel and Iron Strike, 1913–14," 63–64.

14 Long, *Where the Sun Never Shines*, 274–75; McGovern and Guttridge, *Great Coalfield War*, 105.

15 Long, *Where the Sun Never Shines*, 274; Long, "Women of Colorado Fuel," 72; O'Neal, *Damned Foreigners*, 101, 124 (quotation).

16 McGovern and Gutteridge, *Great Coalfield War*, 105–6.

17 See Gorn, *Mother Jones*, and Fetherling, *Mother Jones the Miners' Angel.*

18 Senate Commission on Industrial Relations, *Final Report and Testimony*, 1916, 8:7326 and 7:6359, 6375–76; Long, "Women of Colorado Fuel," 74–75.

19 Long, "Women of Colorado Fuel," 75–76; *United Mine Workers Journal*, January 29, 1914, and March 26, 1914.

20 Senate Commission on Industrial Relations, *Final Report and Testimony*, 1916, 7:6357–58.

21 Papanikolas, *Buried Unsung*, 172.

22 McGovern and Guttridge, *Great Coalfield War*, 174; Senate Commission on

Industrial Relations, *Final Report and Testimony*, 1916, 7:6358 (quotation); Papanikolas, *Buried Unsung*, 173.

23 Senate Commission on Industrial Relations, *Final Report and Testimony*, 7:6358.

24 Colorado Adjutant General, *Report on the Military Occupation of the Coal Strike Zone of Colorado, 1913–1914*, 58–59.

25 Senate Commission on Industrial Relations, *Final Report and Testimony*, 7:6357.

26 O'Neal, *Damned Foreigners*, 127, 131. See also the testimony of Pearl Jolly, Ludlow camp nurse, in Senate Commission on Industrial Relations, *Final Report and Testimony*, 7:6349.

27 O'Neal, *Damned Foreigners*, 133. Pearl Jolly testified that the firing began around 5:00 A.M. on Tuesday morning. Other accounts agree with Mary's statement that it began around 9:00 A.M. (Senate Commission on Industrial Relations, *Final Report and Testimony*, 7:6349).

28 O'Neal, *Damned Foreigners*, 134–35. The Director of Publicity for UMWA District 15 (Colorado), Walter H. Fink, claimed that "Mrs. Thomas was so close to death that a bullet clipped out a part of her hair, and around the feet of her two little children played machine gun bullets" (Fink, *Ludlow Massacre*).

29 O'Neal, *Damned Foreigners*, 137–39; McGovern and Guttridge, *Great Coalfield War*, 219; Papanikolas, *Buried Unsung*, 219–20.

30 O'Neal, *Damned Foreigners*, 140–44. For a full biographical account of Louis Tikas, see Papanikolas, *Buried Unsung*; McGovern and Guttridge, *Great Coalfield War*, 213–15, 251.

31 O'Neal, *Damned Foreigners*, 144–48 (quotations from 148 and 146, respectively).

32 Ibid., 145 (quotation), 149–52; Senate Commission on Industrial Relations, *Final Report and Testimony*, 7:6353–54; Papanikolas, *Buried Unsung*, 243; McGovern and Guttridge, *Great Coalfield War*, 237–39.

33 O'Neal, *Damned Foreigners*, 153. For a general description of the Ludlow Massacre, see McGovern and Guttridge, *Great Coalfield War*, 210–31.

34 O'Neal, *Damned Foreigners*, 155–56.

35 Ibid., 156–57.

36 Ibid., 158–59.

37 Ibid., 161–62. For a general discussion of the fury vented by the miners against the companies following the Ludlow Massacre, see McGovern and Guttridge, *Great Coalfield War*, 239–59.

38 Colorado Adjutant General, *Report, Military Occupation of the Strike Zone*, 58; Fink, *Ludlow Massacre*, 19; O'Neal, *Damned Foreigners*, 163; *United Mine Workers Journal*, May 14, 28, 1914.

39 McGovern and Guttridge, *Great Coalfield War*, 299.

40 O'Neal, *Damned Foreigners*, 165. See also Papanikolas, *Buried Unsung*, 243; McGovern and Guttridge, *Great Coalfield War*, 278; Beshoar, *Out of the Depths*, 233; *New York Times*, May 22, 1914; *United Mine Workers Journal*, May 28, 1914.

41 O'Neal, *Damned Foreigners*, 165–66 (quotations); Senate Commission on In-

dustrial Relations, *Final Report and Testimony*, 7:6356–6360; *New York Times*, May 28, 1914; *United Mine Workers' Journal*, June 4, 1914.

42  O'Neal, *Damned Foreigners*, 169 (quotation); Papanikolas, *Buried Unsung*, 244. See also Upton Sinclair, *Autobiography*, 198–99.

43  O'Neal, *Damned Foreigners*, 171.

44  *New York Times*, May 26, 1914; *United Mine Workers Journal*, June 4, 1914 (quotation).

45  *United Mine Workers Journal*, June 11, 1914. Much of the account attributed to Pearl Jolly in this article actually pertained to the actions of Mary Thomas, for example leading women and children to safety.

46  O'Neal, *Damned Foreigners*, 175, 164, 56.

47  Upton Sinclair, *King Coal: A Novel* and *Coal War: A Sequel to King Coal*; the latter was written shortly after *King Coal* appeared in 1917 but was not published until decades later. This was a fictionalized treatment of the Ludlow Massacre with the same main characters (Duke, *Writers and Miners*, 239 n. 13). Upton Sinclair, *Autobiography*, 212–13; Mary Sinclair, *Southern Belle*, 196–97, 202.

48  Mary H. Thomas to John P. White, January 4, 1915, White to Thomas, January 5, 1915, and White to Thomas, February 5, 1915, President-District Correspondence, 1911–1932, Box 71, F-4, District 15, United Mine Workers of America Archive, Pennsylvania State University.

49  O'Neal, *Damned Foreigners*, 177–80, 184–86, 191–200.

50  Ibid., 45–46, 189–90, 201–3, 208–10.

51  Ibid., 212–13. Eleven lines describe her trip home to Wales, while twelve lines are given to her visit to the Ludlow Monument.

52  Ibid., 214–20.

53  Papanikolas, *Buried Unsung*, 159–60.

54  O'Neal, *Damned Foreigners*, 9, 151. Mary left only oblique references to the influence of religion in her family, but does state that her father was one of the "ten percent" called a "sinner" because he chose the pub over church on Saturday night.

55  Papanikolas, *Buried Unsung*, 160.

56  Ibid., 255.

### EPILOGUE

1  Rev. Erasmus W. Jones, "Longings of Foreigners," *Cambrian* 23 (February 1903): 48–49.

2  Llewellyn, *How Green Was My Valley*, 14.

3  Glanmor Williams, *Religion, Language, and Nationality in Wales*, 226; Berthoff, *British Immigrants*, 210.

4  Emrys Jones, "Some Aspects of Cultural Change," 40.

5  Berthoff, *British Immigrants in Industrial America*, 134.

6  Ibid., 132 (quotation), 125–30, 140.

7 Conway, *Welsh in America*, 165; Berthoff, *British Immigrants in Industrial America*, 56; *Senate Reports of the Immigration Commission*, 1910, XVI, 593.

8 William Jones, *Wales in America*, 84; Conway, *Welsh in America*, 197.

9 R. D. Thomas, *Hanes Cymry America*, 335.

10 William Jones, *Wales in America*, 86.

11 Knowles, *Calvinists Incorporated*, especially chapter 3; Emrys Jones, "Some Aspects of Cultural Change," 16.

12 Emrys Jones, "Some Aspects of Cultural Change," 36–40.

13 Knowles, *Calvinists Incorporated*, 164, 243; Thomas quoted in David Smith, *Wales! Wales?*, 152; Geraint Jenkins and Mari Williams, "Fortunes of the Welsh Language, 1900–2000," 1.

14 Emrys Jones, "Some Aspects of Cultural Change," 26–28.

15 Ibid., 30.

16 Ibid., 31–34.

17 William Jones, *Wales in America*, 91–92, 105 (quotation).

18 Berthoff, *British Immigration in Industrial America*, 171; William Jones, *Wales in America*, 106–10.

19 R. D. Thomas, *Hanes Cymry America*, 336 (emphasis in original).

20 Emrys Jones, "Some Aspects of Cultural Change," 23. For a recent study of women and the language shift in Wales, see Mari Williams, "Women and the Welsh Language," 137–80; Emrys Jones, "Some Aspects of Cultural Change," 23–24.

21 Emrys Jones, "Some Aspects of Cultural Change," 29.

22 *Cambrian* 2 (May–June 1882), 145, and 12 (January 1893), 25–27; William Jones, "Welsh Language and Welsh Identity," 272–73.

23 Emrys Jones, "Some Aspects of Cultural Change," 24–26, 17–21; Jones, "Welsh Language and Welsh Identity," 276; Aled Jones and Bill Jones, *Welsh Reflections*, 104.

24 *Cambrian* 7 (March 1887), 87; *Y Drych*, April 8, 1875; Jones, "Welsh Language and Welsh Identity," 273–74; Emrys Jones, "Some Aspects of Cultural Change," 29, quoting *Y Drych*.

25 *Y Drych*, November 18, 1909, quoted in Emrys Jones, "Some Aspects of Cultural Change," 28.

26 William Jones, "Welsh Language and Welsh Identity," 275.

27 For biographical details see *Druid*, December 15, 1925; *Y Drych*, December 3, 17, 1925; Stoddard, *Prominent Men of Scranton*, xvi–xvii. My discussion of Edwards and the language shift is drawn from William Jones, "Welsh Language and Welsh Identity," 276–84.

28 H. M. Edwards, "*Diffygion y Genedl Gymreig yn America*," *Y Glorian*, 1 (1872), 19, quoted in William Jones, "Welsh Language and Welsh Identity," 278–80.

29 *Druid*, October 21, 1909.

30 *Druid*, September 2, 1909; William Jones, "Welsh Language and Welsh Identity," 280.

31  William Jones, "Welsh Language and Welsh Identity," 280, 284.

32  *Columbia*, May 4, 1893, quoted in ibid., 281.

33  Maldwyn Jones, "From the Old Country to the New," 100.

34  *Druid*, January 1, 1920.

35  Raymond Williams, *Border Country*, 9–10.

36  Hazel Davies presentation, Conference, North American Association for the Study of Welsh Culture and History, 1998, Rio Grande University, Ohio.

# BIBLIOGRAPHY

**MANUSCRIPT COLLECTIONS**

Aberystwyth, Wales
    National Library of Wales
        Harry Blackwell's Cambrian Clippings, Ms. 5945–6D
        "J. G. Davis's Diary of a Trip to the Chicago World's Fair, 1893," Ms. 17537B
        Letters from America Collection
        Miscellaneous Letters, Ms. 16704E and Ms. 3293E
        "Mountain Ash Welsh Choir, North American Tour, 1925–26," Ms. 5595D
        Rees Jenkin Jones Collection, Ms. 14159D
        "Thomas Levi's Summary of Impressions in America, 1867," Ms. 17537B
Akron, Ohio
    Akron Public Library
        Local History Collection
Alliance, Ohio
    Rodman Library
        Morgan Family Papers
Athens, Ohio
    Ohio University Library, Archives and Special Collections
        John Owens Collection
        Local History Collection
        United Mine Workers of America, District 6 Papers
Beckley, West Virginia
    National Mine Safety and Health Academy Library
        U.S. Bureau of Mines Reports and Documents
Bluefield, West Virginia
    Craft Memorial Library, Eastern Regional Coal Archives
        Miscellaneous Files and Clippings
Canton, Ohio
    Stark County Library
        Local History Collection
        Ohio Bureau of Vital Statistics Records
        Probate Court Records

Cardiff, Wales
   Cardiff Central Library
      Newspaper Collection
   Cardiff University, Humanities Library
      Government Documents
      Newspaper Collection
      Welsh History Collection
   Glamorgan Record Office
      Civil Registration Records
      Local History Collection
      Map Collection
Charleston, West Virginia
   West Virginia State Archives
      Thomas Bruce Carpenter and Thomas-Redman-Hughes Family Papers
Long Beach, California
   California State University, Long Beach
      Oral History Archive (Mary Thomas O'Neal Interview)
Madison, Wisconsin
   State Historical Society of Wisconsin
      John L. Lewis Papers, Microfilm Edition
Morgantown, West Virginia
   West Virginia University Library, West Virginia and Regional History Collection
      Erskine Company Records, 1815–1870
Scranton, Pennsylvania
   Anthracite Mine Museum Library
   Lackawanna Historical Society
University Park, Pennsylvania
   Pennsylvania State University Library, Special Collections and Labor Archives
      Papers of T. R. Johns, 1853–1948
      United Mine Workers of America Archive
Warren, Ohio
   Warren-Trumbull County Library, Special Collections
      Local History Collection
Washington, D.C.
   Catholic University of America
      Terence V. Powderly Papers, Microfilm Edition
   U.S. Department of Labor Library
      Labor Union and Industry Periodicals
Youngstown, Ohio
   Mahoning Historical Society
      Ethnicity Files
      Coal Mines and Mining Files
      Welsh Pioneer Association of the Western Reserve

Youngstown Historical Center of Industry and Labor
   Niles Fire Brick Company Records
   Niles Historical Society Collection
Youngstown State University
   Anne Harris Historical Coal Mines Collection (Personal)

GOVERNMENT PUBLICATIONS

**Great Britain**

G.B. General Register Office. Schedules of Population, 1851, 1881.

G.B. Parliament. Parliamentary Papers. 1842, XV–XVII. *First Report from the Commission of Inquiry into the Condition of Children in Mines and Manufactories.*

——. 1843, XII. *Second Report from the Commission of Inquiry into the Condition of Children in Mines and Manufactories.*

——. 1846, I. *Report of the Commissioner Appointed to Inquire into the State of the Population in the Mining Districts.*

——. 1847, II. *Report of the Commissioner Appointed to Inquire into the State of the Population in the Mining Districts.*

——. 1849, II. *Report of the Commissioner Appointed to Inquire into the State of the Population in the Mining Districts.*

——. 1850, II. *Report of the Commissioner Appointed to Inquire into the State of the Population in the Mining Districts.*

——. 1851, II. *Report of the Commissioner Appointed to Inquire into the State of the Population in the Mining Districts.*

——. 1852, II. *Report of the Commissioner Appointed to Inquire into the State of the Population in the Mining Districts.*

——. 1847, XXVII. *Reports from the Commissioners on the State of Education in Wales.*

——. 1871, XXXVI. *Report of the Commissioners Appointed to Inquire into the Truck System.*

——. 1871, III. *Report of the Commissioners Appointed to Inquire into the Several Matters Relating to Coal in the United Kingdom.*

——. 1873, X. *Report from the Select Committee on the Dearness of Coal.*

——. 1854, V. *Third Report from the Select Committee on Accidents in Coal Mines; with the Minutes of Evidence, Taken Before Them.*

——. 1864. VIII. *Report of the Commissioners Appointed to Inquire into the Condition of All Mines in Great Britain.*

——. 1881, X. *Report of Her Majesty's Commissioners Appointed to Inquire into Accidents in Mines.*


**United States Documents**

U.S. Anthracite Coal Strike Commission. *Report to the President on the Anthracite Coal Strike of May–October 1902.* 58th Cong., Special Sess., serial doc. 16. Washington, D.C.: Government Printing Office, 1903.

U.S. Coal Strike Commission, *Proceedings of the Anthracite Coal Strike Commission.* Washington, D.C.: Hanna and Budlong, Official Stenographers, 1902–1903.

U.S. Congress. Commission on Industrial Relations. *Final Report and Testimony.* 64th Cong., 1st sess. Washington, D.C.: Government Printing Office, 1916.

——. House Select Committee on Existing Labor Troubles in Pennsylvania. *Labor Troubles in the Anthracite Regions of Pennsylvania, 1887–1888.* 50th Cong., 2nd sess. Report No. 4147. Washington, D.C.: Government Printing Office, 1889.

——. *Report of the Committee of the Senate, upon the Relations between Labor and Capital.* 48th Cong., Vol. 4. Washington, D.C.: Government Printing Office, 1885.

——. *Senate Report of the Immigration Commission: Immigrants in Industry.* S. Doc. 633. 61st Cong., 2nd sess. ser 5667, 1911.

——. *Reports of the Immigration Commission. Immigrants in Industries. Part I: Bituminous Coal Mining,* vols. 1–2. Document No. 633. 61st Cong., 2nd sess. Washington, D.C.: Government Printing Office, 1911.

——. *Report of the Industrial Commission on the Relations and Conditions of Capital and Labor Employed in the Mining Industry.* House Doc. 181. 57th Cong., 1st sess., ser 4342. Washington, D.C.: Government Printing Office, 1901.

——. *Testimony Taken by the Select Committee to Inquire into Alleged Violation of the Laws Prohibiting the Importation of Contract Laborers, Paupers, Convicts, and Other Classes.* 50th Cong., 1st sess., H.R. 444. Washington, D.C.: Government Printing Office, 1888.

U.S. Department of Commerce and Labor. Bureau of the Census. *Twelfth Census of the United States, 1900: Population.* Washington, D.C.: Government Printing Office, 1902.

——. Bureau of the Census. *Thirteenth Census of the United States, 1910: Population.* Washington, D.C.: Government Printing Office, 1913.

——. Bureau of the Census. *Fourteenth Census of the United States, 1920: Population.* Washington, D.C.: Government Printing Office, 1921.

——. Bureau of the Census. Special Reports. *Mines and Quarries.* Washington, D.C.: Government Printing Office, 1902.

——. Bureau of the Census. Special Reports. *Mines and Quarries.* Washington, D.C.: Government Printing Office, 1909.

U.S. Department of the Interior. Census Office. *Seventh Census of the United States. 1850: Population.* Washington, D.C.: A. O. P. Nicholson, 1854.

——. Census Office. *Eighth Census of the United States, 1860: Population.* Washington, D.C.: Government Printing Office, 1864.

——. Census Office. *Ninth Census of the United States, 1870: Population.* Washington, D.C.: Government Printing Office, 1872.

——. Census Office. *Compendium of the Tenth Census: 1880.* Washington, D.C.: Government Printing Office, 1880.

——. Census Office. *Tenth Census of the United States, 1880: Population.* Washington, D.C.: Government Printing Office, 1883.

——. Census Office. *Eleventh Census of the United States, 1890: Population.* Washington, D.C.: Government Printing Office, 1895.

——. Census Office. *Manufactures of the United States in 1860.* Washington, D.C.: Government Printing Office, 1865.

——. Census Office. Manuscript Census Schedules, 1860. Microfilm edition.

——. Census Office. Manuscript Census Schedules, 1870. Microfilm edition.

——. Census Office. Manuscript Census Schedules, 1880. Microfilm edition.

U.S. Department of Labor. Mine Safety and Health Administration. H. B. Humphrey, *Historical Summary of Coal-Mine Explosions in the United States, 1810–1958.* Bulletin No. 586, 1998.

——. George O. Virtue, *The Anthracite Mine Laborers.* Bulletin No. 13, 1897.

U.S. Geological Survey. *Mineral Resources of the United States, Part II: Non-Metals, 1910–1925.* Washington, D.C.: Government Printing Office, 1925.

**U.S. State Documents**

*Colorado*

Adjutant General's Office. *Report of the Commanding General to the Governor for the Use of the Congressional Committee, The Military Occupation of the Coal Strike Zone of Colorado by the National Guard, 1913–1914.* Denver: Smith-Brooks Printing Company, 1914. Reprinted in *Massacre at Ludlow: Four Reports,* ed. Leon Stein and Philip Taft. New York: Arno and the New York Times, 1971.

*Illinois*

Bureau of Labor Statistics. *Bureau of Labor Statistics, Annual Coal Report, 1883.* Springfield: State Printer, 1884.

——. *Third Biennial Report, 1884.* Springfield: State Printer, 1885.

——. *Fifth Biennial Report, 1888.* Springfield: State Printer, 1889.

——. *Sixth Biennial Report, 1890.* Springfield: State Printer, 1891.

——. State Board of Commissioners of Labor. *Report of the Cherry Mine Disaster.* Springfield: State Printer, 1910.

*Ohio*

Inspector of Mines. *Second Annual Report of the State Mine Inspector, to the Governor of the State of Ohio, for the Year 1875.* Columbus: Nevins & Myers, State Printers, 1876.

——. *Sixth Annual Report of the State Inspector of Mines, to the Governor of Ohio, for the Year 1880.* Columbus: G. J. Brand, State Printer, 1881.

——. *Eighth Annual Report of the State Inspector of Mines to the Governor of the State of Ohio for the Year 1882.* Columbus: Westbote Company, State Printer, 1882.

——. *Thirtieth Annual Report of the Chief Inspector of Mines to the Governor of the State of Ohio, 1904.* Columbus: Fred J. Heer, State Printer, 1905.

——. Mining Commission. *Report of the Mining Commission Appointed under Joint*

*Resolution of the General Assembly of the State of Ohio, Passed May 2, 1871, to His Excellency the Governor Rutherford B. Hayes.* Columbus: Nevins & Myers, State Printers, 1872.

### Pennsylvania

Department of Internal Affairs. *Annual Report of the Secretary of Internal Affairs of the Commonwealth of Pennsylvania*, Part III, XXXI, Industrial Statistics, 1903. Harrisburg: State Printer, 1904.

——. *Annual Report of the Secretary of Internal Affairs of the Commonwealth of Pennsylvania*, Part III, XXXII. Industrial Statistics, 1904. Harrisburg: State Printer, 1905.

——. Inspector of Mines. *Reports of the Inspectors of Mines of the Anthracite Coal Regions of Pennsylvania.* Harrisburg: State Printer, 1870–1900.

——. Department of Mines. *Annual Report of the Pennsylvania Department of Mines, 1906*, Anthracite, Part I. Harrisburg: State Printer, 1907.

——. *Report of the Department of Mines of Pennsylvania*, Part I, Anthracite, 1915. Harrisburg: State Printer, 1916.

### Utah

Coal Mine Inspector. *Report of the Coal Mine Inspector for the State of Utah for the Years 1899 and 1900.* Salt Lake City: The Deseret News, 1901.

### West Virginia

Inspector of Mines. *First Annual Report of the State Inspector of Mines to the Governor of the State of West Virginia for the Year 1883.* Wheeling: Charles H. Taney, State Printer, 1884.

—— . *Reports of Mine Inspectors for the First, Second and Third Districts of West Virginia for the Years 1895 and 1896.* Charleston: Moses W. Donnally, Public Printer, 1896.

#### NEWSPAPERS AND PERIODICALS

*Aberdare (Wales) Times*
*Amalgamated Journal*
*Birmingham (Ala.) Age-Herald*
*Bluefield (W.Va.) Daily Telegraph*
*Cambrian*
*Canton (Ohio) Daily News*
*Cardiff and Merthyr (Wales) Guardian*
*Charleston (W.Va.) Gazette*
*Colliery Engineer and Metal Miner* (London)
*Colliery Guardian* (London)
*Druid*

*Hazleton (Pa.) Daily Standard*

*Logan (Ohio) Republican Gazette*

*Merthyr (Wales) Star*

*Miner and Workingman's Advocate* (London)

*Miners' National Record* (Ohio)

*Montgomery (W.Va.) News*

*National Labor Tribune* (Pittsburgh)

*New Lexington (Ohio) Herald*

*New York Times*

*NINNAU*

*Philadelphia Public Ledger*

*Pottsville (Pa.) Miners Journal*

*Scranton Morning Republican*

*Times* (London)

*Transactions of the American Institute of Mining Engineers*

*United Mine Workers Journal*

*Wheeling Intelligencer*

*Wilkes-Barre Public Ledger*

*Wilkes-Barre Record*

*Wilkes-Barre Union Ledger*

*Workingman's Advocate* (Chicago)

*Workman's Advocate* (London)

## BOOKS AND ARTICLES, THESES AND DISSERTATIONS

Adams, Sean Patrick. *Old Dominion, Industrial Commonwealth: Coal, Politics, and Economy in Antebellum America*. Baltimore: Johns Hopkins University Press, 2004.

Alexander, Ronald R. *West Virginia Tech: A History*. Charleston: Pictorial Histories Publishing Co., 1992.

Aley, Howard C. *A Heritage to Share: The Bicentennial History of Youngstown and Mahoning County, Ohio*. Youngstown: Bicentennial Commission, 1979.

Alinsky, Saul. *John L. Lewis: An Unauthorized Biography*. New York: G. P. Putnam and Sons, 1949.

*The American, Which Contains Notes on a Journey from the Ohio Valley to Wales*. Translated and reprinted in *Quarterly Publications of the Historical and Philosophical Society of Ohio* 6 (1911): 1–41.

Armes, Ethel. *The Story of Coal and Iron in Alabama*. Birmingham: Birmingham Chamber of Commerce, 1910.

Ashton, Elwyn T. *The Welsh in the United States*. Hove, Sussex, England: Caldra House Ltd., 1984.

Ashton, Thomas S., and Joseph Sykes. *Coal Industry of the Eighteenth Century*. Manchester: Manchester University Press, 1929.

Athey, Louis L. "William Nelson Page: Traditionalist Entrepreneur of the Virginias."
	*West Virginia History* 45 (1984): 41–59.
Aurand, Harold W. *Coalcracker Culture: Work and Values in Pennsylvania Anthracite,
	1835–1935*. Selingrove, Pa.: Susquehanna University Press, 2003.
———. *From the Molly Maguires to the United Mine Workers: The Social Ecology of an
	Industrial Union, 1869–1897*. Philadelphia: Temple University Press, 1971.
———. "The Lattimer Massacre: Who Owns History?—An Introduction."
	*Pennsylvania History* 68 (Winter 2002): 5–10.
Baines, Dudley. *Emigration from Europe, 1815–1930*. 2nd ed. Cambridge: Cambridge
	University Press, 1995.
———. *Migration in a Mature Economy: Emigration and Internal Migration in England
	and Wales, 1861–1900*. Cambridge: Cambridge University Press, 1985.
Barkey, Fred A. "Working Class Political Activity in the New River Coal Fields of
	Fayette County, West Virginia, 1897–1916." *Proceedings: New River Symposium*,
	April 9–11, 1987, Boone, N.C.
Battlo, Jean. "Jones Mansion: The Checkered History of a McDowell County
	Landmark." *Goldenseal* 31 (Summer 2005): 52–57.
Becker, Martha Jane Williams. *Bramwell: The Diary of a Millionaire Coal Town*.
	Logan, W.Va.: privately published, 1998.
Beik, Mildred Allen. *The Miners of Windber: The Struggles of New Immigrants for
	Unionization, 1890s–1930s*. University Park: Penn State University Press, 1996.
———. "The Significance of the Lattimer Massacre: Who Owns Its History?"
	*Pennsylvania History* 68 (Winter 2002): 58–70.
Bender, Thomas, ed. *Rethinking American History in a Global Age*. Berkeley:
	University of California Press, 2002.
Bendix, Reinhard, and Frank W. Howton. "Social Mobility and the American
	Business Elite." In *Social Mobility in Industrial Society*, ed. Reinhard Bendix and
	Seymour M. Lipset, 114–43. Berkeley: University of California Press, 1959.
Bendix, Reinhard, and Seymour M. Lipset, eds. *Social Mobility in Industrial Society*.
	Berkeley: University of California Press, 1959.
Bensel, Richard Franklin. *The Political Economy of American Industrialization, 1877–
	1900*. Cambridge: Cambridge University Press, 2000.
Benson, John. *British Coal Miners in the Nineteenth Century: A Social History*. New
	York: Holmes and Meier, Publishers, 1980.
Berthoff, Rowland Tappan. *British Immigrants in Industrial America, 1790–1950*.
	Cambridge, Mass.: Harvard University Press, 1953.
———. "Peasants and Artisans, Puritans and Republicans: Personal Liberty and
	Communal Equality in American History." *Journal of American History* 69
	(December 1982): 579–98.
———. "Welsh." In *Harvard Encyclopedia of American Ethnic Groups*, ed. Stephan
	Thernstrom, 1011–17. Cambridge, Mass.: Harvard University Press, 1980.
Beshoar, Barron B. *Out of the Depths: The Story of John R. Lawson, a Labor Leader*.
	Denver: Denver Trades and Labor Assembly, 1942.

Blatz, Perry. *Democratic Miners: Work and Labor Relations in the Anthracite Industry, 1875–1925*. Albany: State University of New York Press, 1994.

——. "Reflections on Lattimer: A Complex and Significant Event." *Pennsylvania History* 68 (Winter 2002): 42–51.

Blewett, Mary H. *Constant Turmoil: The Politics of Industrial Life in Nineteenth-Century New England*. Amherst: University of Massachusetts Press, 2000.

——. *Men, Women, and Work: Class, Gender, and Protest in the New England Shoe Industry*. Urbana: University of Illinois Press, 1988.

Bodnar, John. "Socialization and Adaptation: Immigrant Families in Scranton, 1880–1890." *Pennsylvania History* 43 (April 1976): 147–62.

——. *The Transplanted: A History of Immigration in Urban America*. Bloomington: Indiana University Press, 1985.

Borrow, George. *Wild Wales: Its People, Language, and Scenery*. London: Collins, 1928, orig. 1862.

Boston, Ray. *Chartists in America, 1839–1900*. Totawa, N.J.: Rowman and Littlefield, 1983.

Bowen, Emrys G. "Welsh Emigration Overseas." *Advancement of Science* 17 (September 1960): 260–71.

Boyle, James. *The Minimum Wage and Syndicalism*. Cincinnati: Stewart and Kidd, 1913.

Bradsby, H. C. *History of Luzerne County, Pennsylvania, with Biographical Selections*. Chicago: S. B. Nelson & Company, 1893.

Brenckman, Fred. *History of Carbon County, Pennsylvania*. Harrisburg: James J. Nungesser, 1913.

Brennan, T., E. W. Cooney, and H. Pollins. *Social Change in South-West Wales*. London: Watts & Company, 1954.

Broehl, Wayne G., Jr. *The Molly Maguires*. New York: Vintage, 1964.

Brophy, John. *A Miner's Life*. Madison: University of Wisconsin Press, 1964.

Browning, Charles H. *Welsh Settlement of Pennsylvania*. Philadelphia: W. J. Campbell, 1912.

Bryce, James. *The American Commonwealth*. 2 vols. New York: Macmillan, 1888.

Bukowczyk, John J. "*The Transplanted*: Immigrants and Ethnics." *Social Science History* 12 (Fall 1988): 233–41.

Burgoyne, Arthur G. *Homestead*. 1893. Reprint, Pittsburgh: University of Pittsburgh Press, 1979.

Butler, Joseph G., Jr. *History of Youngstown and the Mahoning Valley, Ohio*. 3 vols. Chicago and New York: American Historical Society, 1921.

Campbell, Sandra. "For 110, the 'Fine' Avondale Mine Was a Tomb." *Mine Safety and Health* 4 (January–February 1980): 17–21.

Carnegie, Andrew. *Triumphant Democracy, or Fifty Years' March of the Republic*. New York: Scribner, 1886.

Casson, Herbert N. "The Welsh in America." *Munsey's Magazine* 25 (September 1906): 749–54.

Cawelti, John G. *Apostles of the Self-Made Man: Changing Concepts of Success in America*. Chicago: University of Chicago Press, 1965.

Chandler, Alfred, Jr. "Anthracite Coal and the Beginnings of the Industrial Revolution in the United States." *Business History Review* 46 (Summer 1972): 141–81.

——. *The Visible Hand: The Managerial Revolution in American Business*. Cambridge, Mass.: Harvard University Press, 1977.

Chase, H. W. *An Account of the Unparalleled Disaster at the Avondale Colliery, Luzerne County, Pa., September 6th, 1869, By Which One Hundred and Ten Lives Were Lost*. Scranton: J. B. Furman, 1869.

Church, Roy A. *History of the British Coal Industry, 1830–1913: vol. 3, Victorian Preeminence*. Oxford: Oxford University Press, 1986.

Clark, Donald Otis. "John Elias Williams (1853–1919)—Labor Peacemaker: A Study of the Life of an Early Illinois Mediator and Abitrator and His Impact upon the American Labor Movement." Master's thesis, University of Illinois, 1956.

"The Coal Mine Calamity Supplement." *Frank Leslie's Illustrated Newspaper* 29 (September 25, 1869).

Cochran, Thomas, and William Miller. *The Age of Enterprise: A Social History of Industrial America*. New York: Macmillan Company, 1961.

Cohen, Isaac. "Monopoly, Competition, and Collective Bargaining: Pennsylvania and South Wales Compared." In *The United Mine Workers of America: A Model of Industrial Solidarity?*, ed. John H. M. Laslett, 395–416. University Park: Penn State University Press, 1996.

Coleman, J. Walter. "Labor Disturbances in Pennsylvania, 1850–1880." Ph.D. diss., Catholic University of America, 1936.

Commons, John R., et al. *History of Labor in the United States*. 4 vols. New York: Macmillan, 1935–36.

Conway, Alan. "Welsh Emigration to the United States." In *Perspectives in American History: Dislocation and Emigration: The Social Background of American Immigration*, vol. 7, ed. Donald Fleming and Bernard Bailyn, 177–271. Cambridge, Mass.: Charles Warren Center for Studies in American History, Harvard University, 1974.

——, ed. *The Welsh in America: Letters from the Immigrants*. Minneapolis: University of Minnesota Press, 1961.

——. "Welshmen in the Union Armies." *Civil War History* 4 (June 1958): 143–74.

Corbin, David Alan. *Life, Work, and Rebellion in the Coal Fields: The Southern West Virginia Miners, 1880–1922*. Urbana: University of Illinois Press, 1981.

Council, R. Bruce, Nicholas Honerkamp, and M. Elizabeth Will. *Industrial Technology in Antebellum Tennessee: The Archaeology of Bluff Furnace*. Knoxville: University of Tennessee Press, 1992.

Cox, William E. *A Pictorial History of the New River Gorge*. N.p.: Eastern National Park and Monument Association, 1984.

Curran, Daniel J. *Dead Laws for Dead Men: The Politics of Federal Coal Mine Health and Safety Legislation*. Pittsburgh: University of Pittsburgh Press, 1993.

Daddow, Samual Harries, and Benjamin Bannan. *Coal, Iron, and Oil, or the Practical American Miner*. Pottsville: Benjamin Bannan, 1866.

Daniels, Roger. *Coming to America: A History of Immigration and Ethnicity in American Life*. New York: Harper Collins, 2002, orig. 1990.

Danner, John. *Old Landmarks of Canton and Stark County, Ohio*. Logansport, Ind.: B. F. Bowan, 1904.

Davies, Douglas James. *Mormon Spirituality: Latter Day Saints in Wales and Zion*. Nottingham: University of Nottingham, 1987.

Davies, Edward J., II. *The Anthracite Aristocracy: Leadership and Social Change in the Hard Coal Regions of Northeastern Pennsylvania, 1800–1930*. DeKalb: Northern Illinois University Press, 1985.

Davies, E. T. *Religion in the Industrial Revolution in South Wales*. Cardiff: University of Wales Press, 1965.

Davies, Hywel. " 'Very Different Springs of Uneasiness': Emigration from Wales to the USA in the 1790s." *Welsh History Review* 15 (June 1991): 368–98.

Davies, John. "Authority, Community, and Conflict: Rioting and Aftermath in Late-Nineteenth Century Pennsylvania." *Pennsylvania History* 66 (Summer 1999): 339–63.

———. *A History of Wales*. London: Allen Lane, Penguin Press, 1993.

Davies, Phillips G. "The Welsh in Missouri: An Account of Their Arrival, Settlements, and Contributions." *Midwest Review* 14 (1992): 47–62.

Davies, Walter Haydn. *The Right Place, The Right Time: Memories of Boyhood Days in a Welsh Mining District*. Swansea: Christopher Davies, 1975.

Dawley, Alan. *Class and Community: The Industrial Revolution in Lynn*. Cambridge, Mass.: Harvard University Press, 1976.

DeVault, Ileen A. *United Apart: Gender and the Rise of Craft Unionism*. Ithaca: Cornell University Press, 2004.

Dewees, Francis P. *The Molly Maguires: The Origins, Growth, and Character of the Organization*. Philadelphia: J. B. Lippincott & Co., 1877.

Dilley, J. W. *History of the Scofield Mine Disaster*. Provo: Skelton Publishing, 1900.

Dix, Keith. *What's a Coal Miner to Do? The Mechanization of Coal Mining*. Pittsburgh: University of Pittsburgh Press, 1988.

Dodd, A. H. *The Character of Early Welsh Emigration to the United States*. Cardiff: University of Wales Press, 1953.

———. *The Industrial Revolution in North Wales*. Cardiff: University of Wales Press, 1933.

Dubofsky, Melvyn, and Warren Van Tine. *John L. Lewis: A Biography*. New York: Quadrangle / New York Times Book Company, 1977.

DuBose, John Witherspoon. *Jefferson County and Birmingham, Alabama: Historical and Biographical*. Birmingham: Caldwell Printing, 1887.

Duckham, Helen, and Baron Duckham. *Great Pit Disasters*. Newton Abbot: David and Charles, 1973.

Duke, David. *Writers and Miners: Activism and Imagery in America*. Lexington: University Press of Kentucky, 2002.

Easterlin, Richard A. *Population, Labor Force, and Long Swings in Economic Growth: The American Experience*. Cambridge, Mass.: National Bureau of Economic Research, 1968.

Eavenson, Howard N. *The First Century and a Quarter of American Coal Industry*. Pittsburgh: By the Author, 1942.

Eller, Ronald D. *Miners, Millhands, and Mountaineers: Industrialization of the Appalachian South, 1880–1930*. Knoxville: University of Tennessee Press, 1982.

Elliott, Bruce S., David A. Gerber, and Suzanne M. Sinke. *Letters across Borders: The Epistolary Practices of International Migrants*. New York: Palgrave Macmillan, 2006.

Erickson, Charlotte J. "Encouragement of Emigration by British Trade Unions." *Population Studies* 3 (1949): 248–73.

——. *Invisible Immigrants: The Adaptation of English and Scottish Immigrants in 19th Century America*. Ithaca: Cornell University Press, 1972.

Evans, Chris. *History of the United Mine Workers of America from the Year 1860 to 1890*. 2 vols. Indianapolis: n.p., 1918 [?].

——. *"The Labyrinth of Flames": Work and Social Conflict in Early Industrial Merthyr Tydfil*. Cardiff: University of Wales Press, 1993.

Evans, D. Gareth. *A History of Wales, 1815–1906*. Cardiff: University of Wales Press, 1989.

Evans, E. C. "Census Reports of the Welsh Population in the United States from 1850–1890." *Cambrian* 13 (April 1893): 131–38.

Evans, E. W. *The Miners of South Wales*. Cardiff: University of Wales Press, 1961.

Evans, Neil. " 'As Rich as California . . .': Opening and Closing the Frontier: Wales 1780–1870." In *The People of Wales*, ed. Gareth Elwyn Jones and Dai Smith, 111–44. Llandysul, Ceredigion: Gomer Press, 1999.

Evans, Rev. W. R. "Trusts and Trade Union." *Cambrian* 23 (April 1903): 133–36.

Falzone, Vincent J. "Terence V. Powderly: Politician and Progressive Mayor of Scranton, 1878–1884." *Pennsylvania History* 41 (July 1974): 289–309.

Fetherling, Dale. *Mother Jones the Miners' Angel*. Carbondale: Southern Illinois University Press, 1974.

Fink, Gary M., ed. *Biographical Directory of American Labor*. Westport, Conn.: Greenwood Press, 1984.

Fink, Walter H. *The Ludlow Massacre*. Privately printed, 1914. Reprinted in *Massacre at Ludlow: Four Reports*. Privately printed, 1914.

Foner, Eric. *Free Soil, Free Labor, Free Men: The Ideology of the Republican Party before the Civil War*. New York: Oxford University Press, 1970.

Fones-Wolf, Ken. "Transatlantic Craft Migrations and Transnational Spaces:

Belgian Window Glass Workers in America, 1880–1920." *Labor History* 40 (Aug. 2004): 299–321.

Fox, Mair B. *United We Stand: The United Mine Workers of America, 1890–1990.* Washington, D.C.: United Mine Workers of America, 1990.

Francis, Hywel, and Dai Smith. *The Fed: A History of the South Wales Miners in the Twentieth Century.* 1980. Cardiff: University of Wales Press, 1998.

Fraser, Marianne. "Warm Winters and White Rabbits: Folklore of Welsh and English Coal Miners." *Utah Historical Quarterly* 51 (Summer 1983): 246–58.

Fuller, Justin. "History of the Tennessee Coal, Iron, and Railroad Company, 1852–1907." Ph.D. diss., University of North Carolina, 1966.

Gabaccia, Donna. *From the Other Side: Women, Gender, and Immigrant Life in the U.S., 1820–1990.* Bloomington: Indiana University Press, 1994.

Geary, Dick. "The Myth of the Radical Miner." In *Towards a Comparative History of Coalfield Societies,* ed. Stefan Berger, Andy Croll, and Norman LaPorte, 43–64. London: Ashgate Publishing, 2005.

Gibbons, Phoebe E. "The Miners of Scranton, Pa." *Harper's New Monthly Magazine* 55 (November 1877): 916–27.

Gibson, R. M. *History of Shawnee.* N.p.: n.p., 1973. (Copy in Ohio University Archive, Athens, Ohio.)

Ginger, Ray. "Managerial Employees in Anthracite, 1902: A Study in Occupational Mobility." *Journal of Economic History* 14 (Spring 1954): 146–57.

Glenn, Thomas A. *Welsh Founders of Pennsylvania.* 1911. Reprint, Baltimore: Genealogical Publishing Co., 1970.

Goodrich, Carter. *The Miners' Freedom.* Boston: Marshall Jones, 1925.

Gorn, Elliot J. *Mother Jones: The Most Dangerous Woman in America.* New York: Hill and Wang, 2001.

Gottlieb, Amy Zahl. "British Coal Miners: A Demographic Study of Braidwood and Streator, Illinois." *Journal of the Illinois State Historical Society* 72 (August 1979): 179–92.

———. "Immigration of British Coal Miners in the Civil War Decade." *International Review of Social History* 23 (1978): 357–75.

———. "The Regulation of the Coal Mining Industry in Illinois with Special Reference to the Influence of British Miners and British Precedents, 1870–1911." Ph.D. diss., University of London, 1975.

Green, Archie. *Only a Miner: Studies in Recorded Coal-Mining Songs.* Urbana: University of Illinois Press, 1972.

Greene, Victor R. *The Slavic Community on Strike: Immigrant Labor in Pennsylvania Anthracite.* Notre Dame: University of Notre Dame Press, 1968.

Greenwald, Maurine Weiner. Introduction to Elizabeth Beardsley Butler, *Women and the Trades, Pittsburgh, 1907–1908.* 1909. Reprint, Pittsburgh: University of Pittsburgh Press, 1984.

Griffiths, Robert Huw. "The Welsh and the American Civil War." Ph.D. diss., University of Wales-Cardiff, 2004.

Grismer, Karl H. *Akron and Summit County.* Akron: Summit County Historical Society, 1952.

Grob, Gerald N. *Workers and Utopia: A Study of Ideological Conflict in the American Labor Movement, 1865–1900.* Evanston: Northwestern University Press, 1961.

Gudelunas, William A., Jr., and William G. Shade. *Before the Molly Maguires: The Emergence of the Ethno-Religious Factor in the Politics of the Lower Anthracite Region, 1844–1872.* New York: Arno Press, 1976.

Gutman, Herbert G. "The Braidwood Lockout of 1874." *Journal of the Illinois State Historical Society* 53 (Spring 1960): 5–28.

——. *Work, Culture and Society in Industrializing America: Studies in American Labor and Social History.* New York: Vintage Books, 1966.

Gwyther, Cyril E. "Sidelights on Religion and Politics in the Rhondda Valley, 1906–26." *Llafur* 3 (Spring 1980): 32–35.

Hager, Beth A. "Millionaires' Town: The Houses and People of Bramwell." *Goldenseal* 8 (Winter 1982): 43–54.

Haines, Michael R. "Fertility, Marriage, and Occupation in the Pennsylvania Anthracite Region, 1850–1880." *Journal of Family History* 2 (Spring 1977): 28–55.

Hansen, Marcus Lee. *The Atlantic Migration, 1607–1860.* Cambridge, Masss.: Harvard University Press, 1940.

Harrison, Roysdon, ed. *Independent Collier: The Coal Miner as Archetypal Proletarian Reconsidered.* Hassocks, England: Harvester, 1978.

Hartmann, Edward G. *Americans from Wales.* 1967. Reprint, New York: Octagon Books, 1983.

Harvey, Katherine A. *The Best-Dressed Miners: Life and Labor in the Maryland Coal Region, 1835–1910.* Ithaca: Cornell University Press, 1969.

Higham, John. "Current Trends in the Study of Ethnicity in the United States." *Journal of American Ethnic History* 2 (Fall 1982): 5–15.

Hirsh, Mark Gary. "Coal Miners and the American Republic: Trade Union Ideology in the Anthracite Region of Pennsylvania, 1875–1902." PhD. diss., Harvard University, 1984.

*History of Fayette County, West Virginia.* Oak Hill, W.Va.: Fayette County Chamber of Commerce, 1993.

Hobsbawm, Eric J. *Labouring Men: Studies in the History of Labour.* London: Weidenfeld and Nicholson, 1968.

Hoerder, Dirk. *Cultures in Contact: World Migrations in the Second Millennium.* Durham, N.C.: Duke University Press, 2002.

Holland, John. *The History and Description of Fossil Fuel, the Collieries, and Coal Trade of Great Britain.* London: Whittaker & Co., 1841.

Holmes, G. M. "The South Wales Coal Industry, 1850–1914." *Transactions of the Honourable Society of Cymmrodorion* (1976): 162–207.

Horowitz, Irving. *Power, Politics and People: Collected Essays of C. Wright Mills.* New York: Oxford University Press, 1963.

Humphries, Jane. " 'Most Free From Objection': The Sexual Division of Labor and Women's Work in Nineteenth-Century England." *Journal of Economic History* 47 (December 1987): 929–49.

——. "Protective Legislation, the Capitalist State, and Working Class Men: The Case of the 1842 Mines Regulation Act." *Feminist Review* 7 (Spring 1981): 1–33.

——. "Working-Class Family, Women's Liberation and Class Struggle: The Case of Nineteenth-Century British History." *Review of Radical Political Economics* 9 (Fall 1977): 25–42.

Humphries, John. *The Man from the Alamo: Why the Welsh Chartist Uprising of 1839 Ended in a Massacre.* Porth Glyndwr, Glamorgan: Glyndwr Publishing, 2004.

Hunter, Jerry. *Sons of Arthur, Children of Lincoln: Welsh Writing from the American Civil War.* Cardiff: University of Wales Press, 2007.

Hutchinson, John. "John L. Lewis: To the Presidency of the UMWA." *Labor History* 19 (Spring 1978): 185–203.

Ignatiev, Noel. *How the Irish Became White.* New York: Routledge, 1995.

Itter, William A. "Early Labor Troubles in the Anthracite District." *Pennsylvania History* 1 (January 1934): 28–37.

Jenkins, Geraint H. *The Foundation of Modern Wales, 1642–1780.* Oxford: Oxford University Press, 1993.

Jenkins, Geraint H., and Mari A. Williams. "The Fortunes of the Welsh Language, 1900–2000: Introduction." In *"Let's Do Our Best for the Ancient Tongue": The Welsh Language in the Twentieth Century,* ed. Geraint H. Jenkins and Mari A. Williams, 1–27. Cardiff: University of Wales Press, 2000.

Jenkins, Philip. *A History of Modern Wales, 1536–1990.* Harlow, Essex: Addison Wesley Longman, 1992.

John, A. H. *The Industrial Development of South Wales, 1750–1850: An Essay.* Cardiff: University of Wales Press, 1950.

John, Angela V. *By the Sweat of Their Brow: Women Workers at Victorian Coal Mines.* London: Routledge and Kegan Paul, 1984.

"John Owens." *Fortune* 34 (November 1946): 146.

Johnston, Alexander K. *England and Wales.* Edinburgh: William Blackwood and Sons, 1861. Engraving available at David Rumsey Map Collection <www.davidramsey.com/maps398.html>

Johnston, W. Ross. "The Welsh Diaspora: Emigrating around the World in the Late Nineteenth Century." *Llafur* 6, no. 2 (1993): 50–74.

Jones, Aled Gruffydd. *Press, Politics and Society: A History of Journalism in Wales.* Cardiff: University of Wales Press, 1993.

Jones, Aled, and Bill Jones. *Welsh Reflections: Y Drych and America, 1851–2001.* Llandysul, Ceredigion: Gomer Press, 2001.

——. "*Y Drych* and American Welsh Identities, 1851–1951." *North American Journal of Welsh Studies* 1 (Winter 2001): 42–58.

Jones, Bill. "Banqueting at a Moveable Feast: Wales 1870–1914." In *The People of*

*Wales*, ed. Gareth Elwyn Jones and Dai Smith, 145–78. Llandysul, Ceredigion: Gomer Press, 1999.

——. "Ethnic Journalism and the Reconstruction of Identity: The Welsh-Language Press in the USA in the Nineteenth and Early Twentieth Centuries." Paper presented at the Rush D. Holt Conference, West Virginia University, April 2003.

——. "Inspecting the 'Extraordinary Drain': Emigration and the Urban Experience in Merthyr Tydfil in the 1860s." *Urban History* 32 (May 2005): 100–113.

——. " 'Raising the Wind': Emigrating from Wales to the USA in the Late Nineteenth and Early Twentieth Centuries." Annual Public Lecture 2003. Cardiff Centre for Welsh American Studies, Cardiff University, 2004.

——. " 'We Will Give You Wings to Fly': Emigration Societies in Merthyr Tydfil in 1868." *Merthyr Historian* 13 (2001): 27–45.

Jones, Bill, and Huw Walters. "On the American Frontier: Amman Valley Emigrants in Texas, 1879–1880." *Carmarthenshire Antiquary* 37 (2001): 73–78.

Jones, David. *Memorial Volume of the Welsh Congregationalists in Pennsylvania, U.S.A.* Utica, N.Y.: Utica Printing Co., 1934.

Jones, David J. V. *Before Rebecca: Popular Protest in Wales, 1793–1835.* London: Allen Lane, 1973.

——. *The Last Rising: The Newport Chartist Insurrection of 1839.* Cardiff: University of Wales Press, 1999.

Jones, Emrys. "Some Aspects of Cultural Change in an American Welsh Community." *Transactions of the Honourable Society of Cymmrodorion* (1954): 15–41.

Jones, Erasmus W. "The Welsh in America." *Atlantic Monthly* 37 (March 1876): 305–13.

Jones, Francis. "An Approach to Welsh Genealogy." *Transactions of the Honourable Society of Cymmrodorion* (1948): 303–466.

Jones, Gareth Elwyn, and Dai Smith, eds. *People of Wales.* Llandysul, Ceredigion: Gomer Press, 1999.

Jones, I. G. *Explorations and Explanations: Essays in the Social History of Victorian Wales.* Llandysul, Ceredigion: Gomer Press, 1981.

Jones, Maldwyn A. "The Background to Emigration from Great Britain in the Nineteenth Century." In *Perspectives in American History, Dislocation and Emigration: The Social Background of American Immigration*, vol. 7, ed. Donald Fleming and Bernard Bailyn, 2–92. Cambridge, Mass.: Charles Warren Center for Studies in American History, Harvard University, 1974.

——. "From the Old Country to the New: The Welsh in Nineteenth-Century America." *Flintshire Historical Society Publications* 27 (1975–76): 85–100.

——. "Welsh-Americans and the Anti-Slavery Movement in the United States." *Transactions of the Honourable Society of Cymmrodorion* (1985): 105–29.

Jones, R. Merfyn. "Beyond Identity? The Reconstruction of the Welsh." *Journal of British Studies* 31 (October 1992): 330–57.

Jones, Rosemary A. N. "Women, Community and Collective Action: The *Ceffyl Pren* Tradition." In *In Our Mothers' Land: Chapters in Welsh Women's History, 1830–1939*, ed. Angela V. John, 17–41. Cardiff: University of Wales Press, 1991.

Jones, Wendell M. "The Gymanfa Ganu." Master's thesis, Ohio State University, 1946.

Jones, William D. " 'Going into Print': Published Immigrant Letters, Webs of Personal Relations, and the Emergence of the Welsh Public Sphere." In *Letters across Borders: The Epistolary Practices of International Migrants*, ed. Bruce S. Elliott, David A. Gerber, and Suzanne M. Sinke, 175–99. New York: Palgrave Macmillan, 2006.

———. "Wales in America: Scranton and the Welsh, 1860–1920." Ph.D. diss., University of Wales, Cardiff, 1987.

———. *Wales in America: Scranton and the Welsh, 1860–1920*. Cardiff: University of Wales Press, 1993.

———. "The Welsh Language and Welsh Identity in a Pennsylvania Community." In *Language and Community in the Nineteenth Century*, ed. Geraint H. Jenkins, 261–86. Cardiff: University of Wales Press, 1998.

Joyce, Richard Patrick. "Miners of the Prairie: Life and Labor in the Wilmington, Illinois, Coal Field, 1866–1897." Master's thesis, Illinois State University, 1980.

Keen, Richard G. *Llynfi, Garw and Ogmore Valleys in Old Photographs*. Barry, Glamorgan: Geraint Williams, 1981.

Kenfield, Scott Dix, ed. *Akron and Summit County, Ohio, 1825–1928*. Vol. 1. Akron: S. J. Clarke Publishing Company, 1928.

Kenny, Kevin. "Diaspora and Comparison: The Global Irish as a Case Study." *Journal of American History* 90 (June 2003): 134–62.

———. *Making Sense of the Molly Maguires*. New York: Oxford University Press, 1998.

———. "Nativism, Labor, and Slavery: The Political Odyssey of Benjamin Bannan, 1850–1860." *Pennsylvania Magazine of History and Biography* 118 (October 1994): 325–61.

Kerr, K. Austin. "The Movement for Coal Mine Safety in Nineteenth-Century Ohio." *Ohio History* 86 (Winter 1977): 3–18.

Kessler-Harris, Alice. *Out to Work: A History of Wage-Earning Women in the United States*. New York: Oxford University Press, 1982.

Kirkland, Edward Chase. *Industry Comes of Age: Business, Labor, and Public Policy, 1860–1897*. New York: Holt, Rinehart and Winston, 1961.

Knowles, Anne Kelly. *Calvinists Incorporated: Welsh Immigrants on Ohio's Industrial Frontier*. Chicago: University of Chicago Press, 1997.

———. "Immigrant Trajectories through the Rural-Industrial Transition in Wales and the United States, 1795–1850." *Annals of the Association of American Geographers* 85, no. 2 (1995): 246–66.

———. "Migration, Nationalism, and the Construction of Welsh Identity." In *Nested Identities: Nationalism, Territory, and Scale*, ed. Gunstram H. Herb and David H. Kaplan, 289–315. New York: Rowman & Littlefield, 1999.

Korson, George. *Minstrels of the Mine Patch: Songs and Stories of the Anthracite Industry.* Philadelphia: University of Pennsylvania Press, 1938.

Krause, Paul. *The Battle for Homestead, 1880–1892.* Pittsburgh: University of Pittsburgh Press, 1992.

*La Pietra Report: Project on Internationalizing the Study of American History.* New York: New York University and Organization of American Historians, 2000.

Lane, Samuel A. *Fifty Years and Over in Akron and Summit County.* Akron: Beacon Job Department, 1892.

Laslett, John H. M. "British Immigrant Colliers, and the Origins and Early Development of the UMWA, 1870–1912." In *The United Mine Workers of America: A Model of Industrial Solidarity?* ed. John H. M. Laslett, 29–50. University Park: Penn State University Press, 1996.

——. *Colliers across the Sea: A Comparative Study of Class Formation in Scotland and the American Midwest, 1830–1924.* Urbana: University of Illinois Press, 2000.

——. *Nature's Noblemen: The Fortunes of the Independent Collier in Scotland and the American Midwest, 1855–1889.* Los Angeles: Institute of Industrial Relations, University of California, Los Angeles, 1983.

——, ed. *The United Mine Workers of America: A Model of Industrial Solidarity?* State College: Penn State University Press, 1996.

Levine, Susan. *Labor's True Woman: Carpet Weavers, Industrialization, and Labor Reform in the Gilded Age.* Philadelphia: Temple University Press, 1984.

Lewis, Ronald L. *Black Coal Miners in America: Race, Class, and Community, 1780–1980.* Lexington: University Press of Kentucky, 1989.

——, ed. "Letter from John A. Williams of Algoma Mine to Mr. and Mrs. William Thomas of Brynawel, Aberdare, Wales, 1895." *West Virginia History* n.s. 1 (Fall 2007): 69–89.

——. "Networking Among Welsh Coal Miners in Nineteenth-Century America." In *Towards a Comparative History of Coalfield Societies,* ed. Stefan Berger, Andy Croll, and Norman LaPorte, 191–203. London: Ashgate Publishing, 2005.

Lewis, E. D. *The Rhondda Valleys.* Cardiff: University of Wales Press, 1959.

Lieven, Michael. *Senghennydd: The Universal Pit Village, 1890–1930.* Llandysull, Dyfed, Wales: Gomer Press, 1994.

Llewellyn, Richard. *How Green Was My Valley.* New York: Simon and Schuster, 1939.

Long, Priscilla. *Where the Sun Never Shines: A History of America's Bloody Coal Industry.* New York: Paragon House, 1989.

——. "The Women of the Colorado Fuel and Iron Strike, 1913–14." In *Women, Work and Protest: A Century of US Women's Labor History,* ed. Ruth Milkman, 62–85. Boston: Routledge & Kegan Paul, 1985.

MacDonagh, O. O. G. M. "Coal Mines Regulation: The First Decade, 1842–1852." In *Ideas and Institutions of Victorian Britain: Essays in Honour of George Kitson Clark,* ed. Robert Robson, 58–86. New York: Barnes and Noble, 1967.

MacFarlane, James. *The Coal-Regions of America: Their Topography, Geology, and Development.* New York: D. Appleton, 1875.

MacLean, Annie Marion. "Life in the Pennsylvania Coal Fields with Particular Reference to Women." *American Journal of Sociology* 14 (November 1908): 329–51.

Magda, Matthew S. "Welsh in Pennsylvania." Pennsylvania Historical and Museum Commission, 4 pages. <http://www.phmc.state.pa.us/ppet/Welsh/>

Margolis, Eric. "Western Coal Mining as a Way of Life: An Oral History of the Colorado Coal Miners to 1914." *Journal of the West* 24 (July 1985): 11–111.

Marsh, William A., comp. *1880 Census of West Virginia: Fayette County.* Vol. 4. Baltimore: Gateway Press, 1982.

May, Martha. "Bread Before Roses: American Workingmen, Labor Unions and the Family Wage." In *Women, Work and Protest: A Century of US Women's Labor History,* ed. Ruth Milkman, 2–21. Boston: Routledge & Kegan Paul, 1985.

McBride, John. "Coal Miners." In *The Labor Movement: The Problem of Today.* In *Proceedings, National Federation of Miners and Mine Laborers, 1886,* ed. George E. McNeill, 241–67. Boston: A. M. Bridgman & Co., 1887.

McClelland, Keith. "Some Thoughts on Masculinity and the 'Representative Artisan' in Britain, 1850–1880." *Gender & History* 1 (Summer 1989): 164–77.

McCormick, Michael R. "A Comparative Study of Coal Mining Communities in Northern Illinois and Southern Ohio in the Late Nineteenth Century." PhD. diss., Ohio State University, 1978.

McGehee, Stuart. "Cooper Family." *Coal People Magazine* (n.d.): 16–17. Photocopy in Eastern Regional Coal Archives, Craft Memorial Library, Bluefield, W.Va.

———. "Jenkinjones Fights Back." *Coal People Magazine* (1990): 13–15. Photocopy in Eastern Regional Coal Archives, Craft Memorial Library, Bluefield, W.Va.

McGovern, George S., and Leonard F. Guttridge. *The Great Coalfield War.* Boston: Houghton Mifflin, 1972.

*Meigs County, Ohio, from Hardesty's Historical and Geographical Encyclopedia, 1883.* 1883. Reprint, Defiance, Ohio: Hubbard Company, for Meigs County Pioneer and Historical Society, 1982.

*Men of West Virginia.* Vol. 2. Chicago: Biographical Publishing Co., 1903.

Milan, Noel. "Winter Quarters Explosion, Part 2: The Disaster That Killed 200." *Mine Safety and Health* 6 (December 1981–January 1982): 14–20.

Milkman, Ruth, ed. "Organizing the Sexual Division of Labor: Historical Perspectives on 'Women's Work' and the American Labor Movement." *Socialist Review* (January–February 1980): 95–144.

———. *Women, Work and Protest: A Century of US Women's Labor History.* Boston: Routledge & Kegan Paul, 1985.

"Mill Creek Mine First in West Virginia in Pocahontas Field." *West Virginia Review* 7 (September 1930): 144–45.

Miller, Kerby A. *Emigrants and Exiles: Ireland and the Irish Exodus to North America.* Oxford: Oxford University Press, 1985.

Miller, Thomas Condit, and Hu Maxwell. *West Virginia and Its People*. Vol. 2. New York: Lewis Historical Publishing Co., 1913.

Miller, William. *Men in Business: Essays in the History of Entrepreneurship*. Cambridge, Mass.: Harvard University Press, 1952.

Mills, C. Wright. "The American Business Elite." In *Power, Politics and People: Collected Essays of C. Wright Mills*, ed. Irving Horowitz, 110–39. New York: Oxford University Press, 1963.

Montgomery, David. *Beyond Equality: Labor and the Radical Republicans, 1862–1872*. 1967. Reprint, Urbana: University of Illinois Press, 1981.

Morgan, Kenneth O. *Wales in British Politics, 1868–1922*. Cardiff: University of Wales Press, 1963.

Morris, J. H., and L. J. Williams. *The South Wales Coal Industry, 1841–1875*. Cardiff: University of Wales Press, 1958.

Morris, John. "Coal and Steel." In *Wales through the Ages, from 1485 to the Beginning of the Twentieth Century*, Vol. 2, ed. A. J. Roderick, 177–84. Llandybie, Carmarthenshire: Christopher Davies Publishers, 1960.

Munsell and Company. *History of Schuylkill County, Pa., with Illustrations and Biographical Sketches of Some of Its Prominent Men and Pioneers*. New York: W. W. Munsell and Company, 1881.

Murdoch, Alexander. *British Emigration, 1603–1914*. New York: Palgrave Macmillan, 2004.

Nef, John U. *Rise of the British Coal Industry*. London: G. Routledge, 1966.

Novak, Michael. *The Guns of Lattimer: The True Story of a Massacre and a Trial, August 1897–March 1898*. New York: Basic Books, 1978.

*Ogmore Valley Local History and Heritage Society Journal*. 3 (December 2002).

O'Leary, Paul. "Anti-Irish Riots in Wales, 1826–1882." *Llafur* 5:4 (1991): 27–36.

———. *Immigration and Integration: The Irish in Wales, 1798–1922*. Cardiff: University of Wales Press, 2000.

Olson, Diane, and Cory Olson, eds. *Black Diamond: Mining the Memories, An Oral History of Life in a Company Town*. Portland, Ore.: Frontier Publishing, for Black Diamond Historical Society, 1988.

O'Malley, T. T. *Adventures in the Mines, or Perils Underground*. Akron: privately published, 1891.

O'Neal, Mary T. *Those Damned Foreigners*. Hollywood, Calif.: Minerva Printing and Publishing Company, 1971.

Owens, John E. "The Welsh in Politics." *North American Review* 157 (November 1893): 635–36.

Palladino, Grace. *Another Civil War: Labor, Capital, and the State in the Anthracite Regions of Pennsylvania, 1840–68*. Urbana: University of Illinois Press, 1990.

Papanikolas, Zeese. *Buried Unsung: Louis Tikas and the Ludlow Massacre*. Salt Lake City: University of Utah Press, 1982.

Parry, Jon. "The Tredegar Anti-Irish Riots of 1882." *Llafur* 3, no. 4 (1983): 20–33.

Perlman, Selig. *A Theory of the Labor Movement*. New York: Macmillan, 1928.

Perlman, Selig, and Philip Taft. *History of Labor in the United States, 1896–1932*. New York: Macmillan, 1935.

Petofsky, Jacob S., ed. *John E. Williams: An Appreciation with Selections from His Writings*. Chicago: Chicago Joint Board, Amalgamated Clothing Workers of America, 1930.

Phelan, Craig. *Divided Loyalties: The Public and Private Life of Labor Leader John Mitchell*. Albany: State University of New York Press, 1994.

Phillips, Elizabeth. *A History of the Pioneers of the Welsh Coalfield*. Cardiff: Western Mail Limited, 1925.

Pierce, Michael Cain. "The Plow and Hammer: Farmers, Organized Labor and the People's Party in Ohio." Ph.D. diss., Ohio State University, 1999.

Pinkerton, Allan. *The Molly Maguires and the Detectives*. New York: Dillingham, 1905.

Pinkowski, Edward. *John Siney, the Miners' Martyr*. Philadelphia: Sunshine Press, 1963.

"Pocahontas Fuel." *West Virginia Review* 7 (September 1930): 416–17.

Powderly, Terence V. *The Path I Trod*. 1940. New York: AMS Press, 1968.

Powell, Allan Kent. *The Next Time We Strike: Labor in Utah's Coal Fields*. Logan: Utah State University Press, 1985.

Price, Richard. *Two Tracts on Civil Liberty, the War with America, the Debts and Finances of the Kingdom*. 1778. Reprint, New York: Da Capo Press, 1972.

Pugh, William Richards. *The Shaftdiggers*. Privately published, n.d.

Rees, T. Mardy. *A History of the Quakers in Wales and Their Emigration to North America*. Carmarthen, Wales: W. Spurrell and Son, 1925.

Richards, Eric. *Britannia's Children: Emigration from England, Scotland, Wales and Ireland since 1600*. London: Hambledon and London, 2004.

Roberts, Ellis W. *The Breaker Whistle Blows: Mining Disasters and Labor Leaders in the Anthracite Region*. Scranton: Anthracite Museum Press, 1984.

Roberts, Gwyneth Tyson. *The Language of the Blue Books: The Perfect Instrument of Empire*. Cardiff: University of Wales Press, 1998.

Roberts, Peter. *Anthracite Coal Communities: A Study of the Demography, the Social, Educational and Moral Life of the Anthracite Regions*. New York: Macmillan, 1904.

——. "The Slavs in Anthracite Communities." *Charities and the Commons* 13 (December 3, 1904): 219.

Roberts, Ron E. *John L. Lewis: Hard Labor and Wild Justice*. Dubuque, Iowa: Kendall/Hunt Publishing Company, 1994.

——. *Ordinary Ghosts and Everyday People in an Iowa Coal Town*. Dubuque, Iowa: Kendall/Hunt Publishing Company, 1986.

Robertson, Thomas. "Andrew Roy and the Amelioration of the Miners." Master's thesis, West Virginia University, 1990.

Roderick, A. J., ed. *Wales through the Ages*, Vol. 2. Llandybie, Carmarthenshire: Christopher Davies Publishers, 1971, org. 1960.

Roderick, G. W. "South Wales Industrialists and the Theory of Gentrification, 1770–1914." *Transactions of the Honourable Society of Cymmrodorion* (1987): 65–83.

Rodgers, Daniel T. "Republicanism: The Career of a Concept." *Journal of American History* 79 (June 1992): 11–38.

Roediger, David R. *Wages of Whiteness: Race and the Making of the American Working Class.* New York: Verso, 1991.

Rood, Henry. "The Mine Laborers of Pennsylvania." *The Forum* 14 (September 1892): 110–22.

Roy, Andrew. *A History of the Coal Miners of the United States.* Columbus: J. L. Trauger Printing Company, 1903.

Schlegel, Marvin Wilson. *Ruler of the Reading: The Life of Franklin B. Gowen, 1836–1889.* Harrisburg, Pa.: Archives Publishing, 1947.

——. "The Workingman's Benevolent Association." *Pennsylvania History* 10 (October 1943): 243–67.

Schwieder, Dorothy. *Black Diamonds: Life and Work in Iowa's Coal Mining Communities, 1895–1925.* Ames: Iowa State University Press, 1983.

Seccombe, Wally. "Patriarchy Stabilized: The Construction of the Male Breadwinner Wage Norm in Nineteenth-Century Britain." *Social History* 11 (January 1986): 53–76.

Sheppard, Muriel Earley. *Cloud by Day: The Story of Coal and Coke and People.* 1947. Reprint, Pittsburgh: University of Pittsburgh Press, 1991.

Shepperson, Wilbur S. *Samuel Roberts: A Welsh Colonizer in Civil War Tennessee.* Knoxville: University of Tennessee Press, 1961.

Sinclair, Mary Craig. *Southern Belle.* Phoenix: Sinclair Press, 1957.

Sinclair, Upton. *Autobiography.* New York: Harcourt, Brace and World, 1962.

——. *The Coal War: A Sequel to King Coal.* Boulder: Colorado Associated University Press, 1976.

——. *King Coal: A Novel.* New York: Macmillan Company, 1917.

Smith, Charles. *Fire Creek: A New River Gorge Mining Community.* Glen Jean, W.Va.: Gem Publications, 1991.

Smith, Dai. *Wales! Wales?* London: George Allen and Unwin, 1984.

Smith, David. *A People and a Proletariat: Essays in the History of Wales, 1780–1980.* London: Pluto Press, 1980.

——. "Wales through a Looking-Glass." In *A People and a Proletariat: Essays in the History of Wales, 1780–1980,* ed. David Smith, 215–39. London: Pluto Press, 1980.

Smith, Timothy L. "Religion and Ethnicity in America." *American Historical Review* 83 (December 1978): 1155–85.

"Some Figures Relating to Emigration from Wales." *Bulletin of the Board of Celtic Studies,* vol. 7, part 4 (May 1939): 349–415.

Stapleton, Darwin. *The Transfer of Early Industrial Technology to America.* Philadelphia: American Philosophical Society, 1987.

*Stark County Bicentennial Story, 1776–1976*. Canton, Ohio: Zephyr Press, 1988.

Stein, Leon, and Philip Taft, eds. *Massacre at Ludlow: Four Reports*. New York: Arno and the New York Times, 1971.

Stoddard, Dwight J. *Prominent Men: Scranton and Vicinity, Wilkes-Barre and Vicinity, Pittston, Hazleton, Carbondale, Montrose and Vicinity, Pennsylvania*. Scranton: Tribune Publishing Co., 1906.

Stolarik, M. Mark. "A Slovak Perspective on the Lattimer Massacre." *Pennsylvania History* 68 (Winter 2002): 31–40.

Sullivan, Charles Kenneth (Ken). "Coal Men and Coal Towns: Development of the Smokeless Coalfields of Southern West Virginia, 1873–1923." Ph.D. diss., University of Pittsburgh, 1979.

——. "Coal Men of the Smokeless Coalfields." *West Virginia History* 41 (Winter 1980): 143–65.

Summers, Ewing. *Genealogical and Family History of Eastern Ohio*. New York and Chicago: The Lewis Publishing Co., 1903.

Tams, W. P., Jr. *The Smokeless Coal Fields of West Virginia*. Morgantown: West Virginia University Press, 1963.

Taniguchi, Nancy J. "An Explosive Lesson: Gomer Thomas, Safety, and the Winter Quarters Mine Disaster." *Utah Historical Quarterly* 70 (Spring 2002): 140–57.

——. *Necessary Fraud: Progressive Reform and Utah Coal*. Norman: University of Oklahoma Press, 1996.

Thernstrom, Stephan. *Poverty and Progress: Social Mobility in a Nineteenth-Century City*. Cambridge, Mass.: Harvard University Press, 1964.

Thomas, Brinley. "The Growth of Industrial Towns." In *Wales through the Ages*, Vol. 2, ed. A. J. Roderick, 185–92. Llandybie, Carmarthenshire: Christopher Davies Publishers, 1971.

——. *The Industrial Revolution and the Atlantic Economy: Selected Essays*. London: Routledge, 1993.

——. *Migration and Economic Growth*. Cambridge: Cambridge University Press, 1954.

——. "The Migration of Labour into the Glamorgan Coalfield (1861–1911)." *Economica* No. 30 (November 1930): 275–94.

——. "Wales and the Atlantic Economy." In *The Welsh Economy: Studies in Expansion*, ed. Brinley Thomas, 1–29. Cardiff: University of Wales Press, 1962.

Thomas, David. "Early Welsh Settlement in the USA—The Surname Evidence." *Transactions of the Honourable Society of Cymmrodorion* (1987): 53–63.

Thomas, R. D. *Hanes Cymry America*. 1872. Trans. Phillips G. Davies as *History of the Welsh in America*. Lanham, Md.: University Press of America, 1983.

Thomas, Samuel. "Reminiscences of the Early Anthracite-Iron Industry." *Transactions of the American Institute of Mining Engineers* 29 (February 1899–September 1899): 901–28. New York: American Institute of Mining Engineers, 1900.

Tine, Warren R. Van. *The Making of a Labor Bureaucrat: Union Leadership in the United States, 1870–1920.* Amherst: University of Massachusetts Press, 1973.

Tintori, Karen. *Trapped: The 1909 Cherry Mine Disaster.* New York: Atria Books, 2002.

Trachtenberg, Alexander. *The History of Legislation for the Protection of Coal Miners in Pennsylvania, 1824–1915.* 1917. New York: International Publishers, 1942.

Tribe, Ivan Mathews. "An Empire of Industry: Hocking Valley Mining Towns in the Gilded Age." Ph.D. diss., University of Toledo, 1976.

———. *Little Cities of Black Diamonds: Urban Development in the Hocking Coal Region, 1870–1900.* Athens, Ohio: Athens Ancestree, 1986.

———. *Sprinkled with Coal Dust: Life and Work in the Hocking Coal Region, 1870–1900.* Athens, Ohio: Athens County Historical Society and Museum, 1989.

Turner, George A. "The Lattimer Massacre: A Perspective from the Ethnic Community." *Pennsylvania History* 68 (Winter 2002): 11–30.

Ulam, Norman, and Mary Lou Ulam, comps. *1880 Census Index of Trumbull County, Ohio.* Warren: Trumbull County Chapter, Ohio Genealogical Society, 1991.

Upton, Harriet Taylor. *A Twentieth-Century History of Trumbull County, Ohio.* 2 vols. Chicago: The Lewis Publishing Company, 1909.

Vecoli, Rudolph. "Contadini in Chicago: A Critique of *The Uprooted.*" *Journal of American History* 51 (December 1963): 404–17.

———. "The Italian Immigrant Press and the Construction of Social Reality, 1850–1920." In *Print Culture in a Diverse America,* ed. James P. Danky and Wayne A. Wiegand, 17–33. Urbana: University of Illinois Press, 1998.

Vugt, William E. Van. *Britain to America: Mid-Nineteenth-Century Immigrants to the United States.* Urbana: University of Illinois Press, 1999.

———. *British Buckeyes: The English, Scots, and Welsh in Ohio, 1700–1900.* Kent, Ohio: Kent State University Press, 2006.

Vuranch, Karen. "The Influence of the Welsh Immigrants on the Development of the Coal Fields." Proceedings of the First Conference of the North American Association for the Study of Welsh Culture and History, Rio Grande, Ohio, June 1–2, 1995.

Walker, Samuel E. "Terence V. Powderly, 'Labor Mayor': Workingmen's Politics in Scranton, 1870–1884." Ph.D. diss., Ohio State University, 1973.

———. "Varieties of Workingclass Experience: The Workingmen of Scranton, Pennsylvania, 1855–1885." In *American Workingclass Culture: Explorations in American Labor and Social History,* ed. Milton Cantor, 361–76. Westport, Conn.: Greenwood Press, 1979.

Wallace, Anthony F. C. *St. Clair: A Nineteenth-Century Coal Town's Experience with a Disaster-Prone Industry.* New York: Alfred A. Knopf, 1987.

Walters, R. H. "The Economic and Business History of the South Wales Steam Coal Industry, 1840–1914." PhD. diss., Oxford University, 1975. New York: Arno Press, 1977 (facsimile).

———. *The Economic and Business History of the South Wales Steam Coal Industry, 1840–1914*. New York: Arno Press, 1977.

Walters, Rhodri. "Capital Formation in the South Wales Coal Industry, 1840–1914." *Welsh History Review* 10, no. 1 (1980): 69–92.

Ware, Norman J. *Labor Movement in the United States, 1860–1895: A Study in Democracy*. 1929. Reprint, New York: Vintage, 1964.

Warne, Frank Julian. "The Effect of Unionism upon the Mine Workers." *Annals of the American Academy of Political and Social Science* 21 (January 1903): 20–35.

———. "The Real Cause of the Miners' Strike." *The Outlook* 72 (August 30, 1902): 1053–57.

———. *The Slav Invasion and the Mine Workers: A Study in Immigration*. Philadelphia: J. B. Lippincott Company, 1904.

Watchorn, Robert. *The Autobiography of Robert Watchorn*. Oklahoma City: Robert Watchorn Charities, 1959.

Watkins, Harold M. *Coal and Men: An Economic and Social Study of the British and American Coalfields*. London: George Allen and Unwin Ltd., 1934.

Weber, Max. *The Protestant Ethic and the Spirit of Capitalism*. New York: Charles Scribner's Sons, 1958.

Weick, Edward A. *The American Miners' Association*. New York: Russell Sage Foundation, 1940.

Wesolowsky, Tony. "A Jewel in the Crown of Old King Coal: Eckley Miners' Village." Pennsylvania Historical and Museum Commission. <http://www.phmc.state.pa.us/ppet/eckley/>.

Whiteside, James. *Regulating Danger*. Lincoln: University of Nebraska Press, 1900.

Wilks, Ivor. *South Wales and the Rising of 1839*. Llandysul, Dyfed: Gomer Press, 1989.

Williams, Daniel Jenkins. *One Hundred Years of Welsh Calvinistic Methodism in America*. Philadelphia: Westminster Press, 1937.

Williams, David. *Cymru ac America: Wales and America*. Cardiff: University of Wales Press, 1946.

———. *John Frost: A Study in Chartism*. Cardiff: University of Wales Press, 1939.

———. *The Rebecca Riots*. Cardiff: University of Wales Press, 1986, orig. 1955.

Williams, Glanmor. *Religion, Language, and Nationality in Wales*. Cardiff: University of Wales Press, 1979.

Williams, Glyn. *The Desert and the Dream*. Cardiff: University of Wales Press, 1962.

———. *The Welsh in Patagonia: State and Ethnic Community*. Cardiff: University of Wales Press, 1991.

Williams, Gwyn A. "Emergence of a Working-Class Movement." In *Wales through the Ages*. Vol. 2, ed. A. J. Roderick, 140–46. Llandybie, Carmarthenshire: Christopher Davies Publishers, 1971.

———. "Locating a Welsh Working Class: The Frontier Years." In *A People and a Proletariat: Essays in the Social History of Wales*, edited by David Smith, 16–46. London: Pluto Press, 1980.

——. *The Merthyr Rising.* Cardiff: University of Wales Press, 1988.

——. *The Search for Beulah Land.* New York: Holmes and Meier Publishers, 1980.

——. *When Was Wales?* London: Penguin Books, 1985.

Williams, John. *Was Wales Industrialized? Essays in Modern Welsh History.* Landysul, Dyfed: Gomer Press, 1995.

Williams, Mari A. "Women and the Welsh Language in the Industrial Valleys of South Wales, 1914–1945." In *"Let's Do Our Best for the Ancient Tongue": The Welsh Language in the Twentieth Century,* ed. Geraint H. Jenkins and Mari A. Williams, 137–80. Cardiff: University of Wales Press, 2000.

Williams, Peter N. *David Thomas: Iron Man from Wales.* Trucksville, Pa.: National Welsh-American Foundation, 1995.

Williams, Raymond. *Border Country.* London: Chatto and Windus, 1960.

Williams, Stephen Riggs. *The Saga of Paddy's Run.* Privately printed, 1997.

Wittke, Carl. *We Who Built America: The Saga of the Immigrant.* New York: Prentice-Hall, 1939.

Wyman, Mark. *Round-Trip to America: The Immigrants Return to Europe, 1880–1930.* Ithaca: Cornell University Press, 1993.

Yates, W. Ross. "Discovery of the Process for Making Anthracite Iron." *Pennsylvania Magazine of History and Biography* 98 (April 1974): 206–23.

Yearly, Clifton K., Jr. *Britons in American Labor.* Baltimore: Johns Hopkins University Press, 1957.

——. *Enterprise and Anthracite.* Baltimore: Johns Hopkins University Press, 1961.

Zee, Jacob Van Der. *The British in Iowa.* Iowa City: State Historical Society of Iowa, 1922.

## ACKNOWLEDGMENTS

As with any such endeavor, I have accumulated innumerable debts of gratitude during the research and preparation of this study. The more time spent at scholarship, the greater one's appreciation for the work of librarians, archivists, editors, and other scholars. The sources for this study were not found neatly contained in major manuscript collections directly related to Welsh coal miners, but widely scattered and buried in other materials challenging the researcher to tease them out. The bibliography provides a full list of libraries and repositories, but I should note in particular the assistance provided by the library staffs at West Virginia University, Cardiff University, the National Library of Wales, Ohio University, and the Warren-Trumbull Library of Warren, Ohio. I am also deeply appreciative of the assistance provided by Ann Harris of Youngstown State University, who allowed me to use her extensive personal collection on Ohio coal mining at an early stage in my research. Also, few authors receive as much help from external reviewers as was offered by Kevin Kenny and William D. Jones, whose close reading of the manuscript has improved the final product immeasurably. As she has with so many projects over the years, my wife, Susan E. Lewis, has been my best critic and selflessly provided me with the benefit of her invaluable editing skills.

The North American Association for the Study of Welsh Culture and History, which was founded during the incubation period of this work, has furnished an unparalleled network of scholars representing many academic disciplines, both in America and Wales, and its conferences have served as an important venue for presenting my ideas for critical comment. The Regional Research Institute at West Virginia University provided critical support for this project in its formative stages by underwriting a research assistant, Jennifer Egolf, to enter census data into the Ohio Database, which I explain in the text. She also entered biographical data on coal miners from northeastern Ohio and the northern anthracite field of Pennsylvania into a Biographical Database. Here I should acknowledge the problem with using biographical sketches drawn from publications such as *Y Drych*, the *Druid*, and the *Cambrian*—they are largely celebratory in nature. These biographies are, nevertheless, still very useful and often the only sources available. Where possible, however, I have taken pains to gather corroborating evidence, and seldom have I used this evidence for other than identification of individuals. Dependency on such fragile sources highlights the general lack of a solid historical writing on Welsh Americans who have been largely overlooked by scholars.

I am especially grateful for the support of West Virginia University, which provided research assistance through my appointments, first as Eberly Distinguished Professor of History, and then as the Joyce and Stuart Robbins Chair in History. This support has been extremely valuable in the advancement of my scholarly career, and humbling in my hope to fulfill the trust conferred by these appointments. In 1999, a Fulbright Fellowship for Research and Teaching provided the time and financial resources for an extended research trip to Wales. The School of History and Archaeology at Cardiff University provided me with an institutional home among stimulating colleagues and facilitated my research in every way. Many people in Wales have been quite generous with their assistance, and I have returned often since 1999, but none more so than Bill Jones and Valerie Davidge, whose hospitality is legendary among visiting scholars of the Welsh dispersal in the world. Bill not only shared his vast knowledge of the Welsh at home and abroad, but also served as expert guide during our excursions through the South Wales Valleys, which significantly improved my understanding of the Welsh Americans I write about in this book.

# INDEX

leadership, 258, 263–68; as trade unionist, 259, 261–63; and founding of National Progressive Union of Miners and Mine Laborers, 260–65; character maligned, 261, 265–67; as lawyer and politician, 267–69; appointed Ohio Labor Commissioner, 269; death of, 269; and "Welshness," 274

Lithuanians, 223

Liverpool, England, 41–42

Llewellyn, Richard, 307, 319

Lockwood, Nev., 302

"Long Strike" of 1875, 213

Lucas, Iowa, 278–80

Ludlow Massacre, 293–95

Ludlow tent colony (Colorado), 289–91

MacDonald, Alexander, 39, 157, 179, 253

Maesteg, Wales, 284

Mahanoy City, Pa., 54, 214–18

Major, George, 215, 217

March on Newport (1839), 28

Martin, James F., 236–37

McBride, John, 113, 260–68

McKenna, James. *See* McParlan, James

McKinley, William, 64, 68, 114, 269

McParlan, James, 213–14, 216, 219

Mellon, Thomas, 254

Merthyr Rising, 27, 31

Merthyr Tydfil, Wales, 19, 23, 27, 38–41, 87

Merthyr Tydfil Emigration Society, 40

Methodists, 112, 140, 145

Miles, John, 11

Mineral Ridge, Ohio, 111, 113

Miners' and Laborers' Amalgamated Association of Pennsylvania, 212

Miners' and Laborers' Benevolent Association (Ohio), 113, 176

Miners' Benevolent and Protective Association (Illinois), 180

Miners' National Association, 113, 225

Miners' National Association of Great Britain and Ireland, 28, 39, 119, 122, 157, 253

Minersville, Ohio, 65, 115

Mine Ventilation Law of 1870 (Pennsylvania), 168

Mitchell, John, 199, 271

"Modocs," 214, 217

Molly Maguires, 15, 212–20

Monongahela strike, 251

Montgomery, W.Va., 71–72

Morgan, John T., 40–41

Morgan, Morgan R., 106, 230–31

Mormons. *See* Church of Jesus Christ of Latter-Day Saints

Morris, John, 62

"*Mwnwr*" (Miner), 198–99

Nantymoel, Wales, 284

National Association of Coal Miners of Great Britain, 39

National Association of Practical Miners, 28

National Federation of Miners and Mine Laborers, 260–66

National *Gymanfa Ganu* Association, 153

*National Labor Tribune*, 262

National Progressive Union of Miners and Mine Laborers, 77, 114, 265

New Cambria, Mo., 40

North Lawrence, Ohio, 64, 113–14, 131

Oak Colliery disaster, 158

Ocean Colliery, 284

Ogmore Valley, Wales, 284

Ohio database, 331–32 (n. 10)

Ohio Miners' Amalgamated Association (Knights of Labor), 260

O'Neal, Don, 285, 302

Thomas, William M. "Bully Bill," 217
Thomas, William R., 83
Thomas Coal and Coke Company, 78
Thomson, William, 176
Tikas, Louis, 290, 294–95
Tine, Warren Van, 101, 249–50
Tod, David, 62–63
"Treachery of the Blue Books" (1847).
    *See* Royal Commission on the State of
    Education in Wales (1847)
Tremenheere, H. Seymour, 23–24, 146
Tripp's Slope, 203
"Truck" shop system, 25–26
Turner, Samuel G., 159, 165

Union Labor Party (Pittsburgh), 254–55
United Mine Workers of America, 118,
    182, 199, 212, 228, 231, 238, 247,
    249, 251, 257, 268, 270–82 passim,
    289–303 passim
U.S. Commission on Industrial Rela-
    tions, 284, 298–99
U.S. Immigration Commission, 47,
    244–46
U.S. Senate Committee on Capital and
    Labor (1883), 88
United States Steel Corporation, 86
Utah Central Coal Company, 68
Utah Fuel Company, 68

Walker, John R., 118–19
Warne, Frank, 226, 240–42
Watchorn, Robert, 258, 264, 265, 266–
    67, 268–69
Watkins, John Henry ("Father Wat-
    kins"), 277, 279
Watkins, John J., 279
Watkins, Louisa, 279
Waverly Coal Company, 254
Welsh, Americanization of: race and
    ethnicity, 308; socioeconomic status,
    308–10; scattered settlements, 310;

decline of language and institutions,
    311–18
Welsh American coal communities: and
    social structure, 92–96; occupational
    and social mobility, 100–19; literacy,
    130–32; Welsh language, 132–40;
    Welsh American press, 133; temper-
    ance, 139, 146–48; religion, 140–48;
    benevolent societies, 148–50; eisted-
    dfodau, 151–52; *gymanfa ganus*, 152–
    54
Welsh Americans: and labor republi-
    canism, 97–100, 118–19, 128; and
    "Protestant Ethic," 98–100, 128; as
    "archetypal proletarian," 94, 116–17;
    and family wage, 119–28; and mine
    safety reform, 156–59; Avondale dis-
    aster, 159–67; West Pittston Shaft
    ("Second Avondale") disaster, 167–
    70; professional inspectorate in
    Pennsylvania, 170–76; in Ohio, 176–
    79; in Illinois, 179–83; and the West,
    183–88; abandon mining, 238–47;
    upward mobility, 249
Welsh-Irish animosity: roots in Wales,
    191–95; Welsh "bossism," 196–202;
    Welsh strike of 1871, 202–12 passim,
    216; ethnic gangs, 212–20
Welsh miners in Wales: and internal
    migration, 18–23; grievances and
    conditions, 23–26; rebellions and
    unions, 26–29; religion, 30–34;
    migration to America, 34–50
Welsh Neck, S.C., 12
Welsh Philosophical Society of Hyde
    Park, 150–51
Welsh Prize Singers of Cardiff, 149
Welsh settlements: in Pennsylvania,
    51–61; in Ohio, 61–66; in the Mid-
    west and West, 66–68; in Central
    Appalachia, 68–81; in the South, 81–
    90

40
70 n T
wo T w
30 4 T
160 T F
190 F M.